Other People's Children

Other People's
Children

The Battle for Justice and Equality in New Jersey's Schools

DEBORAH YAFFE

RIVERGATE BOOKS

AN IMPRINT OF RUTGERS UNIVERSITY PRESS

NEW BRUNSWICK, NEW JERSEY, AND LONDON

LIBRARY OF CONGRESS CATALOGING-IN-PUBLICATION DATA

Yaffe, Deborah, 1965–
  Other people's children: the battle for justice and equality in New Jersey's
schools / Deborah Yaffe.
    p. cm.
  Includes bibliographical references and index.
  ISBN 978–0–8135–4205–8 (hardcover : alk. paper)
  1. Education—Finance—Law and legislation—New Jersey. 2. Educational law
and legislation—New Jersey. 3. Property tax—Law and legislation—New Jersey.
4. Public schools—New Jersey—Finance. 5. Educational equalization—New Jersey—
Costs. 6. Education and state—New Jersey. I. Title.
  KFN2190.Y34 2007
  344.749'076—dc22   2007006033

A British Cataloging-in-Publication record for this book
is available from the British Library.

Visit our Web site: http://rutgerspress.rutgers.edu

Manufactured in the United States of America

For my children, David and Rachel

CONTENTS

Preface and Acknowledgments   ix
The Plaintiffs and Their Families   xiii

Introduction: The Inheritance   1

PART ONE
The Beginning:
Robinson v. Cahill, 1970–1976

1   Jersey City's Tax War   9
2   Celebrating the Bicentennial   31

PART TWO
The Crusade:
Abbott v. Burke, 1979–1998

3   The True Believer   59
4   Son of *Robinson*   86
5   The Families   110
6   "The System Is Broken"   145
7   The Twenty-One/Forty-One Rule   176
8   The Children of *Abbott*   214
9   A Constitutional Right to Astroturf   249

PART THREE
The Never-Ending Story:
Implementing *Abbott*, 1998–2006

10   "We Do Not Run School Systems"   281

11   The Children Grow Up   304

    Conclusion: Other People's Children   322

    Notes   335
    Works Cited   351
    Index   363

PREFACE AND ACKNOWLEDGMENTS

This is a work of nonfiction that draws on tens of thousands of pages of archival materials, legal documents, and published sources, and on interviews with nearly 200 individuals. I base descriptions of conversations on the account of at least one of the participants; I base descriptions of an individual's thoughts or feelings either on my interview with the person concerned or, occasionally, on accounts given to me by friends or colleagues. In almost every case, I have used the real names of the people whose stories I tell, although I have sometimes omitted the last names of individuals peripherally connected to the narrative. There is only one exception to this rule. In the *Abbott* lawsuit, the Education Law Center identified Blanca's children by her maiden name—Figueroa—rather than by their legal surnames, and because of the uniquely painful circumstances of their lives, I have retained this usage.

This book is about a struggle over the fair provision of public services, and I could not have written it without the help of several public institutions. The National Endowment for the Humanities provided initial funding for the project, and in my research I drew on the resources of the Jersey City and Milwaukee public libraries, the New Jersey State Archives, the New Jersey State Library, and the Rutgers University Libraries.

I owe a special debt to the Education Law Center (ELC) and its executive director, David Sciarra, who gave me free and unconditional access to his organization's files. At ELC, Sciarra, Steven Block, and Paul Tractenberg uncomplainingly endured many hours of interviews, Elizabeth Athos researched a last-minute question, and Danielle Baynes handled myriad logistical matters.

Thomas Cioppettini, Dolores Corona, Lawrence Lustberg, Ernest Reock Jr., Paul Tractenberg, and Martin Wheelwright generously lent me files and documents from their personal collections, and Richard Vespucci of the New Jersey Department of Education responded patiently and cheerfully to a thousand questions.

Many other individuals took the time to find a telephone number, mail out a document, chase down an elusive fact, or smooth my path in any number of other ways. I am grateful to Omar Barbour, Alicia Bass, Herman Bennett, Joannie Burnett, Robert Byrne, Chris Carden, Lan Samantha Chang, Deron Cherry, DeWayne Cherry, Kathy Crotty, Jay Doolan, Jack Dougherty, Jette Englund, Frank Ferdetta, Jason Fink, Kathryn Forsyth, Valerie Garcia, John Gomez, Kia Green, Saundra Green, Edward Hart, Kathy Hennessy, Cynthia Jackson, Joanne Kenny, Daniel Linke, Brenda Liss, Lynn Maher, Helen Marian, Jim McClendon, Craig McCoy, Hermione McNeil, Debra Meyers, Sister Katherine Misbauer, S.L., Don Morris, Jonanthan Ogbonna, Mark Perkiss, Karen Perry, John Petrick, Andy Platizky, David Randall, Fred Reiss, Spencer Reynolds, Sandra Robertson, Robert Roggenstein, Joann Rotondo, Perry Schwarz, Helen Sexton, Ralph Siegel, Kevin Smith, 1st Lt. Earl S. Speechley, USMC, Lilo Stainton, Helene Stapinski, George Strachan, Iris V. Tirado, Stephen Townsend, Ann Waldron, John Watson, Ellen Wayman-Gordon, Carole Weaver, Andy Williams, and Cecilia Zalkind.

Friends, relatives, and colleagues offered guidance, expertise, and practical support that sustained me and my project at every stage. Elizabeth Rourke first suggested that I seek grant funding for my work, and Richard Barbieri, Scott Graham, Dorothy Hinchcliff, and John Oswald graciously provided references for grant applications, sometimes at unreasonably short notice. The late, much-missed Howard Greenfeld read my book proposal, as did Catherine Crystal Foster, Nancy Messegee-Downing, Elaine Yaffe, Gideon Yaffe, and James Yaffe. Catherine Crystal Foster, John Hechinger, Elaine Yaffe, Gideon Yaffe, James Yaffe, and Amelia Zurcher read the entire manuscript and made invaluable suggestions that significantly improved the final product.

The interview list included elsewhere in this volume names the many individuals who gave generously of their time, sometimes more than once; they all have my deepest thanks. I am especially grateful to the families who were named plaintiffs in the *Robinson* and *Abbott* litigation. They invited me into their homes and shared painful details of their lives. I admire them all and have tried to do justice to their stories.

Last, but far from least, I must thank my own family. If husbands got medals, Alastair Bellany would surely have earned one: he listened to my developing ideas, read the whole manuscript more than once, cooked dinner while I revised, and took on extra work responsibilities so that I could pursue this labor of love. No one could have a more beloved partner. Our children, David and Rachel, tolerated my obsession, usually with cheerfulness, and only occasionally asked how much longer it was going to take. Thanks, guys: I couldn't have done it without you.

THE PLAINTIFFS AND THEIR FAMILIES

Robinson v. Cahill

Ernestine Betty Robinson*
    Her children: Patricia, Gwen, Larry (Tank), Tony, Kenneth*, Joan, Lydia, and Saundra

Abbott v. Burke

Camden

Luci and Howard Abbott
    Their son: Raymond*
Blanca Figueroa
    Her children: Vivian*, Orlando*, Frances*, Hector*, and Arlayne*
Lola Moore
    Her children: Lynnette and Michael Hadley*
Nezettia Stevens and Henry Stevens Sr.
    Their son: Henry Jr.*

East Orange

Mattie James
    Her children: Julian (Bunny), Caroline*, and Jermaine*
Lynn Waiters
    Her children: Dorian* and Khudayja*

Irvington

Gladys Knowles and Guy Knowles Sr.
    Their children: Guy Jr.*, Cristina*, and Daniel*

Jersey City

Lucila and Justo Diaz
>   Their daughter: Liana*

Tommi and Eddie Stephens
>   Their children: Leslie* and LaMar*

Patricia Watson and James Hargrove
>   Their daughters: Zakia* and Aisha Hargrove*

———

*plaintiff

Other People's Children

INTRODUCTION

The Inheritance

In 1975, a dentist living in an affluent New Jersey suburb told a newspaper why he opposed using an income tax to fund inner-city public schools. In the process, he unwittingly summed up the clash between self-interest and the claims of community that was to undergird school-finance battles in New Jersey and the nation for decades to come. "You can't expect people who worked very hard to make a little money to pay for other people's children," the dentist told the reporter. "That's why we moved here—to maintain good schools for our children. Look, I'm already paying for three kids, and now you want me to pay more for somebody else's? Possibly this is being selfish, but I don't think so."

That suburban professional could acquit himself of selfishness because, from one perspective, his words expressed nothing but the bedrock promise of the American meritocracy: upward mobility for the hardworking and the self-reliant, no matter their race or class. We call that promise the American Dream, and even those who regard it as little more than a hoax—a dream indeed—see it as a fundamental tenet of our national faith. We do not view the ambition to move up, and to take our families with us, as selfish. That drive, we like to say, is part and parcel of our energetic, individualistic national character. In particular, we view the desire to improve our *children's* lives as the reverse of selfish; we see it as altruistic, and, of course, sometimes it is. Nevertheless, the dentist's words also expose the American Dream's oft-noted dark side. When success is defined as the earned reward of hard work, we need feel no responsibility for those who are left behind, or for their children. Indeed, if we count the power to better their children's lives as one of the deserved rewards that the successful have earned, it can seem logical, even just, for the less successful—defined, of course, as the less deserving—to lack that power. We do not think much about what this logic implies for their children. They aren't our children, after all.

The public schools have a special place in our dream of a meritocratic America, a place free of inherited privilege or disadvantage, where the fruits of success—a little money, a house in the suburbs—go to the deserving. We think of the public schools as the engine of equal opportunity, the institution that levels the playing field for children born with a strike or two against them. The suburban dentist's words remind us, however, that for middle-class America the schools have also become something else: one of the rewards for victory on that supposedly level playing field. Buying the house in the suburbs also buys our children access to the good school down the street. The assumed levelness of the playing field assures the winners that their laurels are earned, not inherited, yet even those who claim to see the level playing field as only fair seldom accept it for their children. Most parents want their children to have a better-than-equal chance, deliberately ignoring—or perhaps not even noticing—how this aspiration undermines the meritocratic ideal. Ironically, the ultimate reward for winning the game fair and square is the chance to rig the next round in favor of our own children, by making sure their schools have better teachers, more rigorous courses, and finer laboratories than anyone else's. "We don't leave our kids the farm anymore, or the estate. We leave them education," one participant in New Jersey's education-funding wars reflected, years after retiring from the fray. "For the middle class and upper middle class, it's the property right, the inheritance they pass onto their children. And they all want to leave more of it to their kids than [to] some other kids. The whole thing is about giving their kids relative advantage."

No wonder, then, that we have spent two generations fighting about school funding, in almost every state in the nation. The fights would be bitter enough if they were just over how to divvy up scarce tax dollars, but because education spending is a down payment on the future, school-funding battles reflect deeper conflicts over society's values and direction. We define the boundaries of community in part by deciding whose children count as "our children," and therefore deserve the best we can give them.

Over the years chronicled in this book, the school-funding fight has ebbed and flowed. Since the early 1970s, when the issue migrated from the federal to the state level, forty-five of the fifty states have faced education-finance lawsuits. Scholars divide the litigation—perhaps a bit too neatly—into two waves: the equity cases of the 1970s and 1980s, and the adequacy cases of the 1990s and beyond. Plaintiffs in the first-wave equity lawsuits located the failure of government policy in the inequality of rich and poor school districts—the extra spending the rich could afford, the heavier tax burdens the poor often shouldered. But state governments won two-thirds of these cases, perhaps because courts were leery of ordering wholesale changes in local spending and taxation. Beginning in the 1990s, however, plaintiffs changed tack, using the educational guarantees enshrined in state constitutions to argue that government had failed to ensure every student an adequate education. With this change in strategy came a shift in the balance of success: by the early years of the twenty-first century, plaintiffs had won two-thirds of these second-wave adequacy suits. Historically, school-finance reform has been a liberal cause, but in 2002, conservative Republican President George W. Bush gave the adequacy movement potentially its biggest boost when he signed the federal education law known as No Child Left Behind (NCLB). NCLB requires states that accept federal education money—in other words, all of the states—to ensure that every child achieves proficiency on standardized tests of core subjects. By ordering states to break out test score data by such demographic categories as race, gender, and economic disadvantage, the law makes it impossible to hide the failures of poor minority children within schoolwide or statewide averages. NCLB is the apotheosis of the demand, historically a conservative one, for accountability in public education—results in exchange for resources. Liberals, however, have wasted no time in noting that such a demand is reasonable only if schools have the raw materials needed to produce results. Thus, accountability demands buttress adequacy claims, producing, in the words of journalist Peter Schrag, "the fusion of conservative tactic with liberal purpose."

New Jerseyans like to say that everything that happens in America happens in the Garden State first, and, indeed, New Jersey has been litigating school funding almost since the beginning of such litigation, in cases combining both equity and adequacy claims. This book tells the story of New Jersey's school-funding battle, one of the oldest, longest-lasting, and bitterest in the nation. The story of one state, even one as wealthy, crowded, and diverse as New Jersey, can never perfectly represent the whole. Still, New Jersey's two-generation-long struggle over a rich society's responsibility for educating the poor strikes chords that echo across our wealthy, crowded, diverse nation.

Other People's Children is the first book to tell the story of New Jersey's school-funding battle, from the filing of the initial lawsuit, *Robinson v. Cahill*, through the tortuous legal odyssey of its successor, *Abbott v. Burke*. Over the course of this long history, the school-funding debate has often been conducted in an atmosphere too rarefied for ordinary citizens to breathe. By contrast, my account is intended for general readers, since they are the voters, taxpayers, and neighbors who must ultimately decide how our democracy will balance the claims of individual and community. Because I am not writing for experts, I do not exhaustively analyze every legal issue that the *Robinson* and *Abbott* cases raise; still less do I detail all the technical ramifications of New Jersey's successive school-funding formulas. Even well-informed citizens find school finance dull and confusing, and no wonder: education-funding laws can be dauntingly complex and numbingly tedious. Their implications for democracy and social justice lie buried amid a welter of algorithms. I have tried to include just enough technical detail to suggest the impact that a few words hidden deep in a statute can have on real lives.

This book is also not a definitive analysis of educational progress in the thirty-one school districts and hundreds of schools covered, at one time or another, by the *Abbott* rulings. The debates over how best to measure school success—whether standardized tests provide meaningful information, whether dropout statistics conceal more than they reveal—are beyond the scope of my narrative. Although in my conclusion I briefly discuss test scores and their implications, I have not tried to tell the *Abbott* districts' individual stories, which run the gamut from extraordinary promise to debilitating failure.

Instead, I have tried to show how the participants in this epic battle over public education framed the issues before them, and how, as

New Jersey's lawyers, judges, and politicians wrestled with those issues, children grew up to make what they could of their opportunities. The book interweaves the public story—an account of legal and political wrangling over laws and money—with the private stories of the children who were named plaintiffs in the *Robinson* and *Abbott* suits. As New Jersey's school-funding fight unrolled in the courts and the legislature, these private stories seldom formed part of the public discourse; like a subterranean river, they flowed unseen beneath the ground on which the public drama was enacted. Only by bringing the children's stories into the light, as this book seeks to do, can we understand the true dimensions of the public battle. The children of *Robinson* and *Abbott* are individuals, not types, but I believe their life stories illuminate the complex interactions among public institutions, private choices, and social conditions that reformers inevitably confront.

As Robert Wilentz, then chief justice of New Jersey's supreme court, wrote in his 1990 *Abbott* ruling, "After all the analyses are completed, we are still left with these students and their lives." Education is essential to our American Dream, and to theirs; the quality and equality of the schooling we give them goes to the heart of what kind of society we want to be. If we tacitly accept that some children—poor children, minority children, other people's children—will never be offered the educational prerequisites for success, we are accepting that they will never have equal life chances. At bottom, arguments over how far we are willing to go to educate the poor are arguments over how fully we will welcome them into the community of democratic citizenship. In New Jersey—and in the nation—that argument goes on.

PART ONE

The Beginning

Robinson v. Cahill, 1970–1976

1

Jersey City's Tax War

For Christmas 1967, Betty Robinson's seven children got just one present among them. Betty had announced that gifts would go only to those kids who brought home good report cards, and that year, only her fifth child, nine-year-old Kenneth, qualified. He got a green bicycle, and the others, from fourteen-year-old Patricia down to baby Lydia, got nothing. Still, Kenneth let his brothers and sisters take turns riding his new bike along the dirt paths that ran between the three-story brick boxes of the Booker T. Washington Apartments in Jersey City, across the Hudson River from Manhattan's skyscrapers. The welfare mothers and working families of the Booker T. housing project, virtually all of them African American, lived in the shadow of the elevated New Jersey Turnpike extension, in one of the poorest neighborhoods of a city whose glory days seemed long behind it, and even in that hard-pressed community the Robinsons felt poor. Other project families had cars, but the Robinsons did not. Betty sometimes wept with anxiety over how she would feed her family, and the kids at school teased twelve-year-old Larry about the holes in his shoes. Years after that Spartan Christmas, Larry wondered if the report-card story was just his mom's way of covering up the fact that she couldn't afford presents for all of them.

When Ernestine Rock left little Eadytown, South Carolina, to start a new life in the North in the years after World War II, she also left her name behind. From then on, she called herself by her middle name, Betty. She had never liked the hard work that life on her grandmother's farm entailed: when it was time to milk the cow, or hoe cotton, or sweep the yard, Ernestine often claimed to be sick, forcing the other children to pick up the slack. Not surprisingly, they grew resentful. Perhaps because Ernestine, born in 1929, was the oldest grandchild, she had a special place in their grandmother's heart, or so it seemed to her sisters, Thomasena and Annie Ruth. Their grandmother was a strict disciplinarian—the children had to cut the switches for their own whippings—but Ernestine seemed to get in less trouble than the others. Her sisters thought Ernestine even stirred up their grandmother against them.

Life in rural Eadytown was austere. Electricity did not arrive until the mid-1940s, and indoor plumbing and telephone service came even later. Like just about everybody else, the Rocks' grandmother grew the food she ate—sweet potatoes, peas, garden greens—and sold the cotton she raised. She made the children's everyday clothes herself; on Sundays, the girls wore the pretty dresses their father sent from New York, where he was a railroad worker. The children amused themselves playing hopscotch or the card game Smut, so called because the winner got to rub soot into the loser's face. Every morning, they walked more than a mile to school, cutting through their uncle's pasture when his ornery cow was quartered elsewhere. Their school was barely bigger than a one-room schoolhouse, and, like most of their neighbors, everyone there, teachers as well as students, was black.

Ernestine finished grammar school in Eadytown and high school fifty miles away in Charleston, where the girls' mother worked in a cigar factory. Then, like half a million other black South Carolinians in the first half of the twentieth century, Ernestine looked northward. Her first stop was Baltimore, where her sister Thomasena, married a month before her fourteenth birthday, was living with her husband. Then the twenty-year-old woman who would now call herself Betty kept on going—to New York, where her father was still living, and eventually across the river to Jersey City and the Booker T. projects.

It was no accident that the projects were named after an African American, and one whose focus on hard work and self-help made him a reassuring icon for whites. The low-rent Booker T. complex was meant "exclusively for colored people," the local newspaper had reported in June 1941, as the city housing authority prepared to solicit construction bids.

The United States' entry into World War II six months later temporarily changed the city's plans—any still-incomplete public housing projects were now reserved for war workers—but by the time Betty moved into Booker T. sometime in the second half of the 1950s, its exclusively black status was well established. The newspaper's phrasing made Booker T. sound like a swanky private club, but in fact the project was far from luxurious. The apartments' rooms were tiny, and the paths connecting the project's seven squat buildings were unpaved; because no gates blocked the entrances to the complex, cars could drive straight through the central courtyard, endangering the children who played there. Each building had a small yard of its own, where tenants could park their cars. Betty and a neighbor pooled their spaces to make a garden, where they grew collard greens, cabbage, and string beans.

Sometime after reaching Jersey City, Betty met Wilbur Robinson, a fellow South Carolina transplant who worked as a machine operator in a factory. Betty and Wilbur's romance eventually produced a child, Patricia, whom Betty sent south to live temporarily with her sister Thomasena. Over the next eight years, Wilbur and Betty married and had five more children, but their relationship was stormy. Betty brooked no nonsense: one of her favorite phrases was "Don't piss in my face and tell me it's raining." Her battles with her husband sometimes got physical. One Fourth of July, Wilbur showed up drunk at a party, started a fight with Betty, and wound up hurting his own shoulder so badly that he was out of work for weeks. Another time, Betty cracked a chair over Wilbur's head and broke both her own wrists; her mother had to come up from the South to help Betty care for the children while she healed. Occasionally, Wilbur took the kids to the Bergen Point amusement park in nearby Bayonne, but most of the time he wasn't around, and sometime after the birth of baby Joan in 1961, he left for good. His children did not hear from him again for a decade.

Wilbur had been an inconsistent provider, and for much of her marriage, Betty was on welfare, which for a New Jersey family as large as hers paid about $355 a month in the early 1960s, too little to lift her above the federal poverty line. After Wilbur left, Betty had other relationships and two more daughters, Lydia and Saundra; decades later, her children would remember the good times, when their mother hosted holiday cookouts in the Booker T. courtyard, with soul music playing in the background, and welcomed her kids' friends into her four-bedroom apartment. Still, her sister Annie Ruth, who had joined her in Jersey City in 1967, disapproved of Betty's life. Getting those welfare checks was very convenient, she thought, but the Rock children had been raised to make their own way, like Annie Ruth herself, who went to work at a factory making baby clothes, bought a house, and raised four children on her own. It wasn't long before Betty began to envy her sister—already a homeowner, after just a few years in the city—and to feel ashamed of the contrast between their lives. A year or two after the bleak Christmas of 1967, Betty decided to change. She got a job in the public schools.

In the late 1960s, the Jersey City school district was near the peak of its enrollment, with more than 38,000 children attending its thirty-one grammar schools and four high schools. With 260,000 residents, the city was still New Jersey's second largest, after Newark, but its population was falling. Blacks and other minorities made up 22 percent of the population but 60 percent of the public school enrollment; the city's white residents, many of Irish, Italian, or Polish descent, sent their kids to Catholic school. Patronage networks channeled the politically connected into public school jobs, and Betty had a toehold in that system, because she had done some campaign work for local politicians. Although her formal education had ended with high school twenty years earlier, her connections were enough to get her hired as a teacher's aide in the federally funded Title I program, launched in 1965 to offer extra educational services to poor children. The new paycheck eased the Robinsons' poverty; Betty bought a car, and on weekends she loaded up her kids and their friends and took everyone fishing on Long Island. Working in the schools also gave her a close-up view of the shabby, overcrowded buildings where her children spent their days, and perhaps that made her especially receptive when, in 1970, a former city councilman came looking for a family willing to put its name on a lawsuit challenging the state's method of funding public schools. Betty signed up, along with her youngest son, eleven-year-old Kenneth Robinson. She didn't know it, but she was about to make him famous, at least in New Jersey.

In the United States, public schools are funded through a mix of federal, state, and local money, with the federal share by far the smallest.

Each state's school-aid formula determines how much of the remaining cost will be borne by local taxpayers and how much by state taxpayers—in other words, how much of the financial burden will fall on the small community surrounding the school and how much on the larger community of the state. Inevitably, as the balance between state and local funding shifts in one direction or another, competing values are favored or disfavored. The greater the state share of funding, the less the wealth or poverty of local districts affects the resources available for schooling—but the greater the danger that educational decisions will be made by bureaucrats in faraway state capitals. The greater the local share of funding, the greater the degree of control that local communities expect to exert over their schools—but the greater the inequities between rich and poor.

For most of New Jersey's history, the gravitational pull of local control, christened "home rule," has been nearly inescapable. From the state's beginnings in the seventeenth century until well into the nineteenth, the separate national and faith communities—Dutch and German, Quaker and Catholic—preferred to run their own affairs and teach their own children, and the developing political and educational systems embodied this determined separateness. The legislature was a loose association of representatives from the state's twenty-one counties, each the fiefdom of a political party chairman—Republicans in rural outposts and Democrats in urban strongholds. Although the state overhauled its constitution in 1947, reforming the courts and strengthening the governor, the legislature remained weak and unrepresentative: regardless of population, each county sent one senator to Trenton, giving the big cities no more power than the growing suburbs or the thinly settled rural counties. Money, that essential political lubricant, flowed liberally in the towns and counties, where governments collected and spent property taxes, but it barely trickled in Trenton, where the state levied no sales or income taxes.

Schooling, too, was traditionally a local or even a family matter. Over the first decades of the nineteenth century, Americans had begun embracing the idea of tuition-free, publicly funded common schools designed to prepare children for citizenship, but that evolution was slower in New Jersey than elsewhere. In 1817 the state had begun allocating money for free public schools, and in 1820 it had started allowing localities to levy school taxes, so that those too poor to pay tuition could still

get an education, but not until 1871, after every other state had barred localities from charging tuition for public schools, did New Jersey follow
suit. In 1875, New Jersey's voters stamped their approval on this evolu-
tionary process by adding to the state constitution a new amendment that
gave the state, rather than towns or churches, the responsibility for educating children. From now on, the amendment said, "The Legislature shall
provide for the maintenance and support of a thorough and efficient system of free public schools for the instruction of all the children in the
State between the ages of five and eighteen years."

By then, New Jersey's method of paying for those free public schools
had been overhauled more than once, as the pendulum swung between
approaches that favored the rich and those that evened the economic
scales. In 1838, with the favor-the-rich approach ascendant, the state began
allocating school aid to counties based on how much they paid in taxes,
ensuring richer counties a bigger slice of the pie. In 1871, the pendulum
swung back, as the law that abolished tuition also established a statewide
property tax to supplement locally levied taxes; the earnings from the
statewide tax were distributed on a per-pupil basis, allowing the property
wealth of the rich to subsidize the education of the poor. By the early
twentieth century, however, wealthier counties had persuaded the state to
revert to the earlier approach and distribute receipts from the statewide
property tax in proportion to the size of the property tax base, again fa-
voring the rich. The chance of equalizing school funding dimmed further
after the 1947 overhaul of the state constitution: although the revision
enshrined the 1875 "thorough and efficient" education amendment in
Article VIII, it also eliminated the statewide property tax. From now on,
state school aid would have to come from the state's general treasury.

That treasury was fed by few funding sources, mostly taxes on corporations and on cigarettes, gasoline, and the like. Legislators, beholden to
local and county politicians, fiercely resisted broad-based state taxes that
would pinch the voters' pocketbooks—and give the state government new
money, with its attendant clout. A state sales tax enacted in 1935, a dozen
years before the death of the statewide property tax, had survived only
four months, and an income tax was anathema to legislators and to many
of their constituents. By the 1960s, the results of keeping the pool of state
money so shallow had become obvious. Although New Jersey's schools

spent more per pupil than the national average, the state—as opposed to the local—share of that total was relatively small: 24 percent in 1963, compared to a national average of 40 percent. Localism remained intense: the 8,100-square-mile state had 568 towns but would soon have 578 school districts, since smaller towns sometimes ran their own grammar schools and then pooled their resources to form regional high school districts. In 1966, Governor Richard Hughes, a Democrat, tried to change the state-local funding balance by enacting an income tax, but his own party rebuffed him. In a compromise, he won the state's first permanent sales tax and began examining how to allocate this rich new source of revenue to benefit the schools, especially urban schools.

The social forces at work in American cities were on vivid display in New Jersey. Before World War II, New Jersey's cities and their schools had flourished, but Depression and war took their toll. Southern blacks like Betty Rock and Wilbur Robinson migrated to northern cities, as jobs vanished and whites fled to the growing suburbs. New Jersey's cities declined into poverty, and their schools followed. With three-quarters of school funding coming from localities, inequities burgeoned. Even at high tax rates, cities and rural towns with deficient property tax bases could not raise enough to spend lavishly on the schools; by contrast, in suburbs and seashore resorts blessed with ample property tax bases, low tax rates supported abundant school spending. In 1966–67, Newark levied a tax of $2.20 on every $100 of assessed property value to fund its schools at $599 per child; its near neighbor, the wealthy suburb of Millburn, taxed at a rate of $1.21 per $100 and spent $786 per child.

In July 1967 urban decline became impossible to ignore, as Newark and two smaller cities erupted into riots that left at least twenty-four people dead and caused more than $10 million in property damage. The state's report on the riots painted a bleak picture of Newark's public schools, their overcrowded, aging buildings filled with underqualified teachers and hostile, illiterate students with little chance of escaping the ghetto. "These young people constitute social dynamite, not to mention the loss of human potential," the report warned.

As the state confronted these realities, the commission charged with devising a formula for spending the new Hughes sales tax did its work. Its eventual chairman was Raymond Bateman, a moderate Republican state senator from wealthy, pastoral Somerset County, in the solidly Republican center of the state. Despite the affluence of his political base, Bateman was convinced the cities needed more money; his study commission began working on a formula that would ensure they got it.

Over the past two centuries, most state school-aid formulas have divided financial responsibility between the state and the local district in one of four ways. First, the state can pay the whole cost of schooling. Second, the state can give every district the same amount of money per child—a flat grant—and let the locals decide if they want to raise and spend more.

Then matters get more complicated. Under the third type of school-aid formula, known as a foundation formula, the state sets a minimum spending level—a foundation—and requires every town to tax its property at a minimum rate; the state makes up the difference for any town so poor that it cannot raise enough on its own to cover the foundation amount. Imagine the foundation amount is $100 per child and the mandated school tax rate is $1 for every $100 of assessed property value. Imagine a town where the property tax base—the sum total of property wealth—amounts to $10,000 per child. That town will be able to raise the $100-per-child foundation amount on its own and will get no state aid; by contrast, a town with a tax base of $5,000 per child will be able to raise only $50 per child, half the foundation amount, and the state will pay the other half.

Under the fourth type of school-aid formula, known as a guaranteed tax base or power-equalizing formula, the state lets localities decide their own tax rates and spending levels, with a twist: at any given tax rate, the state promises to make up the difference between what a town can generate on its own and what it could have generated if its tax base had been equivalent to a guaranteed level. Imagine that this guaranteed tax base is $10,000 per child: that means the state is promising that any town taxing at $1 per $100 of assessed property value will reap $100 per child, and any town taxing at $2 per $100 will reap $200 per child. Thus, a town with a tax base of $5,000 per child and a tax rate of $1 per $100 would generate $50 per child on its own and get $50 in state aid. But if that same town set a $2-per-$100 tax rate, generating $100 per child on its own, it would get $100 in state aid. Towns that impose higher property tax rates reap greater fiscal rewards, and property-poor towns can spend as much as property-rich ones, as long as they tax themselves equally. Thus, power equalizing breaks the link between property wealth and school spending. In the purest form of power equalizing, this link is broken at the top of the scale, as well as the bottom: just as the state makes up the difference for poor towns that cannot generate as much revenue as the guaranteed tax base would, so the state skims off the excess from rich towns that can raise far more, redistributing these takings to less fortunate towns.

In 1968 New Jersey funded its schools through a fourteen-year-old foundation formula that entitled each district to state aid of at least $100 and at most $452 per child. Despite legislative tinkering, actual school spending had far outstripped the numbers enshrined in the law; as a result, towns had to fund most of their school budgets locally, and the formula did little to help poor school districts keep up with rich ones. To replace this outdated structure, the Bateman Commission proposed a complicated guaranteed tax base formula that would offer fiscal incentives for school improvement: "standard" districts, providing a minimal educational program, would be funded against a guaranteed tax base of $30,000 per child, while districts with better programs—the best would be dubbed "comprehensive"—would be funded against higher guaranteed tax bases, up to $45,000 per child. Bateman saw the incentive aid as a gift to struggling urban districts: rich districts needed no fiscal incentives to make the climb from standard programs to comprehensive ones, because they were already offering excellent services, but the extra aid would reward poor districts for improvement. To provide the cities with additional help, the Bateman Commission also proposed giving districts extra aid for children on welfare, to cover the cost of compensating for their poverty.

Bateman was proud of the incentive-aid proposal: as he saw it, a working-class district that improved its science program, say, could qualify for extra state aid as a result, giving the district every reason to upgrade. But the legislature was dominated by suburban Republicans who did not understand why so much money had to go to places that did not even vote for their party. An urban school-aid formula was no great selling point back home in the affluent, rapidly growing commuter towns of North Jersey. After ten years in the legislature, Bateman had a shrewd sense of what his colleagues needed. He knew a formula that took money away from Republican towns stood no chance of passing, so his formula—unlike the purest form of power equalizing—allowed rich districts to keep the excess funds they could raise at each tax rate. His formula also had its sweeteners: a save-harmless clause, guaranteeing that no district would get less aid under the Bateman plan than it had gotten the year before, and a big increase in so-called minimum aid—money that went to every district, even rich ones with tax bases far larger than the guaranteed level.

Still, the bill ignited a hellish fight among Republicans, and in the end, Bateman had to settle for less than he wanted. He got extra aid for welfare kids, a guaranteed tax base formula that gave the cities more money, and, of course, minimum aid and a save-harmless provision. But although the law as passed in 1970 called for the incentive aid he had been so proud of, the law as funded—with $28 million more state dollars, on top of the more than $200 million already being spent—provided enough money only to classify every district as basic, the lowest level on the ladder of incentives. A working-class district that invested in a new science program now would get no financial reward from the state; the money simply wasn't there. Furthermore, it quickly became clear, even the extra dollars that did begin flowing into the cities in 1971–72 were not used primarily to increase school spending. Mayors used the state money to replace local money, so they could cut taxes and get reelected. Bateman was bitterly disappointed. He had designed a school-aid program, not a tax relief program. The legislature should have made the extra aid contingent upon cities' maintaining their own contributions to the schools, he realized in hindsight. The mayors had outsmarted the legislators.

Jersey City's annual State of the City address was scheduled for January 15, 1970, Martin Luther King Jr.'s birthday, and Mayor Thomas Whelan used the occasion to declare war—"a tax war upon the state," he said. Jersey City's finances were in terrible shape. Squeezed between escalating demands for police, fire, and health services on the one hand and adverse state tax policies on the other, the city could no longer afford its 75 percent share of the public school budget, Whelan announced—a share, he might have added, that had become especially burdensome since the recent signing of a generous, strike-generated teachers' contract. So once the schools closed for the summer, Whelan said, they would stay closed, unless the state picked up the whole tab. "We are preparing to file suit to force the state to live up to its constitutional mandate to support the public education system," Whelan said.

The news of the lawsuit came as a surprise to Harold Ruvoldt Jr., and the suit had been his idea in the first place. In January 1970, Ruvoldt was twenty-seven, a Jersey City native less than four years out of law school at Seton Hall, a North Jersey Catholic university. His father was a well-known local lawyer whose close connections to Democratic politics in Democratic-controlled Hudson County went back to his teenage years. As a college freshman, Ruvoldt Sr. had addressed campaign crowds from the back of a truck, and Jersey City Mayor Frank Hague, the legendary machine politician, had dubbed him the "boy orator of the Democratic Party"; as an adult, Ruvoldt Sr. had held county legal jobs before opening his own practice. Ruvoldt Sr. had assured his only son that he could pursue whatever career path he wanted—just as soon as he passed the bar exam. No rebellious hippie, Ruvoldt Jr. passed the bar in 1966, the same year he finished law school and got married; soon after, he joined his father's practice in Jersey City, not far from the two-family house where he had grown up. Four years later, Ruvoldt Jr. and his young family still lived in that house, eating dinner with his parents every night.

In the political ferment of the 1960s, school funding was emerging as an important issue. Although an early federal case out of Illinois had been lost, the California case of *Serrano v. Priest* and the federal case out of Texas, *San Antonio v. Rodriguez*, both of which challenged school-funding systems that relied heavily on local property taxes, seemed likely to meet with more success. Advocates were optimistic that the U.S. Supreme Court would build upon its 1954 *Brown v. Board of Education* decision by affirming what seemed obvious to them: just as racially segregated schools violated the Fourteenth Amendment promise of equal protection of the laws, so too did underfunded urban and rural schools.

Against that backdrop, Harold Ruvoldt Jr. began writing a law review article that he titled "The Right to Learn." Education, he argued, was a fundamental right, and therefore government could not permit educational opportunities to vary from place to place merely because some places were rich and others poor. "Can we on the one hand recognize that one's future may depend on the right to learn and on the other, sanction discrimination in its granting?" he wrote. "I think not." The New Jersey constitution's "thorough and efficient" educational guarantee made these issues particularly compelling, he added; the state's school-funding formula, with its heavy reliance on widely varying local taxing capacity, might be constitutionally vulnerable.

Ruvoldt showed his article to a friend of his father's—a well-connected friend, Jimmy Ryan, the lawyer for the city of Jersey City. Ryan was intrigued enough that, a couple of months before Mayor Whelan's 1970 State of the City address, he arranged a meeting at city hall between Ruvoldt, Whelan, City Council President Thomas Flaherty, and some other lawyers and city officials. The meeting did not go particularly well. No one but Ruvoldt and Ryan seemed to think the city could win a lawsuit challenging New Jersey's school-funding system on constitutional grounds. In the middle of the meeting, Harold Krieger, a prominent local attorney who was Mayor Whelan's personal lawyer, asked Ruvoldt to cite the cases that underlay his legal theory. Ruvoldt remembered how his mother used to complain that whenever Krieger visited her house, he ended up taking all her cigarettes. "Do you think I'm nuts?" Ruvoldt asked Krieger that day. Ruvoldt might be a kid barely out of law school and Krieger might be a big-shot local lawyer, but Ruvoldt wasn't going to give away all his research and let Krieger file the suit.

Still, it looked as though Ruvoldt would not be filing it either—until January 15, when Whelan announced that the city was going to court. Soon after, Ruvoldt's telephone rang. "The mayor wants to see you tonight," Council President Flaherty said. That night, as Ruvoldt and Flaherty hustled in the back door of Whelan's house, TV cameras waited outside: the mayor's promise to close down the schools and sue the state had made quite a splash, though the threat was widely viewed as another example of Jersey City's penchant for playing politics as a contact sport. Inside, the three men drew up a retainer agreement putting Ruvoldt in charge of a case that, although perhaps launched as a public relations stunt, would end by changing the face of New Jersey politics.

Ruvoldt knew the case would be filed against Governor William Cahill and other state officials, and he knew it would be filed on behalf of city and school officials, but he needed another plaintiff as well: a student, to represent all the New Jersey children languishing in underfunded schools. Ruvoldt made a list of the seventy-odd characteristics of an ideal plaintiff.

The plaintiff needed to be young enough that he would still be attending school if the case spent years in court. He needed to be bright but under-achieving, to show that the schools were shortchanging him. His parents should be public employees who might lose their jobs if they moved out of town in search of better schooling. And, ideally, he should be white—Ruvoldt wanted to show that New Jersey's funding system discriminated on the basis of wealth, and race would be a distraction, he felt. Ruvoldt soon concluded, however, that few talented white children remained stuck in Jersey City's worst schools; if you were smart and white, someone found you a way out. The mayor's office sought help from Fred Martin, who had just finished eight years as the city council's first black member, and Martin found Betty Robinson and her son, Kenneth. Although they were black, they fit Ruvoldt's other criteria. The lawyer had his plaintiffs; the suit would be called *Robinson v. Cahill.*

In 1970, Kenneth Robinson was in sixth grade at School 22, a block-long brick building less than a mile from the Booker T. projects. The school had been built in 1919, and its age showed in the fancy terra-cotta floral designs over the front door, architectural niceties that an earlier era had lavished upon its public buildings. Inside, the school was clean and well tended, and a succession of effective principals had kept discipline strong. The school faced substantial challenges, however. For one thing, it was huge, Jersey City's biggest grammar school and reputedly one of the biggest in the state. At its peak in 1968, School 22 enrolled two thousand students in kindergarten through eighth grade; classes routinely had thirty children, and the school housed overflow fifth-graders in three rented classrooms above a nearby bank. The school had no art room, so the young art teacher carried his supplies with him in shopping bags. One day in the early 1970s, as he toted printmaking trays covered in wet paint from floor to floor, the shopping bag ripped open, and he sat down on the stairs, weeping in frus-tration. At School 22, students got one art lesson every three weeks.

More than half the school's students were minority-group members, and many were poor: School 22 served children from both the Booker T. and Lafayette Gardens housing projects, as well as children from the shrinking number of Polish families who still lived in the surrounding Lafayette neighborhood. Although decline nibbled at Lafayette's edges, white-owned businesses—a five-and-dime, a small supermarket, a corner drugstore—still flourished on Pacific Avenue. In place of the social programs that government would later establish inside inner-city schools— the free meals, the supports for the disabled and the Spanish-speaking, the on-site health clinics and full-time social workers—School 22 improvised its own safety net. A teacher might buy a hungry kid a sandwich, or let a ragged one pick out new shoes at a local store whose owner was willing to wait for his money until the teacher's next payday.

Educationally, the Jersey City schools struggled, though an outsider could not easily tell how much: the state gave no standardized tests of its own until the early 1970s. But on national tests, 43 percent of Jersey City's students performed two and a half years below the norm, the school district found when it compiled data for Ruvoldt's lawsuit. On average, students were doing well enough at the end of first grade, but the longer they stayed in school, the more ground they lost. The grammar school curriculum supposedly included science, the all-important subject in the post-Sputnik era, but insiders knew that was a polite fiction: elementary school teachers were not trained to teach science, and most classrooms lacked science equipment anyway. In high school, too, students suffered from a lack of basics. As a teenager attending a Jesuit school in New York in the late 1950s, Ruvoldt had seen the American history textbook that a friend at the public high school in his neighborhood was using. The account of twentieth-century history stopped with World War II, which had ended nearly a generation earlier.

Ruvoldt filed his suit a month after Mayor Whelan's State of the City speech, on February 13, 1970. "Here—this doesn't look like much," Hudson County's chief judge said as he assigned *Robinson v. Cahill* to his colleague, Theodore Botter. Ted Botter was forty-five, the son of Russian Jewish immigrants and a product of Hudson County public schools. After barely missing combat in World War II, Botter had applied to Columbia University's law school almost as an afterthought, but by the time Ruvoldt's case landed on his desk, he was a legal veteran who had spent six years as a high-ranking member of the state attorney general's office before becoming a judge. Botter was a Democrat, and hardly unaware of the country's mid-1960s turmoil, but on the bench, he could express his views only obliquely. To show his sympathy with long-haired anti-Vietnam

War protesters, Botter had grown a beard, an unusual choice for a judge in those days and, he had heard through the grapevine, one that irritated the state supreme court's imperious chief justice, Joseph Weintraub.

The immediate impetus for Ruvoldt's case, Jersey City's brash threat to stop paying for its public schools, soon evaporated: by April, the city had bowed to the inevitable and agreed to find the money somewhere. But the *Robinson* case and its constitutional challenge to the state's school-funding system stayed alive. Ruvoldt planned to base his case on statistics showing how much the taxpayers and students in wealthy districts benefited from their affluence, and how much those in poor districts suffered from their poverty; he would show that poor school districts spent less than rich ones, taxed their residents more heavily, paid their teachers lower salaries, and produced students who were less likely to go to college. But in 1970, processing that kind of data for even a fraction of New Jersey's nearly six hundred school districts was a complex technological task. For help, Ruvoldt turned to the Educational Testing Service (ETS), the company that produced the Scholastic Aptitude Test at its pastoral central New Jersey campus. ETS agreed to donate time on its mainframe after the company's work had ended for the day, and Ruvoldt spent countless evenings in an ETS conference room as the giant computer down the hall crunched through the numbers Ruvoldt and a company technician fed it. Dozens of relationships had to be teased out of data drawn from the U.S. Census, from tax records, and from the state Department of Education's files: correlations among family income, attendance at two-year and four-year colleges, SAT scores, percentages of teachers with advanced degrees. When the technician found ironclad statistical proof that children from homes with two vacuum cleaners were very likely to grow up to attend graduate school, Ruvoldt double-checked the figures: he knew he needed an explanation for such apparently nonsensical relationships, since the state would likely mine the same data and use anomalies to cast doubt on the correlation between wealth and student achievement. He was relieved to discover that the extra vacuum cleaners belonged to rich people with big, expensive houses.

Even with ETS's help, and even with the extra fees generated when the cities of East Orange, Paterson, and Plainfield joined Jersey City as plaintiffs, the all-consuming *Robinson* case was straining the resources of the four-lawyer Ruvoldt firm, so Ruvoldt Jr. went looking for help. In Newark, he met with a group of liberal lawyers affiliated with the American Civil Liberties Union, the Legal Services program for the poor, and the law school of Rutgers, the state's public university. An alliance seemed natural, but somehow it did not pan out: years later, those involved disagreed about whether Ruvoldt was loath to share credit for a potentially landmark case or whether the Newark group lacked his confidence that the suit was winnable. In any case, a group of Rutgers law professors and students was already developing a different challenge to New Jersey's public school system, representing Newark parents who questioned why municipal boundary lines prevented their children from attending the far better public schools in nearby suburbs. That case was still a fledgling when Ruvoldt came calling, but Paul Tractenberg, one of the Rutgers professors involved in the project, thought it had potential. Tractenberg went back to his own case, and Ruvoldt went on with *Robinson*.

Robinson was progressing at a leisurely pace. Botter, who would be trying the lawsuit without a jury, was eager to pare the case down to essentials; he did not intend to sit through months of testimony. But Botter also did not want a show trial, and he had reason to wonder if the state planned a vigorous defense. Modernizers in both parties were steering New Jersey away from its traditional localism—the Hughes sales tax was one example of that effort—and a judicial ruling ordering more state money for poor schools could strengthen their hand. Battle lines over a state income tax, the obvious way to pay for increased state school aid, had been drawn for years; during his 1969 campaign, the new Republican governor, Cahill, had not ruled out such a tax. Once in office, Cahill had appointed an illustrious committee to review the entire state tax structure, and although that group was still at work, its report was expected to question the state's dependence on the property tax. So Botter asked the state's lawyer, Stephen Weiss, if he planned to put up a real fight; if not, Botter would add the state's rich school districts to the case as defendants, ensuring Ruvoldt a vigorous antagonist. Weiss assured Botter that he was under no orders to go slow, and so the rich districts stayed on the sidelines.

In August 1971, eighteen months after the filing of *Robinson*, the California Supreme Court ruled in favor of the plaintiffs in *Serrano v. Priest*, finding that the state's school-funding system violated the equal-protection guarantees of both the state and federal constitutions. California's foundation plan "invidiously discriminates against the poor because it makes the quality of a child's education a function of the wealth of his parents and neighbors," the court ruled. Although the Bateman law had just replaced New Jersey's old foundation formula, the lack of full funding for Bateman's scheme made the New Jersey system a close cousin of the now-unconstitutional California plan. Suddenly, it looked as if *Robinson* might amount to more than just Jersey City political theater.

To Paul Tractenberg, the Rutgers law professor who had been developing his own education case, it seemed clear that *Robinson* was now on a fast track. Inevitably, Ruvoldt's case would be decided long before the still-unfiled Rutgers suit could get to trial, and although the two cases were not identical, the *Robinson* precedent was bound to affect the Rutgers case. The options, Tractenberg decided, were three: rush to file the Rutgers suit; seek Ruvoldt's permission to join *Robinson* as a plaintiff; or offer Botter a friend-of-the-court brief based on legal work the Rutgers group had already done. The first two alternatives seemed unpromising: the Rutgers case was not yet ready for filing, and the ambitious Ruvoldt was distinctly uninterested in sharing his high-profile case, Tractenberg thought. Instead, Tractenberg and his colleagues began work on a friend-of-the-court brief, and Ruvoldt got ready to try *Robinson v. Cahill.*

By November 1971, when *Robinson* finally got underway, the keen press interest attending Mayor Whelan's swashbuckling threat to close the schools almost two years earlier had mostly evaporated; even the hometown newspaper covered the case only in brief reports on inside pages. In truth, the trial had little to interest a reader lacking a college degree in education or economics. Although the case bore their names, Betty and Kenneth Robinson were never mentioned; none of the thirteen witnesses who testified during the six days of trial was a current student or employee of a public school district. Instead, Ruvoldt and Weiss called experts: officials of the Department of Education and the New Jersey School Boards Association, authors of well-known studies on education funding, and academic analysts of tax rates and test scores.

Much of the testimony focused on the debate over whether school spending bore any relation to educational quality and student performance.

Ever since 1966, when sociologist James Coleman had reported that family background had a greater impact on students' academic achievement than schooling did, debate had raged over what, if anything, schools could do to help children from impoverished families succeed. Ruvoldt's witnesses insisted that adequate spending was a necessary, although not a sufficient, prerequisite of educational quality. To get results, those extra dollars had to be spent on better teachers and programs—but the extra dollars did have to be spent. Even Weiss's witnesses barely contested the point. "Isn't it true that with all other things being equal, to improve the quality of an education that a district provides, generally speaking, costs more money?" Ruvoldt asked a former education official testifying for the state. The reply: "Yes." To bolster his arguments, Ruvoldt introduced the reams of computer-generated data he had gleaned during those long evenings in the ETS conference room, the affidavits he had gathered from local school superintendents, and the federal and state studies he had collected on such topics as class size and remedial education—tens of thousands of pages of evidence. He had boxes filled with back-up materials he never even used. The case obsessed him.

Weiss's attitude was less clear. A few years older than Ruvoldt, Weiss too was a city kid from North Jersey and the son of an attorney, although unlike Ruvoldt, who had attended Catholic schools from kindergarten through law school, Weiss was a product of urban public schools. In 1966, the same year Ruvoldt passed the bar, Weiss joined the state attorney general's office, where he specialized in education law. He left for private practice soon after the *Robinson* case was filed, but his old boss knew a young lawyer could use some business and hired him to defend the state's school-funding system against Ruvoldt's novel claim. Years later, Weiss insisted he had gotten no instructions to concede the case, or even to weigh the political implications of contesting a lawsuit that asserted more or less what the governor himself seemed to believe. Still, Weiss saw no point in disputing some of Ruvoldt's major claims. Weiss agreed that the New Jersey constitution's "thorough and efficient" clause made education a state, rather than a local, responsibility, and it was obvious to him that the decaying cities, faced with extensive demands for other services, could not spend as much on schooling as the growing suburbs did. No one could say it was good that some Jersey City grammar schools housed their libraries in closets. But Weiss still thought the state could win its case with a simple argument: the system might be imperfect, but it was not the courts' business to fix it. The constitution did not compel one funding system or another; that choice belonged to the legislature, and the legislature had addressed the issues by enacting the Bateman law.

It was a plausible legal strategy, but as *Robinson* got underway, Ruvoldt was still surprised by some of Weiss's choices. Even as he challenged the state on behalf of four cities, Ruvoldt doubted the cities had standing to sue, since municipalities are legally creatures of the state, but Weiss never challenged their standing. Weiss never challenged the data analyses Ruvoldt had done at ETS, either: stacks of computer printouts went into the record without a peep from the state's lawyer. To one Education Department official monitoring the trial for his boss, it looked as if the state were not putting up much of a fight. Ruvoldt was a youthful firebrand pursuing a case that had sprung from his own imagination; Weiss was an affable professional doing the job he had been hired to do. Although the 1960s were over, their activist spirit lingered; in the wake of *Serrano*, the nation seemed on the cusp of change. Perhaps it seemed pointless to swim against the tide.

As the lawyers wrapped up their closing arguments two weeks before Christmas 1971, neither was sure how Botter would rule. The judge had asked the witnesses many questions, but his demeanor remained inscrutable. Before the trial began, Ruvoldt had expected to lose; it would take a trial judge of unparalleled intellectual courage to declare the state's whole school-funding system unconstitutional, he thought. But as the case ended, it was Weiss who had begun to expect defeat. Indeed, although Botter had known little about urban education when the trial began—he lived in a comfortable North Jersey suburb himself—as testimony progressed, he had become increasingly convinced that the system was flawed. He was offended to learn that the desperately poor South Jersey city of Camden still housed disabled children in a school made of wood. And he was struck by statistics showing that in Jersey City, only half the school budget went for teacher salaries, a far smaller proportion than in suburban districts. With aging, expensive buildings to maintain, the city clearly had many extra demands on its education dollars.

On top of the voluminous evidence, Botter could rely on Tractenberg's hundred-page friend-of-the-court brief, its centerpiece an analysis of the history and implications of the state constitution's "thorough and efficient" clause. First, the brief argued that the so-called T&E clause required the state to provide a comprehensive education, not just a minimal one. In its original form, the brief noted, the 1875 amendment had called for public schools to offer a "rudimentary" education; the fact that legislators had rejected this wording in favor of "thorough and efficient" strongly suggested they had wanted to require something more than minimal instruction. Turning next to the question of how to decide whether the state was providing a T&E education, Tractenberg argued that only such measures of school achievement as test scores and dropout rates—output criteria—provided an appropriate standard. Third, like Ruvoldt's witnesses, he asserted that adequate funding levels—inputs—were clearly correlated with acceptable outputs. Finally, he insisted that the Bateman law could likely never provide districts with enough money to satisfy the constitutional guarantee. By design, the Bateman law's incentive system could leave some districts funded at the constitutionally inadequate "basic" level, rather than the "comprehensive" level required for T&E, and, in practice, the legislature had not provided enough funding to lift any impoverished district above that minimum.

Over the holidays, Botter commandeered his family's dining room table, spread out the evidence, and got to work on his ruling. He took special care with the writing, introducing the five main sections of his opinion with quotations from the likes of Thomas Jefferson and T. S. Eliot. He wanted, he said years later, to suggest what education made possible, to leave the reader feeling, "Here's an example of a good education." Botter also made another strategic decision. With the opinion pending, newspapers had begun calling, asking for a photograph of the judge who, one way or the other, would soon end up on the front page. Before the photographers arrived, Botter shaved the beard he had grown as a silent gesture of protest years earlier: he did not want the public wondering why such an important case had been assigned to some hippie judge.

Harold Ruvoldt Jr. got enough advance notice of Botter's plans to organize a press conference at city hall in Jersey City, and he asked Betty Robinson to attend: although she had played little part in the legal proceedings, he had been in touch with her from time to time over the two years since her case was filed. On January 19, 1972, Botter handed a sealed envelope containing a copy of his decision to a state trooper tasked with delivering it to the governor's office. As a courtesy to Governor Cahill, Botter asked Ruvoldt to tell no one what the opinion contained until the trooper had a chance to make the ninety-minute trip to Trenton. Ruvoldt walked past the reporters waiting in the halls and scanned his copy in the elevator; then he got into the car, where his wife was waiting to drive him to city hall. She was dying of curiosity, but Ruvoldt's lips were sealed. Still, he figured she could tell he was pleased.

Botter had done everything Ruvoldt could have hoped. Although the judge acknowledged that higher spending did not always correlate with higher-quality schooling, the statistical evidence was compelling, he said: the richer the district, the more it spent for teachers, books, and buildings; the less it taxed; and the better its students performed. Of course, schools were not solely responsible for students' achievement; family and community played their roles, Botter agreed. But the evidence had convinced him that schooling had some impact beyond these socioeconomic factors. "It is too much to expect that our school system alone can solve all these problems," Botter wrote. "But much can be done, and doing more will cost more. Education is no exception to this fact of life."

Then Botter turned to the law before him. Were the Bateman law fully funded, he said, its basic structure would probably meet the state constitution's guarantee of a thorough and efficient education. But with the legislature committed to only partial funding, the law fell short of the T&E level, Botter said. And Botter found no justification for two provisions that Ray Bateman had known were crucial to getting his bill through the legislature—the save-harmless clause guaranteeing that no district would lose money, and the minimum-aid provision, ensuring that even the richest district would get a piece of the pie. "As long as some school districts are underfinanced, I can see no legitimate legislative purpose in giving rich districts 'state aid,'" Botter wrote.

Then the judge turned to Ruvoldt's claim that the school-funding system violated the state and federal guarantees of equal protection of the laws. Under equal-protection jurisprudence, judges owed deference to a law unless two tests were met: the law affected a fundamental constitutional right, and the law distinguished among citizens according to a suspect classification, such as race. If so, the law could then pass muster only if justified by a compelling state interest. Botter dispatched these three complex questions with little argument. Education was clearly a fundamental right, he asserted, and apportioning educational opportunities by wealth met the suspect classification test as far as he was concerned. The only compelling interest the state had asserted was its desire to maintain local control of schools, and Botter was sure this value could be protected in a system with fewer inequities. "Distribution of school resources according to the chance location of pupils cannot be tolerated under the State or Federal Constitutions," Botter wrote.

Then Botter went further than even Ruvoldt had suggested. Not only did the state's school-funding system violate the equal-protection rights of students, he wrote, but it also violated the equal-protection rights of taxpayers, because their school tax burdens differed hugely according to where they lived. Since education was a state, rather than a local, responsibility, all the state's taxpayers should share equally in its cost, he wrote. "There is no compelling justification for making a taxpayer in one district pay a tax at a higher rate than a taxpayer in another district, so long as the revenue serves the common state educational purpose," he wrote. The message was clear: New Jersey's traditional reliance on local property taxes to fund its public schools violated the state and federal constitutions.

No one missed the significance of Botter's ruling. On front pages across the state, reporters called the decision a mortal threat to New Jersey's hallowed tradition of home rule, a stage-setter for "one of the most important legislative battles in New Jersey since the state established a system of free public schools." At the city hall press conference in Jersey City, a reporter asked Kenneth Robinson, now a thirteen-year-old eighth-grader at School 22, what he thought of the judge's ruling. Kenneth had not even known he was part of a lawsuit until his mother told him they were going to a press conference, but he did his best to answer. "It's okay, I guess," he said. "I guess it's okay if it did some good."

2

Celebrating the Bicentennial

Somewhere, Kenneth Robinson had acquired a nickname: everyone called him Babe, perhaps because he was the youngest of the Robinson brothers, perhaps because girls were drawn to him. Dark skinned and solidly built, Babe cared about his looks: he kept his teeth white and his hair perfectly waved, ironed his own clothes, shined his shoes, and made sure his sneakers had clean laces. He was funny and outgoing, popular with the boys and girls from the Booker T. and Montgomery Gardens projects who spent their free time watching TV, playing cards, maybe sipping a beer or a wine cooler every now and then. He liked going to Bruce Lee karate movies in the theaters around Journal Square, the bustling heart of Jersey City, or on Forty-Second Street in Manhattan. To his siblings, Babe seemed smart, his nose often buried in a book; although he would one day tell a reporter that he hadn't understood his schoolwork, they thought he got good grades.

But at Harold Ruvoldt's press conference that January day in 1972, Babe stood upon a threshold that often tripped up inner-city kids: he was a few months away from leaving the familiar cocoon of grammar school for the greater anonymity, independence—and temptations—of high school. In Jersey City, the schools lost most of their dropouts in ninth and tenth grade; students who made it to junior year were likely to get across the finish line.

Babe did have one thing in his favor. A few years earlier, the district had replaced an old high school in a different neighborhood with a new building about half a mile from the Booker T. projects, reconfiguring attendance areas accordingly. Booker T. children were no longer assigned to World War I–vintage Lincoln High School; now they would attend the brand-new James J. Ferris High School, a long, boxy brick building described at its 1969 dedication as "a show-piece of modern design." Ferris's main lobby was adorned with a picture window and a grandiose exhortation to arriving students: "Enter to grow in wisdom; depart to serve better thy country and thy kind." The school had a two-level library, enough classrooms that teachers no longer had to share space, a swimming pool big enough to host county meets, and even a playing field—a true luxury in a city short of vacant land. Eventually, however, teachers who worked at Ferris began to wonder if its architect had ever visited an inner-city high school. The building had seventeen separate entrances, and although teachers felt secure—Ferris was reputedly one of the city's safer high schools—they spent their free periods patrolling the halls to catch kids wandering in or out of all those doors. In distant stairwells, the scent of marijuana smoke lingered.

Ferris's classes were sometimes large, and at times, teachers ran short of books or made do with outdated versions; one motivated group of students spent their own money buying copies of The Grapes of Wrath, which was not part of the regular curriculum. Like many high schools, Ferris structured its academic program into tracks, assigning students to the highest, college prep, only if their grades and aspirations warranted. Everyone else settled for a less rigorous curriculum: vocational training for those with specific post–high school plans, and the general track for the rest.

In his freshman year at Ferris, Babe did well enough, but by sophomore year, the distractions of high school were beginning to take their toll. Babe's older brother Larry, now going by the nickname Tank, a gift from a football coach impressed by his bulk, had struggled academically since sixth grade, and now he and Babe started cutting class together. They would check into homeroom first thing in the morning, the better to thwart the school's truancy-detection procedures, and then leave to smoke marijuana or to play basketball in New York. As far as Tank knew, Betty Robinson had no idea what her sons were up to; the schools were cutting truant officers to save money, so perhaps the Robinsons fell through the cracks. Or perhaps Betty was busy with her middle son, Tony, who had begun compiling a juvenile arrest record for burglary and was already using hard drugs. Certainly, Booker T. could be a perilous place for a teenager. One night when Babe was seventeen, he and his brothers were in a neighbor's apartment rolling the marijuana joints that Tank sometimes sold to classmates when the police raided the place and arrested everyone there. Apparently, the apartment's tenant was selling heroin, but the Robinson kids were not involved in that far more serious offense, and the charges against them were dropped before reaching court.

While Babe Robinson made the tricky transition to high school, the citizens of New Jersey were navigating their own transition into the new era Judge Theodore Botter's decision had inaugurated. Everyone who cared about the state's schools had begun spending a lot of time at meetings of education associations and good-government groups, struggling to find a politically viable way of funneling more money to the impoverished cities and their black and Hispanic students. The obstacles to reform were readily apparent. At the lunch break in one of those meetings, two school board members—one a white man from the affluent suburb of Westfield, the other an African American man from the decaying city of Paterson—found themselves sharing a table. After the introductions, the white man turned to the African American with a question. "Why are you people making such a big deal out of money?" he asked. "After all, your kids don't need what my kids need."

Still, reformers had reason for optimism. Botter had ordered the state to stop handing out minimum aid and save-harmless aid by the end of 1972 and to revamp the entire school-funding system by the end of 1973, and armed with the report of his blue-ribbon tax policy committee, issued a month after Botter's opinion, Governor William Cahill decided to take a stab at reform. The blue-ribbon committee's recommendations were sweeping: the state should enact an income tax and a statewide property tax; begin paying the full cost of a host of locally funded services, including the schools; cut local property taxes by 40 percent; and ensure they stayed cut by capping property tax rates. Good-government advocates praised the report, but by July 1972, the most controversial parts of the program—the income tax, the statewide property tax, full state funding of the public schools—were dead, shot down overwhelmingly in the assembly in a humiliating defeat for the governor. Cahill, looking ahead to reelection in 1973, did not try to revive the plan. The next move seemed likely to come from the courts. Soon after the *Robinson v. Cahill* ruling, the state supreme court had suspended Botter's deadlines and agreed to hear the case at once, bypassing the appeals court that would ordinarily have weighed in first. But before the New Jersey Supreme Court had a chance to rule, the U.S. Supreme Court changed the face of school-funding litigation.

The case eventually known as *San Antonio Independent School District v. Rodriguez* had been filed in 1968 by the families of Mexican American students living in a poor Texas school district. In 1971, the same year the California Supreme Court voided that state's school-funding system, a federal court found that Texas's system, too, violated the equal-protection rights enshrined in the Fourteenth Amendment to the U.S. Constitution. But when *Rodriguez* reached the highest court in the land, the momentum propelling the school-funding litigants forward abruptly vanished. In March 1973, in a 5–4 decision, the U.S. Supreme Court ruled that for the purposes of equal-protection analysis, education, mentioned nowhere in the U.S. Constitution, was not a fundamental right guaranteed under the Fourteenth Amendment. The justices were also unconvinced that the Texas school-funding law singled out a suspect class of citizens. Just because a school district was property poor, Justice Lewis Powell wrote for the majority, did not mean that its residents themselves were poor. Further, for the federal courts to overrule a state school-funding statute would upend traditional divisions of responsibility between state and federal and between legislature and judiciary, Powell wrote. Far better to leave the complicated matter of local tax policy to elected representatives in close touch with local conditions.

In dissent, Justice Thurgood Marshall, who, as a lawyer, had brought the landmark *Brown* school desegregation case, lamented that the *Rodriguez* ruling marked a retreat from the court's commitment to educational equity, an "unsupportable acquiescence in a system which deprives children in their earliest years of the chance to reach their full potential as citizens." Property-rich public school districts benefited too much from current funding arrangements for legislative reforms to be likely, Marshall wrote. But in a footnote that seemed designed to rally the defeated troops, Marshall added, "Of course, nothing in the Court's decision today should inhibit further review of state educational-funding schemes under state constitutional guarantees."

As if in answer to Marshall, less than two weeks later the New Jersey Supreme Court ruled in *Robinson*. In its unanimous decision, written by Chief Justice Joseph Weintraub, the court rejected much of Botter's reasoning. His finding of a federal equal-protection violation had been negated by the just-issued *Rodriguez* opinion, and his claim of a state equal-protection violation seemed problematic to the New Jersey justices. While education was directly mentioned in the state constitution, it was provided upon terms no different from those under which the state provided police protection or road repair; to find an equal-protection violation merely because localities chose to spend different amounts on their schools would potentially implicate the entire system of local government funded through property taxes, a step Weintraub's court was not prepared to take. But then Weintraub turned to the "thorough and efficient" clause. Reviewing the history of schooling in New Jersey, he quickly determined that the T&E guarantee was never intended to ensure equality among taxpayers or full state funding of the public schools, as Botter had argued. "But we do not doubt that an equal educational opportunity for children was precisely in mind," Weintraub wrote. "Whether the State acts directly or imposes the role upon local government, the end product must be what the Constitution commands." That constitutional guarantee, he added, "must be understood to embrace that educational opportunity which is needed in the contemporary setting to equip a child for his role as a citizen and as a competitor in the labor market."

It was here, in the provision of equal educational opportunity, that the Bateman law was falling short, the court found. Like Botter, the justices reached this conclusion based upon the evidence of large disparities in per-pupil spending between rich and poor districts. "We deal with the problem in those terms," Weintraub explained, "because dollar input is plainly relevant and because we have been shown no other viable criterion for measuring compliance with the constitutional mandate"—the state had never defined what a "thorough and efficient" education should include, and so the court used spending as a proxy for this missing definition. It seemed doubtful, the court added, that a T&E system could ever be created by relying on local taxation: there was too great a mismatch between areas of great wealth and areas of great need. But the court declined to impose its own remedy; instead, in a second ruling issued a few months later, it gave the legislature eighteen months, until the end of 1974, to come up with a suitable plan.

It was an inopportune time for the state to wrestle with its most difficult political issue. In the 1973 Republican primary, incumbent Governor Cahill had gone down to a shocking defeat, ensuring that the state's top office would change hands before the court's deadline arrived. At the Department of Education, the ouster of the education commissioner had left a leadership vacuum. In the legislature, recently reshaped to comply with court rulings mandating fairer apportionment of representation, all 120 seats would be up for grabs in the November election. And at the supreme court, Weintraub had announced his retirement. Nothing, it was clear, could happen until new leaders were in place in all three branches of government.

Although several well-known Democrats were running in the gubernatorial primary, the party barons disliked the choices. A better alternative, they decided, would be Brendan Byrne. A few years earlier, the lanky Essex County prosecutor had come to public notice when federal prosecutors released transcripts of their wiretapping of an accused Mafia boss. On the tapes, mobsters chatted about their friendly meetings with prominent politicians, but they complained about Byrne: apparently, he wasn't amenable to their usual forms of persuasion. "Trying to buy him only makes it worse," one disgruntled associate groused. "The man the Mob couldn't buy": now there was a stirring political slogan, especially in the wake of campaign-finance scandals that had tarnished Cahill and were swirling uncomfortably close to the Republican president of the United States. Add to Byrne's Mr. Clean image a host of other assets—three years as a judge, distinguished World War II service, degrees from Princeton and Harvard Law School, a twenty-year marriage that had produced seven children, and an Irish Catholic name that would appeal to the party's urban base—and the governor's office seemed well within reach. Byrne resigned his judgeship, joined the Democratic field just six weeks before the primary, and swept to a landslide victory in November, bringing with him an overwhelmingly Democratic legislature (twenty-nine out of forty seats in the senate, sixty-six out of eighty in the assembly) that would soon have to comply with the *Robinson* mandate.

To New Jersey voters, it appeared that the new governor had already ruled out one option: late in the campaign, Byrne had said he saw no need for an income tax "in the foreseeable future." The widely repeated remark surprised and dismayed his campaign manager, Richard Leone, a thirty-something political wunderkind who had worked for Governor Hughes during his unsuccessful income tax fight. Byrne was obviously going to trounce his opponent, Leone thought: why court trouble with such a sweeping campaign promise? Still, although Leone felt sure the state would eventually need an income tax, the incoming Byrne administration had never planned to push for one right away; with the lame-duck Cahill administration confidently predicting a budget surplus, it seemed likely the school-funding problem could be managed without seeking a controversial broad-based statewide tax. Such a tax would pass only under the pressure of an overwhelming, crisis-driven conviction that the state had no other choice, Leone thought, and that kind of crisis hardly seemed imminent. Soon, Leone knew better. Within weeks of Byrne's election, Leone, now in line to become the youngest state treasurer in New Jersey history, learned that Cahill's promised budget surplus had metamorphosed into a gaping deficit. The country, too, was careening into tough economic times: an Arab oil embargo, rising interest rates, spiraling inflation. In other words, a crisis.

Leone quickly convinced Byrne that only an income tax would raise enough money to balance the state budget, pay for the schools, and reduce local property taxes. Leone winced, however, when Byrne quickly passed this insight along to the newspapers: the treasurer was convinced the legislature and the public would accept such a step only reluctantly, after a slow, careful educational process. Still, the administration position seemed strong. Byrne had won a smashing victory, and his party dominated the legislature. Nationally, the Watergate scandal had inaugurated an era of reform, and in New Jersey, liberal politics were at high tide. Byrne's young policy wonks worked with their legislative allies to pass a string of laws designed to clean up government and modernize the state: in short order, they reformed campaign finance, established environmental-protection rights, and created a new citizens' ombudsman, the Department of the Public Advocate. Enacting an income tax and equalizing school funding were just two more items on the agenda—backed by a court order, no less. Byrne's chief legislative liaison was astonished when Leone told her, "Well, maybe we'll get it and maybe we won't." What do you mean, maybe we won't? she wondered.

Danger signs were apparent, though, for those willing to see them. Byrne's relationship with the legislature was souring fast. Although his closest aides—Treasurer Leone and Chief Counsel Lewis Kaden—came from modest middle-class backgrounds, both were thirty-something Ivy Leaguers who struck many legislators as irritatingly arrogant young men. In private, lawmakers derided Byrne's inner circle as the "Whiz Kids." Leone suspected, however, that legislators were really angry about something else: his determination to end Trenton's tradition of cozily intermingling business and politics. The new treasurer enraged old-timers by handing out a booklet explaining the state's bidding and procurement procedures: gone were the days of sweetheart deals for political allies, he seemed to be saying. Byrne, too, seemed uncomfortable with the deals that Trenton lifers took for granted—the promises to give an ally a judgeship or a well-paying commission seat in exchange for a legislator's vote on this or that pending bill. Although Byrne had grown up in a political family and worked for a previous Democratic governor, he sometimes seemed more at home with the Princeton-Harvard side of his life than with the backslapping Irish pol side, Kaden thought.

In June 1974, the details of Byrne's tax package had been public for a month when the grave, unsmiling governor formally presented his grand vision to an unenthusiastic legislature. In a state with a $2.4 billion budget, Byrne was proposing a $1.1 billion tax-and-spending package that would increase the state share of school funding to 50 percent, reduce homeowners' property taxes through an array of new measures, plug the gaping budget hole, and pay for it all with a new property tax on businesses and a graduated income tax of 1.5 percent to 8 percent.

The pro–income tax forces lobbied hard. Byrne invited grassroots tax opponents for iced tea and cookies at the governor's mansion; his aides spoke at town meetings and on radio programs. But the public mood was ugly. One night, a pro-tax state senator was eating with his family in a diner when a stranger buttonholed him to announce, "I hate you." Even people whose total taxes were likely to fall once property tax cuts kicked in were vehemently opposed to Byrne's income tax. "You are a cow's rectum," an angry constituent wrote from working-class Hamilton Township to another pro–income tax state senator. Never one to duck a fight, the senator happily signed an aide's response: "How strange to be called a cow's rectum by a horse's ass." Privately, legislators told Byrne's team they knew an income tax was inevitable, even necessary: they just feared committing political suicide by voting for it. One day, as Democrats caucused behind closed doors, a senator from relatively conservative South Jersey made an impassioned plea for the income tax. We have an obligation to education—it's got to be done, he told his colleagues. Of course, he added, he couldn't vote for it himself: he'd get killed in his district. "But some of you guys have to," he concluded.

Still, in mid-July 1974, the plan squeaked through the eighty-member assembly with a bare forty-one-vote majority. But the senate president, thirty-six-year-old Frank "Pat" Dodd, resented Byrne's income tax flip-flop and his team's high-and-mighty ways. Dodd came out against the income tax, and on July 24, Byrne's senate allies withdrew the bill without risking the vote they knew they would lose. It was a damaging setback, and the court's deadline was only five months away.

The court was now in the hands of a very different chief justice. Weintraub, the author of the first *Robinson* decision, was a towering intellect with a genius for forging consensus among his colleagues, but he retired soon after writing the first *Robinson* opinions. After a brief interregnum, the court got a new leader—Richard Hughes, the Democratic former governor who had tried and failed to enact the state's first income tax. Hughes lacked Weintraub's brilliance, but he was practically a secular saint in New Jersey public life, loved and respected by politicians of both parties and renowned for his ability to craft compromises that left everyone feeling victorious.

Hughes was a year into his new job, and four of his six associate justices were almost as new, when the Weintraub court's deadline for resolving the state's school-funding problem expired. In the five months since Byrne's income tax plan had gone down to defeat, the legislature had made little progress. Still, the political dynamic of the case had shifted significantly in the two years since *Robinson I*, as Weintraub's first ruling was now known. The new governor, though officially a defendant in the case, openly agreed with the other side; although Ruvoldt was still representing Jersey City and its schoolchildren, in essence Byrne was about to become the lead plaintiff. With the court's deadline expired and no plan in place for revamping school funding, Byrne asked Chief Justice Hughes and his colleagues to enforce the *Robinson* order by taking hundreds of millions of dollars in school aid from rich and middle-class districts and redistributing it to poor ones. The Hughes court, however, chose to punt. In *Robinson III*, issued on January 23, 1975, the court gave legislators an extra year to devise a new plan and scheduled arguments on what should happen if they failed to comply. It was another setback for Byrne: for the moment, at least, the legislature would not find its back to the wall.

At the argument two months later, Byrne tried again to prod the court into action. This time, he chose a dramatic flourish: into the packed supreme court chamber strode the governor himself, come to argue his case personally for the first time in state history. He spoke for about twenty minutes, without interruption; the justices had agreed among themselves to suspend their usual practice of interjecting questions. Once again, Byrne urged the justices to redistribute $585 million in school aid if the legislature did not act. "I urge that the court do what is necessary to get . . . an unconstitutional system of financing back on the track," Byrne said. "I firmly believe that the legislature . . . would pick up that responsibility once it knows how far the court is going to go in usurping, if you will, that responsibility." For the next two months, however, the legislature dithered, and in *Robinson IV*, issued on May 23, 1975, the court gave the governor only a partial victory: if the legislature passed no new school-funding plan by October 1, the court would order redistribution of $300 million in school aid—the minimum aid and save-harmless aid that Botter had invalidated three years earlier. Even for that, Hughes could muster only five of the court's seven votes; the two most conservative justices called the partial redistribution "imprudent and untimely judicial activism."

Now the state faced not only a school-funding crisis but also a budget crisis. The country was suffering through simultaneous high inflation and high unemployment; gasoline prices were skyrocketing, and the revenue from existing state taxes was falling. Byrne's staff piled on extra sweaters and turned down the heat to save money. Because New Jersey's constitution required a balanced budget, Byrne's team had a choice: they could cobble together a 1975–76 budget by raising minor taxes and fees, or they could design a budget that relied on the not-yet-enacted income tax and then threaten deep service cuts if the legislature refused to pass the tax. They chose the latter alternative, but it was no easy sell. Everywhere Byrne went, he was booed. When Leone, the state treasurer, spoke at a Bergen County town meeting, a man in the audience informed him that the administration's proposal would end his state-subsidized dialysis treatments. "That's one of the cuts you're making, so I guess I'll die," the man announced.

Still, in mid-1975, the senate voted down yet another tax bill, as anti-tax protesters hanged the governor in effigy outside the statehouse. A week before the budget deadline, the assembly approved the first deficit budget in state history, challenging the senate to pass the income tax bill their house had narrowly approved a year earlier. In a televised appeal the night before the senate vote, Byrne predicted "fiscal chaos" if the senate voted no. In the senate chamber the next day, as yellow Western Union telegrams from constituents piled up on senators' desks and the five-hour debate dragged on, wags circulated Byrne's newspaper horoscope: "You can persuade associates to back almost any reasonable program," it read. "It's up to you to set a sensible budget." But the stars apparently had other plans: on a 21–17 vote, the forty-member senate again defeated the tax, and moments later a Byrne aide hand-delivered to the chamber a list of $384 million in brutal line-item budget cuts to school aid, public transit, community colleges.

Byrne's team had miscalculated again, however: even the national economic slump, the statewide budget crisis, the impending court deadline, and the prospect of higher bus fares and college tuition were not enough to overcome the fierce resistance to the income tax. When the state's fiscal year began July 1, the cuts were in place; it took three more weeks of feverish negotiations before the governor reluctantly accepted the cobbled-together package he had hoped his brinkmanship would fore-stall. Leone was deeply discouraged. The state had faced an unprece-dented crisis, and the governor had still come out of it without an income tax. What was it going to take?

The legislative puzzle Byrne faced after *Robinson* had two big pieces. First, of course, was the question of how to pay for a fairer funding formula, but second was the question of what that formula itself should look like. In the first days of the administration, devising the details of the formula fell to the state's deputy treasurer, Clifford Goldman, a graduate school room-mate of Treasurer Leone's and a fellow veteran of Governor Hughes's ad-ministration. Goldman gave himself a crash course in school funding and quickly settled upon a power-equalization formula that would preserve local control over school funding and taxation. The now-unconstitutional Bateman law was also a power-equalization formula, but the Byrne plan discarded its complicated incentive structure and assumed a higher level of funding: where the Bateman law had phased in a 40 percent state share of total education spending, the Byrne proposal would yield a 50 percent state share. Like Ray Bateman, however, Goldman thought it was politi-cally impossible to skim off the extra money wealthy districts would be able to raise at each tax rate, or to wean them from their addiction to minimum aid, so he did not even suggest such inflammatory steps. The is-sues were murderous enough, Goldman thought; why make things worse in the interest of ideological purity?

The *Robinson* court had called for equalization of school spending, but it had also suggested that the state needed to identify the elements of a thorough and efficient education, and to this problem Goldman now turned his attention. At the Department of Education, bureaucrats and interest groups had spent the months since *Robinson I* discussing this very question, in meetings so grueling that one participant groused, "I just fig-ured out what T&E means: tedious and exasperating." Out of those dis-cussions had emerged three alternative ways of defining T&E. First was an input model: a school district could be considered T&E if it had, for ex-ample, a particular student-teacher ratio, or a set number of books in the library, or classrooms with a certain amount of space. But this approach had a crucial flaw: it was far from obvious which inputs were essential to educational quality. A second approach focused on outputs: a school district could be considered T&E if it met particular standards for student test scores, dropout rates, and the like. But in 1973, state testing was in its infancy. Even more important, the powerful teachers' union opposed the output approach, fearing teachers would be punished for student failure that owed more to home and family than to schooling. Eventually, the department settled upon a third approach, the process model: a school district would be considered T&E if it had set goals for improving its programs and outcomes, devised appropriate steps toward meeting those goals, and begun carrying out those steps and assessing progress.

That consensus dovetailed with the views of one of the Education Department's most influential bureaucrats, William Shine, an ex-marine with more than a decade of experience as a small-town teacher, principal, and superintendent. Shine saw both the input and output models as dangerously flawed. Focus on inputs, and legislative cost-cutters were sure to insist on a lowest-common-denominator standard, he thought; focus on outputs, and the complex process of shaping young minds would be reduced to a series of answers on a test. The process model would allow districts' individual differences to flourish, Shine thought, and eventually that would improve education for all. Pressure from parents and teachers would ensure that spending in the dying cities of Camden and Newark would rise if spending in the thriving suburbs of Cherry Hill and Millburn did, too.

Goldman saw pitfalls in the process approach. The last thing he wanted was to create a massive new bureaucracy dedicated to gauging how well districts were carrying out required procedures. But he trusted Shine's assurances that common sense would prevail: education officials would quickly identify districts needing special help and leave the competent ones alone. Other critics were less sanguine. On the right, conservative legislators complained that if schools were getting new money, they should face heightened accountability, in the form of state tests. The loudest objections, however, came from the left, from advocates for the poor urban schoolchildren the *Robinson* case was supposedly about. The advocates feared that allowing local districts to set their own goals, especially for student achievement, was a recipe for low expectations and persistent inequality. Shouldn't the children of impoverished Newark be held to the same standards as the children of wealthy Princeton? Why should Newark children instead be judged only against special Newark-devised standards? In memos and testimony, the liberal advocates fought a rearguard action; eventually they formed a strange-bedfellows alliance with conservative legislators and won a watered-down guarantee that the Department of Education would administer statewide tests to assess student progress in reading, writing, and math.

Few legislators shared the advocates' engagement with these issues, however. It was the income tax that roused passions; the rest of it was just stuff for education experts. By late September, a week before the court's deadline, the Public School Education Act of 1975, nicknamed the "T&E law," had passed both houses of the legislature. The new funding formula was in place, but not the tax that would pay for it.

The long, unsuccessful fight over the income tax had reshaped the T&E law. Byrne's original formula had set the guaranteed tax base at $106,000 per student, twice the state average. At that level, a district taxing at $1 per $100 of assessed property valuation would be guaranteed a yield of $1,060 per pupil, with the state contributing whatever the local tax base failed to generate; a district increasing its tax rate to $2 per $100 would be guaranteed a yield of $2,120 per student in state and local funds, earning a greater reward for its greater tax effort. In 1974, only 6 percent of New Jersey's 578 public school districts, enrolling just 3 percent of the state's students, had tax bases greater than $106,000 per student. Under the original Byrne plan, these wealthy districts would retain an edge: at any tax rate, they could raise more money than the other 94 percent of districts, and political expediency decreed that the state would not skim off and redistribute those excess funds. For the great majority of districts and students, however, tax effort and tax yield would be closely aligned; in theory, the wealth of a community would no longer dictate how much it could spend on its schools. On average, the state would pay half the cost of public schooling, putting $550 million from the new tax into school funding.

As a succession of income tax proposals went down to defeat, however, political reality eroded the strong, expensive equalization guarantee at the heart of Byrne's plan. The guaranteed tax base fell from twice the state average to 1.7 times the average, then to 1.35 times the average, reducing the amount needed from the new income tax by more than $100 million and the average state share of school spending to about 40 percent, no better than the rejected Bateman formula. To mollify conservatives worried that a flood of new state money would encourage profligacy, caps on local spending were built into the law; to preserve local control, the bill did not require school districts to increase spending, although the commissioner of education could order educationally necessary increases. The law also defined a thorough and efficient education in the vaguest terms, substituting general exhortations for specific indices of success or failure. The Public School Education Act of 1975 was a monument to the art of political compromise, and even so it said nothing about how the state was going to raise the money the law called for. Still, the Byrne administration urged the supreme court to stamp its seal of constitutional approval on the new law, even without a tax in place to pay for it.

Urban advocates disagreed. At the Education Law Center, a two-year-old nonprofit law firm headed by Paul Tractenberg, the Rutgers law professor who had abandoned his own school-funding case when *Robinson* hit the fast track, lawyers were convinced the state's new formula would do little to help poor city schools. Computer runs showed that elements of the new law would combine, with mathematical certainty, to ensure that spending in the poorest districts could never catch up to spending in the richest. Middle-class districts would get the biggest share of the new aid, and the poor would still lag behind.

The opinion the state supreme court produced on January 30, 1976— its fifth *Robinson* ruling, issued four years after Botter's original decision— bore all the hallmarks of a declare-victory-and-go-home sigh of relief. The court was badly splintered, with four justices writing their own opinions, in addition to the unsigned majority opinion; four justices concurred with that majority opinion, two others concurred only with parts of it, and one dissented entirely. The majority of the court found the new T&E law constitutional on its face, assuming it were fully funded, although the opinion noted that only time would tell whether the law would prove constitutional once in operation. The justices praised the new law for giving content to the constitution's T&E guarantee and for giving the commissioner of education power to enforce that guarantee. In his separate concurrence, however, Chief Justice Hughes confessed to "some doubt and misgivings," and some of his colleagues went further. One partial concurrence noted that the new law, like the rejected Bateman formula, relied on local property taxes to cover the bulk of school costs: the guaranteed tax base of 1.35 times the state average now covered only 368 of the state's 578 districts, giving more than one in every four students the edge that came from living in a community that could raise more education money with a lower tax rate. And because the law did nothing to address municipal overburden—the extra demands made on city tax dollars—the education commissioner's power to force school-spending increases was meaningless; how could the commissioner force struggling cities to raise tax rates that were already punishingly high? The dissenter, liberal Justice Morris Pashman, saved his most cutting comments for his fellow justices. "The majority today, in a gesture of intergovernmental coexistence, beats a hasty retreat from a position which it had occupied on a different day," Pashman wrote.

Hasty retreat or not, *Robinson V* had put the court's imprimatur on the legislature's school-funding formula. The only remaining questions were how the legislature planned to pay for it, and what the court should do if the legislature could not agree on a funding source. Six weeks after *Robinson V*, the court heard arguments on the second of these questions, and practically everyone in New Jersey seemed to have an opinion. Lawyers representing twenty-seven towns, school boards, or taxpayer associations weighed in, along with representatives of the teachers' union, the school boards association, the National Association for the Advancement of Colored People, and the ACLU; the state senate, the assembly, the governor, and the education commissioner each sent a separate lawyer. The arguments lasted nearly five hours, with lawyers asking the court to do everything from impose a new statewide property tax to stay out of the matter entirely. Governor Byrne's counsel advocated perhaps the most radical step of all: if the legislature could not agree on how to fund the new school aid formula, he said, the court should bar the state from spending any tax money on the schools, in effect closing them down.

On May 13, 1976, the supreme court accepted Byrne's invitation: by a 5–2 vote, with dissents from both its liberal and conservative wings, the court set a deadline of July 1 for legislative action. After that, every state, county, and municipal official would be banned from spending tax money on the schools. "The continuation of the existing unconstitutional system of financing the schools into yet another school year cannot be tolerated. It is the Legislature's responsibility to create a constitutional system," read the unsigned opinion. "The Legislature has not yet met this constitutional obligation. Accordingly, we shall enjoin the existing unconstitutional method of public school financing."

The ruling caused an uproar. Byrne called the decision inevitable; conservative legislators called it judicial meddling and predicted the court would ultimately back down. Educators wondered how long they could survive without salaries; four thousand teachers rallied in Trenton to urge passage of an income tax. But six days after the ruling, the state senate defeated the latest income tax proposal; the following week, Byrne ostentatiously convened a committee to draw up contingency plans for a school closing. Income tax opponents filed suit in federal court to challenge the state supreme court's order, and the chief federal district judge set arguments for June 30, the day before the schools were to close.

After nearly two years of frustration, however, the long legislative deadlock was finally beginning to loosen. In the anti–income tax camp, a few people were starting to change their minds. Maybe they still disagreed with Byrne, maybe they still feared the voters' reaction, but they had realized an income tax was inevitable, and now they wanted the most politically palatable bill they could get. Most controversially, they wanted the new tax to carry a "sunset" provision, a sort of legislative sell-by date: in mid-1978, two years after passage, the income tax would automatically lapse, unless the legislature voted to extend it. Byrne's inner circle held a long, late meeting to discuss the options. Inevitably, the sunset provision would turn the 1977 gubernatorial campaign into a referendum on the income tax, and the legislature would almost certainly allow the hard-won tax to die unless somebody won the governorship on a pro–income tax platform. The only New Jersey politician willing to run on those terms was Brendan Byrne. Could he win reelection? By the meeting's end, Byrne had made his decision. He would accept the sunset provision and stake his political future on the income tax. Walking back to his office, Leone groaned inwardly. Now the pain would go on indefinitely, he thought; they might get the tax in 1976, lose it in 1978, and find themselves back at square one in the second term. If there even were a second term.

On June 17, 1976, the New Jersey Senate began debating an income tax bill for the sixth time in two years. The bill now under consideration was a far cry from Byrne's original proposal, which had called for a permanent tax with graduated rates of 1.5 to 8 percent and a significant increase in the state's share of school funding. That proposal, passed by the assembly but not the senate in July 1974, had died with the expiration of the two-year legislative session. The far less sweeping tax bill the assembly had passed in early 1976 called for a 2 to 4 percent income tax to fund the T&E law, with its promise of a 40 percent state share of school costs, and even this modest tax was set to expire on June 30, 1978. By the time the bill reached the senate floor three months later, it had been watered down still further; now it would impose a flat income tax of 1.5 percent.

Nevertheless, partisans on both sides knew this vote was crucial. Antitax protesters had been running newspaper ads listing legislators' home numbers, and one Democrat claimed he had gotten 150 calls the night before, all but 6 opposing the tax. The day of the vote, antitax forces made their usual pilgrimage to Trenton, where one of their number, dressed in eighteenth-century powdered wig and knee breeches, passed out leaflets urging passersby to "Celebrate the Bicentennial the American Way—Tax Revolt." To the tune of the "Battle Hymn of the Republic," his compatriots serenaded the statehouse, "Mine eyes have seen the murder of our dear beloved state/It was slain by lawless judges who gave liberty the gate./We must rid our courts of men like these before it is too late,/The dangerous ones must go." Inside the air-conditioning-free senate chamber, temperatures rose to nearly one hundred degrees, stoked by the hot television lights. At 5:52 p.m., the electronic voting board opened, and at last, twenty-one New Jersey state senators—the bare minimum necessary—voted to enact an income tax. In the gallery, angry spectators chanted, "Tax strike! Tax strike!"

The antitax forces were not alone in their disappointment. Pro-tax assembly members were disgusted with the lukewarm bill the senate had finally approved, and just a few days later, they combined with members who had never wanted a tax at all to crush the senate's 1.5 percent flat tax on a resounding 77–2 vote. With less than a week until the school-closing deadline, a conference committee of the two houses convened to craft a compromise. On June 30, with the school-closing deadline less than twenty-four hours away, negotiators were still working to line up votes when New Jersey's eleven federal district court judges met in a rare joint session to hear the case for blocking the state supreme court's order. At 4:30 p.m., legislators waiting in the halls of the statehouse passed the news of the court's ruling down a voice chain—"Nine to two! Nine to two!" The court majority had refused to "force New Jersey to perpetuate a violation of its own constitution" by keeping the schools open. If the senate and the assembly could not agree on a tax plan, the schools would close in less than eight hours, stranding thousands of summer school students.

As the night wore on and the first day without schools dawned, the assembly met in party caucuses, breaking only to defeat the conference committee's proposals. Senate Democrats began hammering out yet another compromise, but at 8 a.m. on July 1, amid uncertainty about details of the latest proposal, the assembly recessed for twelve hours. That night, as July 1 became July 2, the assembly argued the merits of a 2 to 2.5 percent graduated income tax. Victory for the pro–income tax faction seemed tantalizingly close; to assure wavering assembly Democrats that the senate had the votes, two of the assembly's leaders were escorted into a closed meeting of the twenty-nine senate Democrats, where those who planned to vote for the proposal pledged their support in writing. Assembly leaders believed they, too, were close: in time-honored legislative fashion, someone had agreed to provide the forty-first vote putting the bill over the top, as long as the leadership could promise that it had the other forty votes, and that therefore the political risk would not be taken in the service of a failing effort. With the pro–income tax tally stuck at thirty-nine, the arm-twisting appeals to principle and party loyalty that typically occurred behind closed doors spilled into public view. Colleagues surrounded Vincent "Ozzie" Pellecchia, a sixty-year-old Democrat from North Jersey's antitax stronghold of Passaic County, and begged him to change his vote. "Do it, do it for the party," one whispered in his ear, as beads of sweat broke out on Pellecchia's forehead. "I can't do it. I come from a district where I'm dead if I go for this. It will mean the end of me," he pleaded. Nearby, assemblymen whispered into the ears of another wavering Democratic colleague. "You're going to make monkeys out of us," one chided, while another exhorted, "Do it for the sake of the kids." "Don't make me have a heart attack!" the unhappy victim begged. After an hour of such appeals, the pro–income tax forces gave up; after two consecutive all-nighters, the assembly recessed, and members went home to celebrate the two hundredth anniversary of the American colonists' revolt against British tax policy.

On Tuesday, July 6, the assembly reconvened to consider essentially the same bill it had rejected four days earlier. Over the weekend, Pellecchia reported, he had gotten nearly 1,000 messages congratulating him for holding out, and someone had sent flowers to his wife. But other legislators reported little but apathy from their constituents; although the state estimated that 88,000 students and 4,000 teachers were missing summer school, most families were on vacation and cared little that the schools had officially been closed for nearly a week. Once again, the assembly rejected the 2 to 2.5 percent income tax. The next day, July 7, they were back with the same bill, sweetened this time with millions in revenue-sharing money. After days of mind-numbingly repetitive debates in the steamy legislative chamber, everyone was exhausted. The Democratic Party's national convention was coming up that weekend, and many of the legislators were delegates; the last thing they wanted was to spend their days haggling over income tax rates instead of partying in New York. The Byrne administration had compromised with a tax that raised less money and expired in two years. The justices had held firm and closed the schools. Any legislator who voted for the tax now could plausibly tell constituents that the court had left no other choice.

This time, the debate lasted only half an hour; after two years, what more was there to say? At 8 p.m. on July 7, the New Jersey Assembly took its third vote on the 2 to 2.5 percent income tax package, and this time a bare majority of forty-one members, including two Republicans, voted for it. The next night, the senate concurred on a vote of 22–18, with one Republican in favor, and before 10 p.m. on July 8, Brendan Byrne signed the state's first income tax into law, making New Jersey the forty-third state to enact such a tax. "Although it's not a giant leap toward real tax reform, it nevertheless is a significant contribution," the governor said. The next day, with a stroke of his pen, Chief Justice Hughes reopened the schools. The crisis was over.

Although he had worked tirelessly for this moment, Treasurer Leone was not happy. The battle with the legislature had been bitter and personal, and worst of all, it was not over: Brendan Byrne would face reelection in 1977 with the income tax set to expire eight months later, and it was crucial that he win, for if he lost, the reformist cause could be irreparably damaged. As 1977 began, the signs were unpromising. The popularity fueling Byrne's landslide 1973 victory had long dissipated; around the statehouse, they had been calling him One-Term Byrne for years. The public's anger followed him everywhere. Two months after signing the income tax, Byrne cut the ribbon on the brand-new racetrack in the Bergen County Meadowlands, but his two-minute speech was nearly drowned out by the boos of thirty thousand racing fans, and the state police hustled him out the back after the racing was over. In February of Byrne's reelection year, an internal poll showed that 69 percent of the members of his own party said they would not vote for him under any circumstances; in the June primary, he faced a challenge from a former member of his own cabinet, along with eight other Democrats. That crowded field proved his salvation: he was renominated with just 31 percent of the vote.

Byrne's Republican opponent was Raymond Bateman, the state senator who had authored the school-aid formula invalidated in *Robinson*. Bateman had voted against the income tax to preserve his viability in the antitax Republican field, but Leone, who had stepped down as state treasurer and was now running Byrne's campaign, suspected that Bateman's heart was not in the antitax fight. Leone remembered a hundred conversations over the years in which Bateman had said the state needed an income tax. With the new tax expiring in June, Bateman had to offer some alternative, and six weeks before the election, he and his advisor, former U.S. Treasury Secretary William Simon, issued their proposal. When Leone saw the plan, a hodgepodge of one-time savings, rosy economic projections, and unconvincing stopgaps, he knew he had gotten what he had hoped for—an alternative so ludicrous that any open-minded voter would have to reject it. At Byrne's next press conference, Leone mimed the opening of a Bible as he intoned to the assembled reporters, "The Lord has delivered them into our hands." It was Byrne's earthier remark that made the papers the next day, however: the Bateman-Simon plan, he said, "will become known by its initials." On Labor Day, Byrne was behind by twenty-six points, but as the election drew closer, Leone's polls began to show movement. In October, Byrne said to him, "You think I'm going to win, don't you?" "Yep, you're going to win," Leone replied. "But don't tell a soul." The last thing he wanted was overconfidence. On Election Day, Byrne beat Bateman, 57 percent to 43 percent, and a month later, the legislature voted to make the income tax permanent.

Kenneth Robinson graduated from Ferris High School in June 1976, exactly one month before Brendan Byrne signed the income tax into law. After his disastrous sophomore year, Babe had pulled himself together; in senior year, he sacrificed his lunch hour and took an extra early-morning class to make up the credits he needed to graduate on time. What came next? The path wasn't clear. There had been some talk of Babe's applying to college, but nothing had come of it; he and his brother Tank, who had graduated along with Babe after a six-year high school career, considered signing up for the National Guard but never followed through. Babe drifted through a series of dead-end jobs—at a coat factory, a stereo factory, a pillow factory, a department store distribution center. A year or so after graduation, his charm and good looks captivated a girl named Patricia, a friend of his sister Joan's. Pat was the oldest of six, a hardworking high school graduate from a two-parent family with a home outside the projects, and she fell madly in love with Babe. After work, they hung out in the projects with Joan and their other friends, sipping wine coolers and clowning around. They went to parties and movies and strolled hand in hand. He teased her and made her laugh; sometimes, even if they didn't have a date, she would head over to his apartment after her waitress shift at Crown Fried Chicken and chat with his mother until he showed up. By early 1979, Pat was pregnant.

As the *Robinson* case was winding its way through the courts and changing the course of New Jersey politics, Betty Robinson's life had flowed on, unnoticed by reporters or legislators. Betty had become a tenant activist, pushing hard for the city housing authority to replace Booker T.'s thirty-year-old windows, pave the dirt pathways, and erect barriers to

keep cars from speeding through the courtyard. Her children were growing up: Tank was married with a child, her second-oldest, Gwen, had a
son, and Joan was in college, the first person in the family to get that far.

One afternoon, Betty's youngest, Saundra, was playing jacks on the
floor of the apartment while her mother's favorite Al Green tune played.
"Lay your head on my pillow/Hold your warm and tender body close to
mine/ . . . For the good times," Green crooned while Betty moved her lips.
Suddenly, Saundra realized her mother was weeping. "What's wrong? Why
are you crying, Mom?" Saundra asked. "Nothing, baby," Betty said. "It's
going to be OK." But it wasn't. Betty hadn't been singing along to Al Green,
Saundra's sister Joan told her years later: she had been praying, because
she had just learned she had breast cancer. She kept the diagnosis a secret
almost until the end, even as she underwent a mastectomy, lost her hair,
and covered her baldness with wigs that Saundra thought made her look
like a character on the TV sitcom *Good Times*. One stifling Sunday evening
at the end of July 1979, as Betty sat in her favorite chair by the window,
ten-year-old Saundra and twelve-year-old Lydia begged permission to go
play outside with their friends before dark. They were still jumping rope
when they saw the ambulance arrive.

Betty's death at fifty tore a gaping hole in the heart of her family.
Gwen, a twenty-five-year-old single mother, took responsibility for raising
her young sisters; eighteen-year-old Joan dropped out of college to help.
Overwhelmed, Gwen considered sending the little girls down south to stay
with relatives; she changed her mind only when she happened upon a letter Betty had written before her death, begging, "Whatever you do, don't
let nobody take away my babies." But chaos was gaining on stability. Fancy
new furniture appeared in the apartment and then was repossessed. The
police came to search one day; from the snippets of conversation she
overheard, Saundra gathered that Tony was selling drugs, with help from
Gwen. The older siblings began holding parties, shooing Lydia and Saundra off to their bedroom until the festivities ended. One party night, Saundra opened the bathroom door in time to see Babe slide a needleful of
heroin into his arm and send a jet of blood splashing onto the wall. After
that, Saundra didn't like to use that bathroom anymore.

Babe's relationship with Pat had ended with the birth of their son
three months after Betty's death; although he came by every week or so

with disposable diapers and milk for the baby, Pat knew he didn't love her the way she still loved him. She had suspected there were other women, but she was shocked when she learned who the latest was: Jennifer, a project girl whose serious, degrading drug habit was no secret. Whether Babe fell in with Jenny when he joined the drug scene or joined the drug scene because he had fallen in with Jenny was an open question, but his family blamed the girl. Whatever the truth, Babe and Jenny formed a bond that seemed both destructive and unbreakable. Together, they drifted through the apartments of friends and relatives, moving on when they overstayed their welcome. In 1986, their first child, a daughter, was born; the next year, her brother arrived. But the new baby was born addicted to drugs, and by the time he was three months old, child welfare authorities had taken both children away. Saundra desperately wanted to care for Babe's children; at eighteen, she was a high school graduate, the mother of a toddler, newly married, and the proud possessor of an apartment outside the projects. But the place was too small for a family of five, the authorities decided, and Babe's children were adopted by strangers. Over the next five years, Jenny gave birth to two more sons, but both times her family took custody before the state could. Parents themselves, Tank and Saundra figured it must grieve Babe to lose his children, but he never spoke about it. Once in a while, he visited Pat, still working at Crown Fried Chicken, and asked after his firstborn. Pat was doing a good job with her son, the adored baby in her big extended family; he would grow up to graduate from a four-year college and get a steady job in computers. But in 1992, Pat was still nursing her anger at Babe's desertion when he begged permission to see his twelve-year-old son again for the first time in years. She said no.

Babe's life was slipping through his fingers like a rope paying itself out too fast. His good looks were gone; he was painfully thin, his hair as fine as a baby's, his skin discolored. One day he told his sister Saundra that the doctors were saying he had the AIDS virus. Saundra was working hard to make something of her life. She had a solid job with the Jersey City Housing Authority and was studying at the local Jesuit college; in time, she would become the only one of Betty's children to earn a four-year degree. On her visits to Booker T., Saundra wept when she saw what her happy, handsome big brother had become. During one of his hospital stays, as she brought him slippers and sat by his bedside, Saundra and Babe grew closer. Maybe, she thought, if Babe left Jersey City and its familiar temptations, he would be able to turn his life around. She bought him a ticket, packed his few possessions, and put him on a bus bound for the Georgia town where their brother Tank was now living. Babe had never ventured farther than New York City, and he stayed awake the whole trip, fascinated, drinking in the new places he glimpsed out the bus window. But his addiction followed him on the long ride south; although Saundra didn't know it, he had brought his heroin stash with him. Tank hadn't used in a while, but he shared Babe's drugs until they ran out. In Tank's rural town, getting a fresh supply wasn't that easy; Babe needed a fix a couple of times a day, and so he headed back to Jersey City to get it. He told Saundra the pace of life was too slow for him down there in Georgia.

Back in New Jersey, tragedy haunted Betty's family. Patricia had been found dead of cirrhosis of the liver in 1988; Tony had died of AIDS in 1990, while serving a ten-year prison sentence for robbery. In the years to come, Gwen and Joan would die of heart attacks in their forties; cancer would claim Lydia at thirty. By thirty-four, Saundra would find herself raising Lydia's two children as well as her own two, and helping Joan's daughter, barely out of her teens, look after her younger brother. Although she had graduated twenty-fifth in her class from Ferris High School and would eventually teach in the Jersey City public schools, Saundra was convinced that her own high school education had left her ill prepared for college. She sent the children in her care to Catholic school, after winning a lottery offering privately funded scholarships to inner-city kids.

Babe did not live to see Saundra's struggles and successes. Back from Georgia that fall of 1992, he slipped back into his old ways. His illness had earned him a state-subsidized bed in a rooming house, and Saundra insisted he take his meals with her family, but before long he wasn't showing up at either place any more. Instead, he was shooting up with Jenny in some drug pal's apartment in the projects. The new year of 1993 was only a week old when Saundra got a call: her thirty-four-year-old brother had been carried out of Booker T. on a stretcher, just like their mother more than thirteen years earlier. Saundra raced to the hospital, but when she reached his room, his eyes were wide open, staring sightlessly at the television set. Kenneth Robinson had died alone.

PART TWO

The Crusade

Abbott v. Burke, 1979–1998

3

The True Believer

By the 1980s, a casual observer might have mistaken Marilyn Morheuser for a picture-perfect grandmother. Short and stout, with graying hair, thick glasses, and sensible shoes, she loved her books and her cats, nurtured a wide windowsill's worth of luxuriant plants, and spun out her Christmas shopping into an elaborate, months-long project. True, she would have made an irreverent kind of grandma—the kind who chain-smoked, rooted for a sharp-elbowed basketball team, and liked her martinis extra dry, the kind with a hearty appetite for good food, vividly colored scarves, and intense friendships—but irreverent grandmas are their own sort of cliché. Yet it would have been a mistake to see Marilyn Morheuser in such familiar and reassuring terms, for at the core of her personality lay something more complicated: a drive to commit wholly, deeply, irrevocably to a cause larger than self. Three years after the *Robinson* case ended, the unfinished fight for school-finance reform in New Jersey became the last of the three great causes to which Morheuser dedicated her life, and she pursued it with a tenacity that bordered on obsession. She was a childless white lawyer in late middle age, but the black and Hispanic schoolchildren of the inner city became her children, and she defended what she saw as their interests with a fierceness that was part maternal passion, part crusading hunger for justice.

Marilyn Jeanne Morheuser was born in St. Louis on May 31, 1924, the second of three children of Marie Werthe, a former bank teller, and Martin Morheuser, an insurance agent of German descent. In August 1928,

Marie died of tuberculosis at thirty-two, and Martin moved himself and his three motherless children—five-year-old Martin, four-year-old Marilyn, and two-year-old Marie—back home with his own mother and four unmarried adult siblings. Amid that eclectic and argumentative band of adults, in a series of rented homes crowded enough that some of the beds were rolled up and stored in closets by day, the children grew up. Their grandmother died before they were teenagers, but their father and his siblings formed the cornerstone of their lives. Their father, Martin, the middle sibling, was a tall, dark man with big, graceful hands and a taste for unfiltered cigarettes; although he had never reached high school, he read voraciously and took a keen interest in current affairs. His oldest sister, Pauline, known as Aunt Paul, was big and flamboyant, with a gift for numbers and a job running a railroad company comptrometer, a precursor of the computer. She was often short tempered with the children, but after work, she spent long hours at her sewing machine making them exquisite clothes. Martin's youngest sister, Rose, known as Aunt Honey, the only sibling to reach high school, headed the filing department at the local General Motors plant; the younger brother, Joseph, known as Uncle Bud, was a factory worker and a union organizer who had paid for his activism with occasional trips to jail. The glue that held their family together, however, was the second sister, Celeste, known as Aunt Les, whose serene nurturing made her the closest thing the children had to a mother. While her brothers and sisters earned the wages that kept the household afloat, short and stocky Aunt Les cooked, washed, and ironed, baking devil's food cakes for birthdays and fixing meals for hobos who knocked on her kitchen door in the depths of the Depression. She sang as she worked.

With four employed adults, the family lived a middle-class life in a white neighborhood of St. Louis, a city where the lines between the races were deeply etched. Blacks and whites kept to themselves, and the Morheusers did not question this separation—in later years, Marilyn remembered them as suffering from "the typical Mason-Dixon Line blindness" about race. In St. Louis, public accommodations such as department store lunch counters were closed to blacks, and both public and parochial schools were segregated by race. Even among whites, ethnic divisions were so meticulously observed that a generation earlier an Irish priest had ordered Martin's father, Joseph, to enroll his children in the German parochial school six blocks away rather than the more conveniently located Irish parochial school. Only when Joseph Morheuser had threatened to send his children to public school instead had the priest relented.

The Catholic Church was important to the Morheuser aunts, especially Aunt Les, and the children attended all-white parish schools from kindergarten through high school. All three of them flourished. Martin, adored by his little sisters, was handsome, well dressed, and independent, the kind of student who excelled while barely cracking a book. Marie, the youngest, was skinny and sickly but so anxious to grow up that she skipped right to first grade after refusing to attend kindergarten with "babies." Marilyn was plump and dark, with a voracious appetite for life. She loved to eat, and she loved to learn. At Incarnate Word Academy, she edited the school newspaper and joined the student government. On Saturdays, when the family cleaned house in the German way, by moving the furniture into the center of each room, Marilyn often took hours to set her room to rights, distracted by whatever books or magazines she found along the way.

In 1942, Marilyn won a full-tuition scholarship—$250 a year—to Webster College, a small, Catholic women's school in nearby Webster Groves; Marie joined her there the next year. The college had been founded twenty-seven years earlier by the Sisters of Loretto at the Foot of the Cross, a teaching order of nuns whose willingness to offer higher education to women had marked them as progressive in 1915 America. Marilyn and Marie lived at home, commuting to Webster by streetcar or carpooling with other students; never a morning person, Marilyn would sometimes fly out of the house at the last minute. Among the several hundred women of Webster, Marilyn stood out: she was loud, funny, outgoing, and boisterous. Although she was a successful student, majoring in English, she was never bookish or reserved. She happily joined other students for a cigarette or a game of bridge in the dorm lounge known as the Red Room. She was famed for her histrionic rendition of the song "Wagon Wheels," belted out with more enthusiasm than talent. She wrote for the college newspaper and joined student government as a sophomore; by junior year, she was student body vice president, and in her senior year she became president. And everywhere she looked were the smart, confi-dent, vibrant Sisters of Loretto.

The Morheuser daughters soon learned to look beyond the happy co-coon of college life. Marie was deeply influenced by one of her sociology teachers, a charismatic nun who emphasized the centrality of social jus-tice to the Catholic faith; after college, Marie would work as a counselor at St. Louis's first integrated playground, urging white parents to allow their children to play with blacks. Marilyn, inspired by a lecture delivered at Webster by Father Paul Furfey, a liberal sociologist from Catholic Uni-versity, had also begun to think about racial injustice. Across the ocean, World War II raged, and halfway through her college career, the war's re-ality intruded on the Morheusers' life. Their older brother Martin had en-listed in the fight, and on June 22, 1944, he was flying his twenty-ninth mission as a bombardier out of Foggia, Italy, when a pilot's mistake crashed the plane. Martin was twenty-one. He was buried in Italy, and after his death, Aunt Les never sang again.

Two years later, Marilyn Morheuser graduated from Webster with honors and began thinking about her future. During college, she had spent summers working with Aunt Honey at the General Motors filing depart-ment and winter vacations and weekends as a salesgirl at a local depart-ment store, but her Webster course load included a substantial number of education credits, and she soon turned to teaching. During her first year out of college, she lived at home and taught English, math, and social science at Nerinx Hall, the Loretto order's St. Louis high school for girls, earning $150 a month, the equivalent of $1,450 today. Even so, she often had to borrow bus fare from her father when she found she had spent too much on gifts. The year's work, it turned out, was an apprenticeship of sorts, for sixteen months after her college graduation, Morheuser joined the Loretto order. The choice apparently surprised her family, and decades later, she told an interviewer that she had carefully weighed the decision. The prospect of marriage and children tempted her, but "what I really wanted to be is one with the world," she said. "And I thought if I would be unencumbered with personal responsibilities, that would be the best route." She was ready to embrace the first of her life's three great passions.

The Sisters of Loretto at the Foot of the Cross had begun on the Kentucky frontier in 1812, when three young teachers asked their Flemish priest to help them found a truly American order of nuns, with no aid from European sisters. The order, named for the revered Italian shrine of Loreto, moved westward with the pioneers, opening schools and convents along the way. The sisters taught Osage Indians in Kansas and Spanish-speaking children in New Mexico. By the time Marilyn Morheuser joined, Loretto had perhaps twelve hundred members and ran schools in states from California to Kentucky, Michigan to Alabama. With its distinctly uncloistered mission, the order was filled with venturesome women with an intense commitment to service—women like Morheuser. In other respects, however, the order was a less obvious fit for someone with Morheuser's fire and independence. Like other religious orders, Loretto required its members to take vows of chastity, poverty, and obedience; to wear long-sleeved, floor-length black-and-white habits with veils covering their hair; and to live in self-contained communities regulated by strict rules whose origins were lost in the past, rules designed to shield and separate the sisters from the secular world. Lorettine nuns did not travel alone. They visited their families only once every three years. They did not attend weddings. Their convent superiors could open their mail.

The Loretto motherhouse, where Marilyn Morheuser arrived on an October day in 1947 to begin thirty months of training, was a simple, serene community in rural Kentucky. Much of the food the residents ate was grown on the order's land, and drinking water was carried in buckets from a well. To save water, the women bathed just twice a week and used indoor plumbing only at night; by day, they were expected to use out-houses. The trainee sisters, known as postulants for their first six months and novices for the two years after that, slept in dormitories, their beds separated by curtains; they ate in communal dining rooms at tables of six; and they stored their few personal possessions in closet-sized cubicles, each containing little more than a washbasin, some shelves, and a box for shoes. They were expected to patch their underwear and darn their stockings, as they readied themselves for lives of poverty. During the short periods set aside each day for conversation, they were supposed to talk with different people, not with special friends, and they were discouraged from discussing their old lives, their lives before Loretto.

Postulants and novices rose at 5 a.m., and before breakfast at 6:45 they had already spent an hour and a quarter at prayer, meditation, and Mass.

Like most meals, breakfast was eaten without conversation, while one of their number read aloud from an appropriate book. After breakfast the women performed the chores that kept the community running. Vegetables had to be peeled; pots and pans had to be scrubbed. Laundry consumed two days every week, as the billowing habits were machine-washed and hung up to dry, the veils wrung through a mangle and their linings carefully starched. The rest of the day was spent in communal or individual prayer and in formal study—courses on Scripture and theology, but also on secular subjects, to prepare the women for their future as teachers. Twice a week, they were permitted to talk to each other during lunch, and every day a half-hour after lunch and an hour after dinner were spent in recreation—talking, singing, or playing games such as checkers. For the forty-five minutes before the 9:30 p.m. bedtime, however, everyone was expected to observe a "sacred silence."

Like the other novices, Marilyn Morheuser was assigned tasks in the new community. Not every trainee sister was a college graduate, so Morheuser helped teach those trying to earn college credits through the Loretto order's accredited junior college. She struggled to starch veil linings properly in the humid Kentucky summers, directed the choir despite her limited musical abilities, and earned straight As in her religion courses. On April 25, 1950, she stood before the women of the order in the chapel of the motherhouse and read the simple formula that made her a vowed member of the Sisters of Loretto. Some sisters chose to change their names when they took their vows, to mark the break with their old lives, and others were required to do so—because the order used no last names, it was confusing for two sisters to have the same name. Marilyn Morheuser chose a middle course. She became Sister Marilyn John.

The very next day, Sister Marilyn left the motherhouse for her first mission as a nun, a few months' posting in Illinois. At the Louisville station, the nuns who had traveled with her from the motherhouse scattered to another platform, leaving Marilyn and Sister John Bosco, born Theresa Coyle, a twenty-one-year-old Kentucky girl who had joined the order right out of high school, to wait alone for the Chicago train. Uniformed soldiers from nearby Fort Knox eddied around the two young women in their conspicuous black-and-white habits. Suddenly, Marilyn burst into tears, overwhelmed by sadness at leaving the close-knit community of the novitiate.

Theresa tried to comfort her, but Marilyn could not stop weeping. "Marilyn, it's hard to leave, but we have to do this," Theresa told her. But as the train rolled westward, Sister Marilyn kept on crying.

Frequent partings were a way of life for the Loretto nuns. Between 1950 and 1962, Sister Marilyn taught at five different high schools, sometimes for only a year, never for more than four. At St. Patrick's in Kankakee, Illinois, she was the choral director for the school musical; at Loretto Academy in Kansas City, Missouri, she was the advisor for the student magazine. She was a guidance counselor, a Glee Club advisor, the chair of an English department; she taught creative writing, math, chemistry, debate, photography, religion.

But the place she talked about for the rest of her life was Immaculate Conception High School in Las Vegas, New Mexico, a small city nestled beneath a ten-thousand-foot mountain in the northeastern part of the state. There, a few months after taking her vows, she joined a community of ten other Lorettine sisters. Las Vegas had its share of modern homes, but just two blocks from the gray stone school building, Hispanic students and their families lived in abject poverty, in adobe huts with dirt floors and no electricity or running water. The many bars and nightclubs stayed open far into the night, but the town offered almost no wholesome diversions for children, just a public library that closed at 5 p.m., drugstores that closed at 8 p.m., and a swimming pool that was open for an hour each night.

The Loretto high school also struggled. Each year, the school carnival raised the money to heat the building; in her first year, Sister Marilyn taught a freshman class of forty-nine. A year later, that number looked small: after a court decision ended the state's long-standing practice of staffing public schools with Catholic nuns and brothers, the state Board of Education abruptly closed the town's public high school, swelling Immaculate Conception's enrollment to 250. The school lacked enough blackboards, books, and desks for the new arrivals; Sister Marilyn taught chemistry to a class of sixty-two students who perched on folding chairs and shared three to a book while she wrote formulas in thin air. But amid the material shortcomings, she delighted in her students' spiritual gifts and hunger for education. She learned an indelible lesson, too, about what school can mean to children growing up poor. In her first year of teaching, she was startled when her students groaned at the announcement of a holiday. School was "an oasis of comfortable warmth, encouragement, improvement, and innocent fun on their desert of poverty," she recalled later. "There was nothing colorful or exciting in their lives but school."

Back home in St. Louis, the Morheuser family was changing. Marie had married in 1950 and begun a family that eventually included a son and seven daughters. Catholicism was central to her life; on her wall, she hung pictures of the pope and of her sister the nun. With his children settled, Martin Morheuser had remarried and moved out of his siblings' house. When her travels brought Sister Marilyn back to Webster, Marie and the children would visit her there; her young nieces loved the way their aunt wrapped them up in enthusiastic hugs. As far as they knew, she was happy in her life of teaching and religious commitment.

But the world outside the order was changing, too. In 1955, Rosa Parks refused to give up her seat on a bus in Montgomery, Alabama; in 1960, four black college students began a sit-in at a segregated lunch counter in Greensboro, North Carolina. One of Sister Marilyn's most brilliant students was a young black woman who graduated from Loretto's Kansas City high school, made the dean's list at junior college—and then accidentally overheard a white classmate voicing her surprise that blacks could learn at all. "In many of these backward groups, there are always exceptions," she heard another white woman reply. Sister Marilyn's former student came to her in tears, asking, "Can you tell me why they hate us so much?" In her convent communities, Sister Marilyn chose books about social problems to read aloud at dinner; among her fellow Lorettines, she became known as a civil rights supporter. But it wasn't enough: "It was like being in a box," she told an interviewer a few years later. "The box has windows in it. You can see out them if you want to. But things are happening outside. You want to help, but you can't because you're in the box." She was beginning to chafe, too, against the strictures of convent life. It wasn't realistic, she felt, for the community to lock its doors before 9 p.m. each night, shutting out students needing help. The first great cause of her life, the religious and educational mission of the Sisters of Loretto, was losing its hold on her heart; in its place was growing something new, a passion for the civil rights movement.

One night in November 1962, Sister Marilyn was a couple of months into her first college position, teaching English and journalism at her alma mater, Webster, when she picked up a copy of the *New Yorker* magazine. Spread over forty-eight pages, sandwiched between ads for diamond earrings and French champagne, was "Letter from a Region of My Mind," a searing essay by black writer James Baldwin that would soon be published in expanded form as *The Fire Next Time*. Baldwin wrote with precision and rage about everything Sister Marilyn cared about—the promise and illusion of Christianity, the dehumanizing effects of racism on both whites and blacks, the absolute necessity of change. Change was coming, he insisted; the only remaining question was whether it would be peaceful or violent. "Everything now, we must assume, is in our hands; we have no right to assume otherwise," Baldwin concluded. "If we—and now I mean the relatively conscious whites and blacks, who must, like lovers, insist on, or create, the consciousness of the others—do not falter in our duty now, we may be able, handful that we are, to end the racial nightmare, and achieve our country, and change the history of the world. If we do not now dare everything, the fulfillment of that prophecy, re-created from the Bible in song by a slave, is upon us: *God gave Noah the rainbow sign, No more water, the fire next time!*" Sister Marilyn did not sleep that night; she could not read without stopping now and then to catch her breath.

She knew she was approaching a fork in her road. She asked for and received permission to leave teaching for a time, return to her own studies, and think about whether to remain a nun—whether she was ready, in Baldwin's terms, to dare everything. During the winter semester of 1963, at Milwaukee's Jesuit university, Marquette, she took some journalism classes and wrote for the journalism school's biweekly newspaper. Civil rights became her beat. She covered a campus lecture series featuring speakers who urged Catholics to become more involved with the social issues of the day. She profiled a nun who had given six members of her order permission to picket a discriminatory club in Chicago, and she interviewed faculty members active in the civil rights movement. In the course of her research, she met a man whose intensity matched her own, and who would become, for the next seven years, the most important person in her life—the head of the Wisconsin branch of the NAACP, Lloyd Barbee.

Barbee was a year younger than Morheuser, slender, sonorous in voice, and conservative in dress, an intellectual who loved Shakespeare and opera and who melded a lawyer's precision with a reformer's fire. A Memphis native who, like Morheuser, had lost his mother young, Barbee escaped the grinding poverty that crushed many southern blacks—his father, a painting contractor, was the first African American member of his union—but he attended segregated schools, and his racial consciousness blossomed early. At twelve, he joined the NAACP. After college and navy service, Barbee headed north, earning a law degree from the University of Wisconsin at Madison in 1956. With few jobs available for black lawyers, Barbee initially found work in state government, eventually becoming a legal consultant for the Governor's Commission on Human Rights. In 1961, the same year he was elected president of the Wisconsin NAACP, he organized a thirteen-day sit-in in the rotunda of the state capitol to support fair housing legislation. In 1962, his eye on a state assembly seat, Barbee moved to Milwaukee and started a downtown law practice. He often represented the poor, accepting chicken or clothing as payment if more conventional compensation was unavailable.

At the end of their first interview, Sister Marilyn asked Lloyd Barbee to call her the next time he was planning a demonstration. The opportunity came swiftly: in June 1963, civil rights organizer Medgar Evers was shot dead on his own doorstep in Jackson, Mississippi, and Milwaukee civil rights activists organized a local protest on the day of his funeral. The Milwaukee demonstration was small—although three hundred people rallied at a local black church, only six whites and thirty blacks joined the march to city hall—and Morheuser's habit made her instantly conspicuous. Even though neither local newspaper mentioned her participation, word got out quickly; by nightfall, the dean of women at Marquette had called to reprimand her, and two weeks later a telegram summoned her to the Kentucky motherhouse for a face-to-face meeting with Mother Mary Luke Tobin, the head of the order. "Your outstanding virtue has never been prudence," Mother Mary Luke told Sister Marilyn gently. "I think we'd better say that you shouldn't do such things again." "Are you ordering me not to?" Morheuser asked. Mother Mary Luke was no hidebound conservative: a year later, she would become the only American woman invited to attend the reformist Second Vatican Council, and in the wake of Vatican II, she would lead the Sisters of Loretto toward a newly articulated mission of social justice and activism. In 1969, she would publicly support a sister who had joined in ransacking the headquarters of Dow Chemical, the maker of napalm, in a fervent protest against the Vietnam War. But in 1963, the church's reforms were embryonic, and Mother Mary Luke apparently felt she had no choice. Yes, she told Sister Marilyn: she was invoking the vow of obedience and ordering her to refrain from further civil rights activism.

The forked road Marilyn Morheuser had glimpsed the night Baldwin's words burned themselves into her mind now lay before her: she would have to choose between her first love, the Sisters of Loretto, and her new passion for civil rights. The choice was intensely painful. For nearly half her life, she had been a Sister of Loretto, living in the order's communities, doing its work, fulfilling its mission. She had never lived alone, had not earned her own money in sixteen years, had relied on others to tell her where she would go and what she would do. The women of the order were more than her friends and colleagues: they were her home, the family of her adulthood, and if she left the order, she knew she might have to leave them behind, for the pre–Vatican II church treated such defections as betrayals. She knew, too, that her decision would be difficult for her St. Louis family to accept. Marie, the devout Catholic, might take her picture off the wall. On the other side of the scale, however, lay her vision of what justice required, and for Marilyn Morheuser, that would always outweigh every other consideration. By summer's end, Sister Marilyn had made her choice. She wrote to the pope and asked to be released from her vows. She was a thirty-nine-year-old woman beginning her life anew.

The city she lived in was itself undergoing convulsive change. Between 1950 and 1960, the black population of conservative, predominantly German American Milwaukee had nearly tripled, while the white population had remained stable; blacks, once less than 4 percent of the city's population, now made up more than 8 percent, and their numbers were still growing. Residential segregation was rigid, and although the black neighborhoods on the near north side of town, known as the inner core, were not as neglected and desperate as the nation's worst ghettos, they had more than their share of dilapidated housing, unemployed adults, and high school dropouts. Public schools that had once enrolled mostly whites were quickly becoming all black, and when black schools became overcrowded or needed repairs, the district practiced "intact busing": black children were bused to nearby white schools but kept separate from their hosts during classes, lunch, and sometimes even recess and bathroom breaks. The city's established black leadership, including its NAACP chapter, was disinclined to rock the boat, however. Many local NAACP members were teachers who feared that desegregation would cost them their jobs, since black teachers were routinely assigned to black schools.

Lloyd Barbee was a boat-rocker. A few months after his arrival in Milwaukee, in a speech to a white bar association, he accused the school board of violating the nine-year-old *Brown v. Board of Education* ruling by maintaining essentially separate schools for white and black children. The state's top education official dismissed his argument, insisting that Milwaukee's separate schools resulted from housing patterns beyond official control, and the white-dominated school board decided to defuse the controversy in time-honored fashion: it appointed a committee to investigate, naming as chairman conservative white lawyer Harold Story. Story's committee, it was clear, planned to head off pressure for desegregation by offering more money for remedial education in black schools. Public hearings dragged on through the fall of 1963; not until December did Story get around to taking testimony from Barbee and the state NAACP, which demanded an integration plan by the next school year. When Barbee arrived at the following month's meeting to take questions, Story asked him to sit with the committee, but Barbee insisted on staying with his coalition. The symbolism was powerful, and neither man would budge. Finally, Barbee and his supporters walked out, while Story went on with the meeting, posing questions to Barbee's empty chair. The dramatic face-off made Barbee a star.

Already, Morheuser was by his side, beginning a working relationship so close, he would say later, that they could practically read each other's minds. Whether the relationship was more than professional was a matter of some curiosity to their acquaintances. Morheuser's admiration for Barbee was nakedly apparent to everyone. She dropped by his home frequently; Barbee's three school-age children, whom he was raising alone after a divorce, grew used to her constant phone calls, and to her lack of interest in their lives. In later years, some who knew her would say she had hinted at a romantic past with Barbee, perhaps a brief affair that he had ended. But some who knew him would insist it was not so: although Morheuser probably had wanted such a relationship, they said, he never had.

Whatever the truth, Morheuser was soon as deeply committed to the civil rights movement as she had been to the Sisters of Loretto. To earn a living, she had quickly found work at a newspaper covering the city's black community, but within two months, she nearly tripled her $40-a-week salary by jumping to a more prominent black paper, the weekly *Milwaukee Star*. By the time Morheuser arrived at the *Star* in the fall of 1963, the paper had been published for more than two years and boasted a (perhaps exaggerated) circulation of 17,000. Its owner was a factory worker named Kenneth Coulter, who had reportedly acquired the paper in a fistfight with the previous owner. With the city's two daily newspapers virtually closed to black journalists, Coulter had managed to hire talented, ambitious people with deep roots in the community they covered. Every Wednesday, far into the night, the small staff typeset and laid out the paper—Morheuser was a stickler for typographical accuracy, even though mistakes had to be excised by hand and replaced using tweezers—and then handed off the pages to the circulation manager, who drove them to a nearby printing plant and returned with that week's edition. As a community newspaper for black Milwaukee, the *Star* filled its pages with church news, accounts of high school sporting events, household hints, and photos of local bathing beauties, complete with measurements. Every week, a page or two was devoted to pictures of happy patrons bending their elbows at local taverns that paid for the privilege of inclusion. But with Marilyn Morheuser on its staff and soon an editor, the *Star* also became an unabashed supporter of the civil rights movement, both national and local. When Medgar Evers's widow, Myrlie, and national NAACP leader Roy Wilkins came to town, the *Star* covered their appearances prominently. When the Reverend Martin Luther King Jr. paid a fund-raising visit to Milwaukee, Morheuser and three other staff members squeezed onto a couch at a local hotel for an exclusive interview; that week's paper devoted nearly four full pages to King's speech.

The local civil rights movement was providing plenty of fodder for coverage, too. Soon after the Story Committee face-off, Barbee and Morheuser had helped found the Milwaukee United School Integration Committee, or MUSIC, a coalition that planned to agitate for change in the school system. Barbee was MUSIC's chairman; under varying titles, Morheuser also remained one of its leaders. Soon, she and Barbee, along with a passionate young Catholic priest named Father James Groppi, became the public face of the Milwaukee civil rights movement, winning the recognition, and the anonymous death threats, that went with the job. In February 1964, MUSIC organized a demonstration that drew three hundred picketers to the school administration building. But to mark the tenth anniversary of the Supreme Court's *Brown* desegregation ruling on May 17, 1964, MUSIC planned something considerably bigger: a one-day school boycott.

Although Milwaukee's public schools had a good reputation nationally, black schools offered an inferior education, MUSIC argued; the buildings were old and rundown, textbooks were hand-me-downs from white schools, and blacks' historical achievements were barely mentioned in the curriculum. To dramatize these complaints, MUSIC planned to offer boycotting students an alternative—Freedom Schools, housed in local churches and staffed by volunteers, featuring a curriculum devised by Morheuser, the former teacher. By twenty-first-century standards, her plans were hardly radical. "Our curriculum stresses this is not a day of rebellion against the school system and authority," Morheuser told a local newspaper. Indeed, for elementary and middle school students, the day was to begin with the Pledge of Allegiance and the singing of "My Country 'Tis of Thee" or "The Star-Spangled Banner." Later, teachers would tell the stories of African American heroes, from Crispus Attucks to Harriet Tubman; students would discuss freedom, brotherhood, civil rights, and African American history at age-appropriate levels of sophistication; and everyone would sing familiar movement songs ("We Shall Overcome," "We Shall Not Be Moved"), sometimes with new lyrics written for the occasion ("Ain't gonna let Harold Story turn me round" or "No more intact busing here"). The day would end with a hootenanny, a party for Freedom School students.

Morheuser applied her considerable organizational skills to every aspect of Freedom School planning, from recruiting volunteer teachers to assembling peanut butter and jelly sandwiches for students arriving without lunches. And despite opposition from mainstream leaders, both black and white, the boycott came off without a hitch. Although the school district and MUSIC predictably disagreed about just how many students had participated, the most conservative estimate put the number at more than eleven thousand, a significant percentage of the school system's twenty-four thousand nonwhite students.

The *Star* praised the school boycott in its editorials, covered the planning extensively, and, in its May 16 issue, published twenty thousand copies of a four-page, pro-boycott supplement. The journalistic ethics of the situation were touchy, to say the least: Morheuser was simultaneously leading and covering the local civil rights movement, making the news and reporting on the news she made. But the conflict of interest did not create much of a stir: the readers weren't complaining, and Ken Coulter was the kind of newspaper owner who gave out paychecks on time and mostly got out of his staff's way. The *Star*'s top editor, Jay Anderson, did ask Morheuser about the conflict, but she insisted that she never editorialized in her news coverage. Anderson didn't necessarily agree, but he thought MUSIC's cause was just, so he let the matter drop.

Still, before the end of 1964, Morheuser had left the *Star*—years later, former colleagues were not sure why—and after a few months, she took a job with another institution of great importance to Milwaukee's black community, Northcott Neighborhood House. Headquartered in a ground-floor room in a housing project, Northcott had been founded in 1961 by a Methodist women's group and was modeled on the settlement houses of the late nineteenth and early twentieth centuries. By the time Morheuser became its assistant director, Northcott had a staff of 9 paid workers and 168 volunteers and offered a smorgasbord of community programs: camping trips, vocational and guidance counseling, reading readiness classes, a used-clothing store. In the summer of 1965, Northcott won a $30,000 federal grant to run a new summer preschool program under Operation Head Start, and Morheuser directed the effort. She immersed herself in the work with her usual energy and intensity, her boss remembered years later, but this job, too, did not last long; in December she left, telling the local newspaper that she felt she could do more elsewhere.

If her job situation was unstable, Morheuser's commitment to the civil rights cause was not: her passionate dedication seemed remarkable, and sometimes alarming, even to those who shared her views. In the fall of 1965, someone paid tribute to MUSIC's leading lights in fifty-eight rhymed couplets set to the music of "Keep Your Eyes on the Prize"; Morheuser's couplet read, "Marilyn's gonna set herself afire/Civil rights will be her pyre." The black minister who had provided MUSIC with office space was dismayed when she mused about the possibility of hiring someone from nearby Chicago to bomb a particular segregated high school; he feared she might be serious, though luckily nothing ever came of the idea. "I have grown weary of poor people having to pay not for their rights, but for the right to demonstrate for their rights," Morheuser told the black magazine *Jet*. "My activities in no way reflect pity for the Negro's plight, for I believe that the Negro revolution is the only hope we have left for the salvation of American society."

As 1965 wore on and the school board continued to resist calls to end intact busing, MUSIC's activism became more focused and confrontational. In May and June 1965, MUSIC picketers drew national television coverage with days of unannounced protests; little children clapped and cheered as seventy people were arrested for blocking buses carrying black children to isolation in white schools. On May 24, Morheuser, Barbee, and seven others, all wearing signs that read "Stop Busing for Segregation," linked arms in front of a bus at the Brown Street school, singing "We Shall Overcome." The whole group was arrested, though the charges against Barbee were dropped because his election to the state assembly six months earlier had given him legislative immunity. Morheuser pleaded guilty to a misdemeanor traffic charge and was given a fine of ten dollars, promptly suspended. Three weeks later, fifty protesters formed a human chain around a school bus at the Siefert school; this time, the police had to drag Morheuser out from under the bus, injuring her ankle badly enough to send her briefly to the hospital. Twenty protesters spent seven hours singing freedom songs in jail before they saw a judge, and Barbee accused the police of trying to keep them behind bars overnight to prevent further protests the next day. For her second offense, Morheuser was found guilty of two misdemeanors and fined forty-five dollars.

In October, MUSIC launched a second school boycott, intended to last a full week. Again, Morheuser drew up a Freedom School curriculum and trained volunteer teachers, suggesting ways they could incorporate pro-integration messages even into math problems (by calculating how many hours of instruction were lost to busing, for example). She and an aide worked around the clock arranging for volunteer teachers and nurses. A day before the boycott, the Catholic archdiocese ordered its churches not to participate, but thirty-six Freedom Schools opened to crowded classes on Monday. Still, participation was lower than it had been the year before, and attendance fell steadily from Monday to Wednesday; on Thursday, Barbee declared victory and ended the boycott a day and a half early.

In December, MUSIC began yet another protest, this time against construction of a new elementary school in a location that virtually ensured all its students would be black. In the biting wind of December 5, about fifteen people began an all-night vigil at the fenced-in construction site. The protests continued for the next thirteen days, with each day bringing a new tactic. Once, demonstrators formed a human chain to keep construction workers out of the site; another day, a young man chained himself to the entrance gate for more than six hours, and the workers cut a hole in the fence to get around him.

On the fifth day of protests, four cars full of picketers ostentatiously sped to the site, tires screeching, as police moved to keep them away from the entrance. These demonstrators were merely a diversion from the main event, however: behind the police line, Morheuser and a MUSIC volunteer named Ivy Morgan were sneaking through the hole the construction workers had cut in the fence the day before. With a chain wrapped around her waist, Morheuser ran across the muddy construction site—"like a glorious gazelle," a witness remembered years later—and began chaining Morgan to a forklift. Both were arrested before they could finish. Morheuser was tried by a judge the same day and convicted of disorderly conduct, but rather than promise to refrain from what the judge called "unlawful demonstrations," she became the first MUSIC protestor to accept a jail sentence—thirty days. She was released in three days, after accusing the judge of bias and asking for a new trial, but two months later, a jury again convicted her. She could have escaped jail by paying a hundred-dollar fine, but she refused, announcing to the press that she intended to go to jail "to protest Mississippi justice—Milwaukee style." This time, she served a full twenty-three days, with time off for good behavior; in jail, she taught the rosary to a suicidal young woman who had forgotten how to say it, and she marveled at the compassion of her fellow inmates, who would save their desserts for prisoners who needed sugar to ease the symptoms of drug withdrawal. It was, Morheuser said later, "the most deeply human experience" she had ever had. As she left jail on March 2, a fellow civil rights protester presented her with a bouquet of daffodils, and that night Morheuser was back at work, joining a demonstration outside a whites-only club.

MUSIC's days of street activism were drawing to a close, however. A boycott of a single high school in March 1966 drew anemic participation; the segregated school whose construction Morheuser had gone to jail to oppose was going up anyway. Barbee had adopted a new strategy, confronting the school board in a courtroom instead of a construction site. Six months before Morheuser's last arrest, Barbee had sued the Milwaukee school board in federal court on behalf of dozens of children, black and white. The suit, known as *Amos v. Board of School Directors of Milwaukee*, alleged that the district intentionally discriminated on the basis of race by encouraging white students to leave integrated schools, assigning black teachers to black schools, and practicing intact busing. The school board insisted it had done nothing but maintain neighborhood schools; whatever school segregation existed, it argued, was a result of Milwaukee's notorious residential segregation. In the decade since the U.S. Supreme Court's *Brown* decision, courts had begun distinguishing de facto segregation—segregation that had grown up without official sanction, usually as a result of housing patterns—from de jure segregation, segregation intentionally promoted through law or policy; the courts would step in to remedy only de jure segregation. In Milwaukee, even Barbee had to admit, housing segregation was real. To prove that the school board had not simply acquiesced in circumstances beyond its control but rather had intentionally enforced and extended segregation would require extracting a mountain of data from the files of an uncooperative adversary.

With Barbee spread thin between his legislative duties, his law practice, and his children, Morheuser took on the job of supervising the *Amos* research, and a huge job it was. The *Amos* plaintiffs planned a three-pronged argument: first, they would show that Milwaukee's school segregation was the result of official policy, not merely residential patterns; second, they would show that the schools black students attended were inferior; and third, they would show that because of this inequality, black students' achievement was lower. The last point was relatively easy to demonstrate: it was no secret that black students had lower test scores and higher dropout rates than white students. The second point was harder to prove, since the school district was hardly volunteering the necessary information, but eventually MUSIC's hunt through district records and interviews with students, parents, and teachers turned up plenty of information about the inferior conditions in black schools. Black students were crowded into old, dilapidated buildings, learned their lessons from teachers with less experience, endured shortages of supplies as basic as toilet paper, and pledged allegiance to American flags with only forty-eight stars.

By far the biggest challenge of the *Amos* case was proving the first prong of the legal argument, intentional segregation—proving that the school board had not watched passively as the city's housing patterns tipped neighborhood schools into segregation but had actively pushed schools in that direction. By 1968, the *Amos* team was hard at work on two studies designed to prove intentional segregation. The first study analyzed the way the district assigned students and used classroom space in 130 Milwaukee elementary schools for every semester from 1950 to 1969. Morheuser and her team planned to show that as rising numbers of black students squeezed into increasingly crowded neighborhood schools, the district built additions onto existing black schools and pressed substandard classrooms into service, rather than reconfigure attendance areas to let black students attend less crowded white schools. The second study used a twelve-school sample to demonstrate the workings of the district's voluntary student transfer policy in eighteen thousand cases between 1959 and 1968. This study, the plaintiffs believed, would show that the district encouraged white students to leave integrated schools and prevented black students from transferring into white ones.

Digging tens of thousands of pieces of information out of the school district's files, compiling the data into usable form, and converting all the confusing statistics into courtroom exhibits that would make sense to a judge were backbreaking tasks in the misty dawn of the computer era, and MUSIC, even after the national NAACP began supporting the case in mid-1967, had no money to hire help. Morheuser had to assemble a team of volunteers and inspire, persuade, or bully them into giving MUSIC what it needed. Morheuser herself was practically a volunteer, at least initially: although data collection for the lawsuit began in early 1966, she apparently worked without pay, living off freelance work and perhaps MUSIC donations, until the national NAACP's support began providing her with a salary of $550 a month, the equivalent of $3,100 today. The team she directed included MUSIC volunteers—local nuns, Barbee's young secretary, a University of Wisconsin sociologist who provided expert guidance on statistics—and, beginning in 1968, half a dozen idealistic college-aged whites who had arrived in Milwaukee to work for the Volunteers in Service to America (VISTA) program. The VISTA volunteers had initially been assigned to other projects in Milwaukee—a church-run after-school program, a credit counseling program—but most had quickly become dissatisfied with the work, which bore little resemblance to the systemic antipoverty efforts they had hoped to join. Eventually, they found their way to the lawsuit, and while Barbee worked his political connections to keep national VISTA officials from yanking them off the controversial project, Morheuser kept them hard at work through a potent blend of charismatic leadership and emotional pressure.

The *Amos* team was headquartered in Barbee's downtown law office, in a long, narrow conference room crammed with filing cabinets, a conference table, a desk for Morheuser, and a bottomless coffee urn. Morheuser and her volunteers routinely worked twelve- to fourteen-hour days, breaking for dinner at a downtown bar reputedly run by the Mafia; weekends meant a few hours off to do laundry and buy groceries. On the many nights when the team worked so late that the doors to Barbee's office building were locked by the time they were ready to go home, they would climb out the fire escape.

As far as the VISTAs could tell, Morheuser had little in her life besides the *Amos* case. She was a dumpy, middle-aged woman who wore no makeup and clearly took no interest in her appearance; she chain-smoked, drank too much coffee, got to the office around noon, and worked until well past midnight; and her apartment in the heart of Milwaukee's black ghetto was a mess, cluttered with newspapers and *Amos* case files. She didn't even have a driver's license—ever since suffering a mysterious seizure as a teenager, she had taken powerful medication, and although her incessant coffee drinking warded off the mental fuzziness the drug induced, driving was off-limits. She relied on one of the VISTAs, a mild-mannered Denver native named Martin Wheelwright, to chauffeur her between home and work in his beige 1965 Plymouth Valiant.

Single-minded in her devotion to the cause, Morheuser expected nothing less from her volunteers, and she was expert at getting what she expected, through a combination of inspirational pep talks and manipulative guilt trips. The inspiration was real: she was funny, energetic, and enthusiastic, and the VISTAs, youthful idealists all, admired her drive and dedication and basked in her expressions of appreciation. She could be a warm, nurturing friend. One Easter, she treated them to sauerbraten and strawberry-topped cheesecake and made up personalized Easter baskets for each one; at Christmas, they gathered in her apartment to decorate a tree and drink eggnog. But the guilt trips were just as real: to discourage any would-be slackers, she would remind them that the hundred thousand schoolchildren of Milwaukee were depending on them. Although she could hardly fire people who were working for virtually no pay, she found subtler ways to let them know when they had fallen short of her exalted standards. When two of the VISTAs took a couple of days off over Thanksgiving 1968, they found on their return that they were pointedly excluded from a group trip to the movies—even though they had worked extra hours in the month before to earn the brief holiday. On New Year's Eve of that same year, one VISTA took the day off to cook dinner for a fellow volunteer he had been dating. "It's one thing to have a nice evening at midnight on New Year's Eve," Morheuser complained, "but why did you have to take the afternoon off to go prepare for the dinner?" It didn't mollify her that he planned to work on New Year's Day. Although she had left the convent five years earlier, Morheuser seemed to be striving, perhaps unconsciously, to re-create the intensely focused, self-denying community she had left behind, only this time with herself in the role of mother superior. In a psychological sense, one of the VISTA volunteers reflected years later, they had all become her acolytes.

The pace was exhausting, and intermittently the VISTAs resented Morheuser's relentlessness, but they also had no doubt that the cause was just. The more they learned about the Milwaukee schools, the more convinced they became of that. The district did not make their work easy: it refused to release personnel records until the court ordered it to do so, and it claimed, for example, that a particular annual report Barbee had requested did not exist, handing it over only when he rephrased his request to ask for the *semi*annual report. The volunteers had to pore over years of census numbers and old class photos to compile racial data on students and teachers, because the district said it had only started collecting that information in 1964. Some records the district insisted could only be examined in its offices, so for six months, one VISTA volunteer sat in a metal cage in the bowels of the school administration building, going through the applications students had filed when requesting transfers to schools outside their neighborhoods. At night, in the apartment she shared with her small son, Barbee's secretary would interview black students about the woeful conditions in their schools. Back at the office, a VISTA with a math background used a calculator to pull helpful statistics out of the raw data; a volunteer with an artistic bent made up attractive charts and graphs. Eventually, MUSIC found a computer company to help with its work, and the volunteers learned to enter data on the punch cards that the era's vast mainframe computers required. Then came more long hours proofreading the printouts and correcting the inevitable errors.

The meticulous work was producing results. Transfer applications extracted from the district's voluminous records provided nuggets of helpful candor: parents might explain, for example, that they were requesting the transfer because a teacher had told them blacks were coming to their old school. As Milwaukee's growing black population had spread into formerly white neighborhoods, the *Amos* team realized, the district had accelerated the racial transformation by encouraging white students to transfer out of their neighborhood schools; only later, after the children had switched schools, would their parents move out. To track the pattern, the VISTAs pored over years of telephone books, trying to establish when families had changed their addresses; sometimes they called up their targets and claimed to be doing a survey, just to make sure they had the right families.

Morheuser's superb organizational skills and command of detail had impressed Joan Franklin, the African American lawyer the NAACP had assigned to supervise the *Amos* case, and the two women soon became good friends. Although Franklin was fifteen years younger and had grown up poor in Detroit, she and Morheuser shared a fierce anger at injustice and a tendency to demonize their opponents. Since 1967, Franklin had been handling another NAACP-sponsored school segregation case, this one in Benton Harbor, Michigan, a two-hundred-mile drive from Milwaukee on the opposite shore of Lake Michigan, and she had enlisted Morheuser's help with that far smaller research effort as well. In January 1970, with the *Amos* case still months from trial, Morheuser and her VISTA volunteers detoured to Benton Harbor to help whip its case into shape on a crushingly short deadline. For two and a half weeks before the trial, Morheuser and the VISTAs holed up in a local supporter's basement, living on collard greens and sweet potato pie supplied by their hostess and her friends and working feverishly to prepare dozens of exhibits for a case that, to at least one of the volunteers, seemed to be a shambles.

The politics of the situation quickly became byzantine. Franklin had sought Morheuser's help in Benton Harbor and arranged for the NAACP to pay her, but like a number of other NAACP staff members, Franklin had resigned from the organization a year earlier during an internal dispute. By now, Morheuser too had her own reasons to be angry with the NAACP: after funding more than two years of *Amos* research, the organization had just announced an end to its support, leaving Lloyd Barbee to find the money to finish the case. Although Franklin had continued to handle both the Benton Harbor and *Amos* cases as a consultant to the NAACP, now, with the Benton Harbor trial weeks away, an argument began over the terms of her contract, and the organization decided to replace her. When the new NAACP lawyer, a thirty-something white southerner named Louis Lucas, arrived at the Benton Harbor house to check on the progress of the research and announce a change in trial strategy, Morheuser and her team were deeply suspicious of this interloper who had abruptly replaced their friend Franklin, and they refused to share their files. The standoff lasted for days, until Lucas telephoned Barbee in Milwaukee and summoned him to Benton Harbor to mediate. To Lucas, it seemed that Barbee's intervention solved the problem: Morheuser became cooperative enough to finish the exhibits and authenticate them with testimony on the first day of trial. But on her side, the anger was still simmering when the *Amos* team piled into Wheelwright's Valiant and drove through a snowstorm back home to Milwaukee.

After years of *Amos* research, Morheuser's relationship with Barbee had begun to deteriorate. Both Morheuser and Joan Franklin were growing increasingly frustrated with what they saw as Barbee's tenuous grasp of the case's many details, the nitty-gritty facts and figures that Morheuser's team was digging out of the school district files. Franklin flew in from New York regularly for consultations, but in between her visits, Barbee seemed unwilling—unable, the women suspected—to make strategic decisions, or to admit that he needed to rely on others for help. Franklin had a feeling that Barbee knew Morheuser was losing her respect for him. And perhaps Morheuser's disillusionment was all the greater because of the intensity of the admiration it replaced. She had changed her life to commit to Barbee's cause; she had followed him, revered him, perhaps even loved him. She was pulling him down from a high pedestal.

Morheuser was getting tired, she said later, of doing all the work and watching the lawyers get all the credit. For two years, she had been considering attending law school herself, but she had put it off because of her commitment to *Amos*. Now, with Benton Harbor behind her and the Milwaukee case apparently nearing trial, she began applying—to the nearby University of Wisconsin in Madison, but also to eastern schools like Yale, Columbia, and Rutgers, the state university of New Jersey. In the years since the 1967 Newark riots, Rutgers's law school in the heart of that city had embraced a clinical model of legal education, allowing law students, supervised by experienced attorneys, to work on real legal cases for clients who could not afford to pay. Although plenty of its students went on to conventional jobs with law firms or corporations, the Rutgers Law School had put a commitment to public service at the heart of its mission. The fit with Morheuser's aspirations was obvious. From the start, she knew what kind of legal career she wanted: her practice of law would aim to change the world. "Deep-rooted and far-reaching causes of social illness can only be countered by remedies that go deep and reach far to touch many," she wrote in her law school application. "I have learned from personal experience that the very nature of most institutions, public and private, militates against change from within the institutions themselves. . . . It seems clear to me, therefore, that one must become independent (independent, that is, of the need to operate professionally within a single institution) in order to be an effective agent of change in our society as it is presently structured."

In September 1970, Morheuser left Milwaukee for Rutgers Law School. She was almost broke—she would start school, she estimated, with only one thousand dollars in the bank, less than five thousand in today's dollars—but Rutgers had granted her a full scholarship, an important factor in her choice. Marty Wheelwright, her VISTA chauffeur, had also decided to attend Rutgers Law School; as Morheuser flew east, Wheelwright attached a U-Haul trailer to his Valiant, loaded up his own and Morheuser's possessions, and drove in her wake. Before they left, Barbee took them both to lunch at a nice restaurant. He had written Morheuser a glowing law school recommendation, but a pall had settled over their relationship since the Benton Harbor dispute. It was time to move on.

At forty-six, Morheuser was old to be starting school again, but she took to Rutgers at once. It was an exciting place to be a certain kind of law student, the kind who wanted to wear one of the ubiquitous T-shirts declaring Rutgers to be the "People's Electric Law School." Arthur Kinoy, the legendary civil rights lawyer, taught constitutional law, and future U.S. Supreme Court Justice Ruth Bader Ginsburg, a groundbreaking legal feminist, was also a member of the faculty. In his first year of teaching, one professor decided to survey the students in his introductory corporate law class to find out what they hoped to get out of their studies; about a quarter reported that they were taking his course because they wanted to destroy capitalism. And all around, for those who cared to look, were potent reminders of the social ills Morheuser hoped to help cure: in Newark, still reeling from the riots three years earlier, more than 22 percent of the population lived in poverty, the public schools were an acknowledged disaster, and the mayor had just been convicted of corruption.

Despite its abject poverty, Newark lacked affordable student housing. For a month after their arrival, Morheuser and Marty Wheelwright rented gray, depressing rooms in the local YMCA; when they could stand that no longer, they moved, as platonic roommates, into a second-floor apartment in the heart of the ghetto and then into a place a couple of miles north, in a much pleasanter neighborhood. They divided the labor: Marty shopped for groceries and did all the driving, while Marilyn prepared and froze meals each weekend, meticulously dicing vegetables for a week's worth of dishes.

She worked tirelessly, studying late into the night, on her way to a respectable B+ average. Outside of class, she joined an array of liberal committees, working to end the Vietnam War, to speed the impeachment of President Richard Nixon, and to defend arrested black radical Angela Davis. She also made the most of Rutgers's clinical law curriculum, enrolling in the Urban Legal Clinic run by Annamay Sheppard, a professor who had spent years as a lawyer for the Newark poor. On Morheuser's first day at the clinic, far more students than expected showed up, and Sheppard announced she would hold a lottery to choose who could remain. She was immeasurably exasperated when Morheuser insisted firmly that because the clinic was a curricular option, they all had the right to stay. Sheppard had no choice but to give in, and before long she and Morheuser were close friends.

Morheuser cut her legal teeth at Sheppard's clinic. One of her most memorable cases involved a complex interstate child custody dispute—a woman from the Midwest came to the clinic asking help finding her young son, who had been snatched by his paternal grandmother and might be staying with relatives in Newark. In the trusty old Valiant, Wheelwright and Morheuser staked out the family's home, trying to serve legal papers and to figure out where the child was staying; eventually, they tracked the boy to upstate New York, and Morheuser unearthed an arcane legal cause of action permitting his return to New Jersey. "Where did you find this?" the judge asked Morheuser, as he prepared to sign the order. "It's all a matter of looking, Judge," she replied.

Absorbed though Morheuser was in her studies, the *Amos* case was still on her mind. The original 1970 trial date had been postponed, but in September 1973, as Morheuser, fresh out of law school and done with the bar exam, prepared to start her first legal job with the New Jersey public defender's office, it looked as if the trial were finally ready to begin. Morheuser negotiated time off from work and headed for Milwaukee, prepared to support the trial team by plucking whatever they needed from the voluminous case files she knew so well. The night before the trial was to start, Morheuser, Barbee, and Joan Franklin met in Barbee's office to finalize their plans for the next day. The women assumed that the arrangements were clear: Franklin would sit first chair in the trial, give the opening statement, and take their expert University of Wisconsin witness step by step through the research that Morheuser's team had painstakingly assembled. It was obvious to the women that Franklin had mastered the intricate details of the case, and that Barbee never had. Barbee, too, assumed that the arrangements were clear: as the local lawyer and the long-time leader of Milwaukee's civil rights movement, he would sit first chair, give the opening statement, and examine the expert. The misunderstanding spilled into the open that night, and soon the allies were embroiled in a loud, bitter confrontation. Franklin knew the case better than Barbee, the women argued; if he handled the case himself, he would lose. Barbee was angry and hurt: for Morheuser to side with Franklin against him was a profound betrayal, he felt. But he refused to give in, and Franklin and Morheuser walked off the case, leaving him to try it alone. More than two years later, after fifty witnesses, hundreds of exhibits, and months of deliberation, a judge ruled that the Milwaukee school board had deliberately pursued policies that segregated the schools, and he ordered the district to devise a desegregation remedy. Morheuser had been wrong. Barbee had won his case after all. But she did not call to congratulate him; after that night in 1973, they never spoke again. Morheuser's passionate involvement with the second great cause of her life, the civil rights movement, was over. The last of her life's great causes, the fight for equal school funding, lay before her.

4

Son of *Robinson*

Marilyn Morheuser almost did not get the job that would become the center of her life. In 1979, 350 people applied to run the Education Law Center (ELC), the nonprofit law firm that would soon revive school-funding litigation in New Jersey, and she was not one of them.

In the six years since her law school graduation, Morheuser had worked on an array of liberal legal causes, but she had not yet found a ruling passion to fill every corner of her life, the way the convent and the civil rights movement once had. She had spent a year crafting criminal appeals for the state public defender's office, then another year representing mental patients for the Department of the Public Advocate, New Jersey's government ombudsman. For three years, she had worked for the state branch of the American Civil Liberties Union, participating in the landmark housing discrimination case known as *Mount Laurel*, after the South Jersey suburb whose zoning ordinances, the state supreme court had recently decided, were illegally tailored to keep out the poor. In 1978, she had returned to her first job with the appeals section of the public defender's office, this time with new supervisory responsibilities, but the office atmosphere was tense, and friends knew Morheuser was not committed to staying. Her dissatisfaction came at an opportune moment, for elsewhere in Newark, the Education Law Center was at a crossroads of its own.

In the dining room of the Ford Foundation's midtown Manhattan offices, the plates sat atop paper doilies, and many a foundation project had been sketched out on those doilies during working lunches. Ford had a decades-long history of funding left-leaning efforts to promote peace, education, and democracy, and by 1973 school-finance reform was high on its agenda. In his three years at Ford, school-finance expert James Kelly had been systematically building a network of grantees—scholars and lawyers, thinkers and activists—who would push states to improve opportunities for children. In 1973, the young Rutgers University law professor Paul Tractenberg met Kelly for lunch to talk about joining that network.

The quiet, methodical Tractenberg seemed an unlikely activist. He had grown up in the 1940s and '50s as the only child of lower-middle-class Jewish parents in a Newark neighborhood that had not yet begun its slide into poverty and despair. His father, whose own high school education had been cut short by the Depression, managed a bowling alley in nearby Elizabeth; Tractenberg was in his mid-teens before the family could afford a car. Like his near-contemporary, the novelist Philip Roth, Tractenberg went to well-regarded Weequahic High School; his pitching was good enough to earn him postgraduation offers from two professional baseball teams, but instead he parlayed his good grades into college at elite Wesleyan University and law school at the University of Michigan.

Tractenberg planned to practice international law, and he soon landed a well-paying job with the prestigious Wall Street firm of Sullivan & Cromwell, which prided itself on its distinguished tradition of public service—its partners, past and present, included a secretary of state and a United Nations ambassador. An atmosphere of wealth and power suffused Sullivan & Cromwell: the firm expected its lawyers to fly first class and to eat in the best restaurants. Weequahic seemed very far away, and despite the sometimes interesting work—less than two years out of law school, Tractenberg found himself in Manila, explaining a bond deal to the finance minister of the Philippines—he was ready to leave after a couple of years. Whatever the financial rewards, the job provided too little "psychic income," he would say years later. When he told the Sullivan & Cromwell partners he had worked with that he was leaving for a legal job with the Peace Corps, he could sense their incomprehension. They might sing the praises of public service, he decided, but the kind of public service they had in mind was service in the president's cabinet, not as an anonymous government lawyer.

Tractenberg enjoyed his years in Washington, D.C., but when the Peace Corps' top leadership changed, he followed his boss back to another big New York law firm, this time with a mandate to work on public interest projects—first, an overhaul of New York State's antidiscrimination laws, and later, the famous effort to decentralize New York City's schools. When the firm began hinting that he should devote more time to corporate practice, Tractenberg decided to try teaching law instead, and the obvious place to try was Rutgers Law School, in Newark. Not that he lived there any more: Tractenberg had returned from Washington on the heels of the 1967 riots, when few whites felt welcome in the city, and, with his wife and young children, he had moved to Millburn, an affluent Newark suburb. But the law school's burgeoning clinical program and proclaimed commitment to public service drew him just as they had Marilyn Morheuser, and, like her, he arrived on campus in 1970.

By 1973, when Tractenberg heard about Kelly's Ford Foundation project, *Robinson v. Cahill* had made New Jersey a key battleground for school-finance reformers, and Tractenberg himself had already filed his influential friend-of-the-court brief on the state constitution's "thorough and efficient" clause. Kelly was impressed with Tractenberg; the thirty-five-year-old law school professor seemed solid, mature, and genuinely offended by the inequities in New Jersey's public schools. Perhaps most important, Kelly thought, Tractenberg was not afraid to risk angering the state officials who signed his paycheck by challenging their management of public education. The Ford Foundation awarded Tractenberg a two-year, $450,000 grant to launch a public interest law firm that would tackle education equity issues in New Jersey and Pennsylvania. By February 1, 1974, the Education Law Center (ELC) was up and running in Philadelphia and in Newark, where four lawyers occupied offices over a piano store.

ELC's mandate was broader than school-finance reform: the center planned to represent families mired in a variety of disputes with the schools and through those cases to effect broader changes in the delivery of public education. ELC lawyers fought to get disabled students the special education services to which they were legally entitled from school districts that would have preferred to warehouse them. Although Tractenberg had assumed most of his clients would be poor, many of the special education cases involved families from affluent suburbs. Urban kids were treated just as badly, Tractenberg suspected, but their parents sometimes lacked the savvy to ask ELC for help.

From the beginning, the *Robinson* case was central to ELC's work. As the Department of Education hashed out its "process model," defining T&E districts as those that set local goals and worked to achieve them, ELC joined liberal advocacy groups in pressing to supplement that administrative paper-shuffling with concrete progress indicators, including standardized test scores. Meanwhile, as the legislature and the state supreme court played political ping-pong over the funding of the new law, ELC weighed in with friend-of-the-court briefs. Even before Governor Brendan Byrne signed the income tax into law, ELC was arguing that the new school-funding formula would shortchange the poor once again. Someone—perhaps ELC itself—would be back in court before long.

In the meantime, however, Paul Tractenberg had to get back to teaching law. In July 1976, the same month the *Robinson* battle ended with the enactment of the income tax, he handed ELC's reins to a successor. Michael Lottman, a white midwesterner with a background in civil rights law, had seemed like a good fit for the job, but soon he was miserable in New Jersey. His degree from Alabama's unaccredited Jones Law School, where he had studied while editing a civil rights newspaper, had not prevented him from litigating in federal court as an attorney for the U.S. Department of Justice, but it turned out to be an insuperable obstacle in New Jersey's courts, where only graduates of accredited law schools were permitted to appear. And while Lottman was enthusiastic about ELC's work on behalf of disabled children, he had grave doubts about the efficacy of the school-funding litigation that Ford's Jim Kelly championed. The more Lottman learned about the corruption and incompetence scarring school districts like Newark, and the more he thought about the terrible social conditions warping their students' lives, the less the main issue seemed to be money. "Given the gross mismanagement in many of the large urban districts on whose behalf the current formula would be challenged . . . it would be difficult to ask the courts to assume that any denial of a thorough and efficient education in those districts (which would not be difficult to establish) was related to the effects of the school finance system," Lottman wrote in ELC's 1977–78 annual report.

Not surprisingly, Lottman and Kelly did not get along, and with Ford still providing nearly all ELC's funding—another two-year, $675,000 grant in 1975 and a further $600,000 in 1977—Kelly's priorities inevitably trumped Lottman's. At the end of 1978, Lottman left for a new job in Washington, and ELC found itself looking for a new leader, just as Marilyn Morheuser started thinking about a new job. Although she had not applied initially, no one on ELC's list of finalists seemed quite right, and when Morheuser's old law school professor, Annamay Sheppard, suggested her name, the search committee followed up. On August 1, 1979, Morheuser became ELC's third executive director, with a mandate to challenge New Jersey's school-funding system again, in a suit that one ELC lawyer had taken to calling Son of *Robinson v. Cahill.*

By 1979, whatever hopes the passage of the T&E law had inspired in advocates for the urban poor had dissipated. A series of reports from advocacy organizations and academic researchers had concluded that the law, enacted in response to a suit filed on behalf of the poor, had ended up giving the lion's share of its benefits to the middle class. Although the school-funding pie had expanded—in 1977–78, the state was spending $449 million more than it had two years earlier—poor districts had gotten only 12 percent of the new money, while middle-income districts had gotten 68 percent. Furthermore, little of the new money for poor communities had reached poor students. As they had when Ray Bateman's school-funding law was enacted years earlier, the cities had used much of the windfall not to increase their school spending but to reduce their sky-high taxes—in effect, to replace local money with state money. As a result, although tax rates had moved closer to equality, school-spending disparities had barely budged, and by some measures, had actually widened. Rich districts were still spending far more on their schools than poor districts were. "The broad outcome of the new law in operation has been almost negligible," one researcher wrote. "District wealth is still the major factor in determining the level of educational expenditures in New Jersey."

How could this have happened? The elaborate T&E funding formula was supposed to produce the opposite result—to break the link between a district's wealth and its school spending, to enable poor districts to spend more while taxing less. To some extent, however, the persistence of spending gaps had been a predictable outcome. The T&E law established a guaranteed tax base formula, under which state aid made up the difference between the amount a poor district could raise on its own and the amount the district could have raised if its tax base had been equivalent to the guaranteed level. But like all guaranteed tax base formulas, the T&E law left every district free to set its own spending and taxation levels; the legislature and the Byrne administration had wanted it that way, because such freedom continued New Jersey's long tradition of local control of the schools. From that point of view, then, persistent school-spending gaps appropriately reflected different community choices about what to spend on education.

That reassuring explanation told only part of the story, however. Although guaranteed tax base formulas were not expected to eliminate all school spending gaps, they were supposed to eliminate spending gaps *caused by differences in property wealth*—and even by that limited standard, New Jersey's system had failed. The reasons for that failure lay in eye-glazing technical details of the funding formula, details that few legislators had understood even when they voted for the law. At least three such elements of the formula were working now to maintain inequities.

First, the guaranteed tax base, which Governor Byrne had originally proposed setting at double the state average, had eventually been set far lower, leaving 159 rich districts with tax bases above the guaranteed level. Whatever tax rate those 159 districts chose to set, they would inevitably raise more money than districts with tax bases at or below the guaranteed level; therefore, the rich districts could spend more on their schools than poorer districts could, and they could do so without taxing themselves more heavily.

Second, the T&E formula calculated each district's state funding as a percentage of the previous year's school budget; the poorer the district, the higher the share of its budget paid by state aid. But the reliance on prior-year figures meant that no state aid was available for the first year of a new program. That initial investment in updated textbooks, extra guidance counselors, or more microscopes had to be paid for with local money, which poor districts had trouble squeezing out of their depleted local property tax bases. As a result, poorer districts often could not afford expensive upgrades, no matter how necessary.

Third, although the heart of the T&E formula was its effort to equalize the funding available to rich and poor districts, 43 percent of state money was distributed without regard to district wealth. In their quest for political support for the new law, legislators had guaranteed every district, no matter how wealthy, a minimum amount of state aid. In addition, state aid targeted for transportation, remedial education, and special education for the disabled was paid out according to formulas that ignored districts' relative wealth. In other words, nearly half the state's school aid was not used to close spending gaps between rich and poor.

Economic and demographic pressures unforeseen by the Byrne-era legislators had further exacerbated the formula's technical problems. In the 1970s, enrollment in New Jersey's schools had fallen, but the drop had been steeper in the wealthy suburbs than in the poor cities. Because the state calculated aid amounts based on the previous year's enrollment figures, wealthy districts with falling enrollments found themselves with extra state aid to divide among fewer students; their per-pupil spending rose as a result, widening the gap between rich and poor districts. And faced with rapid inflation and tight budgets, the legislatures of the late 1970s had almost never appropriated enough money to pay out all the school aid that the formula said districts were entitled to. Inevitably, that shortfall hurt the most in districts that depended most heavily on state aid—the poorest districts.

As disappointing as the T&E law's fiscal aspects had proved, equally disappointing had been its educational component—the elaborate "process model," under which districts would set goals, draw up plans for achieving them, and then implement those plans, with the commissioner of education ensuring that no corners were cut. In the years after Byrne signed the income tax, the legislative advocates of the new law, their ranks depleted by electoral defeats and their energy flagging after years of combat, lost their appetite for vigorous oversight of the Department of Education's work. William Shine, the bureaucrat who had assured Byrne's assistant treasurer that common sense would guide implementation of the process model, left the department, and school districts began complaining loudly about the paperwork that T&E entailed. Urban advocates groused that the department had set no standards for gauging the effectiveness of school programs or the adequacy of district budgets; they saw little sign the department was using the new powers the law had given it to mandate spending increases and enforce district compliance. The one concrete benchmark of educational success, the Minimum Basic Skills Test established in the legislative compromise over the income tax, was so rudimentary as to be almost useless, advocates argued. By the time Morheuser took over at ELC, the advocacy community knew the *Robinson* compromise had run its course. It was only a matter of time before the whole mess would be back in court.

By 1979, when the fifty-five-year-old Morheuser joined ELC, Harold Ruvoldt Jr., the young Jersey City lawyer who had filed the original *Robinson* suit, had moved on to other projects. ELC would apparently have the field to itself if it decided to challenge the state's school-funding formula a second time. Still, ELC could count on some high-powered help. A few years earlier, the Lawyers' Committee for Civil Rights Under Law, founded in the Kennedy era to involve lawyers in the civil rights struggle, had launched a school-finance project, funded with yet another Ford Foundation grant. The project's director was David Long, a Lutheran minister's son fifteen years younger than Morheuser, who had learned first-hand what discrimination felt like as one of just a handful of mainland whites in his University of Hawaii graduating class: in Asian-run stores, he had noticed, Caucasians often were served last. At the Lawyers' Committee, Long became a circuit rider, traveling around the country to help lawyers bring school-finance cases. During the *Robinson* fight, Long had provided ELC with computer runs showing that the T&E law would fail to achieve funding equity, and in the years after *Robinson* ended, Long had helped ELC lawyers strategize for a rematch.

Gradually, the legal options had sorted themselves out. Under one scenario, known in-house as "the basket case," ELC would choose a poor district suffering from all the typical ailments—high taxes, low spending, a depleted tax base, devastatingly needy students—and sue it for failing to provide the competent instruction, broad curriculum, and adequate buildings guaranteed under the T&E law. Perhaps the district—say, the decaying South Jersey city of Camden—would defend itself by arguing that no one could do better with the money available: in 1978, Camden spent $2,250 per student, while the nearby suburb of Cherry Hill spent $2,534, almost 13 percent more. The difference came to more than $7,000 for a classroom of twenty-five children, enough to pay nearly half an average teacher's salary. To defend the T&E law against this line of attack, the state would have to make one of two unpalatable arguments. The state could assert that the spending shortfall was Camden's fault, because the commissioner of education had no power to order increased spending. But that position was fraught with danger: the *Robinson* court had found the T&E law constitutional in part because the law *did* give the commissioner such power. According to the court's interpretation, the law said that if a local community refused to spend enough to provide adequate schools, the commissioner could step in to ensure children were not shortchanged. To argue that the court had exaggerated the commissioner's powers risked undermining one of the very premises on which the law's constitutionality rested. But if the state instead adopted the *Robinson* court's interpretation and agreed that the commissioner did have the power to solve Camden's spending problems, then the commissioner would have to come up with a plan to do so—a sticky political proposition. Either way, a judge might end up ordering that the state's school-finance law be revised to ensure adequate resources for all the state's Camdens.

Eventually, however, ELC's lawyers rejected the basket-case strategy as too big and complicated. A better approach, they decided, though hardly a simple one, would be to relitigate *Robinson*, to highlight in vivid detail the fiscal and educational problems the T&E law had spawned and the impact those deficiencies had on children. That approach had its own pitfalls, however. The state's lawyers and the courts were unlikely to permit another short, *Robinson*-style trial, with experts on both sides essentially agreeing that educational improvement required higher spending. "Many of the difficult issues that the litigation slid past in *Robinson*, such as the cost-quality issue, would have to be confronted," an ELC lawyer wrote in a 1978 memo spelling out the choices. Whatever the approach, a decent interval would have to pass before any new case could be filed; the state had argued it would take five years to phase in the T&E law, and the supreme court seemed unlikely to entertain a new challenge so soon after the bruising *Robinson* battles. It would be important to wait long enough to compile a clear record of failure, rather than a stack of computer printouts predicting an uncertain future.

As the T&E law took effect, ELC staff quietly gathered information. From parents, school officials, and statewide advocacy groups, they heard the same message: the new money was not reaching the classroom. Before the T&E law, urban children had sat in overcrowded classrooms with no teachers' aides and too few books and desks; after T&E, the classes were still overcrowded, the books and desks and aides still missing. The state was certainly funneling more money into school aid, but just as the statistical analyses showed, in the hardest-pressed communities, that money was buying relief for taxpayers, not books for schoolchildren. From the state, ELC gathered reams of statistical data to back up the anecdotes, and just as the VISTA volunteers had done in Milwaukee, ELC staff and volunteers pored over stacks of computer printouts, using printing calculators to compile long columns of data on tax rates, dropout rates, per-pupil spending.

The chief number-cruncher was Steven Block, a former student activist who, even in his late thirties, radiated the earnest enthusiasm of youth. Block, the only child of Eisenhower Republicans, had grown up conventionally middle class in the Westchester County suburbs of New York. In high school, he played basketball, headed the student council, and drove a pea green 1954 Ford convertible. But at Williams College in Massachusetts in the early 1960s, Block discovered the civil rights movement. He founded the campus chapter of Students for a Democratic Society (SDS), led a demonstration against General Electric's involvement in the racist South African regime, and spent a summer helping organize for Martin Luther King Jr.'s March on Washington. After college, SDS sent Block to do community organizing in Newark; a year later, he took a job teaching seventh grade in the city's public schools, where his teaching partner was a white veteran who, he suspected, would never stop mourning the student body's transformation from all-Jewish to all-black. Block meant well, but his teacher training had begun and ended with a brief course the previous summer, and although he cared about his students, visited their homes, and took them on field trips to New York City, he knew nothing about how to teach them. He had better luck organizing their parents. The Newark Board of Education planned to ease chronic overcrowding by splitting the school day into two four-hour shifts, and the community was soon up in arms at this proposal to truncate instruction.

The night the Newark riots began, Block drew three hundred parents to a meeting called in opposition to the school board's plans. Perhaps it was not surprising that the board failed to renew his teaching contract.

Over the next decade, Block tackled new projects—founding an alternative high school in Newark; teaching and rabble-rousing at the local community college, which county politicians were threatening to move out of the city; and running an interfaith community services organization. With the Vietnam War at full boil, he was drafted and spent a night in jail after refusing to report for duty, although a bureaucratic snafu eventually saved him from prosecution. Then in the late 1970s, as education activists turned their attention to the just-enacted T&E law, a new education coalition called Schoolwatch hired Block to prepare a detailed evaluation of the law's first few years. That job was only half done when Morheuser hired him away to help ELC prepare its school-finance litigation. At first, Block was ambivalent about the ELC job. Policy analysis was fun, he had decided, and though he had a head for figures, he was not sure he wanted to crunch numbers for a living. But Morheuser won him over. The answers lay in the numbers, she told him.

Still, the case she was building would have to be about more than numbers. *Robinson v. Cahill* had degenerated into a duel between computer printouts, an arid argument over statistics. To convince the courts to reopen that tortured debate, the new case would have to breathe life back into the problem, to remind judges that children's lives, not just numbers on a page, were at stake. To dramatize the problem, ELC soon decided to focus on a small group of suffering urban school districts and to compare those districts with a group of affluent suburbs. The contrast between the educational crumbs offered one group of children and the banquet available to others living just a few miles away would throw the issues into high relief.

Marilyn Morheuser embraced the new cause with her old passion, and her old, all-consuming work habits. She was still no early riser, but once in the office, she worked all day, kept up her strength with endless infusions of nicotine and caffeine, and took her papers home at night, spreading them out on the kitchen table in her Newark apartment, far enough from the office that she relied on a succession of friends and colleagues to drive her every day. Like the *Amos* lawsuit volunteers years earlier,

Morheuser's newest coworkers respected and admired her even as they chafed under her yoke. She was funny and ebullient, filled with energy, enthusiasm, and passion, capable of mesmerizing an audience with the sheer intensity of her commitment. But she could also be a demanding perfectionist; anyone who fell short of her standards faced cutting criticism, sometimes delivered at above-average volume. At times, her insistence on getting her own way seemed unbelievably petty: once, she was annoyed when a coworker chauffeured her to an appointment via an alternate route, because Morheuser had wanted to open the upcoming discussion by complimenting her host's driving directions. No one could doubt Morheuser's dedication, though: she lived and breathed the school-funding case, to the exclusion of all else. ELC's mission still included helping disabled children and their parents secure mandated services, but Morheuser barely bothered feigning an interest in those cases. Incremental change, one child at a time, was not what she had in mind.

Although Morheuser could be an imperious mother superior to those she worked with, her warm, nurturing side remained equally real. Morheuser's relationship with her family had been rocky in the years after she left the convent—her sister Marie had stopped speaking to her for a time—but the estrangement had ended before she began law school. Her father had died in 1973, just days after her dramatic break with Lloyd Barbee, but Morheuser remained beloved "Aunt Mar" to her sister's children. Still, visits between St. Louis and New Jersey were sporadic, and by the time she joined ELC, Morheuser had begun welding her friends—law school colleagues, neighbors, fellow travelers in the world of education reform—into the surrogate family that would sustain her for the rest of her life. These were the people who saw Morheuser's charm and generosity up close, who remembered her spontaneous renditions of "Wagon Wheels," her big hugs, her love of jazz and basketball and ethnic restaurants, the spirituality that persisted despite her quarrels with organized Catholicism, the little no-occasion gifts she liked to give.

A year or two into her new job at ELC, Tom Cioppettini joined that surrogate family. Just a few months earlier, Cioppettini had graduated from college and joined his brother's real estate company; ELC had recently moved its offices into the company's Washington Street building, and Cioppettini dropped by one night to introduce himself to his new tenants.

"Who is this young whippersnapper?" he heard Morheuser ask teasingly, as he waited to be invited into her office. The brief chat he had planned stretched into a three-hour conversation, and by the end of the evening, Morheuser had urged Cioppettini to consider renting the newly vacant apartment down the hall in her building. He moved in soon after, and the fifty-something ex-nun-turned-lawyer and twenty-something entrepreneur became inseparable platonic companions. Together, they played Scrabble, rooted for the New York Knicks, and watched the Sunday morning political talk shows. Cioppettini took Morheuser shopping for clothes and groceries, mixed her after-work martini (extra dry, extra olives), ate dinner with her several nights a week, and dropped by to zap her with a water pistol on mornings when she overslept. In those early years, Cioppettini was recovering from a broken engagement to his college girlfriend and negotiating an adult relationship with his big, volatile Italian family; in Morheuser he found an endless supply of wisdom and support. In return, he gave her devoted and unselfish friendship; there was no ambivalence in his attachment, as there was for some of the others who loved and admired her. Years later, he would say that he became the son she never had.

Her other child was the lawsuit. For months, ELC lawyers worked on their opening salvo, the complaint that would lay out the bare bones of the case they planned to flesh out in court. Nowhere was Morheuser's perfectionism more obvious than in those months of work. The draft grew and shrank as she weighed each paragraph and circulated the work in progress to respected lawyers on ELC's board and in the wider advocacy community. The process was not yet complete in April 1980, when the Newark school board, embroiled in a budget fight with both the city's mayor and the state Education Department, announced it was suing the state over school-finance inequities. To at least one ELC lawyer, some of the phrases in Newark's complaint had a familiar ring; perhaps ELC's draft had circulated a bit *too* widely. Regardless, Newark's suit, *Sharif v. Byrne*, could spell trouble for ELC's case. Back when they were strategizing over the single-district "basket case," ELC lawyers had discussed the importance of picking a well-run district: choose a poorly run district, and the state could attribute educational problems to local corruption and mismanagement,

rather than to the failings of the funding law. Newark, whose disgraced
ex-mayor had once said he left the U.S. Congress because you could make
a lot more money running the city, was the poster child for local corruption and mismanagement. ELC was focusing its work on a dozen or so
urban districts whose problems seemed to bear a clear-cut relationship to
funding shortfalls. Add Newark, with its patronage hiring, its sclerotic
teacher-tenure system, and its recent history of Mafia-influenced city
government, and the whole fragile edifice of proof might collapse under
the strain.

Behind the scenes, Morheuser urged Newark to drop its lawsuit and
let ELC handle the litigation, and *Sharif* had barely progressed by the time
Morheuser finally filed her case on February 5, 1981, almost exactly eleven
years after the launching of *Robinson v. Cahill*. After months of winnowing
the case down to manageable scale, her plaintiffs were twenty schoolchildren from ten families living in four urban districts: Jersey City, across
the Hudson from New York, the state's second-largest city; and three
smaller cities—Camden, in Philadelphia's shadow, and East Orange and
Irvington, both bordering Newark. By alphabetical happenstance, the leadoff plaintiff was twelve-year-old Camden sixth-grader Raymond Abbott,
the only white plaintiff; the leadoff defendant was Commissioner of Education Fred Burke.

Years after the conclusion of *Robinson*, the state's school-funding
scheme "continues to rely on widely disparate local property wealth,"
the *Abbott v. Burke* complaint asserted. "In financial resources available
for educational facilities, services, and programs, disparities between
plaintiffs' districts and districts having high property values and high expenditures are even greater in 1980 than they were under the prior, unconstitutional scheme." The complaint spelled out the technical reasons
for the enduring inequities—the continued overreliance on local property
taxes, the problems with prior-year funding, and the like—and documented
the resulting funding gaps between rich and poor districts. The money
shortages, the complaint asserted, were the direct cause of the educational inadequacies in the poor districts—the dilapidated buildings, the
bigger classes, the lower-paid and less-experienced teachers. Yet the children who attended these inadequate schools had overwhelming educational needs, the complaint noted, for they came from families with little

money or education, scored poorly on standardized tests, and dropped out in large numbers. In effect, students who needed the most got the least; the disparities produced by the workings of the T&E law bore no logical relationship to the provision of a thorough and efficient education. To illustrate its points, the complaint paired each of the four urban districts with a more affluent community. While Jersey City spent $1,700 per student, Paramus spent $2,900; Ocean City could draw on a tax base of more than $500,000 per student, while Camden made do with a tax base of less than $24,000 per student.

The argument papered over some difficult questions, questions that would move to the forefront of the case in the years to come. For one, the complaint assumed that the educational inadequacy in the four districts was a direct result of spending disparities, rather than of the mismanagement and corruption that had worried Michael Lottman during his stint at ELC; from that untested assumption flowed the conclusion that educational improvement would require more spending. In places, the complaint also seemed to define spending inequity itself as a form of educational inadequacy. Yet how much did spending disparities matter, in and of themselves? If different districts could spend different amounts and still provide adequate educations, was the spending disparity still a constitutional problem? The complaint never confronted this question.

That ambiguity was a legacy of New Jersey's first school-funding battle. In its *Robinson v. Cahill* rulings, the state supreme court had accepted school spending as a proxy for school quality, largely because the state had suggested no alternative. Thus, the court had found that the disparity in spending between rich and poor school districts was a marker of disparity in educational quality, an indication of the state's failure to provide all children with a thorough and efficient education. In a sense, then, the court had interpreted the T&E clause in comparative terms—not as requiring merely that all districts meet some minimal level of educational adequacy, but as requiring that all districts provide similar levels of educational opportunity. Officially, the court had rejected the claim that the state's school-spending law violated equal-protection guarantees, but at the same time, the court had converted the T&E clause into something very much like an equal-protection guarantee.

To anyone who knew Marilyn Morheuser's history of passionate commitment to civil rights, race played a curiously understated role in the *Abbott v. Burke* complaint. Here and there, the complaint did note that the vast majority of public school students in the four districts—and nineteen of the twenty plaintiff children—were black or Hispanic, and ELC did claim that the state's school-funding system discriminated against the plaintiffs on the basis of race and national origin, as well as wealth. But the complaint subordinated the racial argument, based on state and federal equal-protection guarantees, to the educational argument, based on the state constitution's T&E clause. The tactical reasons for this choice were obvious: the legal precedents on education and equal protection were unpromising, whereas the T&E-based *Robinson* precedent was ELC's most powerful weapon. In an uncomfortable way, however, that tactical choice put *Abbott v. Burke* at odds with *Brown v. Board of Education*'s ringing declaration that separate schools are inherently unequal; the *Abbott* case came close to arguing that, since racially separate schools were inevitable, the schools minority children attended should at least be made equal. That uncomfortable fact was not lost on the *Abbott* legal team, some of whom would have found it more emotionally satisfying to recast *Abbott* as a straightforward race case. They were a left-leaning bunch, and few of them doubted that New Jersey's urban schools would have had an easier time getting state funding if most of their students had not been black and Hispanic. But the lawyers wanted to give themselves the best chance to win their case. Besides, they figured, they could always make those race arguments later, if they had to.

The newspapers covered the *Abbott v. Burke* filing for a day or so, and the state soon filed a boilerplate response containing few surprises. The response disputed the relevance of the district comparisons—some of the paired districts were not even in the same county, the state noted—and argued, as ELC had expected, that any educational failings were the fault of local school officials, not of the state. In any case, the state argued, the case did not belong in the courts. Because ELC was challenging the way the Department of Education was administering a state law, the challenge properly should proceed through the Office of Administrative Law, an arm of the executive branch, whose judges could recommend changes in the way departments of state government did their work.

As the months passed, the lawyers for the two sides worked their way through a thicket of preliminary issues. They exchanged witness lists and agreed on which statistics to use. They argued over whether the case should be certified as a class action, in which ELC would represent all the children in the four target districts; eventually, Judge William Dreier agreed that it should be. Dreier also agreed to let ELC introduce evidence of educational deficiencies in other urban districts. ELC staffers interviewed hundreds of teachers, administrators, and school board members, auditioned seventy-five potential expert witnesses, and toured fifty schools.

For the ELC staff, those school visits were eye-opening. In East Orange, ELC paralegal Debra Matrick stepped out onto an auditorium stage that had been partitioned into a special education classroom using sheets of black plastic. Children sat in unfinished, unpainted basement rooms, or shared chairs in classrooms without enough seating. Workbooks were ripped, their pages already scribbled on. Matrick was far from rich: she had joined ELC as a secretary right after her divorce, and she was raising three children alone in a middle-class town while working on a college degree at night. But her children's schools were safe and appealing; every spring and fall, classes took field trips. On her drives home from the depressing schools that other people's kids attended, Matrick sometimes cried.

Unlike Matrick, ELC lawyer Joyce Miller, an African American who had grown up in Florida in the 1950s and '60s, was used to deprivation. Her high school chemistry lab had been so underequipped that Miller brought a tin can from home to serve as a beaker; one student was burned when he tried to carry acid in a paper cup. But when she stepped into a Camden elementary school for the first time, Miller thought, "This school is worse than the Jim Crow school in the South that I went to." It was not just the dirty and crumbling building or the lack of books and equipment; it was the atmosphere of defeat. The teachers, she thought, could not even imagine that anything better was possible.

Other ELC researchers had similar insights. They met principals and superintendents who, straining to avoid giving a bad impression of their schools or districts, seemed almost paralyzed by the effort. Some did not even seem to realize their schools were in trouble. One principal, ELC staff reported, "is a fine educator who is very involved in what he is doing,

but he has no idea what the word 'adequate' means. He said the kindergarten was well supplied when it was truly very sparsely [sic] supplied."
Nor did everyone they met agree with the premise of ELC's case, that
whatever mismanagement or corruption might exist in urban schools, educational problems were rooted in the lack of money. One spring day in
Jersey City, an ELC lawyer chatted off the record with two veteran school
administrators. The Jersey City public schools, the administrators said,
had become a patronage mill because the children of the city's politicians
and voters were safely ensconced in Catholic school. One of the men, the
lawyer reported, had offered this summary of his possible testimony: "For
Jersey City if we want him to say resources he'll say resources but it's not
resources, it's politics."

Although the *Abbott* complaint had papered it over, the same debate
was simmering within ELC. Years earlier, Steve Block, Morheuser's chief
number cruncher, had moved to the old waterfront city of Hoboken, befriended the mayor, and been appointed to the school board. Hoboken,
Jersey City's mile-square Hudson County neighbor, had a political culture
equally steeped in nepotism, corruption, and patronage, and Block was
appalled by what he saw in the school system. The former mayor was on
the payroll as a full-time labor negotiator, even though the small district
did not have full-time labor negotiations. One local councilman was the
district's business administrator; a former councilman ran the food program. Every Election Day, the victor's campaign workers flooded into jobs
as custodians, aides, and teachers while the loser's supporters were fired
or transferred to unpleasant schools and inconvenient shifts. In memos
and reports and behind-the-scenes screaming matches at school board
meetings, Block hammered away at the issue; in 1982, at a statewide education convention, he gave a speech about political interference in the
schools, using Hoboken as a case study. Everyone sniggered about Hudson
County politics, Block thought, but the impact on kids was no joke: if your
first-grade teacher had been hired because she was the mayor's cousin,
what guarantee was there that she could teach you to read?

Block had no trouble reconciling his critique of urban politics with
ELC's crusade for more urban school funding: city districts would still
need more money to hire enough teachers, he thought, even if the districts cleaned up their politics and hired teachers who were not related to

the mayor. But Morheuser wished Block would shut up. She did not disagree with him on the facts—she knew political interference was real, and she agreed that it hurt children. Still, the issue was a loser for ELC, she felt. It took the focus off funding; it gave the state ammunition for its argument that whatever the cities' educational failings, they were not due to a shortage of money. The two old '60s activists argued back and forth, and once in a while, the argument got heated. In 1983, when Block decided to run for the Hoboken City Council, the decision to leave ELC for full-time campaigning was not as difficult as it might once have been.

The *Abbott* case seemed at last to be coming to a head. Judge Dreier set a trial date for October 1983, then for December. That fall, however, Dreier won a promotion to the state appeals court and a new judge, Virginia Long, inherited the *Abbott* case. Meanwhile, ELC fought to keep the *Sharif* case from tainting its proofs. Newark had briefly won certification of its case as a class action and had tried to consolidate its case with *Abbott*, but within months, the class certification was reversed—as ELC had argued, the *Sharif* plaintiffs, who included not only school board members and schoolchildren, but also city officials and taxpayers, had too many competing interests to fit comfortably under the class-action umbrella. By then, *Sharif* was running out of steam; in the spring of 1983, Newark threw in the towel and moved to dismiss the case because the school district lacked the money to pursue it. "Thus *Sharif* plaintiffs have sought and been granted dismissal for the same reasons for which they sued—insufficient resources," Morheuser told her board.

The political context of the *Abbott* case was far different from that of *Robinson*. In the early 1970s, most of the state's political elite had believed an income tax was inevitable, and many had suspected that Governor William Cahill found it useful to have a court order backing up that imperative. Although Cahill was nominally a defendant in *Robinson*, many observers believed that his administration did not fight the case hard, and Cahill's successor, Governor Byrne, openly embraced the plaintiffs' cause. By the time the *Abbott* case reached the courts, however, Byrne had been replaced as governor by Thomas Kean, a moderate Republican with an aristocratic political pedigree. His family was descended from New Jersey's first governor, Robert Livingston; Kean's grandfather and great-uncle had served in the United States Senate, and Kean's father had spent twenty years in Congress. Kean was a shy, lonely child, and he hated his first years at an elite Massachusetts prep school. By the time he graduated, however, he had learned to appreciate the school's firm discipline and rigorous classical curriculum, and he ended up teaching history there for three years after college. After a decade in the New Jersey Assembly and an unsuccessful run in the Republican gubernatorial primary the year Byrne was reelected, Kean narrowly won the governor's race in 1981.

Education issues were gaining national prominence—in 1983, President Reagan's National Commission on Excellence in Education declared, in the title of its famous report, that the failings of the public education system had left America "A Nation At Risk"—and Kean soon made education one of his priorities. He convinced the legislature to pass a law setting a minimum starting salary for public school teachers, and his education commissioner, a former suburban school superintendent named Saul Cooperman, replaced the widely derided Minimum Basic Skills Test with a tougher high school graduation exam. Cooperman won national notice for another of his initiatives, a program that allowed career changers without a college major in education to become public school teachers. Getting that program enacted meant facing down ferocious opposition from teachers' union officials who feared an erosion of their power.

Kean felt a genuine concern for the poor. Although Republicans in New Jersey traditionally conceded the urban vote to the Democrats, Kean campaigned in the cities during the summer of 1981, and he was horrified at the desolation of Camden, where trash covered the streets and children lived in abandoned buildings. But on his watch, the state continued underfunding the school-aid formula, a budget maneuver that hit poor urban districts especially hard. Just six days before leaving office in 1990, Kean would urge legislators to revise the "outdated and unjust" school-aid formula, but during his eight years in office, he never proposed revamping it. Years later, Kean would say that he had not been sure how to go about doing so and had preferred to focus on his own education reform agenda.

In any case, both Kean and Cooperman were convinced that money shortages were not the fundamental cause of educational devastation in the cities. They blamed politics, and the culture of self-interest fostered

by the political appointees who controlled and staffed urban districts. One
year, Cooperman was invited to a reception in Atlantic City sponsored
by the Newark school district's federally funded antipoverty program.
Cooperman looked around the palatial suite rented for the occasion, noting the catered buffet, the champagne, the Godiva chocolates. Back in
Trenton, he ordered an audit of the program, and despite a mysterious
fire that damaged crucial records hours after the state subpoenaed them,
the audit found pretty much what he had expected. It infuriated Cooperman when he saw waste like that and then read newspaper stories in
which urban school officials complained they would have to cut the music
program if the state didn't fork over more money.

If the Kean administration was less than sympathetic to ELC's claims
of inequity and underfunding, the administration's sometime opponent,
the teachers' union, was no more eager to join the fight. The New Jersey
Education Association (NJEA) was by common agreement the most powerful lobbying organization in the state; its substantial campaign contributions and ability to mobilize its 115,000-plus members weighed heavily
with state legislators. NJEA had lobbied hard for the *Robinson*-era income
tax, assuming—correctly, as it turned out—that the new funding law would
increase overall education spending. But in April 1982, when Morheuser
and her number cruncher, Steve Block, met with three NJEA staff
members to solicit support for their lawsuit, they got a cool reception,
Morheuser reported in a memo she wrote for her files a few weeks later.
The NJEA staff members did not see the T&E formula as fundamentally
flawed, and at least one of them was convinced that urban districts
wasted the money they already got. The union would never give blanket
support to the suit, one of the NJEA people predicted. "They will probably
do as they did in *Robinson*, wait until everybody in the State gets into the
suit and then join it," Morheuser summarized. The NJEA people even declined to recommend sympathetic teachers as potential ELC witnesses.
Morheuser suspected that the staff feared polarizing NJEA's membership,
which, even more than the state as a whole, was predominantly white
and suburban. "It seems eminently clear to me that unless and until a
groundswell for reform becomes visible, the all-powerful NJEA will not
dirty its hands in the fray," Morheuser concluded. "So much for strange
bedfellows."

As ELC readied for trial, the state's lawyers in the attorney general's office were scrambling to catch up. After filing its response to ELC's suit back in early 1981, the state had assembled a panel of experts to analyze the plaintiffs' claims but had otherwise done little trial preparation; as late as June 1983, one state lawyer told Morheuser that his side had prepared only four witness reports, while ELC had prepared fifty-nine. Earlier that year, the lawyer in charge of the case had left the attorney general's office; with all the turnover, trial was only two months away when the state's lawyers finally got around to filing the motion they had seemed to promise in their response to the *Abbott* complaint two and a half years earlier. The case did not belong in New Jersey Superior Court, the state's lawyers told Judge Long. If the Department of Education was failing to ensure a thorough and efficient education in four school districts, that problem should first be litigated through the Office of Administrative Law, where disputes over the exercise of executive power were resolved. Only when those administrative remedies had been exhausted could ELC return its case to the courts, and eventually to the state supreme court.

Morheuser had no interest in litigating her case in administrative law court. Her challenge was a constitutional one, and administrative law judges could not rule on constitutional questions. Technically, they could not rule at all; their decisions were couched as recommendations to executive branch authorities, who were free to accept, reject, or modify the findings. Taking *Abbott* through the administrative process would mean asking a judge to find that the commissioner of education had improperly implemented the T&E law—and then watching while the commissioner himself, a defendant in the case, decided whether to reject the findings. Worst of all, the whole unwieldy process could add years to the litigation. "Daily plaintiffs endure a statutorily mandated system of education which discriminates against them, leaving them with inferior educational opportunities that will follow them throughout life," Morheuser wrote in court papers. "For many class plaintiffs and perhaps even some named plaintiffs, exhaustion could mean no adjudication of their rights until after they have left school. . . . The suspicion arises that what defendants propose is less exhaustion of administrative remedies than exhaustion of the plaintiffs."

Morheuser had more reason than usual to feel exhausted. In the years that Paul Tractenberg had run ELC, the organization's fund-raising had mostly amounted to polite haggling over lunch at the Ford Foundation: Ford's successive two-year, six-figure grants had constituted 80 percent or more of ELC's funding. But by 1979, the Ford Foundation had decided to phase out its grants to public interest law firms. Although the Ford grants did not disappear completely until 1983, by which time the foundation had given ELC $2.8 million over ten years, ELC's survival was swiftly coming to depend upon a patchwork of smaller grants from other supporters, and beating the bushes for those grants—researching the possibilities, preparing applications, schmoozing donors with updates on ELC's work—was time consuming. Each year, ELC lived hand-to-mouth, seldom knowing at the start of the fiscal year whether the funds would materialize to support its projected budget. Halfway through the 1983–84 fiscal year, Morheuser was telling a potential donor that her current budget faced an $80,000 deficit; unless she could raise $100,000 to $150,000, "we will be so deficient in funding . . . that it will be impossible to do the *Abbott* case," Morheuser wrote.

But ELC's perennial money woes were not Morheuser's only burden as 1982 turned into 1983. Sometime that winter, Morheuser had learned she had breast cancer, and in January 1983 she underwent a mastectomy and began chemotherapy. The illness was no secret: Morheuser broke the news in calls to friends and colleagues, and she seemed optimistic about recovery, although at least one coworker could tell she was frightened. After the surgery, Morheuser's twenty-six-year-old niece came to stay with her, to help clean and dress her wound, but Morheuser's fierce commitment to her work never wavered; within weeks, she was back on the job. One friend thought she had made herself better through sheer force of will.

She was officially optimistic, too, about the state's effort to relegate the *Abbott* case to administrative law court. But perhaps her dramatic nickname for the proceedings—she called them "the *Abbott* plaintiffs' 'motion to survive'"—betrayed some private worries. In October 1983, when she dropped ELC board members Tractenberg and Sheppard a line to thank them for their help with the court papers, a note of anxiety surfaced, as she wrote, "I think we win, don't you?"

They lost. The case, Judge Long decided, was a classic example of the kind of complicated, technical matter best resolved in administrative proceedings. The commissioner's expertise on educational issues should be brought to bear on the problems of the four districts, she ruled; he should have a chance to cooperate in improving urban schools. Nearly three years after its filing, *Abbott v. Burke* had been dismissed from the courts, relegated to the backwater of an administrative proceeding. Sitting next to Morheuser at the plaintiffs' table, ELC lawyer Joyce Miller felt her insides collapse. Back at ELC, Morheuser went into her office and closed the door. Although Long's decision would, of course, be appealed, paralegal Debra Matrick could tell that Morheuser felt she had failed.

By January 1984, the appeal was filed, and now there was nothing to do but wait. The office had settled into a strange kind of limbo, Morheuser wrote to her colleague David Long, as staff dabbled in secondary projects and she herself worked on fund-raising. She was trying to prepare herself for another defeat, she told him, because "I cannot again endure the kind of psychological blow which came with Judge Long's ruling." She and a coworker had decided that if they lost again, "we are going to write a book entitled *The Case That Should Have Been* to shame the whole of New Jersey."

5

The Families

In 1970, when Harold Ruvoldt Jr. challenged New Jersey's school-funding law, he envisioned the ideal plaintiffs and found a close enough approximation in Betty and Kenneth Robinson. For her successor suit, Marilyn Morheuser seems to have been less choosy: although she told one parent that she was seeking families from a cross-section of educational backgrounds and economic circumstances, she does not seem to have matched prospective plaintiffs to a Ruvoldt-style checklist. Legally, the only essential element was that they attend public school in the four cities the Education Law Center had chosen as case studies in urban educational misery.

Unlike Ruvoldt, Morheuser did not seek to represent cities and school districts as well as schoolchildren. There were good legal and strategic reasons for this choice: as Morheuser had argued in seeking to neutralize Newark's *Sharif* case, the interests of the adults who ran cities and schools did not always coincide with the interests of children. Furthermore, by representing students, Morheuser could keep at arm's length the messy corruption and mismanagement allegations that the state was sure to make. But a psychological element may have come into play, as well. Attracted to moral clarity, Morheuser undoubtedly found it deeply satisfying to speak for victimized innocents—for the only people who bore no responsibility for the disastrous state of inner-city education.

Representing schoolchildren had a potential pitfall, however. Given the tortuous history of *Robinson v. Cahill*, the new case seemed likely to outlast the school days of at least some of the named plaintiffs, and until mid-1983, when the case was officially certified as a class action on behalf of all the schoolchildren in the four districts, plaintiffs who graduated—or moved out of town, or enrolled in private school—could have lost their legal standing to sue. Even before the class-action certification, however, the state had agreed not to seek dismissal of the case over such technicalities. In retrospect, that agreement was the first sign of something that would become a hallmark of *Abbott v. Burke*, as of *Robinson* before it: the near-total separation between the public reality of the lawsuit and the private realities of the individuals who were nominally at its center. Perhaps that separation was inevitable: as a class action, the lawsuit did not hinge on individual plaintiffs' stories, and early on, when the state demanded the plaintiff schoolchildren's test scores and report cards, ELC argued that such personal details were irrelevant. Still, the decision to represent children who would play no role in the case—"phantom clients," one scholar called them—may ultimately have served Morheuser's preferences. Without clients calling the legal shots, she was indisputably in charge.

At the outset, however, Morheuser did not know just how little attention the courts and the press would end up paying to most of her plaintiffs. She wanted more than names on a piece of paper; as ELC's Steve Block remembered it years later, she wanted parents who could speak articulately about her cause. For the most part, she found them—determined, committed individuals living through the painful decline of New Jersey's cities.

Camden

Once, Camden had beauty, culture, prosperity. It had theaters and shops, stately mansions and an opera company, a railway line and a luxury hotel, and, undergirding all that, it had busy factories where thousands worked turning out canned soup and steel pens and oceangoing ships. On Saturday nights, the downtown sidewalks of the little city across the Delaware River from Philadelphia were crowded with merrymakers.

That Camden had vanished by 1980, when Marilyn Morheuser came looking for families willing to lend their children's names to her lawsuit. By then, the city's lifeblood had been sucked away by the highways that sped the white middle class to the growing suburbs and ferried downtown shoppers to the newfangled indoor mall that had opened in nearby Cherry Hill in 1961. One by one, the factories had closed, taking their well-paying manufacturing jobs with them; left behind in Camden's nine and a half square miles, poor African Americans and Hispanics watched their city's streets and buildings fall apart as the population dropped steeply to 85,000, the tax base shrank, and white politicians divided the spoils. In 1971, Camden's poor rioted. Although in the years to come blacks and Hispanics would win a share of political power, the city's decline would only accelerate. By the late 1980s, a single Atlantic City casino was worth more than all the property in Camden.

The schools suffered along with the rest of the city. In a 1969 report, the state Department of Education described "a system in trouble," marked by large numbers of young, inexperienced teachers; aging, some-times dirty buildings; a shortage of art, music, and gym classes; high absenteeism and dropout rates; and students who seemed passive, inat-tentive, even illiterate. The Board of Education's offices were located in city hall, feeding the widespread perception that politicians dictated every hiring decision. As enrollment grew increasingly black and Hispanic, racial tensions simmered. In May 1968, rattled school officials locked themselves in the Camden High School principal's office after students disrupted an assembly called to air grievances over the lack of black his-tory courses at the predominantly African American school. A year later, white students walked out of predominantly white Woodrow Wilson High School, complaining that school officials were not disciplining black stu-dents who made trouble; four days of protests and arrests followed. In less dramatic ways, too, the schools were withering. At the seven-hundred-student middle school where Henry Stevens Sr. began teaching science in the early 1970s, classes were large and equipment scarce. With no gas lines into the school, a real Bunsen burner was an impossible luxury, so Stevens improvised, burning gas in a small bowl. The school's only micro-scope, shared among all four science teachers, was old and unreliable; often, students peered through magnifying glasses instead.

The Reverend Samuel Appel, a white Presbyterian in his fifties, bore passionate witness to the city's decline. Appel had moved into town in 1960, assigned to a city whose five Presbyterian congregations were hem-orrhaging membership as white parishioners fled to the suburbs. In 1963

Appel had helped found the Camden Metropolitan Ministry, which welded religious and lay leaders into coalitions that could attack the city's many intertwined crises: homelessness, job loss, drug abuse, crime. In 1968, when local activists established the Black People's Unity Movement (BPUM) to press city officials for change, Appel became the chair of the white Friends of the BPUM, which held training sessions on nonviolent protest. Appel himself was arrested and accused of promoting civil disobedience.

Education was one of the Camden Metropolitan Ministry's signature issues, and Appel had more than a professional interest in the subject, since his three children were attending the public schools and getting, from what he could see, a lousy education. In the early 1970s, Appel talked the mayor into putting him on the school board, but after weathering three years of Appel's outspoken independence, the mayor chose not to repeat the experiment for a second term. Instead, Appel worked through his education group, eventually called Advocates for Education, which held monthly meetings to discuss the school board's machinations and published newsletters that enraged school officials by reporting such explosive public information as the salaries of top administrators. Appel knew Camden had good teachers and principals—many of them came to the meetings of Advocates for Education—but they were too often ground down by the system, afraid to speak out against incompetence and corruption lest they incur the wrath of some political godfather who could get troublemakers transferred to the school system's version of Siberia. Through his work, Appel connected with the Education Law Center and eventually joined its board; naturally, Marilyn Morheuser turned to him when she started recruiting Camden plaintiffs for her fledgling lawsuit.

The Abbotts

The Abbotts, who became by alphabetical accident the lead plaintiffs in the suit, were old acquaintances of Appel's, for Howard Abbott was pastor of one of the struggling Presbyterian churches that Appel had come to Camden to oversee. Howard Abbott and Frances Bell had met in Nevada, her home state, in the late 1960s, when both were in their twenties; by the time the church sent Howard to Camden in 1969, they were married and the parents of a baby boy, Raymond. The family lived in the manse next to Howard's church, in an eastern Camden neighborhood evolving from all-white to predominantly minority. Frances—a heavyset, dark-haired woman known since childhood as Luci, after her middle name, Lucille—taught social studies in a Camden middle school. Howard, a white pastor in a city with fewer and fewer white residents, was deeply frustrated by his work at a church that was obviously dying. Although Luci hid the truth from her family, he had been an alcoholic throughout their marriage, and soon his anger and disappointment spilled out in verbal abuse. They separated when their son, Ray, was in second grade, and Luci moved out of the church manse. The separation was far from amicable, and for a child, the situation was confusing: Ray's mother told him his father drank, his father insisted he didn't, and from what nine-year-old Ray could see, Howard was still functioning, still writing sermons. One weekend, the little boy, angry over something he couldn't remember years later, refused to pay his regular visit to his father's house. A day or two later, they told him Howard was dead—an alcohol fatality, the family learned.

Luci Abbott stayed on in Camden, committed to her teaching and compelled to minister to more than just the intellectual needs of her students. One year, she started a coat and galoshes exchange; later, when she began working as a school librarian, she helped students get jobs assisting her. Once, when she was hospitalized for a minor operation, an orderly dropped by to thank her for all she had done for him when he was her student. "If it hadn't been for you, Mrs. Abbott, I would have been in a gang," he said. In those days, Luci and Ray were close: they had season tickets to Philadelphia Phillies baseball games, and Luci taught Ray to calculate a batting average. Luci had also formed a romantic bond with George Cherry, an administrator at another Camden middle school. Cherry—African American and nearly nineteen years older than Luci, with five children from his first marriage—was a kind man, and Ray was soon calling him Pop, blocking out the memories of his life with Howard. Luci's mother, now living on Long Island, did not worry about the racial difference between Luci and George, but she did wonder about the age difference. Luci had just buried one husband, and her mother hated to think of her burying another.

Although Luci Abbott was committed to her work in Camden, she was hardly blind to the district's many shortcomings. At a seminar one year, she heard about the school music program in the affluent northern

New Jersey town of Montclair, where students could choose among classical violin, ballet, tap dancing, choral music, guitar, and singing lessons. That same year, the principal of Ray's elementary school told parents that music, art, and gym classes were being discontinued to save money. The vivid contrast made her angry. "Raymond may not be talented in music," she thought, "but how will I ever know, if he can't have a music class?"

She had less-theoretical worries about Ray, however. He had always floundered in school, struggling to sound out letters and words. It took Luci Abbott a year to get him evaluated for special education placement; eventually, he was diagnosed as marginally perceptually impaired. In the meantime, the other kids noticed his struggles and called him stupid and dummy and peanut-head. Ray learned to wall off his emotions and block out the hurt, but from time to time, he also tried to win the other kids' temporary approval: he would take a few dollars from his mother's purse, without permission, to buy bags of penny candy that he would pass out to his classmates, like a pint-size lord of the manor. Though ultimately he learned to read, the process was always slow and hard. At Veterans Memorial Middle School, where his mother taught, he started out planning to keep up, but it took him so long to get through his work that the teachers became convinced he wasn't even trying. Eventually, he wasn't. Vets was a tough, dirty place, where you had to keep your guard up to avoid losing your lunch money or the jacket you had draped over the back of your chair, but for Ray, the teacher's son, Vets was tougher than average. Every day, it seemed, somebody his mom had scolded in social studies class would pick a fight with him. He could defend himself well enough, and if his mother asked about a bump or bruise, he made something up—"I fell while I was playing handball," that kind of thing.

When Luci Abbott signed Ray on to the Education Law Center's lawsuit, she might not have known about the fights, the lies, the petty thefts, or the nights Ray sneaked out his bedroom window when she thought he was sleeping to play stickball on the school playground or basketball in the park. But it seemed clear to her that her twelve-year-old son was still suffering from the twin blows of his parents' split and his father's death. "Potential of child camouflaged," an ELC staffer noted on the center's intake form. "Had she not known her rights child would have been lost."

The Stevens Family

Henry Stevens had known hardship long before he started using magnifying glasses instead of microscopes to teach middle-school science. An African American born in 1944 in rural North Carolina, he attended a segregated elementary school housed in an old barn without running water or lights, and he studied from white schools' hand-me-down books, which sometimes had racial slurs scrawled inside. Stevens was the son and nephew of teachers, and despite his lackluster grades, his mother urged him on to college. He went to North Carolina A&T University in Greensboro, arriving a year after four students had made news with their sit-in at a segregated lunch counter; the future civil rights leader Jesse Jackson was student body president. Stevens joined some of the marches, and by his junior year, the once-segregated bus terminals he passed through on his trips between school and home had been integrated. After graduation, Stevens married a local girl named Nezettia, and the two soon moved north to Philadelphia, where Stevens's favorite uncle lived. Within a year or two, the couple found jobs in the Camden school system—she as a social worker, he as a teacher—and moved into town with their toddler, Henry Jr.

Henry Stevens Sr. soon involved himself in the civic affairs of their eastern Camden neighborhood, where Luci Abbott was one of his neighbors. He joined picketers pressing for a stoplight on a dangerous corner, became a Democratic Party ward leader, and befriended the man eventually elected Camden's first black mayor. Stevens also became active in the city teachers' union, an affiliate of the powerful New Jersey Education Association; in 1978, he was elected to a three-year term as local president. But he had a sticky problem. Like every parent, he wanted the best for his child, and for the first few years of Henry Jr.'s schooling, the best had meant parochial school, the only viable in-town alternative to the public schools, even for non-Catholics like the Stevenses. However off-balance Stevens might have felt previously as he spoke out for the teachers in a school system he had tacitly announced wasn't good enough for his own child, the situation had become unsustainable now that he was union president. It didn't look right, and more important, it didn't feel right. Henry Jr. had to attend public school. As a Camden teacher, however, Stevens had an advantage other city parents lacked—he could get special permission to send his son to the public school of his choice, and he picked Forest Hill, reputedly one of the district's best elementary schools, housed in a relatively new building and led by a well-regarded principal. There, Henry Jr. thrived in gifted-and-talented classes and played drums in the school band. But the whole experience left Stevens uncomfortably aware of his family's privileges, which he knew were unavailable to most Camden children. The Education Law Center's case sounded like a way to help those other children, and when Marilyn Morheuser came to town to sign up plaintiffs, Stevens added eight-year-old Henry Jr.'s name to her list.

Lola Moore's Family

At the Camden school board meetings where the Reverend Sam Appel often spoke out, Lola Moore was another vocal advocate. Like Henry Stevens Sr., she had grown up poor and black in the South—she was born Lola Wyche in rural Georgia in 1943—and attended segregated schools. Until the end of her school career, when the county opened a brand-new black high school in a last-ditch effort to ward off integration, Lola Wyche had lived with grossly unequal school facilities: a two- or three-room wooden schoolhouse was her first educational home, the books and furniture were secondhand, and her basketball team practiced outdoors on a dirt court, while the white kids played in an indoor gym. Her teachers had high expectations for their students, however, encouraging them to attend college and become teachers themselves—that career, at least, was always open to African Americans. Even as a teenager, Lola Wyche was outspoken: in her senior year, the only one she spent at that beautiful new high school, she led a brief rebellion against her principal's efforts to standardize class rings, until he won her over by explaining how a single ring would forge an identity for this new community institution. She had planned on college and a career as a home economics teacher, but financial aid mix-ups postponed her plans. Instead, she spent two years waitressing in Chicago, where her sister lived, before coming home to marry her high school sweetheart.

Over Christmas of 1971, Lola visited relatives in Camden. With a snowy blanket concealing the dirty streets and frosting the roofs of the abandoned buildings, the city looked newborn and lovely. She was tired of

Georgia—her marriage had ended after the births of a girl and a boy, and a new relationship that had produced another daughter was on the rocks—and Camden seemed to offer a fresh start. She arrived the next summer and saw, to her dismay, what the snow had hidden. At first, she and the children lived in a south Camden apartment complex. Although Lola was working two jobs, most of the other tenants seemed to be on welfare, and she had little sympathy for their gimme-a-handout attitudes. One day, she overheard one neighbor telling another, "Well, no one work all the time but old folks and fools." Another day, a gunshot rang out, and Lola knew it was time to move on. Her Georgia boyfriend had come north before her and was working as a bus driver; soon, they patched up their relationship, married, and bought a square, two-story brick house in the eastern Camden neighborhood where Luci Abbott and Henry Stevens Sr. also lived. Now Lola Moore, she spent her days as a clerk in the Camden schools; to supplement her annual salary of $4,450, the equivalent of $19,400 today, she staffed the school district's evening recreation program, and some weekends she tended bar. Somehow, she found time to speak out at school board meetings and to attend the monthly get-togethers of Sam Appel's Advocates for Education. She also became president of the union representing the Camden school district's clerical workers. By 1978, her second marriage was over, and from then on, Lola Moore and her children fended for themselves.

Moore's oldest daughter, Lynnette Hadley, was a gifted student who, by the time she arrived in Camden at age eight, had already skipped a grade. She did just as well in her Camden middle school, never missing a day and making the honor roll every marking period until eighth-grade graduation. By then, however, Moore was angry at Camden's public schools—the low expectations, the lack of challenge, the unresponsiveness. Once, she had gone to discuss a lower-than-usual grade with one of Lynnette's teachers; at the end of the conference, as Moore was walking away, she had heard the teacher mutter, "What does she think she has—a genius?" Moore had turned around and shot back, "No, I do not, but I tell you what—if you teach my child, she'll learn." Moore was determined that no matter how many jobs she had to work to pay the tuition someplace else, Lynnette would not go to Woodrow Wilson High School. She enrolled Lynnette in a Catholic high school and took a job as a Kmart cashier

nights and weekends; after her day's work in the school district, Moore
would change clothes at home, eat the meal Lynnette had prepared, and
then leave her older daughter to supervise the younger children while
Moore worked her second shift. Before long, Moore enrolled her younger
daughter, too, in Catholic school—a bitter 1978 school strike had divided
the loyalties of the school district's unions, and teachers angry at Moore
were poisoning the life of her little girl.

Moore's middle child, Michael Hadley, stayed in public school. Unlike his older sister, Michael was never much of a student; he repeated
second grade, and his marks were seldom better than mediocre. But he
never envied Lynnette, down in the basement with no TV, her nose buried
in a book. Michael lived for sports. By the time he was seven or eight, he
knew he had a gift, and the other kids in the neighborhood knew it, too.
Every pickup football game began with a question: "Where's Mike? Go get
Mike—you know we gotta have Mike." He was nearly as good at basketball, and in his spare time, he watched sports on TV. His mother talked
about the importance of education, bought a set of encyclopedias, rifled
through his book bag while he slept to make sure he was doing his homework, sacrificed to pay his sisters' tuition, but all that seemed beside the
point to Michael: he saw himself in the NFL, making commercials, earning tons of money. Still, he knew he could play only if he kept his grades
up, and so he did well enough to stay on the team.

When he graduated from middle school, he faced a choice: focus on
football, which everyone in town knew meant going to his neighborhood
high school, Woodrow Wilson, the gridiron mecca; or choose basketball,
which meant fudging the residency rules to attend Camden High School,
the unofficial headquarters of that sport. He stuck with football and went
to Woodrow Wilson. Somehow, despite his sisters' experiences, Catholic
school never seemed a leading option for Michael. Certainly, his mother
never doubted that Catholic schools were more rigorous. While Lynnette
tackled trigonometry and a smattering of calculus, Michael took general
math, maybe a little algebra. Lynnette spent her summers working through
required reading lists; Michael wrote a single book report in junior-year
English. Was it a shortage of scholarship money that kept Michael in public school, or his mom's softhearted reluctance to kill his dream of playing
football for Woodrow Wilson? Years later, no one seemed sure, and Lola

Moore wondered if, deep down, she had suspected Michael would not be able to meet the academic standards of Catholic school.

When Marilyn Morheuser came looking for plaintiffs, Lola Moore put fifteen-year-old Michael's name on the list. She had complained about public education for so long she figured it was time to do something about it. Recruiting new union members in affluent Cherry Hill, she had seen the far superior school facilities there; maybe a suit would call attention to those disparities. After years of challenging the low expectations and downright laziness of some of her kids' teachers, however, Moore did not believe the Camden school district owed its problems to lack of money. The attitudes of teachers made the real difference, she believed; Camden could have done a far better job with the money it already had. Some time later, after the lawsuit had been filed and Morheuser was in town giving her plaintiffs an update, Lola Moore mentioned how she felt about money and schools. Morheuser told her she had best keep that opinion to herself if she were ever called to the witness stand.

The Figueroas

Once, as a little girl in Puerto Rico, Blanca Figueroa had dreamed of becoming a ballerina, but those dreams were dead and buried by the time she arrived in Camden in the early 1960s. Barely twenty-one, a tiny round ball of a woman, less than five feet tall, she had already lived a lifetime of brutal abuse.

Born in 1940, she was just a few years old when her mother left, taking only the oldest boy with her. When Blanca was six, her father reclaimed her from her grandparents' house, but the reunion was far from happy. His sexual abuse was constant; even when she spent months hospitalized with tuberculosis, he molested her during visits. Back home, she passed long days locked in her room with a pan for a toilet, freed only when her father and his girlfriend wanted her to wash their dishes. Blanca had gone to first grade and learned to read a little, but after the hospital, she did not go back. At ten, she moved to Ohio with her father, his latest girlfriend, and their children; at twelve, she confided her suffering to Victor, a twenty-one-year-old tenant of her father's, and soon this man took possession of her. The new relationship was hardly an improvement. Victor drank, and when the teenaged Blanca's cooking, washing, and ironing fell short of his standards, he beat her; by the time she was twenty, she had given birth to five children. During the fifth pregnancy, Victor promised her a fresh start in a new state—New Jersey, where he had family—and before they left Ohio, Blanca put on a blue dress and married him at the Pentecostal church. But the fresh start soon went sour. The drinking and the beatings resumed, and finally Blanca took her five children, the oldest not yet eight, and left for good.

She found an apartment in north Camden, by reputation one of the city's rougher neighborhoods, enrolled the oldest kids in school, and applied for welfare. How did she feel about her life? What did she want? She hardly knew. She loved the children, but she hated herself—she felt ugly, desperate, and numb as she sleepwalked through her days, looking everywhere for a kind man to take care of her. She found one, she thought, but when she got pregnant, he left for the army without a backward glance. For a time, Victor and his new wife took custody of the five older children while Blanca and her new baby returned to Ohio, but the same sad script played itself out again: a man, a promise, a baby, a disappointment. Blanca came back to Camden and reclaimed her older children from Victor, but nothing changed. She was stalked by one neighborhood man who threatened to kill her if she aborted his baby; she nearly married someone else, but that relationship ended after the births of two more children. Within a year, she married a third man, and for a brief time, as she bore him three more children, life improved. The oldest among Blanca's thirteen children struck out on their own, and, with $200 down and an $11,700 mortgage, the rest of the family moved from a trailer home to a real house hard by the railroad tracks, a two-family house with four bedrooms, a wraparound porch, and a big maple tree in the backyard. Best of all, the new house was in the comparatively stable neighborhood of Cramer Hill, a white enclave bordering the blue-collar town of Pennsauken, to the northeast. For a time, Blanca worked the night shift as a nurse's aide and supplemented her husband's contributions with the welfare payments she collected for her fatherless older children.

Within a few years, however, the marriage was disintegrating. Blanca's husband cheated, and she fought back, sending his girlfriend to the hospital with one beating. After the divorce, Blanca started drinking and tried halfheartedly to kill herself. As she struggled with her own despair, her responsibility for so many lives overwhelmed her. Her youngest boy spent long, unsupervised days jumping his bike off makeshift ramps or sliding on old cardboard boxes down the hill by the Thirty-Sixth Street bridge. More important matters also slipped through the cracks. Blanca's childhood had been blighted by sexual abuse, and across the years, the same plague scarred her children's lives. Some were molested by relatives or family friends; then the victims passed their pain down by sexually abusing younger siblings.

Blanca and her children were poor again—poor even by the standards of struggling Camden. With her huge, energetic brood riding mattresses down the stairs and jumping off the maple tree into backyard mud holes, the Cramer Hill house began to deteriorate, and although Blanca did her best to keep it clean, she had no money for repairs. Mice and roaches roamed, the furniture was secondhand, holes gaped in the walls, and the plumbing leaked. The kids shared clothes and ate a lot of rice and beans; on days when money and food ran short, mustard sandwiches or biscuits fried in sugar sometimes filled the gap. The kids learned not to linger in their beds, since late risers might find no breakfast waiting for them. When she had to, Blanca coaxed the milkman or the corner store into giving her food on credit so her kids could eat until the next welfare check arrived. Sometimes Blanca was volatile—eternally torn between loving her kids and yelling at them, one acquaintance thought—but she could also be free-spirited and fun; she would chase the children through the house in some wild game or other, make up long, meandering stories, or retell Puerto Rican folk tales. The Figueroa children loved their mother fiercely, but they were embarrassed by the circumstances of their lives—the dilapidated house, the siblings running wild. They seldom wanted to bring friends home.

Blanca dreamed big dreams for her children—perhaps they would become musicians or artists, stars!—but nearly illiterate herself, she did not really understand that education might provide a road out of poverty. Although she enveloped her children in love, she seldom pushed them in school. By the time Blanca met Marilyn Morheuser, her six oldest children were high school dropouts. The Figueroa kids knew that if you dawdled in the morning, lingering in bed and refusing to get dressed, you could often score an unscheduled day off from school. Other times, Blanca herself required truancy: if her child care fell through on a day she had picked up an odd job, her seventh child, Vivian, had to stay home and look after her younger siblings. Vivian bitterly resented that duty: once, she eased her babysitting chores by putting the little ones to sleep with a dose of Actifed. School was Vivian's refuge, a safe place where she could be a kid, with only a kid's responsibilities. From the beginning, Vivian was bright, well behaved, and pretty, with dark eyes, copper skin, and a sheet of black hair falling to the middle of her back; charmed, her teachers petted and encouraged her, and she repaid their fond regard by aspiring to become a teacher herself. Her test scores were always high, and by the time she finished middle school, she was in the top 10 percent of her class, talented enough that Temple University recruited her for a summer engineering program for minority students.

Still, in the stressed and crowded Camden schools, Vivian had never had to work hard, and at Woodrow Wilson High School, where drug dealers camped out across the street and discipline was lax, she worked even less. She began skipping school, hanging out with friends, smoking pot; in her sophomore year, she was absent half the school year and failed four classes. Junior year went better, but by then Vivian no longer felt safe in school, as she had when she was younger. One day during her sophomore year, a group of boys had backed her into a bathroom; she had been saved from a likely gang rape when her chemistry teacher had heard her screaming and come to her rescue. At home, Vivian did her best to impose some order on the chaos, cleaning up messes and locking her room to keep her things safe from the younger children. Whenever she could, she escaped to the home of a neighborhood girl whose mother was a teacher. There, she heard plenty about the value of education.

Her younger brother Orlando had found an escape hatch, too. One street away from the Figueroas lived a police sergeant who had met Blanca when he broke up a fight between her and her second husband. The cop had a son Orlando's age, and by the time Orlando was eight, he was spending every afternoon at his new friend's house, feeding a craving for stability and structure, for a home with a mom and a dad and just one kid. Soon, Orlando was practically the cop's second son, going on camping trips and vacations with this surrogate family. To his siblings, Orlando sometimes seemed cold and rejecting, a bully who pushed them all away.

For most of the children, the loving bond that welded them to Blanca mitigated the shame they felt about the poverty and disorder of their lives, but Orlando's bond with his mother was looser, and his shame proportionately greater. When Orlando looked around his neighborhood, he saw working people—people who provided for their families and lived better lives than the Figueroas did. Orlando had always been a good student, and before his teens, he was working a paper route and dreaming of a lucrative future, maybe as a stockbroker or a lawyer. He was going to live a different life.

If Vivian and Orlando felt at home in school, to their younger sister Frances it was purgatory. As far back as she could remember, she had understood nothing her teachers said; although she learned to read, she felt deeper comprehension somehow blocked, as if she'd stood in the wrong line when brains were handed out. Years later, she could recall trying hard sometimes, even feeling briefly that she understood, but those fugitive moments of comprehension always slipped away. Once, her class held a spelling bee, with students taking turns writing words on the chalkboard; Frances sneaked a look at the teacher's book and, armed with the illicit information, spelled her word right, for once, to the delight of her classmates. But most of Frances's school memories were painful—the teacher who tripped over a bag someone had left on the floor and unjustly blamed her, the frequent trips to the principal's office, the string of Fs on her report cards. Year after year, she passed from grade to grade, although she knew she had not learned all she should have. At the end of fifth grade, as she moved on to middle school, Frances wondered why they were letting her graduate.

Blanca's youngest boy, Hector, hated school just as much. Unlike Vivian and Orlando, he was not a beautiful, charismatic child whom adults naturally adored; he was a hurt, angry little boy. The roots of his pain were no mystery: Hector was the oldest of Blanca's three children by her second husband, and their split, when he was three, hit him hard. For months, he wandered through the house in tears, searching in closets for his missing daddy. In Camden's crowded classrooms, Hector was quickly tagged as a troublemaker, a goof-off, an attitude problem. He felt that teachers singled him out for public humiliation, and in response to perceived slights, he would close down, become defiant and disrespectful.

Fragmentary records recovered from the school system decades later paint a picture of a child in trouble. In third grade, special-education evaluators judged Hector's academic abilities to be average but classified him as perceptually impaired; although the team recommended placement in a separate special-education classroom, it is not clear whether he was ever transferred. In any case, within months, Hector's behavior had deteriorated: he was exposing himself, urinating against walls, and talking of suicide. School records give no hint whether anyone realized that this behavior might stem from sexual abuse, and it took seven more months for the district to reclassify Hector as emotionally disturbed.

Years later, looking back, Hector wondered if he could have succeeded in school with a bit more one-on-one attention, with some tutoring and extra help. After all, he did not lack ability. Even as a child, he recognized his special affinity for mechanical things—he loved to take apart electrical appliances to see how they worked, and as he got older he became fascinated with cars and motorcycles. But in school, he felt stigmatized. When he walked past groups of teachers in the halls, he saw them exchange glances. By nine, he already had a reputation.

For Blanca's twelfth child, Arlayne, school was neither paradise nor purgatory. Like her siblings, Arlayne was absent far too often, but when she attended, she enjoyed herself, relishing the challenge of math even as a kindergartner. Not every day was so rewarding, though. Arlayne hated getting stuck with the substitute teacher all the kids called Miss Dictionary, because she invariably wrote long lists of words on the blackboard and ordered her students to spend the day tediously looking up definitions. At home, Arlayne found her family's poverty less oppressive than some of her siblings did. Years later, she would remember how Blanca turned even their privations into occasions for fun—letting them stomp the dirt out of the clothes she washed in the bathtub because they had no washing machine, or telling them stories in a candlelit tent under her bedclothes on the days when she was so far behind on her bills that the electricity had been cut off. As a child, Arlayne thought later, she had never known how bad things were.

Sam Appel's daughter Joy was Orlando's kindergarten teacher, and even after the little boy left her class, Joy Appel never forgot her vivid, heartbreaking impressions of his chaotic, charismatic, struggling family.

Years later, no one could remember for sure, but Joy Appel likely suggested to her father that Blanca Figueroa's children might join ELC's suit. Eventually, Blanca came to one of Marilyn Morheuser's meetings and added five of her seven youngest children to the lawsuit. At fifteen, Vivian became the oldest plaintiff; Orlando was twelve, Frances ten, Hector nine, and Arlayne seven. Then Blanca forgot about the case. She had other things on her mind.

East Orange

Like Camden, East Orange had a past filled with affluence and charm, and a present shadowed by poverty and decline. In the mid-twentieth century, East Orange had flourished: in those four square miles neighboring Newark, factories turned out airplane parts and screen windows, dozens of insurance companies had their headquarters, and train lines sped residents to jobs in Newark or New York. The main shopping street, packed with outposts of big Manhattan department stores, was known as "the Fifth Avenue of the suburbs." The parks were lovely, the streets were clean, the public library had a fine reputation, and the commuters lived in luxury apartment buildings. An East Orange High School diploma, a magazine reported at mid-century, "has long been considered practically the equal of one from a junior college." But in 1954, the new Garden State Parkway, the fast toll road to the suburbs and vacation homes of the Jersey Shore, sliced the city in half, and property values began to decline; the process accelerated in the 1960s, as another new highway, Interstate 280, quartered the city. Richer whites began to move out, replaced by middle-class and working-class blacks. The trickle of white flight turned into a flood after the 1967 riots next door in Newark, and by the 1980s, East Orange's population of 76,000 was 85 percent black and Hispanic.

Although East Orange was struggling, it had not sunk as far as Camden: its unemployment, poverty, and welfare rates were only half as bad. But its decline was magnified in the public schools: since families with a little money made sure to enroll their kids elsewhere, only the poorest of the poor were left behind, trapped in a system plagued by low test scores, high absenteeism, and overcrowding. Students at one elementary school ate lunch in two shifts in a first-floor corridor, because their building lacked a cafeteria; the high school track team ran sprints in a second-floor hallway because there were no practice fields. East Orange's school officials were sometimes part of the problem: a state audit in the mid-1980s uncovered a raft of wasteful and corrupt spending practices. The school board president had put her daughter on the payroll and used a district credit card to buy a Ford Mustang. Financial records were sloppy, incomplete, or missing altogether; along the way, the district had managed to overstate its enrollment, collecting $1.4 million in state aid that it wasn't entitled to.

The Waiters Family

Lynn Waiters grew up in the old East Orange, a pleasant bedroom community where the fanciest apartment buildings in the white neighborhoods had doormen, just like in New York City. Hers was one of the African American families that came to town in the mid-1950s, when her father finished his army service in Korea and found a job at the telephone company. Waiters was born in 1951, the oldest of four, and through junior high school her classrooms were integrated; the future singing star Janis Ian (back then, plain Janis Fink) was a sixth-grade classmate. But by the time Waiters got to high school in the mid-1960s, the old order was fading. White students clustered at Clifford J. Scott High School on the north side of town, while blacks mostly attended East Orange High School, a mile south. Waiters had always liked her teachers, but now she languished in a science class taught by an alcoholic and a history class where students and teacher sat each day quietly reading the *New York Times.*

Although her parents had not attended college, they expected Waiters to go and had set aside some money for the purpose; she took a college preparatory curriculum and graduated in the top quarter of her class. Waiters had other ideas, however. Soon after graduation, she married her high school boyfriend, had a baby boy, Dorian, and began work as a clerk; eventually, she quit to stay home with Dorian and his little sister, Khudayja. Waiters's marriage was souring fast. Her husband bounced from job to job; he hit her, and little Dorian witnessed the violence. Finally, Waiters had had enough: "I can do bad by myself," she thought. The week before Thanksgiving 1973, she packed up three-year-old Dorian and seven-month-old Khudayja, called her mother from the telephone on the corner, and announced she was coming home. She never went back to her husband.

Waiters knew it was time to go to college, and with two little children and no child support payments, that meant accepting welfare. She enrolled in nearby Seton Hall University, put the children in an on-campus day care center within walking distance of her parents' house, and majored in political science; one day, she planned to challenge Henry Kissinger's ideas about international politics. For extra money, she did some substitute teaching in the East Orange public schools—New Jersey did not require subs to hold college degrees—and she was startled by the changes since her day. At the junior high school she had once attended, she taught in a dark, stuffy room that resembled an oversized closet jammed with desks; the atmosphere was depressing, and Waiters felt sad to think of students exposed to it day after day. The school district parceled out its sub assignments an hour before school opened each morning, and Waiters, rushing to get her kids out the door, always arrived at her assigned school much too late. Her chronic tardiness never seemed to bother anyone official, but Waiters felt she was cheating her students and soon moved on to other work. For a while, she supervised kindergartners and first-graders in a community after-school program, and there too she saw signs that her town and those nearby had changed. The children were poorer than those she had grown up with, and the boys, especially, brimmed with an unfamiliar aggression.

Waiters was raising her children differently: she did not teach them to fight, and once, when Khudayja said "titty," she washed the little girl's mouth out with soap. Although the kids fought sometimes, with Dorian pounding Khudayja, and Khudayja calling Dorian "faggot" when their mother wasn't listening, they were fundamentally kind and gentle children who shared a close friendship. Every morning, they watched cartoons together, and Dorian loved to style Khudayja's hair and play with her dolls. In school, however, Dorian suffered, persecuted by bullies who shook him down for his lunch money. He clowned in class, disrupting lessons with his jokes and impulsive antics, and Waiters made frequent pilgrimages to school to discuss his behavior. Sometimes he also struggled with his work, but his teachers were not especially interested in his academic progress, Waiters thought; their top priority was keeping order. Waiters noticed that her children's books were sometimes dilapidated, and teachers assigned less homework than she remembered from her own school days. Khudayja, who behaved angelically and was so bright that she had skipped kindergarten, felt unchallenged by her work. In some of her classes, students sat on their desks while teachers ineffectually begged them to return to their seats. The true challenges came outside of class, as Khudayja endured the teasing when her mother cut her hair too short and dodged the bullies who preyed on her brother. Her biggest concern, she remembered years later, was survival.

Lynn Waiters knew that the East Orange schools were not good for her kids. She dreamed of enrolling them in a nonsectarian private school—as an atheist, she felt Catholic school was out of the question—but money was tight. The family shared a one-bedroom garden apartment where Waiters slept on a sofa bed in the living room. Welfare and food stamps covered rent, food, and utilities, but nothing more. So Dorian and Khudayja stayed in public school.

One day while Waiters was still in college, she went to a workshop run by the East Orange Tenants Association. As she settled into her seat, she overheard two elderly black women praising the workshop's white leaders but lamenting that so many of the city's young African Americans moved away once they finished college. The conversation planted a seed, and soon Waiters resolved that when she finished her degree, she would find work in East Orange. When the Tenants Association had a job opening, she applied, and the year the Education Law Center filed its lawsuit, she became the association's director, crisscrossing the city to educate tenants about their legal rights. Across the hall were the offices of a housing newspaper, and one day a man who worked there mentioned to Waiters that his friend Steve Block was looking for plaintiffs for a lawsuit challenging the state's school-funding system. When Block explained the case to her, Waiters agreed to add the names of ten-year-old Dorian and seven-year-old Khudayja. Maybe if the East Orange schools had more money, she thought, they would be able to attract teachers who were really interested in their students. She was young and naive, so she figured the case would progress quickly enough to make a difference for her own children.

The James Family

When Steve Block asked Lynn Waiters if she knew anyone else in East Orange who might be interested in joining the suit, she thought of her friend, Mattie James. James was another African American transplant from the South; born before *Brown v. Board of Education*, she grew up in the small city of Wilmington, North Carolina, the oldest of eight children of a mechanic and a homemaker. Although her mother was a Methodist, James went to Catholic schools—segregated, like public ones—until high school. Her relatives were not civil rights activists, and her father sheltered her so carefully that years later, James could not recall personally suffering any significant racial slights. But she knew that the prejudice was there, that her skin color would always stunt her economic prospects, and even as a teenager that made her mad. She hated Wilmington and could not wait to leave. She was in such a hurry that she didn't finish high school; though she was close enough to graduation that she had already ordered her class ring, she got married instead and moved up north, to East Orange. There, she quickly earned her GED, and by 1968 she was the mother of two children—Julian, nicknamed Bunny because he had been born on Easter, and Caroline.

With her husband running his own construction business, the family had money for extras, like a rented vacation bungalow by the seashore, and they could have afforded parochial school tuition, too. But Mattie James had ambivalent feelings about the religious indoctrination she remembered from her own Catholic school days, and for her children she chose public school instead. She could always change her mind later, she figured. Bunny and Caroline went to the Nassau School, just down the street, and their mother quickly knew everyone in that big, old building. Although she worked from home helping her husband run his business, she had plenty of time to join the PTA, help out with bake sales, and talk to her children's teachers, even after a third child, Jermaine, arrived in 1975. Her older children were bright, and their work seldom challenged them, but James laid down the rules. Children have only one job to do, and that is to earn good grades. Stay on the honor roll. Read. Don't talk back to your teachers: call your mother, and she will do whatever fighting is necessary. On the whole, the East Orange schools were good, Mattie James thought, but then, she made sure of that.

What wasn't so good was her marriage, and in 1977, it ended. The aftermath was devastating for the children, especially nine-year-old Caroline and fourteen-year-old Bunny. Their father had been a loving presence throughout their childhoods, but the moment he walked out of his wife's life, he divorced his children, too. Eventually, he left East Orange and returned to the South; Caroline, who had thought of herself as Daddy's little girl, did not see him again for sixteen years. The divorce brought other dislocations, as well. At first, James moved herself and her children to New York, where she had relatives to help with child care while she looked for a job. She found one quickly—the business school where she enrolled to brush up her typing soon hired her to work in its corporate office—and her children did fine in their new schools. What she had not bargained for was New York City's bad press. Her parents and in-laws down South were apoplectic at the thought of their grandchildren growing up in that dangerous hellhole. During one telephone call, James mentioned that at Caroline's grade school, the children were required to take an escort on bathroom visits; that tidbit sent her family into a frenzy.

Finally, after a year, she gave up and moved back to East Orange. In truth, she took little persuading; she had a church and a network of friends in East Orange, and everyone welcomed her back. For a while, she commuted to New York, but one day Bunny called her at work, distraught because someone had strong-armed him out of his bicycle. It took her two hours to get home to comfort her son, and then and there she decided she needed a job closer to home. Before long, she found work at the East Orange Housing Authority, initially as a collections agent, and she supplemented that salary with other jobs—grocery store cashier, department store sales clerk. At nights and on Saturday mornings, she studied business administration at the local state college. The balancing act was not easy, but she figured it could have been worse. Whining and crying wouldn't make any of the troubles go away.

She was uncomfortably aware, however, that the East Orange public schools were changing, and not for the better. The classes seemed more crowded than before, the students less disciplined, more transient. On her visits to East Orange High School, James saw students roaming the halls; none of the adults seemed to have the will to take control. Bunny had always been bright, and now he was bored. Soon, he was skipping school, and eventually he confessed his truancy to his mother. One week, he told her, he had cut four days of class and still managed to pull an A on a test, the work was so easy. School officials, James realized, had not even known her son was missing.

They were more vigilant, however, when Bunny and a friend were caught with a marijuana joint. Bunny faced expulsion, and James hired a lawyer and got ready to fight. On the advice of a school counselor, however, she gave up the battle. Why force Bunny to mark time at East Orange High when he was getting nothing out of his work, she reasoned. Better to let him get his GED and go straight to college. Bunny did just that, but the ordeal had permanently soured James on the East Orange schools. She was happy to add the names of twelve-year-old Caroline and five-year-old Jermaine to the Education Law Center's suit. "I felt that my kids were getting an inferior education because I wasn't a rich person," Mattie James said years later. "And I felt that it was unjust, and I felt that somebody needed to do something about it."

Irvington

Irvington's story lacked the extremes of high and low that lent extra pathos to the decay of Camden and East Orange. In prosperity, Irvington was never the showplace the other cities had once been, and in decline it did not fall as far. In the mid-twentieth century, three-square-mile Irvington was a densely populated, middle-class, virtually all-white suburb of Newark; its best-known attraction was Olympic Park, one of the East's largest amusement parks. But beginning in the 1950s, the Garden State Parkway and Interstate 78 came through town, disrupting neighborhoods. Olympic Park closed in 1965, and after the Newark riots two years later, African Americans escaping the city began moving into Irvington while whites fleeing the urban distress on their doorstep moved out. By the 1980s, the township's population of 61,000 was more than one-third black, and the poverty, unemployment, and welfare rates, though worse than the state average, were slightly better than those in East Orange. Irvington's public schools did not perfectly mirror the township: while the total population remained more than 60 percent white, the student body was more than 90 percent black and Hispanic. The schools struggled in the usual ways, with subpar test scores and rising dropout rates, but the district's administration had a reputation for honesty and efficiency. Irvington's most pressing problem was overcrowding: one aging elementary school had turned a coal bin into classrooms and another held remedial classes in converted closets.

The Knowles Family

A circuitous, often painful path had brought Guy Knowles to Irvington. He was born in Puerto Rico in 1947, the third of six children of a Puerto Rican woman and an Anglo soldier, but when he was a toddler, his family left the island for a posting in Kansas. Within a few years, his parents divorced, and custody of the children went to their maternal grandmother in New York City. Unable to handle so many children, she sent the four boys to a Catholic children's home in upstate New York. For perhaps four years, beginning at the age of eight, Knowles lived at the home and attended the Catholic school on its campus, seeing his mother on visits and occasional weekends away. At twelve, he joined his father and stepmother in Washington State, but his relationship with them was strained, and after some years he moved back in with his mother, now remarried, in Newark. He never finished high school, and as soon as he turned eighteen, he joined the U.S. Army's 101st Airborne Division, spending a year in Vietnam. It would be more than thirty-five years before he learned to draw a connection between his combat experiences and the aggression, intolerance, and hypervigilance that undermined his relationships ever afterward.

An army veteran at twenty-one, Guy Knowles earned a GED, took some college courses, and drifted from job to job, unable to complete his bachelor's degree or settle down to any particular vocation. Still, when his brother set him up with a girlfriend's older sister, a Puerto Rican named Gladys who worked as a telephone operator, the relationship progressed; in 1972, Guy and Gladys married, and within three years, they had three children—Guy Jr., born in 1973, and the twins, Cristina and Daniel, two years younger. Although his Anglo name and light skin spared him direct experience of discrimination, Guy Knowles Sr. was drawn to left-wing ethnic politics. He joined a Newark-based group called the Puerto Rican Socialist Party, whose members engaged in earnest discussions of class discrimination—"the whole proletariat crap," Knowles would call it decades later. He had been working as a shoe salesman, but his activism caught the attention of the director of the Puerto Rican Congress of New Jersey, and Knowles found work with that group and later with another Hispanic community group in Newark. He joined the Democratic Party organization in Irvington, where the Knowleses rented an apartment not far from Gladys's family, and worked for U.S. Senator Ted Kennedy's unsuccessful 1980 presidential campaign. That year, when Essex County's executive, a Democrat named Peter Shapiro, was looking for a liaison to the Puerto Rican community, he hired Guy Knowles Sr.

The Knowles family was far from rich, but they made ends meet. Gladys had kept her job at the telephone company, working crazy hours— overnights, split shifts. Across the street was the Grove Street School, where the Knowles children eventually enrolled. In his political work, Guy Sr. attended meetings at schools in the wealthy suburb of Livingston, so he was acutely aware of the contrast with his own children's school, where the playground had been converted into a parking lot for teachers' cars. Even the books the children brought home were ragged. Come the revolution, Guy Sr. liked to say, his family would move into one of those fancy houses in the suburbs. When a coworker mentioned Marilyn Morheuser's lawsuit to him, Guy Sr. was interested. He called ELC and volunteered to add the names of seven-year-old Guy Jr. and five-year-old Cristina and Daniel to the case. The Knowles twins would become the youngest named plaintiffs.

Jersey City

On its peninsula between the Hackensack and Hudson rivers, Jersey City commands a noble view of the New York skyline, and its status as New Jersey's second-largest city, trailing only Newark, is a source of civic pride. Like Camden, Jersey City was once an industrial powerhouse, first as the terminus of three railroad lines and later as a manufacturing hub, and its Democratic machine wielded outsize influence in state and even national politics. But as the 1960s and 1970s wore on, Jersey City traced the tragic arc of so many other New Jersey cities: factory closings, fading prosperity, middle-class flight, and deteriorating streets and buildings. To this toxic mix, Jersey City added an ingredient of its own—legendary political corruption, stretching back to the thirty-year reign of Mayor Frank Hague in the first half of the twentieth century and forward to the 1971 federal convictions of top officials, including the mayor. By the time Marilyn Morheuser went looking for plaintiffs, the heart of Jersey City— Journal Square, where elegant shops, theaters, and restaurants had once packed in patrons—had become a depressing, litter-strewn assemblage of cheesy discount stores, where the homeless shuffled along sidewalks begging passersby for change. The poorest neighborhoods, pockmarked with vacant lots and sagging porches, looked like survivors of a bombing campaign, and even the streets where the remnants of the middle class lived fought an uphill battle against dirt, crime, and potholes. In city hall, the Democrats waged internecine warfare but showed no signs of loosening their eternal stranglehold on government.

The public schools fell victim to a complementary set of pressures. In the nineteenth and twentieth centuries, immigrants from Ireland, Italy, and Poland had established a flourishing parochial school system, and by the 1980s, with whites, blacks, and Hispanics making up roughly equal shares of the city's population of 223,000, many whites sent their children to Catholic school, especially once the kids got old enough for high school. Plenty of blacks and Hispanics chose parochial schools, too, but the rest filled the public schools and lived out the depressingly familiar story of low test scores, high dropout rates, and poor job prospects. With so many constituents' children enrolled at Our Lady of Mercy or St. Aloysius, the city's politicians felt little pressure to end the tradition of rewarding their allies with jobs or no-show sinecures in the schools, and patronage hires riddled the system, from the janitor corps to the central administration. Political hiring was so commonplace that some beneficiaries barely bothered to pretend they were regular employees. In the mid-1980s, a sign on one office door in the administration building bore the name of the mayor's stepdaughter; inside, state investigators found only a chair and an empty desk, covered in dust.

Even at its most hopeless, however, Jersey City had reasons for hope. Because it was minutes away from Manhattan, by the 1980s the city had become a magnet for new immigrants from Asia, and, for the same reason, the untapped potential in the city's decrepit waterfront was drawing the attention of banks and brokerage firms fed up with New York's high

rents and taxes. Jersey City stood on the brink of something like a renaissance. All it would take was a little luck, and a little good government.
That renaissance was still embryonic, however, when Marilyn Morheuser
went looking for Jersey City plaintiffs. She enlisted the help of Bobby
Jackson, soon to become the first black city council president, and he sent
her to Eddie Stephens.

The Stephens Family

Born in Virginia in 1941, Eddie Stephens was one of eight children of a
cook and a domestic. "I was poor as dirt," he would say years later. But
Stephens's parents owned their own home on a northwest Roanoke block
filled with black teachers and lawyers, and Stephens learned to carry himself as if he belonged in that world. Despite the hand-me-down books and
the sometimes dilapidated buildings, Stephens got a good education in
Roanoke's segregated public schools, he thought in retrospect: discipline
was strong, and his teachers, like Lola Moore's, had high expectations. It
was not enough to be second best, they told their students: to achieve
anything, blacks had to be better. That message could have been delivered with a full-throated militancy, but under segregation, African American teachers had to tread carefully, cloaking their exhortations in terms
acceptable to the white power structure. It was during the summers he
spent on his grandparents' tobacco farm seventy-five miles out of town
that he imbibed something more, a spirit of quiet but firm resistance to
the racial status quo. While other black families let their children work on
white-owned farms for pay, Stephens's grandparents refused to hire him
out. They did not want their grandchildren accepting slave wages from
white folks.

   As a teenager, Stephens played football and thought vaguely about a
technical career; although a hoped-for sports scholarship did not pan out,
he ended up at Tennessee State University in Nashville, the first person in
his family to attend college. He followed a meandering course through
school, taking periodic breaks to work odd jobs for tuition money and
spending much of his time on civil rights militancy (he preferred Malcolm
X to Martin Luther King Jr.). Along the way, he met Tommi Bogan, two
years younger, who had grown up in Pontiac, Michigan, where her father
worked as an insurance agent and her mother as a nurse. Although the

midwestern public schools were not officially segregated, most of Bogan's classmates were African American until she got to the predominantly white high school, where black students were typically shunted into lower academic tracks and steered toward less exalted rungs of the career ladder. Since the age of six, Bogan had known she was meant to be a teacher, whether she was lining up her dolls for instruction or helping neighborhood kids master reading before kindergarten, but her high school guidance counselor told her she was not smart enough to take the college preparatory curriculum. Bogan found a way to add those classes to her schedule anyway and graduated from Tennessee State in four years, with an elementary education major and Eddie Stephens's wedding ring on her finger.

The young couple spent much of the next four years apart, as Tommi returned home to Michigan to work in the newly minted Head Start preschool program and Eddie stayed in Tennessee to work, study, and agitate. Their daughter, Leslie, was born in 1966 and their son, LaMar, less than two years later. By then, Nashville was heating up: the police had briefly arrested Eddie while investigating a shooting in which he was not involved. Eddie decided it would be wise to move on, although he still had not finished his degree. Eventually, he settled in Jersey City, finished up his college degree at nearby Montclair State, got a job teaching wood shop in the Newark public schools, and sent for his family. Before long, he was immersed in Jersey City politics and community activism, running the local chapter of Jesse Jackson's Operation PUSH and helping elect black politicians. From time to time, if he spent a weekday in Jersey City doing political work, he would hear about phone calls made to his boss back in Newark. Did Eddie Stephens have permission to take that day off? Was he taking an illicit sick day? If he had worked in Jersey City, he knew, the pressure would have been rawer, the threat of punishment inescapable. It was a good thing he worked in Newark.

In other ways, though, the Newark schools were a hard place to teach. Stephens's first supervisor had a simple standard for assessing the competence of his new wood shop teacher: "As long as I see dust and chips on the floor," he told Stephens, "you're doing a good job." If the kids looked busy, it hardly mattered what they were learning, apparently. The same supervisor was puzzled when Stephens, who had spent his own school days poring over textbooks to learn about measurement techniques and joint types, complained that his students had no books. "What you going to do with textbooks in a wood shop?" the supervisor wondered. Stephens finally got his books—three or four years later.

Back home in Jersey City, Leslie and LaMar were cruising through public school without much difficulty. They were bright children, and their mother, by now a day-care-center supervisor for the state human services department, insisted they do their homework at the kitchen table while she made dinner every night. The kids had little doubt about their parents' expectations: if you did anything less than your best, it was a sin. Once, Eddie overheard a friend ask LaMar, "Are you going to be on the honor roll again?" LaMar replied, "Do I have a choice?" But school was no challenge. Tommi had taught LaMar how to read before kindergarten, and by fifth grade he was finishing his work quickly and spending the rest of his time roaming the halls of School 14, running errands for teachers or clapping erasers. When Eddie Stephens asked that the school keep his son busy, he was met with incomprehension. Why was he complaining when his son was earning As? Still, Eddie Stephens never considered moving to the suburbs, even if he and Tommi could have managed it on their salaries, which was by no means certain. Where he came from, you didn't divorce your community that way. You stuck around and tried to make it better.

LaMar was a creative, imaginative child who peopled his fantasy worlds with Fisher-Price adventure figures and devoured Archie comics and Encyclopedia Brown mysteries, tales of a clean-scrubbed, idealized Middle America that must have seemed very far from Jersey City. On his streets, you had to be tougher than Archie, or you would quickly find that your money was buying candy for every punk in the neighborhood and your football was the one that got used for every pickup game. The Stephenses were not rich, but compared to their neighbors on Martin Luther King Drive, they had more—more basketballs, more dolls, more video games—and they needed street sense to hang onto it all. LaMar learned early to look around for a weapon when a bigger kid approached, bent on mayhem; maybe you could find a brick, a stick, a broken bottle with a jagged edge. Leslie—headstrong, outspoken, and opinionated—was just as tough, and together the brother and sister made a formidable team. In seventh grade, when LaMar wore his Afro long, he used a broken bottle to slice the hand of a bully who repeatedly grabbed his hair and called him a girl. Next time LaMar and Leslie passed the bully's house, the neighborhood kids on the street that day watched, breath held, as the bully started down the steps toward LaMar. "And you not going to do nothing to him," Leslie taunted. The bully turned around and went back to his porch.

When Marilyn Morheuser went looking for plaintiffs for her lawsuit, Eddie Stephens was happy to add Leslie and LaMar, now fourteen and twelve, to the case. Money might not be the only reason for Jersey City's problems, he thought, but surely more money would mean better teachers and more books in the school library. Tommi Stephens was less certain about the suit. She wondered what the publicity would mean—would her children be stigmatized, ostracized? In the end, Eddie talked her into it. In truth, however, the suit was not their first priority that year. Their marriage, rocky ever since the early years of separation, was falling apart for good, and in the fall of 1980, Tommi had begun noticing that Leslie seemed irritable and sleepy. The doctor confirmed her suspicions: fourteen-year-old Leslie was halfway through a pregnancy, the baby's father a classmate from eighth grade. Tommi called her parents for advice, and her father's was clear: "We don't kill babies, and we don't give babies away." Tommi was determined that Leslie would stay in school, but it seemed impossible for her to brave the crowded halls and taunting classmates of Lincoln High School; distraught, Tommi called a friend who worked in the Newark public schools and got special permission to enroll Leslie in that district's program for pregnant teenagers. In March 1981, a month after the filing of the *Abbott* suit, Leslie gave birth to a baby girl, and that summer Tommi Stephens left for Michigan, taking her two teenaged children and her infant granddaughter, but leaving her husband behind.

The Diazes

Lucila Rivera hated growing up on welfare, with investigators opening your closets, combing through your family's property, forcing you to justify every possession. Yet one day in 1970, here she was—twenty years old, a new mother with an on-again-off-again relationship with her baby's father and a welfare check to cash. As she waited at the bank with all the other welfare mothers, one in particular caught her eye, a heavyset woman in tight polyester pants. That image of everything she did not want to be seared itself into her memory. Six months after her daughter's birth, Lucila got a job and told welfare she no longer needed their services.

In her two decades of life, Lucila had already weathered plenty of hardship. Her mother, originally from Puerto Rico, was a troubled woman: manic-depressive, sometimes given to drinking binges, sometimes physically abusive to the eight children she had borne to five different men. Lucila had finished high school in Brooklyn and, with the help of a special program for minority students, had gone on to Hunter College, but she felt insecure and out of place in that world and dropped out after a year. She was working for a New York bank when, at a free salsa concert in Central Park, she met the man who would become the father of her daughter Liana. After her brief detour into welfare, Lucila returned to her bank job and, when Liana was four, married Justo Diaz, a Peruvian immigrant who worked at an envelope factory in Jersey City. Justo adopted Liana, and the family bought a house in Jersey City; another daughter and a son arrived over the next couple of years. Liana began Catholic school, but not until first grade. Her mother, remembering her own acute childhood shame at her family's multitude of last names, did not want to enroll Liana until her adoption was final and she had taken Justo's name.

In 1979 Lucila Diaz parlayed her acquaintance with a politically connected neighbor into a secretarial job at the Jersey City school district's central office, and her boss there encouraged her to enroll in a public-policy course St. Peter's College was running for older students returning to school. Lucila began cramming a week's worth of classes into each Saturday, while Justo watched the children. But the marriage was failing; by the time Liana started fifth grade in 1980, her parents were separating, and with money tight, they took Liana out of Catholic school and enrolled her in public school. Lucila got special permission to bypass aging and overcrowded School 3, their neighborhood school, and send Liana to small and well-regarded School 16. Although School 16, too, had its drawbacks— it lacked a lunchroom, and Liana's class had twenty-seven students— years later Lucila could not remember feeling particularly discontented with Liana's education. Still, she was receptive when the director of her St. Peter's program, an old friend of Steve Block's, suggested that she add

ten-year-old Liana's name to ELC's new lawsuit. If better educational opportunity for minority students was the cause, Lucila Diaz thought, she
was glad to help.

Patricia Watson's Family

By Christmas of her senior year in high school, Patricia Watson's future
looked golden. Her past had been anything but: Pat's father, a truck driver,
was an alcoholic who beat his wife and their nine children, and the family was both painfully poor and too proud to let its poverty show. Until
they finally bought a house in Jersey City with money from the GI Bill, they
moved frequently, whenever landlords got tired of waiting for the rent.
Every September for years, the children started school days late, waiting
until their parents could scrape together enough to buy school clothes.
The Watson parents, Clementine and John, were African Americans who
had grown up in Jim Crow Alabama, and Clementine had never finished
high school, but on visits down South, John always detoured to the famed
Tuskegee Institute, which he said he had attended without graduating. In
his household, academic success was nonnegotiable: the children knew
that grades below A were likely to be punished with a beating that raised
welts. "Whatever he said was law," his daughter Cora remembered years
later. "If he said jump, you were already jumping."

Pat, the fourth child, born in 1952, was smart, creative, and strong-
willed, thirsty for attention and given to dramatic displays of emotion. At
Jersey City's Lincoln High School, she earned top grades, wrote plays and
poetry, and was voted both Class Pet and Most Likely to Succeed. College
seemed a certainty, and in her senior year, Pat told her sisters she planned
to snatch the most glittering prize of all, admission to newly coed Princeton University, forty-five miles and a whole world away. That Christmas of
1969, however, Pat's boyfriend, James Hargrove, gave her an engagement
ring, and to her family's shock, Pat announced that she planned to accept
his proposal. James was personable enough, but marriage at eighteen to
an aspiring professional boxer hardly seemed a promising alternative to
Princeton, in an era when young women were not expected to combine
college and marriage. Perhaps, her sisters speculated years later, Pat
feared failing at college and saw marriage to James as a graceful way to
save face, or perhaps she believed his boxing career would guarantee her

a comfortable life. In any case, despite her family's opposition, Pat's strong will carried the day, and soon after graduation, she married James and abandoned her college plans. James was a Muslim, and although Pat had been raised in a devoutly Baptist home, she threw herself wholeheartedly into her new faith, covering her hair and following Muslim dietary laws.

James's boxing career soon fizzled, and before long, the couple had two daughters, Zakia, born in 1972, and Aisha, born in 1974. Raising Zakia had its challenges—she was allergic to strawberries, eggs, even her own perspiration—but Aisha, whose birth had been long and difficult, had far more serious problems. For the first year, Pat insisted the baby was fine, but as the months passed and Aisha missed developmental milestones, even Pat had to admit something was wrong. The eventual diagnosis was cerebral palsy and mental retardation—the result, Pat's family believed, of oxygen deprivation during delivery. Aisha's care was all-consuming. She could eat only specially prepared meals, milkshake-like concoctions whose ingredients had to be weighed and measured precisely. Well into her childhood, she required round-the-clock attention, because her throat had to be cleared of mucus while she slept. She spoke only a few words and could not walk until she was three or four, and because she was prone to seizures, she had to wear a helmet to protect her from falls. After one particularly severe seizure, Aisha lapsed into a coma and lay near death; dressed in her Easter best, five-year-old Zakia arrived at the hospital to say goodbye, only to watch Aisha wake at the sound of her big sister's voice. Pat's marriage had never been strong, and it buckled under the pressures the young couple faced—the demise of James's boxing ambitions, his chronic unemployment, the never-ending strain of caring for a disabled child. By the time Aisha was a toddler, James had disappeared from his daughters' lives.

Consumed by Aisha's care, Pat did no paid work; she collected welfare and disability checks for the girls and lived off and on with her mother, who had finally divorced her abusive husband. Briefly, Pat took college courses at Jersey City State, and for a while she tried nursing school, but she never earned a degree. Pat seemed to be a devoted mother, but her attentiveness had a peculiar side. When Zakia started school, Pat forced her to wear oversized orthopedic boots and insisted on enrolling her in special education classes, even though, unlike her sister, Zakia had no mental or physical disability. It was as if Pat, stymied in her insistence that Aisha was just like Zakia, wanted instead to make Zakia just like Aisha.

Soon, Pat's quirks became too strange to ignore. Her personality had changed, her siblings thought; she had become paranoid and suspicious, insisting that someone was after her, that someone was watching her. At home, Pat told her girls that people were listening to her thoughts; she removed the doorknobs so that bad people couldn't get in and used candles instead of electricity so that no one could see that her lights were on. With outsiders, Pat could seem impressively calm and strong. After years of battling the school system to get Aisha more than rudimentary physical therapy, she had become an articulate advocate for disabled children. But behind closed doors, she could be terrifying, and Zakia bore the brunt of her rage. When Pat's abuse turned physical, Zakia hid the bruises under long sleeves and turtlenecks and told no one what was happening. More often, though, the punishment was emotional. You are evil, Zakia's mother told her. You are responsible for Aisha's illness. Your sister is sick because you are bad. Zakia never questioned this diagnosis. Her mother was the boss.

At times, Zakia found in school the warmth and affection missing at home. Years later, she would fondly remember the kindergarten teacher who had assured her that her ugly orthopedic shoes didn't look too bad, and the reading teacher who had given her loving hugs. But often school was far from a safe haven. By law, special education classes were supposed to be extra-small, so that teachers could lavish individual attention on disabled students, but in the corrupt, mismanaged Jersey City system, Zakia's classes were packed; sometimes the rooms were so clogged with desks there was barely room to walk. Since special education students were not sorted by age, Zakia's classmates were sometimes much older than she. Once, her teachers hid her in a closet while they tried to calm a huge, menacing fourteen-year-old who was threatening to beat her up. From time to time, Zakia's teachers would puzzle over her presence in special education. "Why are you here?" they would ask the little girl with no obvious disability. "My mother put me here," Zakia would answer. But though Zakia had no apparent learning disability, the ordeal of her home life left her unable to learn. Emotionally overloaded, preoccupied with survival, she could not focus on her lessons. "There was just so much stuff happening that my brain had to deal with," she said years later. "My brain couldn't stop and say, 'OK—stop everything and let's learn.'"

Pat never told her family she had added the names of eight-year-old Zakia and six-year-old Aisha to Marilyn Morheuser's lawsuit, and years later no one knew how Pat had heard about the case. But she had always been a fighter, they knew, and her frustration with Aisha's schooling had probably left her relishing a challenge to the power structure. The lawsuit meant nothing to Zakia and Aisha, of course. Months after *Abbott v. Burke* was filed, the Hargrove girls spent Christmas at home. Year after year, when the holiday came, Pat would give Aisha strollers and games and dollhouses, but unless her aunts sent gifts, Zakia would get nothing. The Christmas of 1981 looked at first as if it were going to be different; under Pat's tree, nine-year-old Zakia spotted a beautifully wrapped box with her name on it. Thrilled, Zakia opened the box—and found inside the crushed, powdery remains of charcoal briquettes. Her mother had given her coal for Christmas.

6

"The System Is Broken"

The winter of 1983–84 was difficult for Marilyn Morheuser. True, by the time she paid her Christmas visit to her sister's family in St. Louis, she had recovered from her mastectomy eleven months earlier—over the holidays, she seemed more angry than frightened when, in her matter-of-fact way, she showed her breast prosthesis to her oldest niece. But back home in Newark, a freak accident laid her up again: a coffeepot full of boiling water slipped out of her hand and spilled scalding liquid into the boot she was wearing, severely burning her leg. The doctor threatened hospitalization and skin grafts, but Morheuser dosed herself with megavitamins and slowly healed without those desperate measures.

Her school-funding case seemed in greater danger, however. Through the early months of 1984, Morheuser and her allies waited to hear if a higher court would reverse Judge Virginia Long's decision sending *Abbott v. Burke* to administrative law court, a procedural matter as crucial as it was dryly technical. Administrative law judges, considered part of the executive branch, not the judiciary, usually handled comparatively straightforward disputes over how officials were enforcing the endless stream of regulations the Trenton bureaucracy spewed forth. Administrative hearings typically consisted of a few days' testimony from a handful of witnesses, and, unlike superior court judges, administrative law judges had no authority to decide if state laws were constitutional. If the *Abbott* case were crammed into the administrative template, Morheuser and her allies feared, it could morph from a broadly applicable case about how the state was meeting its constitutional obligations to poor children—a class action using the plaintiffs' four districts as illustrative examples—into a narrow, technical dispute over how appropriately those four school systems were spending their money. In place of incisive testimony about the role of money in schooling, the Education Law Center could find itself bogged down in tedious arguments about whether Irvington had correctly budgeted for roof repair, say, or whether East Orange had paid too much for new textbooks. By the time ELC had finished justifying every dollar, the judge would be asleep, and the big issues of poverty and social justice would be buried in minutiae. Even if the judge woke up long enough to agree that the four districts had real problems, the typical administrative remedy would involve state-supervised improvement plans, long months of implementing those plans, and even longer reports on the results. And, of course, administrative law judges' rulings were, technically speaking, only recommendations that the head of the appropriate executive-branch agency was free to accept, reject, or modify. In *Abbott*, the agency heads were the state school board and Education Commissioner Saul Cooperman—the very people whose administration of the school-funding law ELC was attacking. Yes, their rulings could eventually be appealed all the way to the state supreme court, but under the administrative process, *Abbott v. Burke* would initially be judged by its lead defendants. The whole process promised to delay the case for years.

For fiscally stressed ELC, the six-month wait for a definitive ruling on Long's decision was financially as well as psychologically draining. By early 1984, Morheuser estimated, *Abbott* trial preparation had already cost at least $400,000 over four years, more than 15 percent of ELC's total income in that period. Further delay meant further expense: the longer the case dragged on, the more necessary it would become to update statistics and expert witnesses' reports, and updates cost money. With *Abbott* her top priority, Morheuser was also loath to take on complicated new cases, even special-education matters that might bring fees for the victorious lawyers. She did not want to risk finding her staff in mid-trial when the *Abbott* decision finally came down. The enforced restraint frustrated her newest staff member, a young lawyer named Michael Rubin. ELC was in business to help children, Rubin felt, not to wait around for an *Abbott* ruling.

When the ruling finally came, in May 1984, Morheuser was ecstatic: a three-judge appeals court panel had unanimously reversed Judge

Long's ruling. Although ELC's claims were "sometimes obscure," the judges found, Long had misunderstood the systemic nature of the dispute. *Abbott* was not a case about particular problems in particular districts; it was about the inequities spawned by the entire system of financing education, inequities that the education commissioner could not cure simply by exercising his power to fix individual districts. But Morheuser's ecstasy was short-lived: although the supreme court could have let the appellate judgment stand, it chose instead to hear the case. Fourteen months later, in July 1985, the high court reversed the appellate judges in the unanimous decision that would become known as *Abbott I*. The case was going to be tried in administrative law court after all.

Furious and bitterly disappointed, Morheuser was convinced that the court was dead wrong. Still, when she calmed down, she had to admit that *Abbott I* was far from a total loss. The court had agreed with ELC's bottom line—that *Abbott v. Burke* was a systemic, constitutional challenge to the school-funding law—and had ordered a speedy hearing. The decision about which forum should hear the matter was a close call, the justices found, but in the *Abbott* case, complicated legal and factual issues were tightly interwoven; to tease apart those strands would require a detailed trial record with testimony from educational and fiscal experts, and administrative law court was the best place to air such expert views. Only one of the seven supreme court justices had participated in *Robinson v. Cahill*, and years later, several would say they did not decide *Abbott I* with an eye on the *Robinson* case's slim trial record, the fragile basis for rulings that shook the state to its core. Rather, the justices said, they had simply known they needed a firm factual foundation before they could rule on *Abbott*'s merits. All in all, ELC lawyer Michael Rubin felt, *Abbott I* had handed the plaintiffs a road map to victory. Unfortunately, he thought, they would have to survive an unfair process to get there.

Over the next seven months, Morheuser's team worked feverishly to prepare for the administrative hearing. Along with Morheuser, the team's cocaptain was David Long, who had left the Lawyers' Committee for Civil Rights Under Law and was working in California. Beginning in 1982, Long had drawn on his extensive experience of school-funding litigation nationwide to prepare what he called the "trial preparation 'Bible'"—two black,

three-ring binders containing the *Abbott* team's proof plan, the blueprint
for proving ELC's case and rebutting the state's defenses. Over time, the
proof plan would swell to more than 400 pages, organized into 102 separate sections detailing the witnesses, documents, and arguments the
team planned to deploy in court. With Long thousands of miles away, it
was up to Morheuser and her staff to flesh out the skeleton of his plan
with the details that would bring the case to life, and ELC was still a small
operation, with no more than six or seven lawyers, paralegals, and secre-
taries in the New Jersey office. The long hours, the low pay, and the strain
of working for the volatile and demanding Morheuser ensured frequent
turnover. By the time *Abbott I* came down, most of ELC's legal staff were
newcomers to the office and the case.

One of the new hires was Rubin, white and not yet thirty, a teacher's
son who had grown up on Long Island, interned with a teachers' union,
and worked in Democratic politics. He could face down Morheuser's
anger with calm assertiveness, and she quickly became fond of him. Since
Morheuser still had no driver's license, she delegated him to take her
home after work each day—a mark of her favor, but one that Rubin grew
to resent. Rubin soon became friends with another recent hire, Sheila
Dow-Ford, an African American a year older than he was, who had grown
up middle class in Philadelphia and taught at a private school before becoming a lawyer.

Rubin and Dow-Ford were enthusiastic and idealistic, but they were
also inexperienced, and Morheuser soon decided she needed more help.
She planned to farm some witnesses out to Joyce Miller, the African
American lawyer who had been so shocked by the Jim Crow conditions in
Camden's schools; although Miller had left ELC, she was willing to donate
time during the trial. Morheuser had other allies she could call on, as
well. By now, the *Abbott* case had become a cause célèbre among New Jersey's liberal public policy groups, and every time Morheuser went to
court, she could count on friend-of-the-court filings from the likes of the
ACLU, the Urban League, and the League of Women Voters. Among the
stalwart supporters was the Department of the Public Advocate, the state
government's in-house watchdog; when Morheuser asked for help, the
department lent her the services of two of its lawyers, and more bodies
squeezed into ELC's crowded Newark offices.

One of the Public Advocate's lawyers was Clifford Gregory Stewart, known as Greg, an African American in his thirties who had worked at the Lawyers' Committee for Civil Rights Under Law after David Long's time. The other loaner was Ida Castro, in her early thirties, who had been born in New York to Puerto Rican parents with a deep reverence for the schooling they had never had. Education, they taught her, was all poor folks had to stop them from being poor. Castro began her own schooling in the Bronx, where, as a first-grader, she was about to translate for a Spanish-speaking classmate when the teacher ordered her, "Don't say anything to that spic." In 1974, a college graduate and the single mother of a two-year-old, Castro moved to New Jersey; eventually, she started law school at Rutgers. By then, her daughter, Isa, was the only Latino child in her central New Jersey elementary school, and Castro had encountered a subtler form of the discrimination she had faced in her own Bronx classroom a generation earlier. In the first few years of school, Isa's language development lagged, and one Friday when she was in second grade, the school announced that, starting Monday, she would be tutored at home. They had reckoned without Isa's law-student mother, who quickly vetoed that novel approach to public education. By the time Castro signed on to the *Abbott* case, her daughter's problems were behind her; Isa was a feisty teenager who sometimes called in the middle of the day to ask, say, whether school officials had the constitutional right to send a student home for wearing a T-shirt with an obscenity on it. Castro's *Abbott* work quickly became so all-consuming that some nights, she would sleep over in Newark while Isa stayed with a girlfriend; other days, Castro would make it home in time to kiss her sleeping daughter goodnight. If ELC won its case, Castro told her daughter, maybe no other student would have to struggle for her rights the way Isa had.

The *Abbott* team understood its mission. The administrative hearing's record—the sum total of the witness testimony, the evidentiary exhibits, and the lawyers' arguments—had to make a compelling case for overturning the state's school-funding law: nationwide, school-finance cases were increasingly turning on the completeness of their records, and the New Jersey Supreme Court's *Abbott I* decision had made that requirement explicit. As outlined in David Long's proof plan, the case inevitably included the mathematical arcana that had bored legislators and newspaper readers since the *Robinson* era. ELC's expert witnesses would lay out the fiscal disparities between rich and poor school districts and show how technical flaws in the T&E formula exacerbated those disparities. The experts would show that, twelve years after *Robinson*, school spending was still largely determined by local property wealth, with the rich spending more and the poor less. They would argue that the T&E law had been conceived as a tax-relief plan, rather than an education-funding plan, and had largely worked accordingly, lowering property taxes without closing school-spending gaps. To bring the statistics to life, urban mayors and school board members would explain how impoverished cities struggled to pay for everything from schooling to trash collection out of the same depleted tax base. In sum, the *Abbott* case would assert that by using a guaranteed tax base formula, which left school-spending choices up to local taxpayers, New Jersey had made a fatal error: since the state's job was to ensure educational quality, basing its funding system on fiscal and not educational considerations was unacceptable.

The soul of ELC's case, however, would lie not in analyzing the fiscal differences between rich and poor districts but in showing what those differences meant for the education of poor children—how lack of money translated into impoverished art, music, and science programs, overcrowded classrooms, and deteriorating school buildings. Principals and teachers would describe the academic feast available to suburban students, many of whom already came from comfortable, book-filled homes, and the lukewarm leftovers provided for city kids, whose parents were often poor and uneducated themselves. Compared to privileged suburban students, educators would explain, the children of poverty needed more—more counseling, better teachers, extra tutoring. Providing more cost more, but the cities had less. Witnesses would discuss how the state's basic-skills testing program had, perhaps unintentionally, encouraged the creation of a two-tiered educational system, with high-scoring suburban districts offering a rich curriculum while low-scoring urban schools drilled endlessly in reading and math. Finally, representatives from the worlds of higher education and employment would describe how ill prepared were even the graduates of urban high schools, let alone the legions of dropouts.

In essence, ELC's case sought to reopen the *Robinson*-era debate over the definition of T&E. Twelve years earlier, bureaucrats and legislators had decided not to define T&E using input measures, like the teacher-student ratio and the number of books in the library, or output measures, like test scores and dropout rates. Instead, lawmakers had adopted the process model, defining T&E largely as what resulted when school districts made and carried out appropriate plans. ELC's *Abbott* case was a long argument for redefining T&E as a matter of inputs, measured in dollars and reconceived as the raw materials of opportunity. All children deserved access to comparable public services, ELC would argue: smart high school students in Newark deserved Advanced Placement courses just as much as their peers in Princeton, and a second-grader struggling to learn how to read was entitled to extra tutoring in Camden as well as in Cherry Hill. "The state can't guarantee results. It can guarantee opportunity, however," Morheuser told a reporter. "It's a little hard to tell what the results might be when opportunity is never made available." ELC would not try to define a T&E education with great specificity—as a list of programs, each with its own price tag—since that complex task was surely a state responsibility. Instead, ELC would show how totally the present system failed at giving poor students an equal chance.

In recasting inputs, and the dollars that bought them, as building blocks of opportunity, ELC sought to sidestep the vexed question of the relationship between inputs and outputs—the test scores, dropout rates, and college-attendance figures that most taxpayers thought of as the true gauges of school success. Certainly, the lawyers expected that spending more on urban education would improve poor students' lives, but David Long knew ELC could not assert that money bore a direct, linear relationship to student success, that every extra dollar of spending bought an extra point on a standardized test. Like other states, New Jersey had its share of frugal, high-achieving districts and free-spending, mediocre ones. In court, Morheuser would argue that underfunding was the root cause of urban schools' failure; in the court of public opinion, she would call more money a necessary but not a sufficient condition of reversing that failure. "We would never say the only important thing is money," Morheuser told an interviewer, "but we will never be in agreement that money makes no difference, which is really the position of the state."

Day by day, the *Abbott* team built its case. In sprawling private firms, lawyers might learn only a tiny corner of a big case, but Morheuser wanted her whole staff to understand the complex funding and tax issues. She arranged tutorials with the team's key expert witnesses—Margaret Goertz, a wiry, dark-haired researcher at the Educational Testing Service, whose articles had documented the failures of the *Robinson*-era compromise; and Ernest Reock, a relentlessly thorough Rutgers University economist who had helped draft the T&E law but had later become disillusioned with it. File drawer after file drawer was filling up with academic studies, internal state reports, test-score summaries, legislative testimony, computer printouts, witness résumés, demographic data, legal research. Years later, when the case was consigned to a dusty archive, the accumulated collection would fill nineteen cardboard boxes to bursting.

Joining the *Abbott* team late, Ida Castro, whose background was in labor law, had known she would need help in mastering the case's intricacies, and she found that help in a surprising place: the Department of Education, where more than one bureaucrat quietly disagreed with the state's anti-*Abbott* line. Castro never told Morheuser the names of her two secret sources, and years later, she still refused to identify them. But at midnight, after a long day at the office, Castro and her moles would meet in a diner; there, the Deep Throats offered a guided tour through the mountains of paper the department produced, pointing out the significance of this report or that study, telling Castro what answers to expect if she posed particular questions to the state employees testifying for the other side.

ELC staff members were still visiting schools, too, interviewing teachers and principals, seeking just the right people to illuminate the plight of urban schools. In January 1986 Michael Rubin interviewed a guidance counselor in tony Princeton, a woman who had previously worked in the nearby city of Trenton. Her former colleagues just didn't care about children, she told Rubin. "Bottom line was that she could not agree that more money was needed in Trenton until waste was eliminated so she could see how much money there really was," Rubin wrote in his report. "I don't think she should be a witness." Morheuser surely agreed. Her ideal witness, it was becoming clear, would have to be passionate and unwavering, like Morheuser herself. That month, in a memo to the file, she wrote,

"As we come to the zero hour, I am more and more convinced that we need true believers as witnesses."

Just as she always had, Morheuser also wanted true believers as colleagues. She was the same complicated, difficult, inspiring boss she had been back in Milwaukee more than a decade earlier—the same blend of idealistic fervor and unreasonable perfectionism. She could not brook a moment's wavering from her standard of absolute dedication, and if her charm and enthusiasm could not draw out the commitment she required, she did not hesitate to unleash her fury. Her staff were hardly shirkers—Sheila Dow-Ford had pored over so many school-funding tables that if fellow dinner-party guests mentioned the names of their hometowns, she instantly knew their tax rates and per-pupil spending. But Morheuser seemed unable to treat her employees like professionals who could make their own decisions about, say, whether to work over the weekend. Why wasn't this being done, or that, or that? she would demand, sometimes loudly. "If you don't care about this—leave!" she would shout. "If you're not willing to put in the hours, then leave!" Younger lawyers chafed under this treatment, but her senior colleague, David Long, quickly decided he would not tolerate it—especially since, to save ELC's scarce cash, he was living in Morheuser's guest room and eating her home-cooked meals during his periodic trips back east for consultations. Morheuser's intensity was a gift, Long thought: together, anger and love fueled her hatred of injustice, and it was that which would sustain her through the hard work ahead. But after taking the brunt of her fury one day, he called a halt: he could not live and work with her around the clock, he told her, if she unloaded her rage so freely. Morheuser apologized, and the episode was not repeated. When she chose, Long thought, she could control her anger, even though you sensed that underneath she was seething.

Mostly, she seethed at the state of New Jersey, personified by the lawyers she faced off against in court. The whole *Abbott* team felt theirs was a holy struggle in which they occupied the moral high ground, but no one held that conviction more deeply than Morheuser. She seemed personally affronted that the state was defending a system she believed was patently bankrupt. Where a more dispassionate attorney might have seen tactical maneuvering or bureaucratic bungling behind the fits and starts in the state's trial preparation, she saw bad faith of the most contemptible kind, since its victims were too young to protest. "What a great service you have done in countering the state's war on poor children," she wrote one urban superintendent who had provided helpful information. "This is exactly the kind of analysis we need to shoot their witnesses out of the water. Pardon my military language, but we really are engaged in war." And if the state was the enemy, it was a powerful one. In one of her many fund-raising letters, written in November 1984, Morheuser reiterated her fear that ELC would run out of money before the end of the litigation. "The delays caused by the Attorney General's deliberate foot-dragging and procedural maneuvering may deprive the plaintiff children of their attorney," she wrote. "Of course, government always tries to win by wearing down law reform advocates, and government has all of our tax money with which to play that game." The message was clear: ELC was David to the state's Goliath.

During his years in the state attorney general's office, Bertram Goltz Jr., nicknamed Skip, had become accustomed to the way opposing lawyers liked to assume the mantle of underdog, spouting off about their poor little client, "one guy against the vast resources of the state of New Jersey." Those speeches always made Goltz glance around his government-issue office, which for a while lacked even a secretary, and wonder wryly where those vast resources might be hiding. As they prepared to defend the *Abbott* case, Goltz and the rest of the state's lawyers felt remarkably unlike the invincible Goliath of Morheuser's rhetoric. For one thing, their four-member team was half the size of hers. For another, their office had seen almost as much turnover as ELC had—since the filing of the *Abbott* complaint more than four years earlier, two deputy attorneys general had come and gone as head of the trial team. Not until eight weeks after *Abbott I* had the state settled on a new lead lawyer, Alfred Ramey Jr., a tall, slender, light-skinned African American in his mid-thirties who had spent eight years climbing the ladder in the state attorney general's office. Where Morheuser was emotional and passionate, Ramey was controlled and undemonstrative, and his colleagues admired his ethical uprightness.

Ramey's team was a varied lot. The forty-something Goltz, another veteran of the attorney general's office, had graduated from Rutgers Law School a few months before Morheuser enrolled there, but unlike her, he did not groove to the beat of the People's Electric Law School. Even then, he was more conservative than his peers, at least on some issues. Although he opposed the Vietnam War, for example, he was also staunchly antiabortion, perhaps because of his Catholic upbringing, or perhaps because of his unique perspective: he had been born with cerebral palsy, which twisted his body and slurred his speech. The other members of the team were relative newcomers to the attorney general's office. David Powers was in his forties, but he had spent fourteen years teaching junior high school in inner-city Philadelphia before attending law school. The youngest lawyer on the case, at nearly thirty, was Eldad Philip Isaac, known as Phil, who had lived half his childhood in Israel before his Romanian-émigré parents had moved the family to southern California. A trace of an Israeli accent still lingered in his voice.

Ramey was soon convinced that the state's case was in trouble. When *Abbott* landed on his plate, he inherited eleven boxes and two file drawers filled with documents, apparently a reassuring sign that matters were well in hand. But it was more than three weeks before Ramey had a chance to examine those files carefully, and when he did, he realized that his team would have to start nearly from scratch to prepare the case they now envisioned, a case focused on the nonfiscal causes of urban district's educational failings. The state's lawyers felt lost and overwhelmed—Morheuser's team was steeped in the minutiae of school funding, while the defense team faced an Everest-steep learning curve. The state's lawyers also discovered quickly that local school officials were hardly eager to help them prove that mismanagement and corruption, not underfunding, explained urban educational failure. In city districts, where administrators saw the *Abbott* case as a ticket to bigger budgets, crucial documents never seemed to lie close to hand when the state asked for them; school officials typically offered only the vaguest of answers to the lawyers' questions. Even suburban school administrators were reluctant to help the state make its case; they feared being branded anti-poor, Isaac thought. New Jersey was a busy, crowded place, but its education community was small and close-knit, and no one wanted to hurt friends or make enemies.

Despite the obstacles, the case took shape. Although the state's lawyers planned to deploy their own statisticians to assert that school spending gaps were neither wide nor growing, as ELC's experts claimed, the state would concede that in some urban school districts, children were not getting the thorough and efficient education to which they were entitled. The question was why, and the state's lawyers rejected ELC's answer—that a flawed funding formula had starved urban districts. Instead, the state would argue, whatever problems existed were not systemic but confined to just a handful of districts, and in those districts two key factors were at work. First, the lawyers would assert, the chaos, violence, and deprivation that scarred urban students' lives inevitably interfered with learning; schools could not be expected to pick up all those broken pieces. Second, urban school boards and administrators were often guilty of gross mismanagement—politically motivated hiring and firing, spineless acquiescence to city officials' tax-cutting demands, even criminal corruption. Good management, not abundant dollars, allowed New Jersey's affluent suburban schools to offer the outstanding programs ELC's witnesses would describe, and good management need not cost much more than New Jersey was already spending.

The state would also attack ELC's claim that T&E should be understood in terms of inputs, and thus dollars. What mattered was not inputs but outputs—test scores, dropout rates, the creation of productive workers and citizens. ELC, the state would argue in its opening statement, was guilty of typical left-wing "keyhole vision," the erroneous belief "that money, in its quantity and distribution, is the solution for all educational maladies and, indeed, for an assortment of other ills which beset society." New Jersey was already hugely generous to its urban schools; the defense team's own funding expert, Education Department statistician William Fowler Jr., liked to point out that New Jersey was spending 30 percent of its budget on education. Certainly, education was immensely important, Fowler told the lawyers on his side, but it was not the state's only priority. How much spending was enough? Half the budget? Sixty percent? Ninety percent?

ELC's demands were especially unreasonable, the state would argue, given that social science research had found few firm links between school spending and student achievement, as measured in test scores. In the *Robinson* era, few people had questioned the link between school spending and educational quality, but by the 1980s, that position was a far harder sell. Economist Eric Hanushek, the leading researcher in the field, would testify as an expert witness for the state, arguing that the very inputs the *Abbott* plaintiffs saw as crucial elements of equal opportunity—smaller classes, more experienced teachers, higher teacher salaries—actually had little impact on test scores. "The things we're buying just don't systematically influence the learning of students," Hanushek would testify. "We have no reason to suspect that just spending more on average will in fact improve the performance of students, at least if the spending follows the patterns that we have observed in the past."

Against ELC's understanding of T&E as a matter of inputs, the state would defend the existing law's process model, which held that a district earning certification from Department of Education monitors could be considered T&E. Monitoring had evolved over the years, from the paperwork nightmare of the Burke era to the more streamlined process of the Cooperman period, and the new system worked, the state would insist. Given time, monitoring would solve whatever problems the plaintiffs' districts faced. In any case, ELC's picture of thriving suburbs and suffering cities distorted reality: many of the superb educational programs that ELC's suburban witnesses would describe were exceptional even in the suburbs, and many of the problems the cities faced, from inadequate facilities to shortages of library books, were common everywhere. Some differences were merely the result of local choices about budgeting and curriculum, and local control was historically a cornerstone of New Jersey government; the T&E law had rightfully preserved local control, and increased state funding of the schools would inevitably erode it. Other differences, like the narrow, test-driven basic skills curriculum that ELC's urban witnesses would describe, were reasonable responses to the academic failures of inner-city children, the state would argue: students had to learn to read and compute before precious minutes of classroom time could be spent on art and music.

The state's case would also address the ambiguity that had threaded its way through the *Robinson* decisions and the *Abbott* complaint: the question of whether New Jersey's constitution required an equal education for rich and poor, or just an adequate education for all. The state would insist that as long as every district provided the programs and services required by the legislature and the state Board of Education, the fact that some districts might provide more was beside the point. Nothing in the T&E clause implied that every New Jersey school district had to spend identical sums of money or offer identical programs, the state would argue—indeed, such uniformity was incompatible with local control. Morheuser seemed to want every school district to excel, expert witness Fowler told the state team, like the mythical radio town of Lake Wobegon, where all the children were above average. It just wasn't possible.

To ELC's lawyers, it seemed clear that the state's arguments—that money mattered less than management, that local control trumped equity—were dictated less by genuine conviction than by political necessity. To close the gaps between urban and suburban school districts, the legislature would have to limit spending in the suburbs or spend hundreds of millions of dollars more in the cities, both politically daunting prospects. Governor Thomas Kean was up for reelection in 1985; buoyed by a strong economy, he had built a national reputation as an education reformer and had been mentioned as a Republican vice presidential prospect. The last thing anyone in Trenton wanted was a huge new bill for school spending, ELC thought. State lawyer Ramey seemed to understand these political realities. In November 1985, Morheuser wrote in a memo to her file, the two lead lawyers had discussed the case during a phone conversation about logistics. "Probably a lot of people would agree with us in principle, but it looks like we're talking about total State liability of $3 to $5 billion dollars. That's the kind of money that's hard to swallow. It could start a move to repeal the T&E Clause of the Constitution," Morheuser wrote, summarizing Ramey's comments. Morheuser herself probably knew more than he did about the thinking in the governor's office, she quoted Ramey as saying. "There is growing recognition that more money is needed for urban kids. But there may be a question about control of that money," she described him saying. "I asked him why he would think I'd be against control?"

Whatever the political backdrop, years later, members of the state's *Abbott* team would insist that they had built their case independently, with no mandate from on high to argue a position that would hold down the state's school costs. Their views, they said, evolved from the facts as they found them. That winter of 1985–86, as Morheuser's colleagues continued to visit schools seeking data and witnesses for their case, state lawyer Skip Goltz worked behind the scenes drafting legal arguments and finding witnesses, and his colleague Phil Isaac made the rounds of urban schools. To Isaac, the buildings he visited did not look like disaster areas, at least compared with his own experience: although he had grown up middle class in Los Angeles, the campus of his public high school had been severely damaged in an earthquake, and by the time he enrolled, a third of the buildings were uninhabitable, the school lacked a gymnasium and a cafeteria, and students attended classes in "temporary" bungalows that had remained in use for years. East Orange High School was in better shape than that, Isaac thought.

Certainly, Isaac's tours uncovered plenty of problems—an East Orange school whose damaged roof sent water cascading in sheets down classroom walls, jam-packed classes in Irvington, Jersey City high schools littered with broken glass and smelling of urine. But he also saw plenty of schools that were clean, well lit, and cheerfully decorated. Urban districts were not monoliths, uniformly victimized by the systemic failings ELC asserted. Building by building, district by district, Isaac thought, strong leadership could make a difference. The argument was plausible, but even the relatively conservative Goltz had his doubts about whether it would ultimately prevail. By arguing that money mattered less than management, the state was putting a lot of eggs in one fragile basket, he thought.

The state's lawyers were hard workers who immersed themselves in their case, but Morheuser's passionate identification with *Abbott v. Burke* sometimes left them bemused. Remembering his younger days as an island in a sea of liberal orthodoxy, Goltz thought of her attitude as "the Rutgers Law School syndrome," the unwavering belief that your side had a monopoly on truth, justice, and the American way. Once, listening to Morheuser invoking, for the umpteenth time, the interests of "the children," Goltz joked to his colleague Ramey that it all reminded him of a song from *The King and I*. Although Isaac did not doubt Morheuser's sincerity, he sometimes detected a note of calculation in her crusading: some of the passion was played out with one eye on her audience, he thought. He found the contrast between Morheuser's grandmotherly-former-nun persona and her take-no-prisoners legal zeal a bit jarring. "Sugar-coated poison," he called her.

The supreme court handed down its *Abbott I* opinion in July 1985, but it wasn't until early October that the lawyers met for their first conference with the administrative law judge assigned to the case. Judge Steven Lefelt was in his mid-forties, dark and balding, with a neatly trimmed beard and mustache; in the twenty years since his own graduation from Rutgers Law School, he had served in the army in Vietnam, worked as an associate law school dean, litigated prisoners' rights for the ACLU, and spent five years in administrative law court. To those he worked with, he seemed evenhanded, fair-minded, and meticulous, the epitome of the judicial temperament, but years later Education Commissioner Saul Cooperman would say that as soon as Lefelt was assigned to the case, allies called to warn him that this judge would surely rule against him. Whatever his own views of the *Abbott* case, Lefelt knew it would be far more complicated and unwieldy than the average administrative law matter. To house what were sure to be voluminous court papers and exhibits, his staff commandeered a conference room near the judge's chambers in the strip-mall-infested suburbs of Trenton, and Lefelt put his legal assistant to work researching school-funding litigation in other states.

For five months, the judge and the lawyers wrangled over logistical and legal issues, while Morheuser, complaining repeatedly that the state was failing to turn over reports on its witnesses, accused her adversaries of deliberately delaying the trial. The judge had set a March 10 deadline for completing the pretrial exchange of evidence, and ELC staff worked feverishly to comply, spending fourteen hours a day in the office and working weekends. Money was as tight as ever, but Morheuser authorized extra spending on long-distance telephone calls, express mail deliveries, and additional secretarial services. One afternoon in the midst of the frenzy, a man stopped by the office to present ELC lawyer Sheila Dow-Ford with a bottle of sambuca, a token of appreciation for the help she had given him on his daughter's special-education case. As Dow-Ford chatted with her client, Morheuser simmered; when he finally left, Morheuser walked into Dow-Ford's office to berate her for wasting time. Dow-Ford defended herself—she always met her deadlines, and she would this time;

besides, special education was an important part of ELC's work. Then she closed her office door. "And don't you yell at me ever again."

Shockingly, Morheuser began to cry. "I'm sorry. I'm so scared," she said, as Dow-Ford folded her into a hug. "I'm scared we're going to lose."

By March 10, 1986, two weeks before the scheduled start of the trial, ELC had given the state 47 witness reports totaling 150 pages; in return, the state had handed over almost nothing. Two days later, the lawyers and the judge met to hash out the disagreement, and Ramey dropped a bombshell. "To be perfectly honest, we're not—we will not be prepared to go to trial on March 24th," he admitted. "In fact, I think it's necessary to make a motion for a four-month extension." Morheuser was furious, and the judge seemed hardly less so. Since October, he noted in apparent exasperation, Ramey had repeatedly promised that the case would be ready by March. "I have to postulate that either there's not enough lawyers working on this case or they're not working fast enough, or perhaps there's an intentional desire to delay this case," Lefelt said. He denied Ramey's request for a four-month delay but then backed off his most incendiary suggestions. "I believe that the state is truly interested in a thorough and efficient education for all children in this state," Lefelt said. "I'm not even sure that the state is, in fact, attempting to delay this case. . . . I have to look at this as plaintiffs have been litigating this issue for six [actually, five] years now, and at some point, they have to have a ruling on the merits." But by the time the issue had ground through the legal mill, the March 24 trial date was history and the summer, when public-school witnesses were sure to be unavailable, was approaching. In the end, Ramey's proposed four-month delay stretched to six months.

On September 29, 1986, more than five and a half years after the filing of the initial complaint, the *Abbott v. Burke* hearing began in administrative law court. Like the *Robinson v. Cahill* trial nearly fifteen years earlier, the *Abbott* hearing lacked glamour. In the Newark court building where ELC would present its case, the parties met in a long, narrow room with stained acoustic ceiling panels and walls lined with cardboard boxes full of papers. The judge sat at a table, not a raised bench, and everyone else draped coats over plastic chairs; the rumble of the city subway underneath sometimes punctuated the exchanges between lawyers and witnesses.

Once ELC was finished, the state's case was to be heard in Trenton; eventually, the parties agreed to meet at the angular, modern Justice Complex. The trial was expected to last three or four months, and despite the huge sums of taxpayers' money at stake, reporters had little interest in covering weeks of tedious, highly technical testimony. After a few articles pegged to the opening day, the media decamped; by October, the Associated Press was describing the case as "half-forgotten."

That fall, ELC called witness after witness, fifty in all, to flesh out the case outlined years earlier in the *Abbott* complaint. College professors and school principals, mayors, superintendents, and teachers, all took their turn. No one remarked on the absence of the twenty plaintiff schoolchildren and their parents. Just as New Jersey's first school-funding case had left Kenneth Robinson behind, so *Abbott v. Burke* had turned out to have little to do with Ray Abbott and the others. No visitor dropping by Lefelt's courtroom for the day could have mistaken the proceedings for a TV-ready spectacle, complete with dramatic admissions and surprise endings. The lawyers subtly jockeyed for advantage: on her cross-examination days, ELC lawyer Ida Castro rolled in a wheeled cart stuffed with files that bulged intimidatingly and took notes on a yellow legal pad in five different colors of ink, just to keep the state's lawyers wondering what it meant when she dropped the red pen and picked up the blue one. (Nothing, actually.) Progress was measured in inches: years later, ELC lawyer David Long would recall his pleasure at forcing Fowler, the state's expert witness, who was busily downplaying an old research paper he had coauthored, to admit that he himself had presented the paper's findings at a conference of the American Education Research Association. The testimony could be painfully dry—defending her own statistical methods, ELC expert Margaret Goertz spent half a day's cross-examination arguing about the relative merits of regression analysis, the McLoone index, and the Gini coefficient. The testimony of the state's municipal finance expert featured discussions of r-squares and multi-collinearity. Yet, from time to time, an anecdote or a phrase pierced the tedium like a camera flash, illuminating the landscape of poverty, crime, and despair surrounding the children of the inner city and the educators who struggled to reach them.

In Irvington, a witness testified, children walked to school wearing their old sneakers and carrying the new ones in a bag. If you wore the good ones, they were likely to be stolen right off your feet.

One Camden elementary school had decided to notify parents when their children arrived safely each day, after the morning a kindergartner was raped on her way to school.

At a grammar school in one of Irvington's roughest neighborhoods, a male teacher had been assigned to a crowded, noisy room in a distant wing of the building after a female colleague had been brutally attacked there. The school's field trip money often ran out by spring. No big deal? The teacher didn't think so. "It's a vital thing for these children to know that the whole world is not just that neighborhood," he said. An hour's drive from Irvington lay the beaches of the Jersey Shore, but some of his students were fifteen years old and had never seen the ocean.

In Jersey City, elementary schools reused workbooks year after year, until the pages fell apart. Teachers wrote on chalkboards whose green paint was peeling off. "Nobody wants to have their kids in those schools," a former superintendent testified bleakly. "Whenever they can, they get out."

At Camden High School, students often failed physical education because they refused to change their clothes, afraid of having them stolen out of their lockers. The building lacked a cafeteria; the teachers had to share rooms, even desks; and the neighborhood was so dangerous that the school could not schedule nighttime activities. Still, "the school is the hub of everything that the kids in Camden have," the principal testified, echoing Morheuser's insight all those years earlier in Las Vegas, New Mexico. "They have no movies, they have no skating rinks, they have nothing to do, nowhere to go, and the school is still the best place that they have."

Suburban South Brunswick spent nearly $900 per student more than the city of Trenton, $4,772 to Trenton's $3,888. "What would be the impact on South Brunswick's school district if it were funded at the level of Trenton?" one ELC lawyer asked the suburban district's superintendent. "Well, they would be looking for a new superintendent tomorrow, that's one thing," he replied. "It would be absolute disaster as we see it."

Soon, everyone knew that the *Abbott* trial's projected three-month timetable had been hopelessly optimistic. "I don't mean to interrupt your cross-examination—it is your case," the judge interjected in the midst of one lengthy interrogation, "but frankly, I'm facing fifty-something other witnesses by plaintiffs and Lord knows how many by the state, and I really don't want to grow old in this case." State lawyer Isaac thought the judge was the real problem. Although the lawyers had agreed in advance to limit the time spent questioning nontechnical witnesses, the judge had quickly given up on expediting anything, Isaac thought. With an explicit directive from the supreme court to create a full record, Lefelt told the lawyers he saw the proceedings as something akin to a legislative hearing; better to allow almost everything into evidence than to exclude something that might later seem relevant. Whatever the merits of that approach, its results were clear enough: it was January 1987 when ELC finally finished presenting its witnesses. By then, the trial transcript filled more than 8,000 pages, the plaintiffs had introduced more than 370 exhibits, and the state had not yet begun presenting its case.

Exactly four months after the start of the hearing, state lawyer Al Ramey called the first of his forty-nine witnesses. Just as ELC's testimony had illuminated the desperate conditions urban districts faced, the state's witnesses trained a spotlight on the mismanagement and corruption those districts condoned.

In Hoboken, the Jersey City neighbor whose politically driven hiring practices ELC researcher Steve Block had once criticized, stainless-steel wheeled carts had filled the new high school's storage area—useless accessories the school board had bought from someone influential. "Stories from my colleagues in other buildings were replete with material that they didn't order, stuff that they couldn't get that they wanted, vendors who were involved with the board, or calls from City Hall to see someone," a former administrator reported.

In the wake of Jersey City's 1981 municipal election, the newly elected mayor and his handpicked school board president had casually eliminated most of the school district's top administrative positions, apparently because their occupants had not backed the winning candidate. Under civil service rules, if the vanished jobs were reinstated, the dismissed administrators had to get first crack at them, so instead the school board forced the superintendent and his deputy to run the state's second-largest district by themselves for three years. One of the dismissed administrators was special education director Charles Williams, who testified that he routinely fielded calls from councilmen, ward leaders, and school board members asking that he sell tickets to fund-raisers or give his staff time off to attend political functions. Employees with political protection were difficult to discipline, and teachers and supervisors who had backed losing candidates risked transfers to unpleasant new assignments. To win them back, Williams would have to send intermediaries to negotiate with whatever godfather his employees had offended. Eventually, Williams himself endured a campaign of petty harassment, culminating in repeated ticketing of his car. "If you look at most urban administrators," he said, "you'll see that they all have some kind of heart problem or ulcers, or something else, because of the constant fighting to get things accomplished."

Most of the state's witnesses were Education Department employees charged with monitoring progress in the plaintiffs' four districts, and nearly everywhere they had looked, they said, they had found sloppy planning, lax implementation, and widespread apathy. "These are among the most inefficient, mismanaged districts in the state," one education official testified. "The last thing in the world we would want to do at this point would be to put any additional funds in there without some significant needs of accountability." Some of Camden's principals "are incompetent, or at least verge on incompetence," another official said. "They have given up. They have no expectations for their staff and their students. They feel for one reason or another that they are unable to impact positively the programs that are in place."

But where ELC's witnesses offered emotional insights into life in inner-city schools, the state's witnesses offered numbers and checklists. Morheuser and her team saw the case as a quasi-religious crusade, and their witnesses shared that conviction, state lawyer Isaac thought. By contrast, his own side's witnesses were detached and objective, like doctors examining a troubled patient. If the judge got caught up in the emotion, the state was bound to lose. Fired with zeal, ELC's lawyers wondered privately if their opponents really believed their own arguments or were just parroting the company line. The enigma of the state's lead lawyer, unflappable Al Ramey, particularly obsessed them. How, they wondered, could an African American remain indifferent to the plight of minority children? One day, Ramey dropped by ELC's office for a conference and, in the idle time before the meeting began, showed ELC lawyer Sheila Dow-Ford pictures of his children. Afterward, she and Morheuser speculated about the gesture. Was it Ramey's way of letting them glimpse the human being behind the professional mask? Or was he suggesting something about his true allegiance?

The hearing, and the punishing workload, continued. Daily transcripts of the testimony were prohibitively expensive, so Dow-Ford, who was not examining witnesses, took voluminous notes on everyone else's work—each day, she practically memorized the testimony. When his witnesses were scheduled, David Long flew in from California and spent days holed up in Morheuser's spare room; Long's wife took to referring to Morheuser as his second wife. One night, Long stayed up until 1 or 2 a.m. preparing the cross-examinations of two crucial witnesses, and then got up early for the ninety-minute drive to Trenton.

The state's lawyers, too, worked late into the night after the end of each day's testimony. Ramey would go home to eat dinner with his family and then return to the office until 11 p.m. David Powers had struggled for years with illness—asthma, kidney stones, lung infections—and late in the trial his doctor ordered him to limit his workload. Months after the case ended, Isaac's fatigue became debilitating, and his doctor diagnosed Epstein-Barr syndrome. Isaac attributed the illness to the chronic exhaustion he had lived with through the months of the *Abbott* hearing.

Lefelt's concern over the hearing's gargantuan length was growing. By mid-February 1987, he worried that the record was "bordering on being unmanageable." In late April, he reported, "Every time I go back to the office and I look at the mountain of documents, it really is an unbelievable record. I have been wracking my brain for ways to make it of more use to the viewers at the end of the case." And in July, a month after testimony had finally ended, he confessed, "This is the only case I've ever been involved with that I didn't feel I had complete command over the record." If the lawyers did not provide cogent summaries of the evidence and arguments, it could take him nine months to write a decision, Lefelt predicted. "That's what I'm trying to grapple with, and it terrifies me," he said. And no wonder. By the time the *Abbott* hearing ended on June 5, 1987, more than eight months after it had begun, ninety-nine witnesses had testified over ninety-three days in court. The judge had admitted 745 exhibits into evidence—witnesses' résumés, curriculum and management handbooks, scholarly articles, statistical charts, even postcards of student artwork. The exhibits filled seven file drawers; the transcript of testimony ran to more than 16,000 pages. And the flood of paper was not over yet. In the months following the end of the trial, the lawyers distilled their cases into more than 1,300 pages of proposed factual findings and 400 pages of legal briefs (legal "'briefs,'" Lefelt called them in one procedural ruling). By the spring of 1988, when the state asked permission to submit yet another reply, Lefelt refused. "After all that has occurred in this matter, my reasoning is simple," he wrote. "I have concluded that enough is enough."

The winter of 1988 had been another difficult time for ELC. As the lawyers plowed through the endless transcripts and exhibits, drafting their final court submissions, ELC's eternally precarious finances teetered on a cliff-edge. The Reagan years had not been kind to liberal interest groups, and foundations were less and less willing to pay for litigation. Consumed by the *Abbott* hearing, Morheuser had had no time to fund-raise in 1987, and by December the financial picture looked so grim that, in a letter to supporters, Morheuser warned, "Our remaining resources will barely carry us into 1988." ELC needed $100,000 to stay alive, but more than a month later, the December appeal had raised only $10,000. By now, ELC had spent $1.25 million on the *Abbott* case and could go broke by April, Morheuser told a newspaper; striking her favorite underdog pose, she blamed the center's plight on state gamesmanship. "It's unfair to anybody who tries to challenge the state," she told the reporter. "The state doesn't have to worry about expenses or delays because the state has all of our tax money. And when children bring a lawsuit, they can't pay for it." The center's survival hinged on one final grant application, to the Edna McConnell Clark Foundation, and in early 1988, the foundation's board voted to give ELC a lifesaving $100,000 transfusion. David had survived to fight Goliath another day. Some years later, in notes she made on

ELC's work, Morheuser succinctly summed up the eleventh-hour rescue: "LUCK."

By May 1988, with its immediate future no longer in doubt, ELC settled once again into limbo, waiting for Lefelt's decision. Although the lawyers felt confident that the trial had gone about as well as they could have hoped, they knew they needed a big win, for Lefelt's analysis of their evidence would guide the work of every higher court that heard *Abbott*— and since Lefelt, as an administrative law judge, lacked authority to resolve the constitutional issues at the heart of the case, his decision would undoubtedly be only a first step on the way to the inevitable state supreme court showdown. Lefelt, too, surely knew the scrutiny his ruling would face; in the months after the hearing ended, and all that summer after the final submissions, he worked diligently in his chambers next to the conference room stuffed with *Abbott* exhibits and court papers. Unlike superior court judges, who could pick and choose which facts to highlight in their rulings, administrative law judges had to make specific factual findings on all the issues dividing the parties before them, no matter how arcane. The previous fall, the first assignment Lefelt had given his new law clerk was to research the differences between multiple regression analysis and the coefficient of variation.

Lefelt's decision, when it finally arrived on August 25, 1988, was appropriately mammoth. In 607 detailed pages, the judge made more than 160 specific factual findings on everything from the validity of competing statistical methods to the prevalence of mismanagement in urban districts. And he gave ELC almost everything it had hoped for, in the process rejecting virtually all of the state's case. New Jersey's poor urban school districts were shortchanging their students, and fundamental flaws in the school-funding law were largely to blame, Lefelt found. "The system is not T&E because opportunity is determined by socioeconomic status and geographic location," he wrote. Whatever mismanagement and corruption existed in the urban districts was a secondary issue. "I do not believe in fixing what is not broken," Lefelt wrote. "However, plaintiffs have proven the system is broken."

Lefelt's analysis began by noting that guaranteed tax base funding formulas, like New Jersey's, were never intended to equalize school spending—spending levels were left to the choice of local voters. Indeed, he found, spending gaps had widened since the *Robinson* era. But guaranteed tax base systems *were* supposed to ensure that similar tax effort would yield similar levels of funding, and here New Jersey's system had failed, the judge found: even though urban districts were taxing themselves heavily, because of flaws in the funding formula, they still could not spend as much as suburban districts making smaller tax efforts. Urban districts were also offering their students far inferior educational programs. As they struggled to raise scores on the state's reading and math tests, city schools narrowed their curricula even for students who had mastered the basic skills, although urban students needed art classes, music lessons, and library books far more than did suburban children whose parents could supply those needs at home.

Next, Lefelt turned to the disputed question of why these fiscal and programmatic disparities existed. The main reason, he concluded, was the desperate economic situation of New Jersey's cities, where school districts and municipalities shared the same depleted local tax base. In the cities, schools competed for funding with every priority from police protection to street repair, and raising already punishing tax rates was often seen as politically and economically impossible. The state criticized local school boards for caving in to these pressures and spending less than the funding law permitted them to, but Lefelt argued that the state itself bore some responsibility for local boards' plight: the state Board of Education had never set uniform standards for school programs, leaving urban boards little basis for arguing against cuts that municipal officials demanded. Lefelt refused to equate such political accommodation with mismanagement, as the state did, and he rejected the state's argument that other forms of mismanagement were pervasive in urban districts. Neither Camden nor Irvington had been mismanaged, he found, and even East Orange's history of corruption and incompetence did not necessarily explain all the district's woes. Jersey City was a different matter—political intrusion there was "shocking and harmful to the school children of Jersey City and qualitatively and quantitatively different from the pressures present in most other property poor districts," the judge wrote. But the record, he said, provided no evidence that Jersey City's problems were typical of the state's urban districts. Lefelt could not conclude, he wrote, "that property poor districts are being so mismanaged that proper efficiencies, management practices and the expulsion of politics will redirect sufficient funds and administrative energies to address the failings and disparities that have been proven."

The state had argued that the monitoring system instituted by the T&E law, the heart of the "process model" embraced by the legislators and bureaucrats of the 1970s, was working effectively to identify and solve the problems of urban districts. And, indeed, Lefelt rejected ELC's claims that monitoring was little more than cynical paper shuffling—it was a good-faith effort to address an enormous administrative challenge, he found. Nevertheless, the process failed to ensure the T&E education that the constitution guaranteed, Lefelt ruled. The state's monitors studied each district in isolation and on its own terms, without evaluating whether the district had properly assessed its students' needs or whether the programs it had devised to meet those needs were inferior to programs in other districts. Nor did the monitors recommend, much less require, extra spending. "The existing monitoring system permits some districts to have better schools than others," Lefelt wrote. "In fact, the entire education system in New Jersey expects and thereby condones vast variations in educational quality among school districts."

But if the monitoring process had failed as a gauge of T&E, what standard should be applied in judging whether a school district was meeting the constitutional mandate? The plaintiffs had sought to define T&E as a matter of inputs—providing equal opportunity meant providing equal funding and programming. The state had sought to define T&E as a matter of student-achievement outputs evaluated through the monitoring process: if a district had successfully passed state monitoring, it could be presumed to be meeting the T&E guarantee. Neither side's definition fully satisfied the judge, and in his ruling he tried to steer a middle course. Although he accepted the state's view that contemporary social science had found no systematic relationship between inputs and outputs, that fact did not compel the state's conclusion that inputs had *no* significance, he wrote. On the other hand, ELC's absolutist position was no more satisfying: "Inputs alone do not measure the quality of an education," Lefelt wrote. The key issue, the judge ruled, was whether students with similar needs and abilities received "substantially similar educational programs and services" regardless of where they lived. A system that could not ensure that measure of equity was not thorough and efficient. Still, such equity would not necessarily require all districts to offer identical programs, Lefelt added: the state could set standards for evaluating "the variety of acceptable approaches to providing substantially similar opportunity for comparable students."

Although Lefelt had no authority to find a violation of the state's constitution, he came as close as he could, concluding that the vast record contained enough evidence for a higher court to find such a violation. Still, he rejected ELC's claim that the state's school-funding system was intentionally biased against African Americans and Hispanics. The system operated on the basis of property wealth, not race, he said, although white flight from cities to suburbs had ensured that in New Jersey, the two categories often overlapped. That defeat was significant for ELC: plaintiffs who prevailed on claims of racial discrimination were entitled to collect attorney' fees from the losing side, so Lefelt's finding meant ELC would not recoup the costs of seven and a half years of litigation.

Lefelt wrapped up his ruling with reflections on an alternative school-funding system, coming down in favor of the plan proposed by ELC's experts—replacing the guaranteed tax base system with a "high foundation" formula, in which the state set a generous funding level and ensured that every district could spend at that level. Such a plan, Lefelt noted, could be funded through a uniform statewide property tax that would replace the patchwork of locally determined school taxes. Whatever the ultimate remedy, Lefelt urged that it "level up" low-spending districts rather than require affluent districts to cut successful, expensive programs. Although he had concluded that urban districts were underfunded, Lefelt said he did not know if the state would have to spend more money systemwide to achieve T&E, and he stressed that whatever money was spent would have to be well spent. "I do not, at this time, share plaintiffs' confidence that equalizing expenditures is all that is necessary to achieve T&E," Lefelt wrote.

Like Judge Botter's ruling nearly a generation earlier, Lefelt's decision was front-page news across the state. Almost immediately, suburban superintendents and legislators began to wonder what Lefelt's talk of "substantially similar" programs might mean for their schools. Did the latest decision require only that poor districts spend adequately, or that they spend the same amount as rich ones? Did adequacy in fact require equality, as a close reading of the state supreme court's *Robinson* opinions suggested? Was Lefelt saying that "everybody should have the same—not good for the rich and mediocre for the poor," as the Irvington superintendent had told a reporter a few days after the ruling? Lefelt had never said that equity required limiting what rich districts could spend on their own students; he had specifically urged "leveling up" rather than "leveling down." But with some rich districts spending twice as much per student as some poor ones, leveling up would be an expensive proposition. Raising that money through the statewide property tax recommended by Lefelt would surely mean increasing taxes in dozens of rich towns that were used to raising huge sums with minimal tax effort—a politically painful prospect. Still, keeping taxes down by telling those rich towns they could not spend whatever they chose on their own children would hardly be easier. Morheuser said she thought any new formula should bar rich communities from spending much more than the statewide foundation level; that way, rich and poor districts would have a joint interest in lobbying the legislature for yearly increases, she said. Predictably, suburban legislators hated that idea. "If the community wants to spend money out of its own pocket for quality education, how can you say no?" asked one Republican assemblyman.

While the debate raged, *Abbott* had to run the rest of the procedural gauntlet: Lefelt's ruling was technically only a recommendation to Education Commissoner Saul Cooperman and the state Board of Education, and their decisions in turn were certain to be appealed to the state supreme court. Because he would eventually have to adjudicate the case, Cooperman had kept aloof from the state's trial preparation, but after six years heading the Education Department, he did not lack strong opinions on the issues.

At fifty-three, Cooperman, like many white New Jerseyans, had spent most of his life far from the troubled cities. He had passed an idyllic middle-class boyhood in a comfortable North Jersey suburb, and after college and navy service, he had decided to teach. By happenstance, it was a suburban district that offered him his first job, and as one position led to another, Cooperman built a career in a succession of middle-class, white districts. Articulate and personable, he rose quickly from high school social studies teacher to principal to superintendent, and, after Kean's election, to the state's top education job. As commissioner, Cooperman juggled a thousand issues, overhauling the bureaucracy, streamlining the state's monitoring process, instituting a more rigorous high school test, and pushing a reform agenda whose cornerstone was the controversial effort to recruit mid-career professionals into teaching.

Of course, Cooperman knew urban districts were troubled—any New Jersey educator knew that—and in his first few years on the job, during what he would later call his "idealistic naïve phase," he offered them help: workshops on successful programs, visits to exemplary city districts around the country, that kind of thing. Nothing changed, however, and soon Cooperman was seeing up close the waste, corruption, and mismanagement that he had previously only heard about—the no-show jobs in Jersey City, the illicit spending in East Orange, that lavish Godiva-and-champagne reception sponsored by Newark. As his naïveté faded, Cooperman decided to get tougher: instead of letting urban districts pick the programs they wanted, he launched an Urban Initiative, designed to promote exactly the programs he thought they needed. His frustration simmered, however. A handful of troubled districts seemed unwilling, or unable, to attack their own problems; they could not even devise an improvement plan, no matter how much help the Education Department offered. Did money matter? Cooperman's philosophy was "Yes, but." Certainly, money solved some problems—you couldn't patch a leaky roof without money for shingles. But leadership and school culture mattered at least as much, Cooperman thought. Dirty hallways signified poor management, not straitened finances. Why spend money to solve problems that could not be solved with money?

One day, Cooperman had an epiphany. No matter what happened with *Abbott v. Burke*, he thought, some of these school districts were beyond help, and the state had to find a way to clean them up. Right there in his backyard, Cooperman wrote the first draft of a bill that would permit the state to seize control of those hopeless districts—to fire the superintendent, replace the school board, and put a state appointee in charge of everything from hiring principals to buying pencils. By the time Lefelt's decision came down, Cooperman's idea had become law and the state was a year away from taking over the Jersey City schools.

Cooperman pored over the voluminous *Abbott* transcript and, laid up with a bad back, called the state's lawyers to his bedside to offer devil's-advocate arguments on all facets of the case. Nevertheless, Morheuser had little doubt about which way the father of the school takeover law would rule, and Cooperman's February 22, 1989, *Abbott* decision held few surprises. Cooperman rejected nearly all Lefelt's findings. Urban schools' problems were district-specific and not systemic, he found, and the state's existing monitoring system could resolve them. Although the funding formula had its flaws, they were not responsible for district failures. Urban school boards that cut their budgets in response to political pressure to hold down taxes were guilty of "a clear moral failure" to protect the interests of schoolchildren. And to say, as Lefelt did, that mismanagement played only a minor role in school failure was "to deny logic and enthrone naïveté."

At bottom, Cooperman's ruling squarely rejected the assumption, implicit in the supreme court's *Robinson* rulings and in Lefelt's decision, that providing an adequate education for poor children required some measure of equality with the rich, even when it came to programs that went beyond what the state required. "There is no mandate in this State that all children receive the same educational program and services," Cooperman wrote. "To require every district to provide everything that any other district may provide would lead either to an educational structure which would collapse under the weight of its own lack of fiscal restraint or shrink to a bare minimum of offerings that all could afford." He rejected the view that disparities in programming were themselves evidence that poor students were shortchanged. Different communities could choose different programs, depending on their students' needs, and in districts with painfully low test scores, a narrowed curriculum might be a logical option. "The harsh reality is that an increase in advanced placement courses may not be the soundest choice educationally when the more compelling need is to concentrate on raising basic skills competencies," Cooperman wrote. Two months later, the state Board of Education ratified Cooperman's decision, freeing ELC to appeal the case back to the courts. Nearly four years had passed since the supreme court's *Abbott I* decision had ordered an expedited administrative hearing of the case, and now at last *Abbott* was headed back for a final resolution.

Through those long years of hard work and excruciating delay, Morheuser had leaned on her ad hoc family of close friends. After each day's testimony before Judge Lefelt, she would sit in her apartment sipping her martini, smoking her cigarettes, and regaling Tom Cioppettini with tales of how devastatingly her team had eviscerated the state's case. She had drawn strength from another source, as well. In the twenty-two years since her painful decision to leave the convent, Morheuser had kept in touch with some of the Lorettine sisters, and in 1985, she apparently reconnected with the order in a more formal way, perhaps through a celebration with friends after one of the order's annual conferences. In April 1985, as she awaited the supreme court's ruling on where the *Abbott* case would be heard, Morheuser paid tribute to the Sisters of Loretto in a poem she titled "Found Again." "I took you with me and found you again:/We've always been together," she wrote. She recalled the order's birth on the frontier, traced her own history from jail in Milwaukee to law school in New Jersey, and affectionately recalled friends from her Loretto days. In her new life, Morheuser wrote, she drew on "The womanstrength in Lorettoworld."

> In board rooms where I search for funding
> In courtrooms where the wrestling is for justice.
> Over Martinis,
>> Negotiating with the manworld of lawmaking
>> —for the children—
> I need you and
>> You are there.
> Thank you for not leaving.

7

The Twenty-One/Forty-One Rule

Through eight long years, *Abbott v. Burke* had been dismissed, appealed, rerouted, delayed, heard, decided, and appealed again; the Education Law Center had kept its slippery grip on financial viability; and Marilyn Morheuser had weathered cancer, accident, and crushing disappointment. By the fall of 1989, as Morheuser prepared for arguments before the state supreme court, no one, not even the state's lawyers, expected her to lose. In the supreme courts of Montana and Kentucky, school-funding plaintiffs had just won resounding victories, the first signs that the tide of litigation was turning nationwide. The press saw New Jersey as a bellwether: one of the first states to face a 1970s court challenge to its school-finance system, it was now the first state back in court defending a funding formula adopted in response to a previous lawsuit. The ELC team that had tried the *Abbott* case before Judge Steven Lefelt had split up, but for the next stage, Morheuser had recruited an old ally—Steve Block, the researcher who had left ELC years earlier to tackle political reform in Hoboken. After that effort ended disappointingly, Block had spent a frustrating three years working for the state Education Department, and he welcomed Morheuser's invitation back to the *Abbott* fight. Each day, he picked Morheuser up at her apartment, and on the drive to the office, the two veterans of the '60s gossiped about Block's young son or Morheuser's beloved New York Knicks. At work, Block pored over the voluminous transcripts of the administrative hearing, extracting nuggets that bolstered ELC's arguments. Block sometimes felt the sting of Morheuser's impatient perfectionism, but most days, their shared commitment sustained him.

The political climate at last seemed favorable to ELC's cause. After eight years under the Republican Kean administration, which had fought *Abbott* every step of the way, New Jersey was about to elect a new governor, and that November, the Democrat, Jim Florio, won a landslide victory. In contrast to the patrician Thomas Kean, Florio, the son of a ship painter, had grown up working class on the Brooklyn waterfront; sometimes, his family ate oatmeal for dinner, and Florio took his first paying job at age twelve. He dropped out of high school, earned a GED in the navy, and briefly took up boxing, providing future journalists with a nearly irresistible metaphor for his relentless political style. After the navy, Florio became a lawyer, got a city job in Camden, and, with the help of the Democratic machine, won election to the state assembly and then the U.S. Congress. Smart, rigid, and aloof, he became a respected but unloved expert on transportation and the environment.

Florio had no real record on school-finance issues—as a Byrne-era assemblyman, he had voted against the income tax—but his urban roots and liberal politics made sympathy with the *Abbott* plaintiffs likely, and his education adviser, a former state bureaucrat named Thomas Corcoran, had testified for ELC at the administrative hearing. That fall of 1989, the pendency of the *Abbott* ruling gave both gubernatorial candidates an excuse to sidestep the issue, but whatever the year, school funding never played much role in New Jersey governor's races. Vows to improve inner-city education won few middle-class votes, and complicated tradeoffs between tax fairness and school quality resisted easy sloganeering. Florio had special reason to avoid the issue: any solution was likely to require tax increases, and he had narrowly lost the 1981 governor's race after Kean branded him a closet tax-raiser. Of course, Kean himself had later raised both sales and income taxes, but no matter—this time, Florio would not be cast as the pro-tax candidate.

New Jersey's last Democratic governor, Brendan Byrne, had campaigned on a vague no-taxes pledge, trusted the Republican incumbent's promise of a budget surplus, and watched a national economic crisis devour that surplus even before Inauguration Day. Now history repeated itself. Florio had told voters he saw no need for new taxes, pointing to Kean's claim of a budget surplus, but in the weeks after Election Day 1989, the fiscal news steadily worsened, as the national recession arrived early in New Jersey. By January, the state faced a $600 million current-year deficit and a projected $1 billion deficit in the budget Florio had to design for the following year. Administration officials quickly devised a three-step plan: close the current-year deficit with spending cuts; plug the projected 1990–91 deficit with a sales tax increase; and pay for new programs, including any court-ordered school-aid increase, with an income tax hike. Officials wanted to administer the unpalatable tax increases in two separate doses, enacting a sales tax increase immediately, to solve the pressing fiscal crisis, and delaying the income tax increase until after the *Abbott* ruling. The slow-building pressure of the *Robinson* rulings had fostered the crisis atmosphere that eventually forced through the income tax and saved Byrne's political career; Florio's team envisioned a similar progression for their school-aid crisis.

Political realities complicated the administration's plans, however. Although Democrats controlled both houses of the legislature, the senate and the assembly distrusted each other and differed sharply on the tax timetable. The senate favored the administration's two-step approach, but the assembly leader, Joseph Doria Jr., refused to delay the income tax vote. The regressive sales tax was a "Republican tax," he thought, and he feared that once it was increased, the senate would never muster the votes to raise the progressive "Democratic tax" on income. The legislature should approve the whole tax package at once, Doria argued. Florio's aides, nicknamed Floriocrats by the Trenton commentariat, planned a complex reform agenda—not only tax hikes and school-aid increases, but also a major auto insurance overhaul and an assault-weapons ban sure to draw virulent opposition from the powerful gun lobby. With so much work ahead, the administration could not afford to alienate assembly Democrats. The Floriocrats reluctantly agreed to a single tax vote.

That decision radically compressed the legislative calendar. To balance the 1990–91 budget, the sales tax increase had to be enacted before the new fiscal year began on July 1, less than six months after Florio's inauguration; if the income tax increase had to be enacted at the same time, so did the new school-aid formula, or legislators would inevitably find other ways to spend the income tax windfall. Since the court had not yet explained what kind of school-aid formula the constitution required, the Floriocrats would have to devise a new formula based on their best guess about what the court would mandate, and they would have just a few months to do it.

Florio's advisers had planned to develop their school-aid proposal quite differently, through a deliberate, public process kicking off after the release of the *Abbott* decision. "Once the decision is handed down, the process of developing a response should be as open as possible because exclusionary, closed door approaches are going to build mistrust and opposition," education advisor Corcoran wrote. On the compressed timetable dictated by the single tax vote, however, an exclusionary, closed-door approach was precisely what the administration adopted. Years later, officials offered competing explanations for that decision. Perhaps the administration's crowded agenda had left the Floriocrats too busy to manage a public process; perhaps they feared prematurely publicizing tax increases; perhaps they did not want to give likely opponents time to rally their forces. In any case, through the late winter and early spring of 1990, the school aid formula took shape far from the spotlight, in twice-weekly meetings of a handful of individuals from the Education Department, Treasury Department, and governor's office. Between meetings, computers churned out data, checking every new proposal to see how it played out in Ridgewood and Elizabeth and Cape May.

The Byrne-era guaranteed tax base formula had preserved local control by letting school districts set their own tax rates and spending levels, but political and economic pressures had forced poor districts to spend far less than rich ones. Florio's team planned to accept reduced local control in return for greater equity. They would propose a foundation plan, similar to that urged by the *Abbott* plaintiffs: the state would set a school spending level and ensure that every district, regardless of wealth, could spend up to it. To ensure tax fairness, the new formula would require every district to set an affordable property tax rate, with state income taxes making up the difference between local revenues and the foundation amount.

Like the architects of the Byrne-era school-aid formula, Florio's team decided not to bar rich districts from spending above the foundation amount, if their voters chose to do so. Morheuser wanted sharp limits on such local leeway, to ensure greater equity and to give both rich and poor a political stake in the foundation formula, but no one had the stomach for that fight. Months earlier, a Republican assemblyman had predicted a "revolution" if the supreme court tried to cap school spending. If the rich wanted extra bells and whistles for their children, so be it, Treasurer Douglas Berman thought. As long as every kid was getting a good, solid education, what did it matter?

To fill in the details of the new formula, Corcoran set about deciding on an appropriate foundation level. Corcoran, who had done graduate work in sociology and education, had spent four years in Byrne's Education Department after the income tax wars, and like many high-level department officials in those years, he sympathized with Morheuser's cause: he wanted fairness and educational excellence for poor children, and he knew the existing formula achieved neither. But he did not share Morheuser's conviction that equity required poor districts immediately to spend as much as rich ones. The key, he believed, was not spending equity but program equity—providing all children the same services. School districts spent most of their money on salaries, and therefore high pay for veteran teachers accounted for much of rich districts' high spending, Corcoran argued. Poor districts ramping up their programs would likely hire younger, lower-paid teachers, since few veterans would leave the comfortable suburbs for the challenging inner cities. Over time, as their teachers accrued experience, poor districts would spend more, but they need not spend it all immediately.

To determine what they did need to spend, Corcoran ranked New Jersey's many school districts by spending levels, by test scores, and by quality indicators—teachers' experience, classroom ratios, Advanced Placement enrollment. He looked at what wealthy suburbs provided in the way of guidance counseling, class size, and computer technology. He examined urban districts' budgets and estimated the cost of providing suburban levels of service in Newark or Camden. The foundation level, he finally decided, should be set around the sixtieth percentile of school spending in the state, far below the rich-district averages Morheuser had used as her standard. At that level, Corcoran argued, districts were providing good services and students were achieving well. Corcoran's analysis didn't convince everyone, however. One Florio team member, treasury official Robert Goertz, was married to Margaret Goertz, the education researcher who had testified for Morheuser. Each night, as Bob described how the work was going, Peg pounded the table in dismay at Corcoran's numbers.

As Corcoran calibrated the foundation amount, Treasurer Berman played with income tax rates, looking for a configuration that would raise enough to fund schools adequately while keeping tax bills down. Computer runs played proposed foundation amounts against possible income tax packages. At a $7,000-per-child foundation, the income tax would be too high; at $6,000, school spending would be too low. Eventually, the team settled on $6,835. Meanwhile, team members considered how best to assess each district's wealth, which would in turn decide how much of the foundation amount local property taxes would cover. Using property values as the sole gauge of district wealth, it turned out, skewed state aid toward the low-cost towns of South Jersey and away from the big, impoverished northern cities. One night, Florio's team huddled around a tiny globe, trying to determine which line of latitude passed through central New Jersey; perhaps using a different wealth formula on either side of the line would skirt the South Jersey problem. Instead, the team found another solution: a district's local tax contribution, they decided, would turn not only on its property values but also on its residents' average income.

As the analysis advanced, political considerations were never absent. Trenton lived by the twenty-one/forty-one rule: every bill needed the votes of at least twenty-one senators and forty-one assembly members. The school-aid formula would survive only if most school districts, especially those represented by key legislators, got state aid increases; the income tax package would survive only if most voters paid no more than before. Achieving those goals, it soon became clear, would require a big gamble: tinkering with the teacher pension fund.

Since 1955, the state, not local districts, had paid teachers' pensions and the employer component of Social Security, even though pensions were based on locally negotiated salaries that the state could not control. Since rich districts usually paid higher salaries, a disproportionate share of state pension payments went to their teachers; in effect, state payment of teacher retirement costs—about $900 million in 1990—subsidized rich districts. ("High-class welfare," Morheuser called it.) The only way to keep income taxes down and school spending up, Florio's team decided, was to add that $900 million to the pot of school aid distributed on the basis of district wealth. Local taxpayers would pay part of the cost of teacher pensions, just as they paid part of the cost of textbooks, roof repairs, and teacher salaries. Corcoran saw an additional benefit to the pension shift: once local taxpayers began bearing the real cost of big raises, teachers would probably start getting smaller ones, he thought.

For most school districts, the new formula, funded with income tax increases, would boost their aid enough to cover much of their new pension costs, but some rich districts would face a double whammy. Florio's team was certain the supreme court would invalidate minimum aid—state money paid to every district, no matter how wealthy—and therefore the Florio formula, too, eliminated this subsidy for the rich. With the pension-cost shift, districts losing minimum aid would simultaneously incur a heavy new expense. Their voters would be angry, and the pension shift was also certain to outrage the state's most powerful special-interest group, the teachers' union. But some members of Florio's team felt sure the supreme court would ratify their gamble. Surely the justices would find pension aid, like minimum aid, to be an unconstitutional sop to the rich.

The spring wore on, and still the court did not rule. Finally, with its tight time line stretched to the limit, the administration could wait no longer: on May 24, 1990, Florio unveiled his education proposal, known as the Quality Education Act (QEA). The funding formula was just one part of a larger package, but no one paid much attention to the bills promoting school construction or changing the school-monitoring process. No one wanted to talk about anything but revamped school aid and higher taxes. Florio planned to raise $1.4 billion by adding a penny to the 6 percent sales tax, applying it to previously exempt products, like paper goods, and increasing excise taxes on alcohol and tobacco. He would raise another $1.25 billion by doubling the top income tax rate, from 3.5 percent to 7 percent. And his QEA would end minimum aid to rich districts, force local school boards to pay teacher pensions, and pour new money into poor and middle-class districts.

Much of the package should have been politically appealing. The income tax increases affected only 17 percent of New Jersey taxpayers. The state planned to offer new tax rebates and take over counties' social service costs, reducing local property taxes. More than 80 percent of the state's students lived in districts that would get extra aid under QEA; although 151 districts would eventually lose millions, they were small and affluent, and their aid would be phased out over several years. Between the new money raised from the income tax and the old money redistributed from rich districts, poor and middle-class districts would get $1 billion more in aid. QEA paid for aid increases for the poor and the middle class with money raised from the rich.

The rich were outraged. "Excellent school systems in the state will become mediocre," one suburban superintendent declared. "I don't agree with the theory of tearing down school systems with high commitment to education to solve the problems of the inner cities." Those inner-city schools—corrupt, inept, riddled with patronage—would just waste the money anyway, some critics insisted. A whiff of hypocrisy perfumed the argument: apparently, money spent in the suburbs was crucial to maintaining good educational programs, but those same dollars were wasted when spent in the cities. Still, the suburban fears ran deep, and soon they spawned a new activism: by October 1990, the superintendents of twenty-five affluent districts had banded together to oppose parts of QEA, and in less than two years their group had a name, the Garden State Coalition of Schools. Garden State's paramount issue was the pension shift: superintendents feared that the millions required to pay pensions for retired teachers would mean fewer dollars for microscopes, field trips, or, indeed, salaries for active teachers. The Florio team had assumed rich districts would raise their often low property taxes to cover the new costs, but school officials who had survived bruising budget battles with local taxpayers, especially senior citizens without schoolchildren, were pessimistic about the prospects for tax increases. Inevitably, they thought, programs would be cut.

Garden State's founders were acutely aware of the moral and public-relations pitfalls of their lobbying. They wanted to avoid looking like rich folks "crying into our beer," as one put it years later, and they empathized with their colleagues in inner-city schools. Even as they fought for their own interests, they decided, they would resist the divisive finger-pointing at corrupt inner-city schools; they would insist that the poor needed the extra help Florio planned to give them. At legislative hearings, Garden State's first president, Mark Smith, the superintendent of affluent West-field, coordinated his testimony with that of the Newark superintendent, to ensure that rich and poor spoke with one voice. Not everyone shared Smith's commitment to striking this tricky balance. On his refrigerator hung a clipping from the local newspaper, a letter from an angry citizen demanding to know whose side Smith was on, anyway.

If Garden State's activism was persistent but genteel, the New Jersey Education Association's resistance was street-fighting furious. Florio's QEA team had fundamentally misread the teachers' union. Despite the unpalatable pension shift, the team had reasoned, NJEA would surely em-brace QEA, since the bill directed hundreds of millions in new money to poor and middle-class districts, many of which would inevitably spend the windfall hiring new teachers or giving raises to old ones. To help assuage anxiety over the pension shift, Florio's team had written in important guarantees: although local money would for the first time help fund teacher retirement costs, the state would guarantee pension fund contri-butions. If local mismanagement squandered a required payment, the pension fund would still get paid; it would be up to the state to collect the debt. "NJEA will be divided," Corcoran had predicted in an April 1990 strategy memo, "but a personal appearance [by Florio] might help per-suade them that no one will be harmed, and many helped by the proposal."

But Corcoran had misunderstood the depth of NJEA's attachment to its pension fund. The union had two sacred cows, tenure and pensions, and QEA gored one of them. NJEA believed in anticipating the precedent today's compromises might set for tomorrow's legislation, and despite QEA's short-term guarantees, the pension shift spelled long-term danger, union officials thought. New raises would drop off sharply as districts ab-sorbed the true cost of old ones, and teachers would lose their jobs if vot-ers rejected tax increases needed to cover pension costs. Further down the slippery slope, local districts might try to negotiate smaller contribu-tions to their pension plans, potentially endangering members' retire-ments. By accident or design, NJEA's campaign against the pension shift blurred the difference between long-term and short-term dangers, ignoring QEA's pension guarantees and highlighting NJEA's worst-case fears. Union members were galvanized. Busloads of teachers demonstrated in Trenton, accusing Florio of risking their retirements, and when the governor spoke at a middle-school graduation, teachers picketed outside.

Corcoran had predicted that QEA would divide the union, but NJEA had seldom been more united. That unity was especially ironic, because for years NJEA officials had feared that the *Abbott* case would tip the union into civil war, pitting members from the suburbs against members from the cities. In 1982, when Morheuser solicited NJEA support for her case, those fears helped keep the union on the fence. Not until 1989 did NJEA file its first pro-*Abbott* friend-of-the-court brief, and then only because its president forcefully argued that NJEA's hands-off position was morally indefensible for an organization committed to children's welfare. Florio's pension-shift proposal, because it rallied teachers under a single unifying banner, helped NJEA sidestep the real danger QEA could have posed—that the union would have to take a stand on the redistributive impulses at the heart of the bill, and thereby alienate either teachers in wealthy suburbs or teachers in neglected inner cities. "We dodged a bullet," a former NJEA official said years later.

NJEA's virulent opposition to the pension shift had its counterpart in the equally virulent opposition to Florio's tax increases. Although the income tax hike had been carefully designed to leave most citizens unaffected, the administration was inexplicably slow in getting that message out. It took weeks to release a chart showing who would pay more, and in the meantime, media-fueled outrage filled the vacuum. A month after the unveiling of the tax package, the tabloid *Trentonian* wrote about increases in the assembly's own operating budget, describing "gold Assemblyman badges in leather wallets" and "lavish lunches, junkets to vacation spots . . . and luxury cars with mobile telephones." For weeks, callers to the FM radio station 101.5 had been venting their fury at higher taxes, and that day, a disk-jockey team read the *Trentonian*'s editorial on the air. When a mail carrier named John Budzash called in to bash lawmakers, the DJs urged him to contact other outraged listeners, and a grassroots organization, Hands Across New Jersey, was born. On July 1, 1990, the ten-day-old organization drew six thousand people to an antitax rally in Trenton.

To signal their solidarity, participants decorated their car antennas with rolls of newly taxed toilet paper.

Some administration officials suspected that the talk-radio taxpayer revolt remained more media creation than genuine grassroots phenomenon. Two days before the Hands Across New Jersey rally, Florio's communications director was shocked to find on the front page of one of the state's largest dailies a map directing participants to the event. Why was a newspaper ginning up turnout for a political gathering? he wondered. Even the angriest New Jersey voters told Democratic focus groups that the governor had four years to win them back, but that nuanced message was drowned out by the bumper-sticker-ready cries of "Impeach Florio." Years later, Florio would argue that insistent media coverage had made him look more embattled than he really was.

Still, not all the anger was media hype: by mid-July, only 23 percent of voters approved of Florio's job performance. A generation after Watergate, voters distrusted their government; when officials promised property taxes would fall if income taxes rose, citizens didn't believe them. The tax protests also had an irrational, wishful side, administration officials thought. Meeting with Florio, founders of Hands Across New Jersey acknowledged that their own income taxes had not risen—they earned too little—but said they opposed the tax hikes anyway: someday they might be millionaires, and then they wouldn't want to pay more. Three times, Corcoran visited the growing middle-income suburb of Toms River to explain that its schools were getting a big infusion of aid, and that they needed the new money, because their students took relatively few advanced courses and attended college at relatively low rates. Over and over, Corcoran heard the same reply: "These schools were good enough for us, and they're good enough for our kids." After a while, he began to wonder why he was bothering. Fine, he felt like saying—stay in your swamp.

The antitax protests also had an ugly undertone, administration officials sensed, a compound of class resentment and racial antagonism, whipped into hostility by recession-fed economic fears. "It's ridiculous to try to take money away from people that work and earn their money and give it to people that don't," John Budzash told reporters. At town meetings, members of even well-educated, sophisticated audiences would rise to their feet to opine that if "those people" wanted good schools, "schools like ours," they should get jobs and work hard so they too could move to the suburbs. Suburbanites might claim to believe in equality, Corcoran decided, but deep down they wanted their own children to have the competitive advantage they knew a suburban education would provide.

With opposition gathering from so many quarters, the administration was eager for a clear statement from the supreme court. For months, rumors had swirled that a decision was near, raising anxiety "to the nail-biting level," Morheuser wrote. On June 4, eleven days after Florio unveiled QEA, Morheuser went to Trenton to beg legislators to wait for the court's ruling before voting on the bill. Legislators were unenthusiastic; one told Morheuser that rumor had it the court was badly divided and might not rule for months. Morheuser had nearly finished her testimony when someone passed her a note. "I've just been informed that the court has announced that its decision will be coming out tomorrow," Morheuser declared, to gasps from the standing-room crowd. To Republicans, the timing seemed impossibly coincidental: after eight months of waiting, the court's ruling had arrived just when the governor needed it. Years later, surviving justices insisted politics had played no role in the timing; the decision was released when the decision was ready, simple as that. Stoking Republican suspicions, however, was the indisputable fact that the liberal Democratic governor had just gotten a boost from a court headed by a well-known liberal Democrat, Robert Wilentz.

Wilentz, who had become the court's chief justice upon Richard Hughes's 1979 retirement, had Democratic blood in his veins. As a child, his father, David, had arrived in the industrial city of Perth Amboy before the turn of the twentieth century, the son of Latvian Jewish immigrants who made their money in wholesale tobacco. David Wilentz became a lawyer and a Democratic Party power broker, ruling as unquestioned boss of his Central Jersey political machine. In 1934, a governor whom Wilentz had helped elect named him state attorney general; the next year, Wilentz personally prosecuted Bruno Hauptmann for kidnaping and killing the Lindbergh baby.

David Wilentz's son Robert was a brilliant student—valedictorian of the Perth Amboy public high school, graduate of Harvard College and Columbia Law School—who followed his father into the family firm and then into politics, serving two terms as a member of the assembly in the late 1960s. A reliable liberal vote on issues like clean air and urban aid, Robert Wilentz supported Governor Hughes's unsuccessful effort to create an income tax, and he quickly became so respected that, with one fiery oration, he killed a bill that would have made it a crime not to stand when the national anthem was played. When Wilentz spoke, a lobbyist recalled, near-total silence would fall in the boisterous assembly chamber. In 1969 Wilentz cemented his reputation for integrity: he supported a conflict-of-interest bill that would have barred lawyer-legislators like himself from doing business with the state and then retired from the assembly rather than gamble that the bill would die—a gamble, as it turned out, that he would have won. Even after leaving office, Wilentz stayed active in politics from his perch at the family law firm, serving on Governor William Cahill's tax policy commission and working behind the scenes to vet Byrne's candidates for education commissioner. Soon after Wilentz's appointment as chief justice, his predecessor summed him up: "He has the mystique of moral leadership," Hughes said.

Wilentz had a forbidding public image—austere, arrogant, aloof—but his colleagues on the court found him warm, humane, self-deprecatingly funny, and given to small kindnesses, like supplying pickled herring and coffee cake for the justices' conferences. Still, the justices recalled him as private and reserved: "You didn't get close to Chief Justice Wilentz," one told an interviewer. The Wilentz court had made plenty of controversial decisions before the *Abbott* case arrived on its docket—voiding a surrogate-mother contract, declaring hosts liable for accidents caused by their drunken guests, and, most prominently, putting teeth into the earlier *Mount Laurel* ruling requiring the suburbs to open their doors to low-income housing. Governor Kean condemned the 1983 *Mount Laurel* ruling as "communistic," and in 1986, when Wilentz came before the state senate for reappointment to the court, Republicans seized upon an emotive, populist issue to derail him: his residency. For years, Wilentz had spent half the week at his New York City apartment, and since 1980, when his adored wife began breast-cancer treatment, he had lived there virtually full time. Although the state had no residency requirement for judges, New Jersey's inferiority complex was inflamed. After two tense days of hearings, hours of legislative debate, and fevered behind-the-scenes negotiations, Kean, committed to judicial independence even for a judge he disagreed with, brokered a compromise under which Wilentz promised to spend more time in New Jersey. The chief justice kept his seat by a single vote.

By 1989, when the *Abbott* case reached the court, Wilentz's job was safe until the mandatory retirement age of seventy. His wife had lost her battle with cancer the year before, but Wilentz was still stretched thin between his administrative duties at the head of New Jersey's court system and his responsibility to help decide supreme court cases. The court's eight-month delay in resolving *Abbott* might have irked the Florio administration, but to the justices themselves it seemed an unremarkable result of the chief justice's heavy commitments and the special demands of the vast *Abbott* record. Contrary to legislative rumor, however, the court was never seriously divided. At the first conference after the September 1989 oral arguments, at least four of the seven justices supported Morheuser's position. Several were genuinely outraged at what the record revealed about conditions in inner-city schools. The leaking roofs, broken plumbing, and lack of heat in urban school buildings shocked Justice Gary Stein, a Republican who had worked as Governor Kean's chief policy adviser before joining the court. "It was shameful for the state to have school buildings that were so decrepit," Stein said years later. "I just felt it was evidence of callousness and neglect."

The morning after her dramatic committee testimony, Morheuser picked up her copy of the decision that would become known as *Abbott II*. The court had wanted what one member called the "thunderclap" of unanimity, and all seven justices had concurred with the opinion. But Wilentz had written it, and an extraordinary piece of writing it was, a long, detailed appeal to the state to live up to its constitutional promise of education for all children. "We find that under the present system, the evidence compels but one conclusion: the poorer the district and the greater its need, the less the money available, and the worse the education," Wilentz wrote. "That system is neither thorough nor efficient."

The court's reasoning echoed Judge Lefelt's decision nearly two years earlier, and the ELC case on which that decision had been based. Poor children needed more resources for their education, but the state's school-funding system provided them with less, the justices ruled. The state had claimed that mismanagement and socioeconomic destiny accounted for urban educational failure, but the justices rejected those arguments. Whatever mismanagement existed in urban districts, it could not account for the disparities between rich and poor, and better management alone could not cure those disparities. And however difficult the task of educating the children of poverty, the state was obligated to try. "If the claim is that these students simply cannot make it, the constitutional answer is, give them a chance," Wilentz wrote. "The Constitution does not tell them that since more money will not help, we will give them less; that because their needs cannot be fully met, they will not be met at all." The state had blamed urban school boards for failing to tax at necessary levels, but the court saw that failure as the inevitable result of forcing school districts to share a depleted tax base with a struggling municipality.

At the heart of the state's case had lain the proposition that spending levels had little bearing on educational quality. The justices admitted that research showed money alone would not improve schools. But, the justices ruled, the state had not proved that money was irrelevant, and without clearer proofs, the court would not disregard the conventional wisdom that money mattered. "If the claim is that additional funding will not enable the poorer urban districts to satisfy the thorough and efficient test, the constitutional answer is that they are entitled to pass or fail with at least the same amount of money as their competitors," Wilentz wrote. Not every justice entirely agreed: Marie Garibaldi, the first woman justice and the court's most conservative member, believed the state's argument had merit. Sure, money helped, Garibaldi thought, but without better teachers and administrators, even a well-funded district would fail. Garibaldi could have dissented, but she decided she could win more ground by concurring with the majority and pressing her liberal colleagues to call for school district accountability. No sign of her qualms surfaced in public.

Like Lefelt, the supreme court justices wrestled with the proper definition of a thorough and efficient education, expressing dissatisfaction with both the state's process model and ELC's input model. Significantly, Wilentz pushed far beyond the *Robinson* court's definition of T&E as "that educational opportunity which is needed in the contemporary setting to

equip a child for his role as a citizen and as a competitor in the labor market." Rather, the Wilentz court held,

> Thorough and efficient means more than teaching the skills needed
> to compete in the labor market, as critically important as that may
> be. It means being able to fulfill one's role as a citizen, a role that
> encompasses far more than merely registering to vote. It means the
> ability to participate fully in society, in the life of one's community,
> the ability to appreciate music, art, and literature, and the ability
> to share all of that with friends. As plaintiffs point out in so many
> ways, and tellingly, if these courses are not integral to a thorough
> and efficient education, why do the richer districts invariably offer
> them? ... If absolute equality were the constitutional mandate,
> and "basic skills" sufficient to achieve that mandate, there would
> be little short of a revolution in the suburban districts when par-
> ents learned that basic skills is what their children were entitled to,
> limited to, and no more.

ELC had suggested no concrete standard against which to measure districts for T&E, but ELC had shown that whatever the standard, poor urban
districts weren't meeting it, the court ruled. Accordingly, a remedy was
called for.

This was the issue that had dominated the justices' deliberations
from their very first conference. In the *Robinson* era, the supreme court
had declared the state's school-funding law broadly unconstitutional and
left the solution to the legislature, but the legislature's statewide solution
had failed to close the gap between rich and poor. The Wilentz court was
determined to mandate a workable remedy, and the justices had decided
that a narrowly tailored decision was more likely than a sweeping one to
force compliance.

Years later, surviving justices could not remember who first proposed
their solution: limiting *Abbott II*'s declaration of constitutional insuffi-
ciency to the state's poorest urban schools. Morheuser's case had focused
on failure in poor, inner-city schools and success in rich, suburban ones;
she had barely mentioned conditions in the hundreds of districts that
lay in between those extremes, or in the dozens of poor rural districts.
The court cobbled together a list of the districts it meant the legislature to

help: those districts that were defined as "urban" on a 1984 Kean admin-istration list and that also fell into the bottom two groups on the Depart-ment of Education's socioeconomic scale, derived from the 1980 Census. Then the justices excluded urban, poor Atlantic City, because gambling casinos pumped up its property-tax base. Twenty-eight districts made the final cut.

If the list of beneficiaries was limited, however, the benefit was star-tlingly ambitious: instead of making do with less than other school sys-tems, the justices ordered, the twenty-eight poor urban districts must be funded at a level "substantially equivalent" to per-pupil spending in the state's richest suburbs, those districts in the top two socioeconomic categories on the Education Department's scale. Had the remedy been in place for the 1989–90 school year, it would have cost the state an additional $440 million, a roughly 13 percent increase in the school-aid budget. Even that level of parity, which would boost urban spending in New Jersey above the systemwide average in almost every other state, might not be enough to address poor students' needs, the justices added: "in addition, their special disadvantages must be addressed." The court's mandate—extra help for the disadvantaged, on top of parity spending for regular education—would soon earn its own shorthand: parity plus.

While *Abbott II* dictated new spending priorities, however, it left to the legislature crucial decisions about how to comply. Unlike Lefelt, the supreme court justices did not explicitly recommend a foundation for-mula rather than a guaranteed tax base formula. They left it to legislators to decide whether to cap local spending or to let it rise unchecked, whether to fund poor districts at the current spending levels of the rich-est or instead to level down the rich. Although, as the Florio team had ex-pected, the justices invalidated minimum aid, the basic grants paid to every district regardless of wealth, they left intact most of the traditional funding structure, with its separate, non-wealth-based allocations for programs like special education. The justices also did something else that would have far-reaching political significance: they sidestepped the teacher-pension issue. Years later, surviving justices did not remember spending much time discussing pension funding, and in the written opin-ion, the issue took up only a few sentences. The court agreed with ELC that state payment of teacher retirement costs undermined equity, since rich districts with better-paid teachers got proportionately more state pension aid. But the *Robinson* court had continued the system to avoid administrative confusion, and the *Abbott* court decided to do the same, "without foreclosing the possibility that such aid may be constitutionally infirm."

Although *Abbott II* deferred to the legislature on specifics, it left no doubt of the court's attitude—Wilentz's attitude—toward the inequalities in the state's public education system. "The fact is that a large part of our society is disintegrating, so large a part that it cannot help but affect the rest," Wilentz wrote, in one of the decision's many eloquent evocations of the plight of the urban poor. "Everyone's future is at stake, and not just the poor's. Certainly the urban poor need more than education, but it is hard to believe that their isolation and society's division can be reversed without it." The lives of the poor were empty and desperate, filled with crime, drugs, early pregnancy, and lifelong despair, he wrote; social institutions had failed them, leaving them with abiding bitterness and little hope for the future. Children, he wrote, deserved better:

> The students of Newark and Trenton are no less citizens than their friends in Millburn and Princeton. They are entitled to be treated equally, to begin at the same starting line. Today the disadvantaged are doubly mistreated: first, by the accident of their environment and, second, by the disadvantage added by an inadequate education. The State has compounded the wrong and must right it. . . . After all the analyses are completed, we are still left with these students and their lives. They are not being educated. Our Constitution says they must be.

ELC celebrated. A day after the ruling, the telephones were still ringing constantly, feeding the growing stack of pink message slips, many reading simply, "Congratulations." Supporters sent flowers; notes and cards flooded in. Florio's newly appointed education commissioner sent a handwritten message. Another admirer addressed Morheuser as "Madam Freedom Fighter." For three days, Morheuser couldn't stop smiling.

Predictably, Republicans were dismayed. The leader of the state senate's Republican minority slammed the court for ignoring the needs of the middle class. "The court is requiring working-class people who reside in middle-income communities who drive around in Fords to buy Mercedes for people in the poorest cities because they don't have cars," he said. Privately, some Floriocrats agreed. Although the governor had praised the ruling, some of his aides were unhappy. By avoiding the pension issue, Treasurer Berman knew, the court had exposed the administration to NJEA's fury. By insisting poor districts had to spend as much as the richest, rather than simply provide equivalent services, the court had ensured that any solution would be unnecessarily expensive, education advisor Corcoran thought. And by entitling poor districts to as much funding as the rich—to more funding than the middle class—the court had cast the issue in politically unpalatable terms. "The court produced a decision almost perfectly designed to foster resentment in the great majority of parents—and voters," two Florio aides wrote years later.

The administration was stuck with the decision, however; now it had to revise QEA to comply with it. Berman thought the administration should ask the court for immediate clarification of how "constitutionally infirm" continued state funding of teacher pensions might be, but he was overruled. Instead, the bill was tweaked: the court's twenty-eight poor urban districts, plus two more that had been overlooked, were labeled "special needs districts," eligible for extra funding that could raise them to parity with rich districts within five years. With the new fiscal year only three weeks away, the administration and its legislative allies began a full-court press for the complex, controversial package. The Democrats voted to limit the length of legislative debates; in protest, Republicans gagged themselves with red bandanas. Angry tax opponents sent the assembly speaker envelopes stuffed with toilet paper. Late one night, technicians drafted a new amendment adjusting the calculation of property values for certain northern New Jersey school districts, to ensure an extra $6 million for one powerful Democrat's constituents.

On June 18, less than two weeks after *Abbott II*, the legislature began a series of marathon, late-night sessions to pass Florio's budget, the income and sales tax increases, and the new school-funding formula. Though Morheuser had qualms about aspects of QEA, she swallowed her doubts and lobbied in Trenton; ailing Democratic legislators tottered from their beds to cast crucial votes. The night of the sales tax vote, a closed-door assembly caucus stretched to seven hours as the leadership tried to win over the holdouts, but Speaker Doria denied twisting arms. "We just explained the political realities," he told reporters blandly. One after another, the bills slipped through, most by one vote; not a single Republican voted for the tax increases.

After a decade of Reaganite tax cuts, Florio's tax package was national news. If New Jersey's governor could raise taxes and survive to reelection, pundits suggested, he might herald a sea change in American politics. The early signs weren't good. Poll numbers were terrible, NJEA had vowed revenge, and 101.5's listeners still raged. Even U.S. Senator Bill Bradley, a popular Democrat campaigning for reelection against a little-known opponent, was facing questions about where he stood on Florio's tax hikes, although as a federal officeholder he had had nothing to do with them. Corcoran's staff monitored the call-in shows, telephoning angry on-air callers after the broadcasts to point out that their taxes weren't going up and their districts' school aid was. The Democrats ran radio ads touting Florio's program, cabinet members strolled Jersey Shore boardwalks explaining the package to voters, and in August Florio attended a Middlesex family's barbecue to tell his story in a just-folks setting. Theoretically, Florio's story was a good one: QEA would give many middle-class districts a boost, and most citizens would pay no more in income tax. That message just wasn't getting through, however. The state income tax increase would not take effect until January 1, 1991, but on January 1, 1990, a federal Social Security tax increase had begun taking an extra bite out of paychecks; on the boardwalks that summer, taxpayers told Berman over and over that their state income tax was up, even though they made too little to feel anything but the federal tax hike.

Still, the Floriocrats felt optimistic. From Byrne's political near-death experience a generation earlier, they extracted a hopeful message: if you did the right thing and toughed out the criticism, voters would ultimately come around. Legislative leaders were less sanguine. To them, the public-relations efforts seemed too little, too late. Years later, they would insist the administration had promised a marketing offensive that never materialized. QEA would not take effect until the 1991–92 school year, but the budget crisis had forced a freeze in state school aid for 1990–91; as a result, local property taxes were rising to cover new costs, and voters were mistakenly blaming the new law. The governor had promised that his initiatives would reduce property taxes. Unless he was proved right before November 1991, when the whole legislature faced reelection, lawmakers feared for their seats. That fall of 1990, proposals for revoking the QEA's pension-cost shift multiplied. Senate President John Lynch, one of the state's most powerful Democrats, tried to give angry voters a new target, stridently criticizing school boards for granting teachers double-digit annual raises. In the flush 1980s, when the pay structure was absorbing Kean's minimum-teacher-salary mandate, generous contracts had been common, and districts anticipating a QEA windfall were still spending profligately, Lynch charged.

Voter anger could not be deflected. In the 1990 election, Democrats lost ground even in stronghold counties, and, most shocking, Bradley came within 56,000 votes of losing his U.S. Senate seat. The next day, a contrite Florio promised to reconsider his initiatives, and by year's end he had agreed to suspend the pension shift until a blue-ribbon commission could examine QEA. As 1991 dawned, state senate leaders were hammering out amendments designed to rein in school spending and guarantee property tax relief. The assembly's preferences had compressed the previous year's legislative timetable; now the senate took the lead in forcing through the amendments.

Behind the scenes, Florio urged that QEA be permitted to take effect, but legislative leaders were adamant: an election was coming, and if they left the law intact, they would lose. On March 14, 1991, Florio reluctantly signed the amended law, known as QEA II. The new law redirected $360 million from school aid to property-tax relief, delayed the pension shift for two years, and placed more restrictive budget caps on school districts. Supporters called QEA II a responsible curb on government spending, but, predictably, Marilyn Morheuser was enraged. "The legislature caved in to the anti-fairness forces in New Jersey," Morheuser wrote. "The Quality Education Act is no longer a funding scheme designed to support Quality Education throughout the state of New Jersey. It has become a tax relief law, built on the backs of poor and minority children. Once again children of color have been sacrificed on the altar of political expediency."

As a political expedient, however, QEA II was a failure. Although the pension shift had not yet taken effect, in the 1991 legislative elections the still-outraged NJEA refused to endorse anyone who had voted for it.

The National Rifle Association, furious at Florio's assault-weapons ban, helped fund and organize the antitax forces. And in November 1991, for the first time in twenty years, the Republicans won control of both houses of the state legislature, by veto-proof margins. For Democrats, the outcome of their eighteen-month struggle with tax reform and school funding could hardly have been worse: they had adopted worthwhile but unpopular policies, watered them down before they could prove their worth, and paid the political price anyway.

The strangest aspect of the QEA debacle was the stark divide between public perceptions of the law and its reality. The conventional wisdom ran something like this: Florio, who had promised not to raise taxes, had raised them $2.8 billion, more than any governor in New Jersey history. That money came from working people struggling against the deepening recession and from suburban districts with excellent schools, and it went to poor inner-city districts likely to waste it on nepotism and patronage. The truth was quite different. Although everyone paid higher sales taxes, the income tax increase touched only the wealthiest one-sixth of taxpayers, and most of the $2.8 billion in new taxes, including the entire unpopular sales tax increase, wasn't funding schools at all—it was plugging the budget deficit and funding state takeover of the cost of local services. Of the $1 billion that was going to schools under QEA I, only half was earmarked for the thirty special needs districts covered by the *Abbott* ruling; like the Byrne-era school-funding law, QEA I directed much of its new money to middle-class districts, with their rich cache of voters. QEA II further skewed the allocation: under the amended law, school aid rose by $800 million, and the urban special needs districts got just over a third.

A year or two later, conventional wisdom added another charge to the QEA indictment: all that money had made no difference to the quality of urban education. Few realized that QEA II's stringent new budget caps had prevented poor districts from spending all their extra school aid on schooling: the special needs districts got $287 million in new money but could increase their budgets by only $195 million, with the overflow diverted to tax relief. Still, even if poor districts had not received quite the windfall of popular imagination, taxpayers had a right to wonder what the new money had bought, and no one seemed entirely sure. Urban test scores remained generally low. The Department of Education had sent teams of experts into each special needs district to suggest spending priorities, but the teams had worked fast, their reports were sketchy, and the state did not require districts to adopt the recommendations. Health-insurance costs had eaten up much of the aid increase, and murky school-district accounting made it difficult to track spending: budgets did not identify new QEA money as such, and dollars earmarked for, say, special education sometimes went to other programs. The Education Department hardly helped matters with its ham-handed efforts to demonstrate QEA's value. One public-relations document erroneously claimed QEA money had built an elementary school that had actually been paid for out of a fire insurance settlement. The mistake made the whole report look like a tissue of lies.

Years later, a team of academic researchers, including Margaret Goertz, the school-funding expert who had testified for ELC in court, would conclude that poor urban districts had spent their QEA money in reasonable ways: by hiring new teachers to cope with growing enrollments, by reinstating programs canceled in earlier budget crises, by reducing maintenance backlogs. Poor districts might not have been models of efficiency, but neither were rich ones, and to the researchers, none seemed egregiously mismanaged. The public had seen QEA as radically redistributive, but in the end, the law did not close the gap between rich and poor. Although rich districts lost some state aid, they forestalled the biggest threat—the pension shift—and kept their spending up by raising taxes. Despite Senate President Lynch's accusations, teacher salaries had risen only slightly faster in poor districts than in rich ones, the researchers found; after three years of QEA, the poor districts still paid their teachers less.

Whatever the reality, Marilyn Morheuser preferred not to ask whether QEA money had been spent well, just as, years earlier, she had preferred that Steve Block speak less openly about rampant political interference in urban schools. Morheuser still wanted ELC to focus, laser-like, on funding inequities and to avoid strengthening the state's case by questioning poor districts' management choices. The legislature's rapid retreat from the QEA reforms had only heightened her suspicion of accountability talk, and eventually her exquisite sensitivity to anything that

smacked of backsliding embroiled her in another behind-the-scenes battle with a would-be ally.

The Association for Children of New Jersey (ACNJ), one of the state's
best-known child-advocacy organizations, usually addressed child-welfare
and juvenile-justice issues, but in 1992 ACNJ decided to look into how
QEA money was being spent. When Morheuser saw the results late that
summer, she was furious. "If this report is released, its main effect will be
to give aid and comfort to those in New Jersey who continue to fight
against the provision of equal educational opportunity for poor urban
children," she wrote to urban school superintendents. She minutely cri-
tiqued the report's methodology; she sent ACNJ's board a fiery letter, accusing the organization of endangering her cause; she stopped speaking
to ACNJ's leaders and resisted a mutual friend's efforts to heal the breach.
In her fury, she apparently did not notice that the hated report was really
rather mild—in places, even helpful to her cause. The report detailed the
terrible problems facing poor urban districts and emphasized how badly
they needed money. Then it criticized the Department of Education's un-
willingness, or inability, to set firm priorities and ensure that districts
funded them. "Our conclusion is that there is presently no way to tell
with any certainty and accuracy how the special needs districts utilized
their 1991–92 funds for educational improvement," ACNJ wrote. Despite
Morheuser's anger, the report was released. Press accounts focused on
the Education Department's failures, and the story quickly faded.

Perhaps Morheuser's anxiety was especially high that fall because she
was once again back in court. Three months after the enactment of QEA
II, Morheuser had filed court papers arguing that the new law was an
inadequate response to the landmark *Abbott II* ruling a year earlier. Characteristically, Morheuser had wanted to accuse the state of deliberately
ignoring *Abbott II*, but colleagues persuaded her the public would never
accept so extreme a claim. Instead, ELC argued that even if the state were
making a good-faith effort to comply, good faith was not enough; *Abbott II*
required results. Although Morheuser had hoped to convince the state
supreme court to hear the new case directly, a bare majority of justices
voted to send the case to a lower court for trial.

As trial preparation began, Morheuser was pleasantly surprised at the
attitude of the state's lawyers. In the Lefelt hearing, she had accused the

state team of deliberate delay aimed at bankrupting ELC, but the new state lawyers seemed far more willing to move quickly. By spring 1992, the state's lead lawyer was Benjamin Clarke, a thirty-seven-year-old New Jersey native who had attended law school in part to emulate his godmother, Dorothy Kenyon, a pioneering civil rights lawyer. Colleagues in the state attorney general's office admired Clarke's penetrating intellect and stylish writing; legend had it that one lawyer had decorated his own office door with a page from a brief Clarke had edited so brutally that, amid the scribblings and crossings-out, only a single word—"and"—remained untouched. Clarke's thirty-something second, William Brown, had also had a youthful interest in progressive politics: after college, he had worked as a community organizer in Chicago.

Morheuser had a new assistant as well, Jonathan Feldman, not yet thirty, who had joined ELC after *Abbott II* and thought of the case as the new *Brown v. Board of Education.* Even before he took the job, Feldman had heard Morheuser was a difficult boss, and soon he too experienced her perfectionism, her yelling, her insistence on getting her own way. Most days, she sent him out to fetch her lunch; at times, Feldman felt like a gofer with a law degree. Balancing the petty irritations, however, was the excitement of working on a major case with a compelling, dedicated advocate. From Morheuser, Feldman learned never to give up.

ELC's preparations were marching ahead. Once again, the trial plans were compiled in sky blue loose-leaf binders filled with inches of paper—dozens of numbered sections outlining the case and organizing the computer printouts documenting each point. "The major problem is shifting political sands," Morheuser wrote in February 1992. "We have analyzed funding data released by the Department of Education in December. As of this writing, however, all of that analysis must be redone because of new data. . . . But this may not be the end. Almost daily we hear of changes the Republican controlled Legislature is contemplating. Such changes will again require new analyses."

Data analysis lay at the heart of ELC's case. Even by the standards of school-funding litigation, QEA was extraordinarily technical: years later, state lawyer Ben Clarke would say that only the federal tax code was more complicated. Even ELC had not initially understood why the QEA's formula was failing to close the spending gap between rich and poor districts.

School-funding expert Margaret Goertz finally put the pieces together during a meeting at Morheuser's apartment one day. Deep in the law, Goertz found the flaw that meant QEA could never ensure parity for poor schools, the supreme court's bottom-line demand.

Under the now-defunct Byrne-era funding law, the Department of Education had calculated each district's aid entitlement and presented the legislature with the statewide total; nearly every year, the legislature had appropriated too little money to fund the formula fully, forcing districts to make do with less. To make the process more predictable, QEA's authors had decided that each year, the state should decide the size of its total school-aid pie and only then divvy up the slices among districts. The total pie would increase annually at a rate tied to income growth, ensuring that school aid would not grow faster than the income taxes that paid for it. Under QEA II, the first slice cut from the school-aid pie covered teachers' retirement costs; next came slices covering the cost of transportation and of targeted programs like special education. Whatever was left was foundation aid, covering general education costs. Coincidentally or not, the formula paid first for aid programs benefiting the rich at least as much as the poor; only the last slice went disproportionately to the poor.

To divvy up that last slice—foundation aid—on the basis of district wealth, the state first used the per-pupil foundation amount to calculate how much each district should spend. Then the state calculated how much of this amount each district could contribute from local taxes—its "fair share." The richer the district, the higher its fair share would be. Finally, the state subtracted each district's fair share from its total budget and allocated foundation aid to make up the difference, if any. To help close the spending gap between rich and poor, the state increased the foundation-aid entitlement for the thirty poor special needs districts by a percentage known as the "special needs weight," permitting poor districts to increase their spending faster than other districts. The special needs weight was set at 5 percent for the first two years of the law; after that, in alternate years, the state could change it.

In her Eureka moment, Goertz saw the flaw in this complex machinery. The special needs weight provided the only link between the goal, spending parity for rich and poor districts, and the means of achieving that goal—state foundation aid. Only by adjusting the special needs weight as necessary could the state ensure that poor districts got enough foundation aid to spend at parity. And although QEA *permitted* the state to adjust the special needs weight, it did not *require* the adjustment. Therefore, the law did not guarantee parity spending, as the supreme court had required. Worse, the structure of the law made it unlikely the state would ever adjust the special needs weight. Since the total size of the school-aid pie was predetermined and foundation aid was the last slice to be funded, every extra dollar of foundation aid for poor districts meant one less dollar of aid for middle-class districts. With big spending gaps persisting even after the first years of QEA, *Abbott II* compliance would eventually require huge increases in funding for the poor and equivalent cuts in funding for the middle class—a political impossibility, ELC was sure.

Clarke knew ELC was right that QEA did not guarantee spending parity, so he argued that a lack of guaranteed success did not equate to guaranteed failure: the state might achieve parity by increasing the special needs weight, even though QEA did not require the increase. A moment of truth was fast approaching, however: if Florio did not recommend an increase in the special needs weight on April 1, 1992, he could not do so again until 1994. That March, the governor's legal aides distilled the issues: "Failure to recommend an adjustment could be extremely detrimental to the case. . . . Plaintiffs have consistently argued that the necessary adjustments to achieve parity will not be made, thus the absence of a recommended adjustment substantially bolsters that position. . . . On the other hand, increasing the special needs weight will be perceived politically as a giving of further aid to already heavily-subsidized urban districts." Fighting for his political life, Florio did not increase the weight, and Clarke figured his case was lost before it had even been tried.

Behind the complicated technical issues lurked a big political question: would the state continue paying the full cost of teacher pensions? NJEA's raw political power had already muscled a two-year postponement of the pension shift, but ELC was pushing for the shift eventually to take effect. In May and June 1992, as ELC prepared for trial, David Long, the school-funding lawyer who had organized the case before Judge Lefelt, took depositions from pension experts to prove that full state funding of teacher pensions unfairly subsidized rich districts.

A confluence of factors was weakening ELC's support for the pension shift, however. In theoretical terms, it made sense to reorient the state's school-aid system toward the poor by distributing the big pot of pension aid according to district wealth. Politically, though, the position was difficult. Not only NJEA but also every other major education organization opposed the pension shift because of the new pressures it would put on local spending. NJEA's anger over the issue had helped force the legislative retreat to QEA II, and NJEA's refusal to endorse legislators who had voted for the pension shift had helped put the legislature in Republican hands. Now, in the spring of 1992, a new threat to the *Abbott* decision materialized: powerful Republican state senators proposed amending the state constitution to eliminate the "thorough and efficient" clause on which the *Abbott II* parity guarantee rested and to substitute a clause entitling poor districts to spend only 10 percent more than the state average. Every major education group condemned the plan, but, to Morheuser's astonishment, NJEA's opposition seemed lukewarm: only the pension issue roused the union's passion. Although legislators quickly withdrew the proposed amendment, the episode had brought home to Morheuser the crucial importance of building a unified pro-*Abbott* coalition—and she feared that ELC's lonely support for the pension shift was undermining that effort. "It became clear that although we might well win on the one issue in question, we could also lose forever the chance to assure equal, high quality education for poor children," Morheuser wrote to funders.

If Morheuser had begun questioning the political wisdom of ELC's position, researcher Steve Block had begun questioning its substance. Months earlier, two suburban superintendents from the Garden State Coalition of Schools had visited Block to explain how the proposed pension shift could force rich districts to cut programs, degrading educational quality. Block was sympathetic: ELC should not espouse a position that would reduce educational opportunities for anybody's children, he felt. Furthermore, Block had begun to realize that fiscal reality was undermining QEA's reformist potential. Pension costs were growing faster than the income factor that would be used each year to increase the size of the school-aid pie. If the state stopped paying for teacher retirement costs, over time, every school district, including the poor urban ones, would have to spend more and more foundation aid on pensions for adults, rather than programs for children.

Block soon persuaded Morheuser that ELC's position on the pension shift might be mistaken. "My God," Morheuser wondered. "What am I going to do?" Then she thought of Jim Zazzali. Zazzali, a former state attorney general, had spent years on ELC's board in the 1980s; now in private practice, he represented NJEA. He was the perfect go-between. Zazzali brokered talks between Morheuser and NJEA, and eventually the two sides reached an agreement: ELC would stop litigating the pension shift, and in return NJEA would support only pro-*Abbott* legislation.

ELC's board, stacked with Morheuser's old friends and colleagues, usually did little more than rubber-stamp her wishes, but the proposed rapprochement with the teachers' union gave even this compliant group pause. ELC was abandoning its clients' claim on hundreds of millions in state money and allying itself publicly with a group that did not always put children's interests first. To some board members, that smacked of sellout. But Morheuser had made up her mind, and in the end, she carried her board with her. "ELC was maturing politically," Steve Block concluded years later. One day in mid-July 1992, Morheuser and NJEA announced their new alliance, and Morheuser withdrew her legal claim to the pension money. Within a year or two, NJEA's executive director had joined ELC's board, and the teachers' union began making annual five-figure donations to ELC.

By the time Morheuser and NJEA announced their new alliance, the QEA trial was already underway, before a judge, Paul Levy, whose prickly personality contrasted markedly with Lefelt's even temper. As a young lawyer in the 1960s, Levy had worked with civil rights supporters in Trenton; later, he had held the number-two job in the state attorney general's office. When the *Abbott* case reached his docket, the fifty-something Levy had been a judge for more than a dozen years; in one prominent case, he had awarded the government of the Philippines control of a New Jersey estate that deposed Filipino president Ferdinand Marcos had bought with money looted from the national treasury. Levy was smart and hardworking, but he was known not to suffer fools gladly. In 1988, facing a barrage of complaints, he had apologized from the bench for publicly demeaning lawyers who appeared before him unprepared. Recalling the incident

years later, Levy said his cutting comments had been justified. He regretted his apology.

In Levy's courtroom, the protracted run-up to the Lefelt hearing had
not been repeated: the new trial had begun in July 1992, thirteen months
after ELC challenged QEA II. Missing as well were the sharp disputes that
had characterized the previous hearing; the new trial was notable for its
large areas of agreement. Clarke and Morheuser agreed that the spending
gap between rich and poor school districts had narrowed but not vanished since the passage of QEA, they agreed that only an increase in the
special needs weight would achieve parity, and they agreed that QEA did
not mandate such an increase. What they disagreed about was how to in-
terpret these facts—as evidence of failure to meet the *Abbott* mandate, or
as evidence of a good-faith effort to comply.

Just because the parties agreed didn't mean the trial was simple,
however. Almost every day brought testimony from an expert or a bureaucrat about school spending, aid calculations, and tax rates, testimony
that even the state's legal trade paper described as "dense" and "tedious."
Only two of the seven witnesses discussed what urban districts wanted to
buy with new state money—preschool programs, guidance counseling,
school-based health clinics, smaller classes. "We are losing kids every single day, and we know that we pay later," the Jersey City superintendent
testified. "We pay through the criminal justice system. We pay through
the welfare system. We, the taxpayers, are paying all over the place, and if
we invested our money earlier . . . we might offset some of the later costs
and problems in our society." Connoisseurs of small ironies could savor
the fact that the Jersey City superintendent, now an ELC witness, had been
appointed by the state during the school takeover the Kean administration had promoted as an alternative to increased school funding.

Like the Lefelt hearing, the Levy trial drew intense press attention as
it opened—the first day, lawyers stepped off the elevator into a gaggle of
reporters and camera crews—and almost none as it continued. Soon it became clear that journalists weren't alone in finding the proceedings dull
and confusing: Judge Levy made no secret of his frustration. "When I went
to college, I studied statistics and one of the textbooks was *How to Lie with
Statistics*," Levy said irritably one day, as a state bureaucrat explained yet
another chart. "What are you talking about?" he interjected another day,

as Morheuser cross-examined a witness. "You're having a conversation here that the two of you know all the buzz words. I don't know what you're doing." Levy was an able judge with a head for numbers, but he knew nothing about school funding, and he was simultaneously handling a complex insurance-company dissolution that required him to organize hearings involving thirty law firms and to coordinate settlements with judges across the country. His *Abbott* decision, he knew, would go directly to the state supreme court, and as witness followed witness, he began to realize that he did not understand the opaque QEA statute. Levy hated unprepared lawyers, and he hated feeling unprepared himself. "I was just worried I would write something dumb to the supreme court," he acknowledged years later.

On the eighth day of testimony, Levy finally told the lawyers he needed help: the trial would be suspended while they explained QEA to him. The exasperated Morheuser characteristically had little patience for the judge's human frailty. "His reason—that he does not understand the issues—arises from the State's deliberate and continuing attempt to confuse the judge, and his own reluctance to immerse himself in the issues," she reported to her funders. "This state of affairs is almost unheard of, especially in such an important case." That fall, Clarke and Morheuser spent an off-the-record day guiding Levy through QEA's tangled thickets. At last, he understood the statute. In November, four months after the trial's start, Levy heard a ninth and final day of testimony; the trial transcript filled thirteen hundred pages.

Morheuser expected a quick victory, but the months wore on with no ruling. Levy was still immersed in insurance litigation. Then, in the summer of 1993, Levy won a coveted promotion to New Jersey's appeals court, effective September 1. The judge buckled down to finishing his two big cases, releasing his *Abbott* opinion on August 31, his last day on the trial bench. The rambling decision was hardly a masterpiece of legal writing, and here and there minor factual errors suggested haste. Morheuser had little to complain about, however: Levy agreed that QEA II did not guarantee spending parity and therefore violated *Abbott II*, and he found that the state had not provided enough money to meet the extra needs of disadvantaged students. Three years after *Abbott II*, the case was headed back to the supreme court.

But QEA, the subject of Levy's ruling, was dying, whipsawed between political opposition and new fiscal pressures. By January 1993, yet another blue-ribbon commission was working on yet another funding formula, and Florio signed a stopgap law that gave poor urban districts an extra $115 million and continued state funding of teacher pensions. "You will be interested to know that during the weeks of negotiations on this matter, the Governor's Counsel called me in for a special meeting at which he assured me that if I didn't agree to the funding finally worked out, Governor Florio would veto the bill," Morheuser bragged in a letter to a funder. The one-time '60s rebel had taken her place at the table where New Jersey politicians divvied up public money out of the public eye.

But not for long. Governor Florio was up for reelection in November 1993, and signs pointed to a tough race. He was facing Christie Whitman, the Republican who had almost upset Bill Bradley in the 1990 U.S. Senate race, and pundits saw the election as a referendum on the unpopular tax increase. Over the summer, polls suggested Florio would eke out a victory. Six weeks before the election, Whitman promised to cut state income taxes 30 percent in three years, and Democrats derided the proposal as a desperate gamble. But ethics charges against close advisers hurt Florio's campaign, get-out-the-vote efforts in urban Democratic strongholds fell short, and NJEA, still furious over the pension shift that had never happened, withheld its endorsement. On Election Day, Whitman beat Florio by one of the narrowest margins in state history.

As the *Abbott* case moved in and out of the courts, ELC's fiscal fortunes had ebbed and flowed. The early 1990s had seen the usual money struggles. Every October, as her fiscal year began, Morheuser would beg donors to help close the inevitable budget gap—$133,000 in 1990, $50,000 in 1991, $130,000 in 1992. Even small expenses loomed large: she solicited $3,000 from an insurance company for copying costs, $1,103.58 from a sympathetic law firm for deposition transcripts. The foundation money ELC had once relied upon was increasingly scarce—in at least one case, Morheuser wrote, "Because the foundation trustees are frustrated by the failure of State officials to comply with the *Abbott* decision, they have decided to provide no funding for our work."

To make up the shortfall, Morheuser turned to the poor urban school districts that stood to benefit from increased state funding. They were not officially her clients—as she had always insisted, her *Abbott* clients were schoolchildren, not school districts—but during and after the near-death funding crisis of 1988, a handful of districts had given ELC money. In 1990–91, Morheuser began soliciting such contributions more aggressively; the following year, she urged districts to sign contracts committing them to a dollar-per-student donation to ELC. The appeals bore fruit: in 1993, twenty-four of the thirty special needs districts gave ELC a total of $205,000, more than half that year's donations.

ELC's increasing financial dependence on school districts had problematic aspects, however. Although *Abbott* consumed most of ELC's time— 69 percent, Morheuser wrote in one fund-raising letter—ELC also represented students in disputes with school officials over services such as special education. Now ELC lawyers' salaries were being partly funded by institutions they might have to confront in court, a conflict of interest that Morheuser, desperate to keep ELC alive, chose to ignore. From time to time, however, oddities surfaced. In April 1992, Morheuser wrote to Newark's superintendent, soliciting a donation. Two months later, she wrote him again, pointing out that Newark lacked the legally mandated policy on transporting homeless children to school. "I realize that affording homeless children what they need is a huge problem for Newark," Morheuser wrote. "I hope that the summer will provide you and your staff the time to establish a transportation policy for these children." Would Morheuser have written so empathetically had she not needed Newark's $50,000? Perhaps even she didn't know.

As Morheuser maneuvered to keep ELC afloat, she fought her own battles with ill health. In 1991, arriving for an appearance at the Plainfield public library, she slipped on the steps and broke her nose and wrist. She hired a nurse to help her make dinner, change clothes, and feed the cats; as her wrist healed, Morheuser added the nurse, Paula Bryant, to her ad hoc New Jersey family. Bryant was in her late thirties, an African American who had grown up working class in Central Jersey. Over dinner, night after night, Morheuser told the stories of her childhood, her convent years, her work in the civil rights movement, her interview with Martin Luther King Jr. After a while, Bryant refused to take any more of Morheuser's money;

by then, they were just hanging out. They shopped for Morheuser's huge Christmas list, went to stage shows and museums, and sampled Newark's ethnic restaurants. Once, they were hypnotized together, Morheuser in an effort to stop smoking, Bryant in an effort to lose weight, but Morheuser kept her cigarettes, and all those restaurant meals sabotaged Bryant's diet.

Early in 1993, as Morheuser waited for Levy's decision in the QEA trial, her health again took a turn for the worse. In June she canceled an ELC board meeting because of an unspecified "health problem for which I am receiving daily therapy." "The problem should be resolved by the fall," she added. Perhaps she did not yet know the truth, or perhaps she was not yet ready to admit it: ten years after her cancer treatment, the disease was back. She had recovered quickly from her 1983 ordeal, but this time was different. By July 1993 she had begun radiation treatments; by December she was undergoing chemotherapy; by March 1994 she was describing her regime as "a new and more invasive chemotherapy." She rescheduled board meetings, she felt too sick to accept an NJEA achievement award in person, and her friends began to sense an unwelcome change in her personality. Morheuser had always been a complicated woman: her warmth and generosity, her intense enthusiasms and inspiring dedication, had coexisted with her hectoring demands and her tendency to punish perceived betrayals with excommunication. But her illness seemed to magnify her anger and mutate it into paranoia. Soon, events were approaching a crisis.

The supreme court had scheduled arguments in the QEA case for May 2, 1994, and despite the rigors of her treatment, Morheuser insisted that she would argue *Abbott*: "The children need me," she told her old friend Annamay Sheppard, a longtime ELC board member. But Morheuser's colleagues were becoming increasingly worried that she could not carry off the arguments, and their anxieties only intensified when a bad reaction to chemotherapy forced her to ask the court to postpone the arguments until mid-May. Gently, colleagues began trying to persuade Morheuser to let ELC founder Paul Tractenberg, still a member of the board, argue instead. Morheuser resisted; she accused her old friends of betrayal. One afternoon, Sheppard spoke to Morheuser by phone and hung up convinced that she had finally persuaded her to pass the argument to Tractenberg. A couple of hours later, Sheppard and Steve Block dropped by Morheuser's apartment, stopping en route to buy her a bouquet of red roses. By the time they arrived, Morheuser was coldly furious. She had rethought her conversation with Sheppard; now, as she saw it, everyone was trying to get rid of her.

Tractenberg was uniquely empathetic to Morheuser's agonized struggle to hold onto her work, for he too was battling cancer; he had been diagnosed with lymphoma in March and was himself undergoing chemotherapy when his colleagues asked him to argue *Abbott*. He was reluctant—he had his own health to consider, and he knew Morheuser would be angry. But eventually he agreed, and eventually Morheuser was persuaded to turn over the documents he needed. Tractenberg was feverishly preparing for the argument when Morheuser called back some days later. She was feeling better, she said. She would do the argument after all. Tractenberg was stunned: surely Morheuser still wasn't up to the task. ELC had told the supreme court that Tractenberg would speak, and now Tractenberg telephoned the court's clerk to ask what he should do. Would the court risk another postponement by scheduling Morheuser for the argument? The clerk brought back the justices' answer: they wanted the arguments to take place on schedule, and therefore they wanted Tractenberg to speak. But if Morheuser was strong enough, they would give her extra time to speak, too.

On May 24, 1994, Marilyn Morheuser and Paul Tractenberg traveled separately to Trenton. Morheuser felt too angry and betrayed to ride with her old companions-in-arms. Tractenberg argued the bulk of ELC's case, but as they had promised, the justices found time for Morheuser. To some of her colleagues, it was clear that Morheuser was not at her best: her rambling, unfocused remarks were not the Marilyn they knew. But the justices were kind, even deferential. Less than two weeks later, in a speech to Rutgers Law School's graduating class, one of them offered an unusual tribute to "the courage, the persistence, the skill, and the devotion to her clients' cause" she had shown over the many years of *Abbott* litigation. Although her case was still pending before him, the justice said, he thought it was "pardonable" to offer "a salute to a valiant lady and a splendid lawyer."

The arguments had given ELC reason for optimism. Chief Justice Wilentz had demanded to know how long the court should wait for the state to achieve spending parity between rich and poor districts, and the relatively conservative Justice Garibaldi had expressed frustration that the state had still not found a nonfiscal way to gauge educational parity. "They have frankly stonewalled us on this point all the time," she said.

Seven weeks after the argument, in July 1994, the supreme court issued its *Abbott III* ruling. The unsigned opinion was far less dramatic than *Abbott II*. Although the court found that QEA II had shrunk the spending gap between rich and poor, the justices agreed with ELC that the law did not guarantee the gap would close entirely. Clarke, the state's lawyer, had acknowledged that QEA, while technically still the law, was likely to be superseded soon, and now the justices gave the state until September 1996 to enact a new spending law and until the 1997–98 school year to reach parity. They also noted that the state had done no study of the special educational needs of children growing up in poverty. The goal of educational success for the poor could not be reached unless state officials identified the programs that would achieve it, the justices said. Clarke was satisfied: he had hoped to win his new boss, Governor Whitman, breathing space to meet the *Abbott* mandate, and now she had it.

Marilyn Morheuser was enjoying a brief respite from the pain that had wracked her in April; her doctor had prescribed male hormones, and during that summer of 1994, they seemed to be working. A week after the *Abbott III* ruling, she left for St. Louis to visit her sister's family and attend an assembly of the Sisters of Loretto. There, she officially committed herself to a new form of fellowship with the order she had left thirty-one years earlier, pledging, in a contract written in a hand grown shaky with illness, to support the order's work as a non-vowed "co-member." That decision, she wrote, would "formalize what has never ceased to be. Lorettos are my sisters. Loretto is my home." By the spring of 1995, her brief respite over, Morheuser was ailing again, coming into work less and less. With no one in charge, ELC began to disintegrate. As staff departed, vacancies remained unfilled. Morheuser was too ill to raise money, and the board worried about the budget. No one was making decisions. Morheuser stayed home sick, or called in with pointless, irrational mandates. One day, she demanded that a magazine subscription be canceled to save money. Her desperate illness had pitilessly exposed all ELC's structural weaknesses: the board's excessive deference, the organization's near-total dependence on one individual, Morheuser's failure to delegate responsibility, the lack of succession planning.

Everyone but Morheuser was beginning to realize she would never return to ELC. The trustees were in an impossibly painful position. ELC was falling apart; they had to replace Morheuser with someone healthy enough to hire staff, raise money, testify in Trenton, and pursue litigation. Morheuser disagreed, however, and they could not bear to hurt her. She had recruited many of them for the board precisely because they were her friends, and they loved and admired her. Firing her was unthinkable, for reasons not only of friendship but also of public relations: across New Jersey, *Abbott* was identified with the indomitable, charismatic ex-nun who had fought so tenaciously for urban schoolchildren. That spring of 1995, Paul Tractenberg, who had survived his own cancer battle, circulated a memo calling for Morheuser to retire, draw her full salary and benefits as emeritus director, and mentor her replacement. Somehow, Morheuser dragged herself to the meeting at which the board discussed Tractenberg's memo. Half-tearful, half-belligerent, she begged the board not to replace her. "The Education Law Center is my life," she said. "It's what's keeping me alive. Don't take it away from me."

Tom Cioppettini, Morheuser's surrogate son, felt caught in the middle. On one side were board members, probing for the latest prognosis; on the other was Morheuser, deeply wounded by the board's efforts to remove her. That April, after her last hospital stay, Morheuser had made Cioppettini promise she would never be hospitalized again; a month later, she told him she no longer wanted treatment. She wanted to be home, with her cats and her plants. She took pain medication, and she kept on chain-smoking. Cioppettini hired round-the-clock nursing help. All summer long, Morheuser tried to work from home, but by September, she knew she was dying. At last, she accepted the solution Cioppettini and the board had brokered: she requested a disability leave, officially keeping open the possibility that she could return to ELC if she recovered. Everyone knew she would never recover.

Morheuser no longer wanted visitors; she hated people to see her bald and shrunken. In October, her sister Marie came for a final visit. For dinner with Marie, Tom, and his wife, Morheuser put on a housecoat, a turban, and one of the colorful scarves she loved, and they talked and laughed about Marie's children, Marilyn's elaborate Christmas celebrations, the way she had always teased Tom. Morheuser had begun to dream that her dead father was waiting for her. The next week, Cioppettini left for a long-planned visit to his sister in Ohio. The last night of Morheuser's life, Paula Bryant held her hand and told her she had to let go. "We'll miss you," Bryant said, "but you're tired." Two hours later, on October 22, 1995, seventy-one-year-old Marilyn Morheuser slipped away. She had waited for Tom to leave.

Cioppettini rushed back from his trip, chose the scarf she would wear in her coffin, and went to the funeral home to say good-bye. As he gazed at the tiny, childlike body that had once contained that huge spirit, he told her he was glad her pain was over. He knew she would always be a part of his life. Three days later, Morheuser's friends, colleagues, and admirers gathered at a Newark church to remember her. Giant bouquets of red roses decorated the church, and Cioppettini had asked the priest to end the service by inviting every woman in the audience to come forward and take a single blossom, in symbolic affirmation of the way one life can touch so many others. "This is what she gave to me," Cioppettini said, years later. Five weeks afterward, in fulfillment of Morheuser's wishes, Tom Cioppettini and Paula Bryant buried her ashes at the Loretto motherhouse in rural Kentucky. Morheuser had lived frugally on her ELC salary, and Cioppettini managed her money carefully during probate; in the end, her estate totaled over three hundred thousand dollars. In her will, Marilyn Morheuser made a few small bequests, but the bulk of her property she divided between the two institutions she had loved most. She left half to the Sisters of Loretto and half to the Education Law Center.

8

The Children of *Abbott*

For journalists awaiting the *Abbott II* ruling that spring of 1990, Ray Abbott's story was a gift from the news gods. The alphabetical accident that had put Ray's name at the head of Marilyn Morheuser's plaintiff list provided the peg on which to hang a human drama more compelling than school-funding statistics and constitutional analyses could ever be. Reduced to the shorthand of daily journalism, what the reporters found seemed to fit comfortably with their middle-class readers' cherished assumptions about inner-city life. No one had time to find out whether Ray's story was more complicated than that. Yet complexity would prove to be a hallmark of all the *Abbott* children's stories. The *Abbott* plaintiffs fashioned their lives from the raw materials their families and schools provided, and like young people everywhere, they made foolish mistakes—sometimes deadly serious ones. Unlike their more fortunate peers, however, they did not always have a safety net to cushion their fall.

Ray Abbott

In the years since the filing of *Abbott v. Burke*, Luci Abbott had married George Cherry, the African American school administrator eighteen years her senior, and given birth to another son. Luci was still teaching in the Camden public schools, but when Ray reached high school, she enrolled him in a local Catholic school. One day that fall, Ray arrived home to find police cars at the door. His house had been burglarized, and the thieves' takings included something Ray cared about—a gift from one of his stepbrothers, a gold dog tag engraved with Ray's name. Perhaps the break-in was the last straw; in any case, on Super Bowl Sunday 1984, the family moved to Pennsauken, the blue-collar town bordering Camden.

Academically, Ray was floundering in Catholic school, and the lessons he was learning there were surely not what Luci had hoped. Behind the football field one lunch hour, a friend had offered Ray his first marijuana joint. Although Ray had coughed his brains out that time, he had kept smoking on weekends, eager to join the in-crowd. For the second semester of ninth grade, Ray begged to transfer to Pennsauken's public high school, where he was quickly assigned to special-education classes for children with perceptual impairments and social problems. Ray hated the stigma of special classes, and his grades and test scores stayed low; by tenth grade, he was cutting school weekly, sometimes sneaking home to watch TV all day. Once, Luci returned unexpectedly and found him in his room having drinks and cigarettes with friends.

Luci's frustration was mounting. She arranged sessions with counselors; she lost her temper and yelled; she confined Ray to his room and confiscated his radio, his stereo, everything but the bed and dresser. Ray applied his ingenuity to getting around that punishment: his girlfriend smuggled in a clock radio and a supply of soda, candy, and chips, and Ray eventually learned to escape by climbing out his bedroom window and sliding down the garage roof. On his return, loaded with whatever goodies he'd bought, he would come in by the basement and sneak through the house to the bedroom his parents didn't know he'd left.

Finally, Ray came up with a plan that, to his sixteen-year-old mind, seemed promising: he would leave home to live with his uncle and aunt in California. True, he hadn't cleared this plan with them, but he figured it would all work out if he could find the money for the trip. Over the years, Ray had taken a few dollars from his mother's wallet here and there, but the afternoon he decided to run away, he crossed a line. As Luci napped, he stole her credit card and headed off to the automated teller machine. By the time Ray reached the bank, his stepfather was there with the police, and as the cops took Ray into custody, the furious boy looked at the man who had raised him and spat out the unforgivable: "Nigger." For the first and last time in their relationship, George slapped Ray across the face. A few days later, Luci and George handed Ray over to the custody of

New Jersey's child welfare authorities. They must have been frightened and desperate, hoping against hope that someone could reach their boy. But to Ray, their decision was a terrible rejection. He felt alone.

For the first month or two, Ray lived in a group home in Camden, but soon he was enrolled in a six-month Outward Bound–style program run by Project U.S.E. (Urban Suburban Environments), a nonprofit that contracted with the state to provide wilderness trips and residential living for wayward teenagers. Hiking and canoeing in the Everglades, Ray learned something about interacting with other kids. He was having fun, looking forward to the upcoming whitewater-rafting expedition in Virginia. One afternoon, back at Project U.S.E.'s headquarters on the Jersey Shore, he was playing football with the other boys when he tore ligaments in his knee. The injury meant no rafting trip, and no more Project U.S.E.

But Luci refused to take Ray back for another exhausting round of truancy and punishment. Instead, her parents offered him a home in the tony Long Island summer community of East Hampton, where Ray's grandfather taught high school math. His mother's decision hurt, but Ray knew East Hampton from summer visits to his grandparents, and he accepted the new arrangement. Quickly, however, he slipped into his old patterns. He had earned almost no credits in his sophomore year at Pennsauken High School, and he had spent much of what would have been his junior year in group homes. Now, as an East Hampton junior, he found himself far behind, and once again he quickly lost interest in even trying to catch up. Then one night, at a dance party in someone's basement, Ray tried cocaine for the first time. Immediately, he was hooked. For a few months, he stayed in school and hid his addiction from his grandparents, but soon he was partying in rented hotel rooms all weekend, staying out all night, stealing the television and the VCR to support a crack habit that now cost him two hundred dollars a week. He officially dropped out of school in February of his senior year, but the rock-bottom grades he left behind suggested he had unofficially abandoned his education months earlier.

His grandparents tried to help. They found him a job at an acquaintance's shoe store, until Ray forged his grandfather's signature on a check and tried to buy sneakers to sell for drugs. They gave him a home, until the police found their missing truck abandoned on a dirt road, where Ray had skidded on the mud and smashed into a tree. After the accident,

Ray never slept another night under his grandparents' roof. His grand-mother thought Ray incapable of taking responsibility for his behavior, but years later Ray said he had been too ashamed to go back.

Ray's life was spiraling downward. He had held a few short-term jobs—he worked at a grocery store until he was caught stealing, and he did some landscaping off the books—but his regular income came from a drug dealer. Although Ray frequently dipped into the stock, he sold enough, or stole enough, to fuel his habit without cheating his boss. On days when he could not stay with friends, Ray broke into summer homes that stood vacant all week long, just to sleep, shower, or snack on the con-tents of the refrigerator. Each time, he left the house before the owners re-turned, and years later, he insisted that he had never stolen from these strangers the way he had from his own family. In May 1988, when Ray was nineteen, his luck ran out. One morning, as he arrived at his latest job, the police arrested him. Though he was quickly released on his own re-cognizance, the precarious balance of his life was tottering. One July day, Ray could not pay his drug dealer boss what he owed. The dealer threat-ened him, and Ray was frightened. He knew he was too far under; he longed to talk to his stepbrother back in South Jersey; he had a girl to see in Camden. He remembered that his boss had left the keys in his truck. Ray took the truck and drove home, had dinner with his stepbrother, saw the girl. The police found him in Camden.

Ray's legal problems mounted with dizzying speed. He had gotten probation for stealing from his grocery store job, and New Jersey gave him two years' more probation for taking the drug dealer's truck. He served ninety days for attempted burglary in the 1988 summer-home case, and the following year he got an eight-month sentence on another summer-home burglary charge. In jail, he got up at 4 a.m. to cook omelets or grilled-cheese sandwiches for other inmates and spent his downtime watching soap operas. In between jail sentences, he smoked marijuana instead of cocaine, drank, and hung out with friends; his mother heard from him at most once a month. He felt angry and hurt, and he told him-self he had no family any more.

When the *Abbott II* decision came down, Ray was in jail again—in Camden, charged with violating his probation in the truck-theft case by committing the second New York burglary. By then, reporters had been visiting for a couple of months; the headlines said "Abbott, now 21, in prison" and "For him, a lawsuit far too late." The connect-the-dots was easy: another tale of inner-city woe, another impoverished minority kid gone bad. Only a diligent reader would realize that Ray Abbott was a middle-class white kid from a two-parent family.

During visiting hours at the New York jail, Ray had met a woman called Carol, and when he finished his minimal term for violating his New Jersey probation, he moved in with her. Carol was older than Ray, a high school graduate with a school-age son and a job measuring chemicals for a cosmetics company. By the fall of 1991, Carol was pregnant; she and Ray married the day before his twenty-third birthday. But soon after, Carol introduced Ray to her friend Jean, a nurse, and Ray and Jean fell in love. Five months after his marriage, Ray left Carol and moved in with Jean. Three months later, he moved back in with Carol—to help her, he said years later, in the final months of her pregnancy. Carol gave birth to Ray's daughter in July 1992; the following month, he left for good and moved back in with Jean. Soon Jean too was pregnant. Ray worked odd jobs and smoked marijuana, although not, he insisted years later, anything harder. The way he remembered it, he and Jean were happy.

For months, Ray's mother Luci had been feeling sick, and by the time she saw a doctor in July 1992, her pancreatic cancer was inoperable. Her parents closed up their house and moved in to nurse their forty-five-year-old daughter through her final months as she grew weaker and her once-heavy frame wasted away. One day in September, Ray came to visit. He carried a plate of his grandmother's food upstairs to Luci's room, lay down next to her on the bed, and tried to help her eat. Ray and Luci wept together over their estrangement and apologized for the pain they had caused each other. It wasn't the first time Ray had told his mother he was sorry, but it was the first time he had meant it. He promised Luci he would never lie to her again; he said he would visit the next week. On the three-and-a-half-hour drive back to Long Island, Ray felt a great peace, as if a weight had been lifted from his chest, and before the week was over, Luci was dead. Although Ray and Carol were no longer living together, they brought their baby to the funeral, but outside the funeral home, one of Luci's grief-stricken relatives accused Ray of causing his mother's death. The bitter accusation was irrational—Luci had died of cancer, after all—but perhaps it cut too close to the guilt and shame Ray felt about his life. Enraged, he seized the woman by the shoulders. Onlookers pulled them apart before he could harm her, and Ray and Carol jumped into their car and drove home.

Jean's baby girl arrived on May 1, 1993, and less than two weeks later, Ray and Carol signed an official separation agreement. They were still wrangling over Ray's access to his older daughter, however, and three days later, Ray let himself into Carol's apartment and took two VCRs, a television set, a video game system, and a Sonic Hedgehog video game. In court papers, prosecutors alleged that Ray had stolen Carol's property to sell; the defense argued that Ray had acted out of frustration, hoping to push Carol into giving him more time with his daughter. "I admit it. I fucked up. I took some of the stuff from the house," Ray told the cops when they arrived the same night. He helped the police unload the missing items from his car, quietly submitted to handcuffing, waived his Miranda rights, and signed a statement admitting what he had done. For ten months, Ray languished in jail on an unreachable bail, until Jean hired a new lawyer who got the bail dropped. Ray, insisting even years later that he was not guilty of burglary, refused a plea bargain that would have drawn him a one-to-three-year sentence; instead, he went to trial, washing out his one new suit each night so it would be ready for court the next day. The trial in the late summer of 1994 lasted a week. In his summation, the prosecutor portrayed Ray as a user leeching off the women in his life, sordidly ping-ponging between his pregnant wife and his pregnant girlfriend. The jury took only forty minutes to convict Ray of burglary, larceny, and possession of stolen property, and later that year, the judge sentenced him to four to eight years in state prison, by far the hardest time he had ever faced. Ray was shocked by the result; perhaps he hadn't realized just how unsavory his life looked to outsiders. After the verdict, one juror called Ray "cocky" and "very unworthy." "Thank God we don't have to look at his green suit any more," the juror said. "We're spared that."

Henry Stevens Jr.

Henry Stevens Jr. was flourishing in the Camden public schools. In fourth grade, he read his paper on the first black pilot in front of the whole school and won an award presented at City Hall. In fifth grade, he was student council president, and every year, he made the honor roll. For sixth grade, he moved to the bigger, rougher East Camden Middle School. With two caring parents at home, Henry's family was different from his classmates': even in sixth grade, some of his friends could stay away from home for days, never bothering to get permission from parents who were barely home themselves. In school, fights broke out often, and stealing was rampant. When a teacher's pocketbook disappeared, every student in the class would be patted down in the search. Hardly challenged academically, Henry studied for tests the day they were given and measured himself against only a few other top students. One of his teachers spent each day reading the textbook aloud to her class; Henry suspected that her students were smarter than she was. Still, school was never dull: the violence and petty crime made sure of that.

The atmosphere inside East Camden Middle mirrored the edginess of the city outside. In Camden, walking on the wrong block—and everyone knew which blocks those were—could mean getting beaten up or losing your jacket. In sixth grade, Henry was riding his bicycle in the park near his school one Saturday when a bigger kid pushed him off and rode away. Although Henry and his father cruised the neighborhood for hours, they never found the kid or the bike, and Henry figured he should have known to get out of that park when someone bigger showed up. Camden children learned the rules young. Henry's little brother stopped trick-or-treating the year some older kids beat him up and took his candy. Fewer and fewer people were leaving their porch lights on for Halloween, anyway. In Camden, you didn't knock on strangers' doors.

Eventually, even Henry could not avoid trouble entirely. Siblings he knew from summer camp picked a fight with him at school one day. He defended himself and, thanks to the school's policy of punishing everyone involved in a fight, was suspended for the first time in his life. Henry's father suspected that his own visible political activism, his close ties to Camden's mayor, might have made his son a target, if not for the youthful bullies, then for school administrators anxious to avoid any appearance of favoritism. Whatever the truth, Henry Stevens Sr. wanted his son out of the Camden schools. Choosing private school was still politically problematic, so the Stevenses decided to send Henry Jr. to Haddonfield, an affluent nearby suburb whose public schools accepted out-of-town students in return for two thousand dollars in tuition.

In the suburbs, Henry Jr. was no longer an academic star—what passed for excellent work in Camden was merely very good in Haddonfield. He learned more complicated lessons elsewhere. His seventh-grade year, Henry was the only black student in the school. On his short walk from the train station, older kids in passing cars yelled "nigger" out their windows. Kids at school sometimes tried out racial slurs, too, and Henry learned to give back some of the same: if they fired off "spook" or "jigaboo," he could hurl "wop" right back at them. He didn't tell his parents, because he didn't want to go back to East Camden Middle School.

Despite Camden's abundant problems, Henry enjoyed living there. In Haddonfield, he felt he represented the entire black race, even after three more black kids enrolled in the school his second year there. At home, he was just another kid. High school lay ahead, however, and the choices looked unappealing. Henry knew nothing good about his neighborhood high school, Woodrow Wilson, and Haddonfield High School posed its own problems. Henry was beginning to get interested in girls, and there wouldn't be many African American girls to date in Haddonfield. Dating white girls, Henry already suspected, could prove problematic. Once, a middle school teacher had chewed him out for sharing a chair with a white girl, claiming they were violating the fire code. The other kids in the class had to explain the racial subtext before Henry got it. Teachers, he recalled, had never intervened when students tossed racial slurs back and forth.

In the end, the high school dilemma evaporated, because Henry Stevens Sr. found a new job with the Ohio teachers' union. The family moved to Columbus, where they were the only black family in an affluent white neighborhood. The city had spent years under a desegregation order, however, and the local high school was filled with African American students bused in from poor neighborhoods. With his Camden street smarts and his suburban Haddonfield gloss, Henry Jr. mixed easily in both worlds. He finished high school, earned a bachelor's degree in business from a local university, and found a customer service job. More than half the Woodrow Wilson High class of 1990—his class, if he'd stayed in school in Camden—dropped out before graduation.

Michael Hadley

The night before Lynnette Hadley left for college, she asked her mother, Lola Moore, how much money they had saved to cover her four years' tuition at a small Pennsylvania school. "Child, we don't have no money saved," Lola told Lynnette. "Mom, how we going to do this?" Lynnette asked. "On a wing and a prayer," Lola replied. The next day, with Lynnette on her way to school, Lola Moore registered for classes at the local community college. She worked two and sometimes three jobs, spending her weekdays as a receptionist in the Camden public schools, reading between phone calls, and her Saturdays standing at a Kmart cash register, using her downtime to study from the index cards stashed in the pocket of her smock. Sometimes other employees laughed at her diligence. They wouldn't work two jobs for anybody, they said. But four years later, in 1984, Lynnette collected a bachelor's degree in political science and came home to watch her mother get an associate's degree in law and justice.

Moore's middle child, Michael Hadley, was still ambling through the Camden public schools, and Moore was still unimpressed with the education he was getting. At East Camden Middle School, all the children failed the library skills section of their standardized test because, Moore found when she investigated, teachers wouldn't escort their students to the library and the librarian wouldn't pick the students up from their classrooms. (Too lazy, Moore concluded.) In high school, Michael earned Cs, and he knew he owed even those to Woodrow Wilson's low standards. He had friends whose mediocre Catholic school grades had miraculously become As when they transferred to Woodrow Wilson. As far as his mother could tell, however, Michael wasn't struggling with his work. Years later, she suspected friends had helped him finish his assignments.

Michael won his glory on the football field, as the quarterback of the Woodrow Wilson team, and in his senior year, he fielded scholarship offers from several Division I colleges. The recruitment was unrelenting, a barrage of letters, phone calls, and meetings. Coaches attended his games and stopped by his school, pulling him out of class to talk. Michael's teachers joked that he might as well not even start his work, since he was likely to be called away at any moment. After football season ended, Michael visited three of the schools that had offered him scholarships, eating at nice restaurants, meeting the coaches and their families, checking out the pretty girls. No one ever suggested he visit classes. His mother accompanied Michael on only one recruiting visit, to the University of Pittsburgh. She was looking for something more than restaurants and girls: she wanted Michael somewhere with a strong academic support system, and she was impressed with Pittsburgh's tutoring program. Michael was not prepared for college, Moore told the Pittsburgh coaches. They assured her they could help him, and Moore added her considerable influence to Pittsburgh's recruiting campaign. Michael went to Pittsburgh.

Although Michael had known he was poorly prepared, college still came as a shock. Wilson friends who had graduated before him had come home from college talking about parties and girls, not papers and tests. He had never written anything longer than five pages in high school, and the ten- to fifteen-page college assignments were daunting. The first paper he submitted to an English class came back covered in red pen; the professor had ripped it to shreds. The football program supplied tutors, and as he had in high school, Michael tried to do enough to stay eligible to play. He finished his homework, though sometimes only a half-hour before class; he usually wrote his own papers, though he sometimes submitted friends' work instead; he attended class, though he sometimes slid into large lectures five minutes before they ended, knowing he could still get oblivious professors to sign the card verifying his attendance. When Michael's grades slipped, someone in the football program would notify Lola Moore and urge her to give her son a pep talk. As the years passed, Michael kept his scholarship, but he was earning too few credits to graduate on time.

His biggest disappointment came on the football field, however. In college, Michael was no longer the star he had been in high school. He did not start on the Pittsburgh team; instead of quarterback, he played wide receiver and then, as a sophomore, defensive back. He struggled to learn the new position, to catch up with guys who had been playing defense for years. Football was his job now. How could football have stopped being fun?

He found his fun off the field. In four years of high school, he had drunk only a single six-pack of beer, Michael said years later, but in college he did his share of all-night partying. In the autumn of his junior

year, he gained more than 200 yards on kickoff returns in a nationally televised game, and afterward he celebrated with a marijuana joint. Over
Thanksgiving vacation, the team trainer called to tell Michael he had
failed a random drug test. Michael was suspended from the team and
barred from that year's bowl game appearance. Years later, Michael insisted he hadn't cared; back at school after the holiday vacation, he
recalled, while his teammates were swaggering around in their Astro-
Bluebonnet Bowl sweat suits, he was wearing the fashionable new Run-
DMC outfit he had gotten over Christmas. But his junior-year stumbles
continued. For the first time, Michael lost his academic eligibility for football and was suspended from summer workouts with the team. He considered dropping out of school, but his mother paid to enroll him in two
courses, and he got his grades up enough to rejoin the team.

Three years had passed—three years of limited playing time. His pro
football career prospects were dimming. In his senior year, Michael
worked out with the Pittsburgh Steelers, and two days later he tried out
with the New Orleans Saints, who told him he was "the best defensive
back at Pittsburgh that never played." But his legs were still sore from the
Steelers' workout, and he had become so muscular he had lost some of his
speed. The tryout went badly, and the Saints never called. Michael had
earned perhaps two years' worth of credits in his four years at Pittsburgh.
Although his scholarship entitled him to a fifth year, he left in 1989 and
spent a few months with a Canadian pro football team before he pulled an
Achilles tendon and was cut from the roster. Years later, Michael insisted
that the death of his dream did not break his heart. By senior year, he had
known it wasn't going to happen.

Lola Moore had wanted Michael to earn a bachelor's degree, but she
could not think of his college years as a total loss. For four years—four
volatile years, in which Camden's drug culture had devoured so many of
the young men he had grown up with—Michael had been far away, and
safe. For four years, Lola Moore had been able to sleep at night.

In 1989, the year Michael should have earned his degree, Moore graduated from nearby Glassboro State College with a bachelor's in criminal
justice. Glassboro hired her to start a program preparing teenagers for
college; a few years later, she returned to the Camden schools to manage
a Woodrow Wilson High School youth services center, where students

could get everything from physical exams to drug counseling, pregnancy tests to mentoring. Moore remembered the clerks who had mocked her for studying on the Kmart checkout line. They were still clerks.

After Canada, Michael came home to Camden, where, with the help of his mother's connections, he found a job in the school system. Despite his mediocre high school grades and his college stumbles, the Camden schools hired Michael Hadley as a substitute teacher.

The Figueroas

Blanca Figueroa wanted to get out of Camden. Years after her second divorce, she still grieved; sometimes she felt so hurt she couldn't breathe. In her imagination, California was the land of new beginnings, the place where pioneers traveled in covered wagons to start their lives over. A year after the *Abbott* case was filed, Blanca bought four hundred dollars' worth of clothes, farmed five of her six youngest children out to older siblings, and got on a bus to the West Coast with her six-year-old daughter, the baby of her huge family. In California, Blanca quickly found work as a babysitter and a housekeeper, filling in the gaps with welfare. A few months later, she sent for the older kids and moved into an apartment in a largely white and upper-middle-class southern California suburb.

When Blanca sent for her, Vivian was seventeen. She had finished her junior year at Woodrow Wilson High School, and her longtime boyfriend wanted her to marry him and stay in Camden. Instead, she embraced the new opportunity California represented, but her senior year there was isolating and painful. To the white students who made up most of the high school's student body, copper-skinned Vivian looked Mexican, and Mexicans were at the bottom of the social hierarchy. Vivian felt depressed. She missed her family back home, made no new friends, skipped the prom. When graduation day arrived, she felt like skipping that ceremony too, but she was the first of Blanca's children to finish high school, and she knew she owed it to all of them to march. Clad in a red cap and gown, Vivian accepted her diploma, and afterwards her family threw a party whose centerpiece was a cake topped with a tiny gowned graduate.

Vivian had been working since the age of twelve, when she cleaned a day care center to earn enough for a purple bicycle. Now, with her high school diploma in hand, she got her own apartment, worked a succession of odd jobs, and enrolled in community college. Through a housecleaning job, she met a man who found her work as a management trainee at his financial services company; she moved up in the field and rented a townhouse by the beach with one of her sisters. One day, an older brother phoned her at work, furious: somehow, he had just learned of the sexual abuse another relative had inflicted upon her when she was a child. Suddenly, there at her desk, all the memories Vivian had suppressed for years came flooding back. For months afterward, flashbacks ambushed her in the shower, and she raged at her mother for allowing her own painful childhood history to repeat itself.

Vivian stayed in California until 1991. Two years earlier, at a family wedding in New Jersey, she had met someone. When she moved back to the East Coast, their romance blossomed, and eventually they bought a house together in Pennsauken. In 1993, Vivian became pregnant, and they married. Vivian's husband was an operations engineer at a gas company; she earned thirty thousand dollars a year as a credit manager for a computer company. Twelve years after the filing of the *Abbott* case, Raymond Abbott, the son of a minister and a schoolteacher, was doing time for burglary, and Vivian Figueroa, the daughter of a welfare mother with a grade-school education, was living a middle-class life.

Orlando, too, had escaped the vise of poverty. Fifteen when Blanca moved, Orlando had done well enough in his California school to earn placement in honors courses, but he skipped class so often he was thrown out. Years later, he said he had stayed home some days because he had no clean clothes to wear. By senior year, he was fed up with school; he dropped out, got a GED, and earned his keep working in a restaurant, doing construction, fixing cars. He had been toying with the idea of college, but his childhood mentor, the police sergeant around the corner, urged him to consider a law enforcement career back home in New Jersey. In 1990, twenty-one-year-old Orlando became a Camden cop.

Blanca's younger children, however, were floundering. Frances had suffered in school in Camden, and California proved no better. In class, she clowned around and talked out of turn; teachers sent her to the principal's office, and she was kicked out of school after school. She gravitated to kids with links to California's notorious youth gangs. Blanca whipped her with a belt when she was caught shoplifting clothes and makeup at the mall. By thirteen, Frances was experimenting with marijuana and PCP. Blanca placed her in a group home, and Frances promptly ran away.

Hector, who arrived in California at eleven, was flirting with gang life, too. For his initiation into a neighborhood affiliate of the notorious Bloods, he endured a beating administered by the whole gang and proved his mettle in a one-on-one fistfight. He stayed out until 3 or 4 a.m., experimenting with alcohol, marijuana, sex, and petty theft. The Figueroas had moved so soon after the Camden schools diagnosed Hector as emotionally disturbed that he had never been placed in the small classes the diagnosis mandated, but in his California school, the classes seemed smaller than in Camden, and in the darkness of his dangerous new life, Hector found a bright spot: a teacher who cared about him. In adulthood, though he could no longer remember the man's name, Hector remembered his calmness, his knack for putting students at their ease, and the way he shared his snacks with the whole class. "He treated every student the same," Hector remembered.

Arlayne had never hated the Camden schools the way Hector and Frances had, but in California, where she arrived at the age of nine, she slacked off, too stubborn or too bored to earn the grades her test scores suggested she was capable of. She hung out with the same kinds of tough kids that Frances and Hector knew, kids on the margins of gang life. In sixth grade, Arlayne arranged to fight another girl after school, and the student body assembled to witness the spectacle. As the principal grabbed Arlayne to break up the fight, her shirt swung up, leaving her humiliatingly exposed in front of the whole school. She fought to get loose, hitting and scratching the principal in the process, and earned herself an expulsion.

Blanca was worried about her children—not only the younger ones, falling in with the wrong crowd in California, but some of the older ones, experimenting with drugs in New Jersey. Her pioneer's journey west had helped rebuild her spirit; she had stopped drinking and found a new man. It was time to go home. Two years after leaving Camden, Blanca came back. In 1985, she married her California boyfriend; in 1989, she committed her life to the Jehovah's Witnesses, who gave her counseling, taught her to read, and offered her troubled soul a measure of peace. "The only one that can help you straighten out your life is God," Blanca said years later.

Back in New Jersey, Frances started eighth grade in the Pennsauken schools, using a fictitious address to get around the inconvenient fact that she lived in Camden. The dodge was common enough: New Jersey's patchwork of tiny districts left plenty of children living tantalizingly close to schools far better than those they were legally entitled to attend. Using the address of a friend or relative to get around the residency requirements had become so common that districts with relatively disadvantaged neighbors sometimes hired staff just to ferret out the deceptions and ship offenders back to the places where their parents paid taxes. As it happened, however, the taxpayers of Pennsauken subsidized Frances' education for only a year. A carload of relatives watched her graduate from eighth grade, but ten days into her ninth-grade year, frustrated with the latest test or assignment she couldn't understand, she dropped out for good.

For the next three years, Frances drifted. Sometimes she lived with Blanca, sometimes with friends. She worked in a fast food restaurant and a T-shirt store; she drank, smoked pot, found a boyfriend, broke up with him, found another. Then, at seventeen, she discovered to her shock that she was pregnant. The catastrophe seemed total—her boyfriend was married, her mother would kill her if she found out—yet something in Frances shrank from the prospect of abortion. She decided to move in with Vivian in California. Frances threw her clothes into a motley collection of boxes and suitcases, talked Blanca into buying her an airplane ticket, and kept her secret from everyone but a sister or two. On the drive to the airport, as Frances sat in the car, edgy and miserable, her mother told her how proud she was of her, how well she would do in California, what a good role model Vivian would be. The flight took off; Blanca got back in the car with a grandson who had come along for the ride. "So Frances is going to have the baby in California?" he asked innocently. Apparently, one of Frances's confidantes had let her secret slip. Blanca slammed on the brakes.

The next few months were devastatingly difficult. Frances was young, pregnant, and scared, and her mother was not speaking to her. Finally, Frances got on a plane and came home to have her son. Her relationship with the baby's father soon ended. He was a drug dealer, and Frances wanted something better for her little boy. A year later, however, she was pregnant again, supporting herself on welfare, living with her new boyfriend in Pennsauken, and enduring nightmarish physical abuse. Her daughter was still a toddler when Frances finally extricated herself from the relationship.

One winter's day in 1992, Frances learned that the board allocating federally funded rent subsidies for the poor, the precious Section 8 vouchers, was meeting in nearby Maple Shade Township. The application deadline had passed, and the day was cold, but Frances walked the three miles from her mother's house in Camden to plead for the chance to move her children somewhere else, somewhere with better schools. "Please," she begged. "I need this opportunity. I want to change. I want better for my kids." She got the voucher and used it to pay for a sixth-floor apartment in a well-kept high-rise in Cherry Hill. Frances was still a single mother supporting her two toddlers with a telemarketing job; only a few miles separated her from the neighborhood where she had grown up. But she lived in the suburbs now. Her children would go to school in the suburbs.

Hector's New Jersey school career lasted only a little longer than Frances's. At Veterans Memorial Middle School, Hector once again felt humiliated and alone. His teachers embarrassed him publicly; he sat at his desk drawing, or lashed out angrily, cursing and throwing books. He stacked up punishments at a world-record pace, returning from one fifteen-day suspension only to earn another on his first day back. When he threatened suicide, the school sent him to counseling. In 1985, he failed seventh grade; the next year, he seemed poised to fail it again. This time, however, the school suggested an alternative: he could move on to ninth grade if he enrolled in Archway, a local private school that contracted with the Camden district to supply special education services for students with serious emotional or behavioral problems. Archway, however, was no improvement. Some of the students were far older than fourteen-year-old Hector and had been in even more serious trouble, and Hector found the academic program laughably easy. When he objected, the teachers told him he would have to wait for the rest of the class to catch up. Hector lasted two weeks at Archway before he begged Blanca to find him something else. She asked about having a tutor teach Hector at home, but as

Hector remembered it years later, the district told her home instruction was reserved for students too ill to attend school. Hector was through looking for options. He dropped out, and felt a load lift from his shoulders. At last, he was in control of his own life.

Drugs had been everywhere at Vets—kids brought joints to the playground—and in the years after his return to New Jersey, Hector had used regularly with a tight circle of friends and relatives, sampling crank and pot and developing a cocaine addiction. As he got older, however, he tired of spending hours in a vacant daze. Years later, he would say that he simply outgrew his habit. Soon after dropping out of school, he found a job that matched his mechanical aptitude: he worked at a body shop for two hundred dollars a week, cash. The money covered the rent on a shared apartment, and, once he was old enough to drive, he got his first car, a white '67 Nova with a red roof. He fell in love with a girl, reconnected with his father, and considered following in Orlando's footsteps and becoming a cop. For that, however, he would need a high school equivalency degree. Schoolwork terrified Hector, and his first foray into night school flopped. He was embarrassed to find himself covering sixth-grade material, and he bombed on a GED predictor test. But Hector was determined to build a life for his girlfriend; the next year, he tried again. This time, he was amazed to discover that he actually liked learning math. In fits and starts, he stuck with it and earned his GED. He took the civil service exam, passed with a respectable score, and settled down to wait for the police department to call. His big break seemed tantalizingly close.

Arlayne had returned to New Jersey before the rest of her family, moving in with an older brother in Pennsauken after her California expulsion. The transition was hard. In California, Arlayne had worn gang clothes, baggy black pants and red Chuck Taylor sneakers; in New Jersey, the girls were aping Madonna, wearing belts, bracelets, and neon-bright colors. Although Arlayne did not find her work particularly difficult, she arrived at school late, played hooky, and focused more on friends than books. To her dismay, she failed sixth grade. For a year or two, she bounced between relatives in New Jersey and California, attending part of seventh grade on the East Coast, picking up some night-school credits on the West Coast. Back in Pennsauken, Arlayne expected that her ninth-grade work in the California night school would be enough to get her into high school, but Pennsauken insisted that she return to seventh grade. Arlayne was tall and statuesque; at twelve, she could pass for twenty-one in a liquor store, and by fifteen, she was fending off advances from grown men. The prospect of returning to school with children three years younger was too humiliating to face. Arlayne dropped out.

Like Frances before her, she drifted, working at a mall food court, living sometimes with her mother, sometimes with friends, drinking and using cocaine, her habit financed by a relative's drug sales. One day, she and a girlfriend were high and giggly when Blanca dropped by and found them. Arlayne never forgot the hurt and anger in her mother's eyes. Like Frances, Arlayne got pregnant early and could not face the prospect of abortion; she was seventeen when her son was born, his father long out of her life. Arlayne lived on welfare; her family helped her get by. Once, when someone stole the money she had set aside to buy her baby a coat, a brother bought it for her. When her baby was three months old, Arlayne began dating again; like Frances, she had her second child, another boy, less than two years later. Arlayne's boyfriend was a drug dealer who spent part of her pregnancy in jail, and when he got out, they moved in together. She earned her GED with little trouble and enrolled in a computerized accounting program, finishing months later than planned because she had dropped out temporarily to nurse her kids through chicken pox. Like Frances's relationship, Arlayne's was abusive. Although her boyfriend never broke bones, drew blood, or left bruises on her face, he hit and kicked her head and legs, and then called his grandmother, weeping, to ask why he did this to the woman he loved. Arlayne was black and blue the day she finally took her two toddlers and moved out.

Dorian and Khudayja Waiters

Lynn Waiters' one-bedroom apartment in East Orange had gotten even more crowded. Through her job at the East Orange Tenants Association, Waiters had met a white housing lawyer named Jack; they fell in love and eventually married, and Jack moved into her cramped quarters, sharing the sofa bed with Waiters while Dorian and Khudayja slept in the bedroom. Their search for a bigger place proved curiously difficult—although no one was stupid enough to say so explicitly, Waiters was sure East

Orange landlords balked at renting to an interracial couple. Finally, the family found a three-bedroom apartment with broken windows and a burnt-out hole in the floor, and the landlady agreed to rent to them if they would fix the place up. They moved in a few months after *Abbott* was filed.

Waiters's new relationship shocked her children, who had grown accustomed to life in their tight three-person unit. Years later, Khudayja remembered her early childhood with rosy nostalgia: then, she and Dorian had been their mother's sole focus. She had read to them every night, and the three of them had walked hand in hand. Back then, they had been too poor for expensive sneakers, but they had been rich in love. Now everything was different: Jack was their mother's focus.

The move did not settle the children. The new apartment was burglarized three times in six months, despite the deadbolt locks on the door. After the second break-in, the television, stereo, bicycle, and jewelry were all gone; with nothing to take, the third burglar contented himself with scrawling "Omar was here" on the walls. Dorian and Khudayja were afraid to come home alone, lest they surprise a thief; in the car, they would duck down, lest a robber spot them. By then, Waiters was ready to leave the tenants' association, and in 1982, she took a new job with the state and the family moved to the Newark suburb of Maplewood.

The South Orange-Maplewood district, one of New Jersey's few racially integrated school systems, had a reputation for academic excellence that drew well-off families, both black and white. Waiters saw the difference in her children's education: classes seemed slightly smaller than in East Orange, the books and buildings were in better shape, and the teachers seemed more interested in discussing students' progress. Khudayja, who was nine when she moved, felt behind in her new fifth grade, but the orderly classrooms were nothing like the ill-disciplined circus in East Orange. Students seemed more motivated, and teachers had higher expectations. Years later, Khudayja still remembered the chemistry teacher who had told her she was smart enough to do much better than the C she had just gotten on a test. Dorian, who was eleven when he got to Maplewood, was still a class clown who saw school as more social event than academic imperative. In high school, he was found to have perceptual problems, a diagnosis that had apparently eluded the East Orange schools. Dorian was also charming and popular. He ran track, did back-flips for cheering crowds of classmates, and took a starring role in the high school production of *Guys and Dolls.*

The biggest struggles came at home, where both children clashed with their stepfather with increasing animosity. Dorian hogged the telephone for endless conversations with his friends and refused to listen to anything Jack said. He saw a therapist, who told his mother Dorian was self-destructive and would likely die young. One day, Dorian told Khudayja that he was gay: gossips were about to spread the news through their high school, and he did not want her to learn it that way. Khudayja was in the ninth grade when her parents finally tired of Dorian's disrespectful behavior and threw him out. He moved into a group home, and Khudayja, her best friend gone, was devastated. She threw a rock that broke windows on the sun porch; she raised her fists to her mother; she swallowed too many aspirin and spent time in a psychiatric unit.

Although counseling helped, Khudayja still suffered. Some days, too depressed to go to school, she would hide in the closet until her parents left for work. She began failing classes. Her relationship with her parents was so bad they did not even discuss college, although Khudayja hoped to go and was admitted to historically black Virginia State. Years later, she could not remember why she didn't enroll. The summer after her high school graduation, she was working at Bloomingdale's, spending weekends with a boyfriend in New York, coming and going as she pleased, paying little attention to her parents. They asked her to pay rent. She refused, and they told her to leave. With nowhere else to go, Khudayja moved in with her boyfriend, and when the relationship ended, she found an apartment in a bad neighborhood in Brooklyn. At work, however, she began to move up.

Dorian had flirted with college, spending a semester or two as a parttime student at Montclair State while working at a corner candy store, but eventually he settled into a job at Macy's flagship store in New York. He lived in a succession of low-rent apartments in the down-at-heel suburbs of Newark, sharing space with male friends in rooms with more rats than furniture. The volatility of his teenage relationship with his parents had subsided; sometimes he babysat for the younger brother who had arrived in 1992. Dorian was good-looking, funny, extroverted, and magnetic. He dressed beautifully, exercised until his six-pack was a work of art, and got a toll-free telephone number, to his parents' bemusement. But despite the clubbing, the cruising, the many boyfriends, Dorian seemed to Khudayja to be conflicted over his sexual identity, craving acceptance from his family, seeking security in relationship after relationship. She didn't think he was happy.

Caroline and Jermaine James

Mattie James had soured on the East Orange public schools when she saw them shortchanging her oldest son, Bunny. Now she saw her middle child, Caroline, falling into the same patterns, whizzing through her work, bored and unchallenged. To keep Caroline out of chaotic East Orange High School, Mattie found someone with a Newark address she could use and prepared to enroll Caroline in Arts High School, a selective magnet program restricted by law to residents of Newark. Before Caroline could enroll, however, a neighbor learned of Mattie's plan and tipped off Arts High's principal. Mattie was furious, but determined: she found a Catholic girls' high school she could afford and enrolled Caroline there.

Caroline's schooling wasn't the only crisis in the James family in the years after *Abbott*'s filing. Bunny was sick. After leaving high school and earning his GED, he had begun college and fathered a child, but now he had a brain tumor. In his late teens, Bunny underwent six operations, including one that lasted all day; the doctors told Mattie that he would not be able to return to his studies. He enrolled in engineering school anyway, but repeated illness eventually forced him to drop out.

Jermaine was a contented, optimistic child, more self-contained than his emotional older siblings, and he knew little about the health problems of the much older Bunny. Mattie shared painful information with her kids on a strictly need-to-know basis, and Jermaine didn't need to know. His mother, working at the East Orange Housing Authority each day and studying for a college degree nights and weekends, relied on a village to help raise her kids. The Jameses' landlady babysat, the AME church where Jermaine sang in the choir was within walking distance, and acquaintances who caught Jermaine throwing rocks or saw Caroline outside during school hours would report everything to Mattie. The village had its less savory members, too: by the time Jermaine was eight, local drug dealers had offered him work as a runner, but he always turned them down. Instead, he hung out at the public library, one of the last bastions of East Orange's more prosperous past. He and his best friend read every book they could find on Greek mythology and then went to the park to play at being Zeus and Apollo.

Like Bunny and Caroline before him, however, Jermaine finished his schoolwork quickly and then talked too much, disrupting class because he was bored. "Well," Mattie asked herself, "am I going to be a dummy and sit here and watch this happen all over again? No, I don't think so." As a single mother, she no longer had time for the intensive supervision she had provided when her older children were attending elementary school and she was a stay-at-home mom in close touch with their teachers. Caroline was in Catholic school, and Mattie wanted Jermaine out of the East Orange schools, too. When he reached fifth grade, she parlayed his singing talent into a place at the Newark Boys Chorus School and took a second job to cover the tuition. Jermaine immediately felt behind when he arrived at the chorus school, which assigned far more homework than he was used to, but the classes were tiny, and the teachers offered individualized attention. Between regular academic classes, the boys worked on their singing; Jermaine learned to love Bach and toured Japan with the chorus. Years later, he thought of the school as one of the foundation stones of his life.

Caroline was having a far less positive experience in private school. She hated getting up early to catch the Irvington bus, going to class with only girls, losing touch with the neighborhood kids who were attending East Orange High. Although she read *Macbeth*, earned good grades, and enjoyed frog dissection so much that she considered becoming a doctor, she was still distracted and unhappy. Her teachers noticed how often she stared out the window. For senior year, Mattie finally granted Caroline's wish to return to public school. By then, Caroline had covered most of East Orange High's graduation requirements in her Catholic school's more rigorous program. With algebra, chemistry, and physics already under her belt, she was finished with classes by noon every day, in time for a work-study job at Newark's airport. Mattie wanted her to go to college, and Caroline took the SATs and collected some applications. But at East Orange High, college counseling was minimal, and besides, Caroline didn't want to leave her boyfriend. She never finished her applications.

Caroline graduated from high school in 1986 and took a part-time job as a switchboard operator at a Newark hospital. Before summer's end, her mother had laid down the law: either go to college or get a full-time job with benefits. The hospital had an opening for a medical assistant, with free training. Caroline took the job. She could always go to college later, she figured. The next year, she moved to Newark; at twenty-three, she had a baby boy. After the birth, she broke up with her boyfriend. She was still working at the hospital. She still hadn't gone to college.

Jermaine spent four years at the chorus school, graduating from eighth grade in a class of eight. Mattie looked into private high school—the chorus school had connections to some of New Jersey's best—but the tuition staggered her. She knew she could not pay thousands a year for high school and then cover college costs, too, and although she felt too poor to pay for private school, on paper she looked too well off for financial aid. At last, she looked again at Newark's public magnet high schools. She and Jermaine still lived in East Orange; legally, Jermaine was not entitled to attend public school in Newark. Using a relative's Newark address, however, Mattie got Jermaine into selective, well-regarded Science High. Mattie had little trouble justifying the subterfuge to herself. "I felt that I pay taxes in the state of New Jersey," she said years later. "I just felt that it was unfair that you had to lie to get a good education for your child, because I couldn't afford to pay for the education I would have liked. Hey, if that's what I needed to do, then that's what I did. I was at that point, because the system was just making me really sick." Eventually, the Jameses began to suspect that school officials were happy to look the other way. A Newark coach lived down the street from them in East Orange. When Jermaine was a junior, he realized that the school had known for years where he really lived. No one had said anything, because he was a running star.

Running cross-country for Science High gave Jermaine his first insight into the inequalities that so galled Marilyn Morheuser. Science High was an excellent school, where students memorized Shakespeare and took a double period of science, but it was housed in a decrepit old factory building where the plumbing sometimes flooded and the heat didn't always work. With nowhere to run, the cross-country team sometimes practiced on the stairs at the Newark Y, which had no field, either, or ran in the street, which made students susceptible to shin splints. In his last two years, the poor training left Jermaine injury-prone. Science High's runners competed against teams from other small schools, usually suburban ones, and during meets on the manicured campuses of Chatham Township and Mountain Lakes, Jermaine and his classmates marveled at the beautiful tracks. Imagine if they had these facilities, they would joke: imagine how fast their times would be! The discrepancies never made Jermaine angry, but sometimes he could see the despair and hopelessness etched on his classmates' faces. "I hate this place," they would say, back in Newark. "Damn—I can't wait to leave."

Science High offered a way out. Its students were not rich, but they were motivated. They had to keep their grades up to remain there. At Jermaine's East Orange elementary school, carrying a book bag was the definition of uncool, but at Science High everyone took four or five books home every night. In senior year, the guidance counselor shepherded students toward their futures, urging the African Americans to apply to historically black colleges. Jermaine had been considering Syracuse, but a snowbound week there during a national track competition had dampened his enthusiasm. The brochure for historically black Hampton University pictured quite a few beautiful women, and a visit to the lovely Virginia Beach campus sealed the deal. As Jermaine left for college, his brother Bunny told him how proud he was.

Bunny's health problems had never completely disappeared, but his life seemed on an upswing: recently, he had started his own construction company. In September 1993, however, Bunny failed to show up at a wedding he and Caroline were supposed to attend, and Caroline called their mother in alarm. It was Mattie who found her thirty-year-old son's body. Jermaine came home for the funeral and decided to dedicate himself to finishing college in four years, because he knew that would have made Bunny proud.

The Knowles Children

For the Knowles brothers, the blow came wholly unexpectedly. One moment, it seemed, their family was happy and close-knit, their parents working, their father taking the kids camping each summer, joining them in pickup baseball games, and shepherding them on trips to the library and

the New York museums. True, the Irvington schools were overcrowded—
years later, Guy Jr. would remember attending class in a trailer, and Dan
would recall rooms so crammed that some students could not even find
chairs—but they did well and were content. Guy Knowles Sr.'s job with
Essex County Executive Peter Shapiro had ended after the 1985 gubernatorial election, when Shapiro lost spectacularly to incumbent Thomas
Kean, so Knowles found work as a mailman in Newark, and the family
moved there and enrolled the children in public school. And then suddenly, around the time that Guy Jr. was thirteen and Dan and his twin
Cristina were eleven, their parents' marriage collapsed, messily, bitterly.
Cristina was not quite as surprised as her brothers: she had always been
close to her father, and her emotional antennae had picked up earlier
hints of trouble. For all three children, however, the divorce changed almost everything. Their mother moved again, to the upper-middle-class
suburb of West Orange, where she crammed her four-person family into a
two-bedroom apartment rented from her sister. Their father, who had
tired of the post office, decided to change his life. His mother and sisters
lived in Florida, and he joined them there.

    Years later, Guy Knowles Sr. would say that he regretted leaving his
children behind in New Jersey, but he would insist that, even during his
Florida years, he was never completely out of touch. His children, however, remembered it differently: to them, it seemed that he vanished.
They were struggling in their new life. Although she had never volunteered answers from her preferred seat at the back of the classroom,
Cristina had always been a good student. In West Orange, however, she
suddenly felt unprepared, surrounded by students who seemed to know
facts she had never learned. In her city schools, she had grown accustomed to listening quietly, but in the suburbs, students spoke up freely,
and their teachers engaged them in discussions that Cristina often had no
idea how to join.

    Her brothers' problems were more serious, however. Guy Jr. was be-
coming increasingly disaffected with school. The West Orange public
schools had a solid reputation, but Guy Jr. felt out of place surrounded
by white kids. Some teachers, he was convinced, saw him through the lens
of prejudice. Once, when he misbehaved, the baseball coach scolded,

"You're not in Newark any more." Dan's anger and grief were so great that West Orange sent him to a counselor and assigned him to unusually small classes. Years later, Dan remembered with particular fondness the teacher who played Mozart to relax his five unhappy pupils. Still, Dan was antsy and unsettled. He refused to listen and walked out of class on days when he couldn't calm down.

The children's home life was equally difficult. Although they lived in a safe, well-kept suburban neighborhood, their aunt's house was run-down. The boys slept in the living room while their mother and sister took the bedrooms, and sometimes the heat failed. Their mother was still working crazy shifts as a telephone operator, and money was tight. Sometimes the food Gladys bought with her weekly paycheck would not last all week, and, years later, Guy Jr. would remember days when there was nothing for breakfast, when a dollar was all he had to feed himself for a whole school day, when dinner was a meal he ate with friends' families while his mom worked the overnight shift. Gladys had applied to get her children a free school lunch, but she earned too much to qualify, Cristina recalled years later.

Gladys Knowles had a new man in her life, and her children hated him. He cursed at them and shoved them around. No one was allowed to sit in the chair he had brought from his home to theirs. When he roughed them up, Dan would threaten to tell his father, and the boyfriend would taunt, "He ain't around! He ain't caring about you guys!" He was right, Dan thought. In his early teens, Dan seemed to be spiraling toward a grim fate. He broke windows, got into fights, and hung out with kids who used drugs, although years later he would insist he himself did not use. Perhaps Gladys had finally had enough when, sometime after Dan's eighth-grade year, her boyfriend packed up Guy Jr. and Dan, drove them down to Florida, and left them with their father.

Guy Sr. was remarried and working, initially as a clothing salesman, later as an HIV educator at a homeless shelter. Eventually, he and his new wife rented a big house and moved in all their children—her two; his three, when Cristina joined her brothers for a short visit; and a daughter they'd had together. The Brady Bunch it was not. Dan felt pure hatred for his father and the new woman in his life. He skipped school, smoked marijuana, and dedicated himself to making everyone feel as miserable as he did. One day, he got into a shoving match with his stepmother, and after that Guy Sr. drove his kids back to New Jersey.

After the initial adjustment, Cristina had regained her academic equilibrium in West Orange. She took honors classes, earned decent grades, graduated from high school in four years, and enrolled at a state college where she had once attended a summer program. Her first semester, she lived on campus and set to work spending a windfall that had dropped into her lap: the insurance-company settlement held in trust for her since the age of seven, when a drag-racing teenager had driven onto the sidewalk near her home and broken her leg. She paid tuition, bought a car, had fun with her friends, and the money evaporated. Years later, she thought wistfully of what she could have done with that forty thousand dollars. "I don't think an eighteen-year-old should ever have that kind of money," she said.

After Florida, Guy Jr. was finished with formal schooling. He dropped out, loafed for a while, and then found a job transporting corpses to the morgue at a Newark hospital. He didn't even think about how unsavory the work was—it was a paycheck, and his horizons extended no further than that. At first, he lived with his mother, and later, he moved in with his father, who had returned to Newark when his second marriage ended and resumed his old job as a mailman. In her second semester of college, Cristina moved into her own apartment across the hall. Looking back, Guy Jr. remembered his younger self as a decent kid who avoided doing anything that would shame his mother. "We never did any drugs or anything," he said years later. "We just didn't have any goals."

Dan had flunked ninth grade in Miami, so he started high school all over again in West Orange. For the next four years, he stayed in small classes, but he earned good enough grades to play basketball for his school and, to the astonishment of his family, he managed to graduate—the last of the *Abbott* plaintiffs to finish his public education. Now he knew he faced a crossroads. His friends were hustlers, selling drugs, marking time until the inevitable day their luck ran out and they ended up behind bars. If he stayed where he was, he knew he would probably follow them down that dead-end road. He knew he needed to get away. The U.S. Marines, he decided, would be his ticket out.

Leslie and LaMar Stephens

Tommi Stephens and her children spent nearly a year in Michigan while she healed from the pain of her divorce and thought about the future. Each day, a special bus took fifteen-year-old Leslie and her tiny daughter to the high school, where the baby spent her day at a nursery and Leslie went to class. Thirteen-year-old LaMar soon found he preferred his new junior high school, with its tree-filled campus, library, and hot meals, to Jersey City's School 14, a concrete jungle where kids sometimes set their fried-chicken lunches on the windowsills to thaw the ice-cold centers.

In the spring of 1982, however, Tommi decided to go back. The Jersey City public schools offered her a job as a substitute teacher, and School 29 placed her with a class of first-graders so recalcitrant that one of their previous six teachers was reported to have deserted before lunch on her first day. Little though they were, the children already felt like failures. They could not read, write their names, listen to a story, or sing a song; instead, they fought and hit each other. Tommi was determined to tough it out. As she told the colleagues who predicted she wouldn't survive Room 105, she had three kids at home who had grown accustomed to eating every day. She collected extra teaching materials from the school's reading specialist, took her class to the gym for group games, set up toy centers where well-behaved children were allowed to play, and consulted with parents by telephone. By the end of the year, her students could walk down the hall just as politely as any other class. "They were sweet little first-graders," she recalled much later, "almost a whole year behind."

As Tommi settled into her job, LaMar and Leslie enrolled at Lincoln High School. To Leslie, Lincoln looked more like a prison than a school, and LaMar felt lost in the tidal wave of students that inundated its chaotic halls every time classes changed. Still, he felt safe: neighborhood posses known as "crews" mediated disputes for their members, keeping in-school violence to a minimum. The crews were less dangerous than California street gangs. Although one, the Little Demons, specialized in strong-arm robbery, LaMar's crew, the Big Demons, preferred to hang out listening to hip-hop music.

Leslie graduated from Lincoln in 1984 and went on to college nearby, but years later she said she felt academically unprepared. LaMar—angry at the world, but mostly at his father, who had not visited his children in Michigan—was also getting little out of his schooling. In ninth grade, he spent weekends and after-school hours at parties centered on beer, marijuana, and hip-hop. Then the parties spilled into school hours, and LaMar began skipping school three times a week. With careful management, this news might never reach truant officers, he found. Although one particular English teacher would call your parents if you skipped class, everyone knew that certain teachers didn't much care whether you showed up or not. LaMar took chemistry with a teacher whose idea of a lesson plan was handing his students the Periodic Table of the Elements and leaving the room while they memorized it.

Looking back, LaMar could see how directionless he had been. But he was also a basketball point guard, and during his absence-pocked freshman year, his grades got so low that school rules forced him to watch every game from the bench. That frustration motivated him to raise his grades—not to As, certainly, but high enough to get playing time. In his junior year, however, LaMar quit the team, despite his coach's pleading. Tommi was working three jobs to keep her family afloat and save money for a house, and LaMar had decided to help her earn enough for a down payment. Tommi's day was long. She taught for seven hours at School 29, which had hired her permanently after her success with Room 105, and then she tutored at a parochial school for two hours. Finally, she hurried to Sears, where she worked in the business office until 9 p.m. LaMar took a job in the Sears credit department—he was so bad at the work that he figured people were still cursing his incompetence decades later—and in his senior year, they saved enough to buy a house in the working-class city of Orange. By then, Leslie had moved on: she had married her daughter's father, given birth to another baby girl, earned a medical assistant certificate from the community college, and taken a job with a health insurance company.

LaMar's imagination still flourished, as it had in his childhood. He considered a career in filmmaking, and Tommi's father, a self-taught photographer, sent him books. In sophomore year, LaMar wrote a comic script about a chaotic inner-city high school sprucing itself up for a visit from the mayor. He lined up a willing cast and took a pie-in-the-sky proposal to a school administrator: he needed cameras, he said, and permission to shoot on location at Lincoln. "Yeah, I need that too," the administrator told him. "Get out of my office." The next year, LaMar joined the school paper, contributing hip-hop criticism and a tragic fiction about a Kentucky transplant to the big city who became ensnared by drugs and, high on PCP, jumped off a building to his death. In his senior year, LaMar connected with Lincoln's rudimentary audiovisual department and shot school football games, though the high school had no TV channel to show his work. Instead, the coach used the films for training.

By 1986, when LaMar graduated from Lincoln by the skin of his teeth, he was dreaming of film school. With neither the grades nor the money for a top program, he enrolled at Essex County Community College, got straight As en route to a two-year degree, and considered transferring to a four-year college. Instead, he parlayed an internship at Jersey City's cable television franchise into a full-time job. He dreamed of becoming a producing mogul. With an editing whiz named Gerard, he created a show about local teenagers, and then he moved on to produce coverage of football and basketball games. But LaMar's first love was still hip-hop, and he proposed a new program to champion his favorite artists, those too often neglected by the mainstream. His boss, who called hip-hop "rap crap," said no: he wanted LaMar to stick to sports.

LaMar began producing the show on his own time. Some days, he raced from an interview with a local high school football coach to an interview with a rap artist in New York, and record companies gave him promotional videos to flesh out his program. His boss still refused to air the show, so LaMar spent his own money leasing public-access time, and then covered his costs by soliciting ads from local businesses. Eventually, however, LaMar decided to commit himself wholeheartedly to his dream. He quit his job and spent a year trying to drum up sponsors, take his show statewide, and find a network to buy it.

It didn't work. At twenty-five, now living with his high school sweetheart and their three-year-old son, LaMar was unemployed. He sent out a thick stack of résumés to every television facility he could think of and got a thick stack of rejections in return. At last, he took a job in the kitchen of St. Peter's College, flipping burgers on the cafeteria line. From time to time he still hosted his show, which now aired at 3 a.m. on the statewide cable network. Sometimes, as he loaded sodas into college vending machines, students would recognize him. "I saw you on TV last night," they would say. "Yeah," LaMar would answer. "It's a tough world out there."

Liana Diaz

Lucila Diaz's divorce became final in 1982. She and her ex split the proceeds from the sale of their house, and she bought herself a new place in the center of Jersey City. Lucila and her children were not poor, but they lived carefully: every month, each child chose an outfit to put on layaway at the local Marshall's, and an earlier month's selection came home fully paid for. Lucila had come to hate her secretarial job at the school district's central office. Although she herself had pulled political strings to get there, she hated the politics, the power plays, the favors done for friends. With a mortgage to pay and three children to feed, however, she was too frightened to look for anything new, even after she finished her bachelor's degree in 1984. She hunkered down and stayed on at the school district.

Thanks to the special permission her mother had gotten, Liana had spent fifth grade at School 16 instead of at her neighborhood's School 3, but that arrangement ended after one year, and Liana enrolled in School 3 after all. The new school worked out fine. Liana, who had taken remedial reading in fifth grade, was placed in the gifted-and-talented program by sixth grade. The gifted-program kids were a competitive lot, and in the Jersey City public schools, the ultimate prize was admission to Academic High School, the district's selective program for high achievers. Created in 1976 as a desegregation tool, Academic allocated an equal number of seats to blacks, whites, and Hispanics, and in short order it became a sought-after alternative to Catholic high school for ambitious students and their parents. While students at Jersey City's four other public high schools struggled to pass the state graduation test and get a diploma, Academic's students breezed through the test and expected to attend college. Still, as a latecomer to the school district—and perhaps something of a stepchild in Jersey City's politicized climate—Academic was forced to make do with barely adequate facilities. When Liana Diaz enrolled in 1984, Academic was housed in space rented from a Ukrainian church, and students were bused to a nearby college for gym.

Getting into Academic was a coup, but Liana never really applied herself to her studies. She had fun playing volleyball and working as a statistician for the basketball and baseball teams. Her grades were adequate, especially in math, but her frustrated teachers told her she was capable of more. She attended school regularly (the one time she could remember playing hooky, she had cowered in her basement, scared to death that Lucila would catch her), and she steered clear of drugs and drinking. Her mother told her plenty about the importance of education, but Liana was lazy. "I had the push," she said years later. "I just resisted the push."

Still, college was a given for Academic students, and after her 1988 graduation, Liana enrolled at a state college in South Jersey, covering the tuition with loans and financial aid. At a minority-student orientation program the summer before her freshman year, Liana absorbed the well-meaning advice about embracing college life, and she fit in easily, becoming president of the Hispanic students' group, participating in student government, joining a sorority. Academic had prepared her well for college, but her studies were still not her top priority: as she had in high school, she earned adequate grades, first as a math major and later studying computers, business, and accounting. In the summers, she returned to Jersey City and worked for the local employment training program, using what she had learned in accounting courses to become an accounts payable clerk. She had learned a double-edged lesson—she could make a living even without a college degree. The burden of her growing student loans oppressed her, and with only a year to go, Liana decided to drop out of college. She moved back home to Jersey City.

Zakia and Aisha Hargrove

In February 1983, Patricia Watson was changing clothes in a bedroom at her mother's house when one of her sisters noticed the lump in Pat's breast. Panicked, Pat's sister grabbed the telephone book and began looking for a doctor. Pat had ignored the lump for three months. By the time she saw a doctor, the cancer was in her breast and her bones, and although she underwent surgery, radiation, and chemotherapy, her fate was sealed.

Had the cancer spread to Pat's brain, as well, turning her into the paranoid, abusive monster that her daughter Zakia Hargrove knew? Or did

Pat's mental illness grow from the trauma of her abusive childhood and predate her tragically coincidental physical illness? Years later, family members disagreed. Whatever the explanation, Pat's behavior only grew more bizarre. In her final months, she gave away or threw away yearbooks and family photos, the record of her past, and her children's. Her family worried that, in the throes of her illness, Pat might harm her children; they did not know that she had been abusing eleven-year-old Zakia for years. As Pat's health declined, her mother gained legal custody of the girls, moved them into her house, and warned them not to go anywhere with their mother. But one autumn afternoon while the girls were on the porch, Pat came to see them. Nine-year-old Aisha ran to her mother and Zakia followed. Pat grabbed Zakia's hand and started walking. All that day, Pat and her girls wandered from house to house, dropping in on people Pat apparently knew, though the girls did not. At one house, Pat changed the girls' clothes; at another, she told them to hide in the bedroom, where they spent the night. The next day, Zakia managed to give her grandmother's phone number to their hostess, and Aisha and Zakia lay on the floor of the woman's car while she sneaked them out from under their mother's nose and passed them to the police waiting nearby.

At last, Pat came back to her mother's house to die. She asked her oldest sister, Evanett, to take care of her girls; she made her mother promise never to institutionalize Aisha. Then, on November 3, 1983, in the huge bedroom she and her daughters shared, thirty-one-year-old Patricia Watson died. Caring for both little girls was more than their grandmother could handle, Pat's siblings felt. Evanett, who worked for the federal government and lived in Memphis with her own school-age son, volunteered to take Zakia. Aisha was now enrolled in a school for disabled children, but her daily care remained too overwhelming for Evanett, a single working mother, to take on. The judge supervising the custody arrangements asked Zakia to write him a letter explaining her wishes, and in her letter, Zakia asked to move away. She wanted to escape the house where her mother had died, the memories of what her mother had done to her, the sister whose disabilities her mother had accused her of causing.

So Aisha remained with her grandmother in Jersey City. Every day, she took the bus to a publicly funded program for disabled students, and every afternoon she returned home to her room. Pat had stormed against anyone who suggested limits to what Aisha could do, refusing to acknowledge that her daughter was mentally retarded, but Aisha's grandmother accepted Aisha's limitations all too readily, letting her speak in one-word, baby-talk sentences and continuing to bathe and dress her as she grew into an adult. She refused any suggestion that Aisha be placed in a group home. To her, that meant institutionalization, and she had promised Pat she would never institutionalize Aisha.

Zakia left for Memphis after the Jersey City school year ended in 1984. Her aunt Evanett soon realized that Zakia's skills were far below grade level for an eleven-year-old, but Evanett also doubted that Zakia belonged in special education. Instead, Evanett started Zakia in summer classes, bought her a Speak & Spell, and enrolled her in a private school that she figured would handle placement more flexibly than a public school might. Zakia struggled with reading, writing, and math, uncomfortable in the classroom full of nine-year-olds where she had been placed. She felt lost and isolated, but outwardly, she seemed fine. That first year, she joined the track team. She was a perfect, well-behaved little girl. Evanett never had to raise her voice.

Zakia had hidden the nightmare of her mother's abuse behind a tightly controlled facade of normality, but with the nightmare over, her control began to crumble. In Evanett's house, she felt safe enough to fall apart. Gradually, Evanett realized that Zakia was losing weight. After everyone else went to bed, she could hear Zakia moving around the kitchen. One night, she went to investigate and found Zakia at the refrigerator, cramming everything edible into her mouth. Evanett knew she was looking at bulimia, and Zakia was soon hospitalized. She began cutting her arms and wrists, sometimes deeply, with anything she could find, even a sharpened toothbrush. Although Zakia's hospital stay ended after a couple of months, her illness did not; she was in counseling, then back in the hospital, then in a group home for troubled adolescents. At the group home, where she spent her last two years of high school, education was an afterthought. Although tutors left work for her to finish each week, when she chose not to complete it, no one much cared. One night, when she was supposed to be asleep, Zakia overheard the staff discussing her case. She wasn't going to make it, they concluded. Clearly, no one thought it mattered much whether she learned anything, since she had no future.

Zakia had left Jersey City to escape the terrible memories of her mother's abuse, but those memories had followed her to Memphis, blossomed like cancers, and nearly choked her to death. With the skewed logic of her disordered mind, she concluded that leaving Memphis would mean leaving those memories behind; although she had been accepted to a branch of the University of Tennessee, she decided to return to Jersey City and move back in with her grandmother. She enrolled in remedial courses at the state college, but, surrounded by the people and places associated with the worst experiences of her life, Zakia soon fell into a deep depression. She was evil; she always would be. The only way to eradicate the evil was to erase herself. One day, she called a suicide hotline for help. When the hotline put her call on hold, she hung up, emptied the medicine chest, and took every drug in her grandmother's house. She took heart medicine, blood pressure medicine, sleeping pills, and an entire bottle of aspirin, washing the whole mess down with Nyquil. Then she barricaded herself in her room and waited to die. The suicide hotline traced her call, reached her grandmother on a separate telephone line, and called 911. Zakia, her stomach lining hemorrhaging, spent days in the hospital and then in a psychiatric ward. The state psych ward was far scarier than the private hospitals she was used to. People banged their heads on the walls; one woman was convinced someone was coming to stab her in the back. "What are you doing here?" the staff asked Zakia, as if echoing her special education teachers all those years before. "You're too normal to be here."

9

A Constitutional Right
to Astroturf

Marilyn Morheuser's last terrible year had wreaked havoc on the Education Law Center. Its staff was decimated, its finances were a shambles, and its case was approaching another critical juncture: the court-ordered deadline for a new school-funding law was less than a year away. Despite her faults, Morheuser had been an extraordinary leader for ELC—dedicated, courageous, and profoundly committed to children. Even under ideal circumstances, replacing her would have been difficult, and ELC's circumstances were far from ideal. The new executive director would have to accept months of job insecurity while wooing funders, rebuilding the organization, and mastering the complex *Abbott* litigation. The board feared no one would want the job. It was serendipity, ELC founder Paul Tractenberg reflected years later, that a few weeks after Morheuser's death, they found the right person.

David Sciarra was another lapsed Catholic with a fierce sense of mission, but in other respects he was no Morheuser replica. Morheuser had been a child of the Depression, a midwesterner from a middle-class home, an activist who turned to the law in her forties and married herself to her cause. Sciarra was nearly thirty years younger, a blue-collar Jersey kid who went to law school soon after college and found time for family life. Morheuser's charisma, commitment, and unusual life story had made her a compelling public figure, equal parts grandmotherly former nun and relentless crusader, a burnished icon of righteousness. Sciarra shared her passion for social justice and her tenacity in legal battle, but he cut a more familiar figure: the lawyer with a cause that engaged but did not

consume him. Her plainspoken warmth had charmed even those who disagreed with her; his long-winded lecturing sometimes irritated even his
allies. Morheuser had been larger than life; Sciarra lived on a more
human scale. ELC's trustees hoped that would be enough.

By 1995, the forty-three-year-old Sciarra was ready for a change. For
three years, he had worked with the state's legal aid office, but the organization spent most of its time providing one-on-one help to impoverished
clients, and Sciarra preferred tackling big, systemic issues. Still, had he
needed a reason to say no when a friend on ELC's board approached him
about the job, he wouldn't have had far to look: he had litigated no
education cases, had no fund-raising experience, and, with a family to
support, could not take the job's precariousness lightly. The board never
sugarcoated ELC's peril, but Sciarra thought the work was important, and,
like Morheuser herself sixteen years earlier, he was looking for a new
direction. His first official day as ELC's executive director was January 1,
1996.

Sciarra had grown up in Wildwood, a Jersey Shore town that came
alive each summer and relapsed into dead calm when the tourists went
home. His father, also named David, was the son of Italian immigrants, a
bricklayer with his own business who worked long, backbreaking hours.
Sciarra's mother, Helen, had survived a quietly tragic childhood whose
details her own six children learned only piecemeal, as they grew older.
Helen's mother had died giving birth to her; soon after, her alcoholic father surrendered his three youngest children to a Catholic orphanage in
Philadelphia, where the living conditions were austere. Years later, Helen
told her own daughter, David's younger sister Ellie, that as a child she
would sometimes steal up to the orphanage attic to eat handfuls of
sugar—starved not so much for physical nourishment, Ellie thought, as
for sheer, intoxicating sweetness. Helen stayed in touch with her family
through the orphanage years, and in her early teens, she went to live with
an older sister. After high school, Helen longed to attend college, but
money was tight, and instead she worked as a waitress until she met her
future husband at a dance hall one night.

Wildwood was so safe that the Sciarras never locked their doors, and
the beach-loving kids surfed and water-skied. The family never wanted
for food, clothing, or shelter, but extras were scarce. "There was nothing

lavish or extravagant about our lives," Ellie Sciarra said years later. Every summer, jobs arrived with the tourists, and the Sciarra kids went to work. David was a paperboy, a busboy, an assistant in his father's business. Over dinner, the family discussed news and politics; Helen Sciarra supported civil rights, opposed the Vietnam War, and was devastated by the assassinations of John F. Kennedy and Martin Luther King Jr. As her oldest children reached their teens, she discovered a passion for environmentalism, and, eventually, she joined a band of local activists lobbying to preserve New Jersey's Pinelands. Perhaps, her daughter speculated years later, her activism gave her an outlet for an unarticulated anger.

Helen Sciarra was also a devout Catholic, and her children attended local parochial schools, where most of their classmates were also working-class whites. Blacks lived in another part of town and attended the reputedly inferior public schools. Even the Catholic schools were no-frills, however, and looking back, David Sciarra did not remember them as paragons of academic excellence. In elementary school, where classes were large, the nuns drilled. In high school, despite some gifted teachers, the program was spotty—better in English and history than in science or art. David, the Sciarras' second child, was an able student, cerebral but not excessively bookish, and his parents encouraged him to attend college. Eager to shake off small-town New Jersey, he packed his surfboard and followed his older brother to the University of Hawaii, but two years later, he transferred to the more intellectually satisfying University of California at Berkeley, where he majored in American history, earned work-study money at a liberal think tank, and wondered what to do with his future. Back home in Wildwood after college, he took an internship at the local legal aid office, and as he helped shepherd impoverished clients through evictions, bankruptcies, and domestic violence cases, he glimpsed the law's power to promote justice. Three years later, he was a legal aid lawyer in Atlantic City.

A lawyer for the poor had no shortage of work in the Atlantic City of 1978. Less than two years earlier, New Jersey's voters had approved a referendum legalizing casino gambling in the decaying resort town, and speculators were snapping up properties a step ahead of the big casino companies. Slumlords bent on forcing out inconvenient tenants issued dubious eviction notices, let the heat fail in winter, or burned buildings to the ground. In the newspaper he read each morning, Sciarra saw the out-lines of the day ahead: another mysterious fire meant another batch of newly homeless clients filling his office. One case even brought Sciarra, four years out of law school, his first state supreme court victory. Already, however, his attention was turning to broader systemic issues. A loophole-ridden state law required casino companies to reinvest some of their rev-enue in Atlantic City's impoverished neighborhoods, and Sciarra's office began working with community groups to demand enforcement. The election of a new Republican governor, Thomas Kean, brought a new leader for the state's citizen watchdog, the Department of the Public Ad-vocate; the new public advocate was interested in casino reinvestment, and Sciarra wangled an introduction that led to a job.

For ten years in the advocate's office, Sciarra pursued cases that were public-issue campaigns as much as attempts to get justice for individual clients. The office intervened when casinos' licenses came up for renewal, challenging dubious claims to reinvestment credit, like Caesars' effort to get credit for erecting a statue of Caesar Augustus outside the entrance to the casino. Finally, the legislature began to move, and Sciarra helped write the law that put teeth into the reinvestment requirement. He had a hand in other issues, too: he won supreme court rulings giving the homeless a right to shelter, forced the state to set realistic standards for welfare ben-efits, and helped write a report detailing appalling conditions in public boarding homes. The hours were long, the cases were complicated, the negotiations with the legislature were sometimes difficult. Sciarra loved it all.

His personal life was bumpier. During law school, he had recon-nected with a high school sweetheart, and in 1981 their son was born. But the relationship ended three years later, and Sciarra settled into the painful routine of shared custody—one week a single father, the next week just single. In the comfortable Trenton suburb where his ex lived, their son attended public school and, like legions of middle-class Jersey kids, played soccer. The soccer coach had a sister-in-law named Fay who worked in television in San Francisco; during one of Fay's visits to New Jersey, her family introduced her to David Sciarra. In 1992 they married, and within a few years they had a son of their own. By then, however, the Department of the Public Advocate was dying. Crippling funding cuts began in the Florio administration; then, Governor Christie Whitman helped balance her first budget by eliminating the whole department. Before the lights went out, Sciarra left for the state legal aid office, where ELC found him, discontented, after Morheuser's death.

His first priority was stabilizing ELC's finances, and he began with applications to longtime funders whose grants had lapsed during Morheuser's illness. Like Morheuser before him, Sciarra soon realized that foundations were reluctant to fund litigation, especially litigation that seemed as endless and thankless as *Abbott*; they preferred paying for direct legal assistance to parents and children. ELC had always helped clients navigate the special-education bureaucracy or challenge schools' disciplinary decisions, but Morheuser, consumed with *Abbott*'s grand ambition, had paid little attention to that one-on-one work. Sciarra decided to build up that side of ELC and fund it separately, the better to attract grants. Gradually, ELC began to revive, but the first eighteen months were a brutal grind as Sciarra juggled his family responsibilities, his long commute from central New Jersey, his fund-raising duties, and his self-administered crash course in the fifteen-year-old *Abbott* case.

Sciarra wasn't the only one learning a new job. A year earlier, Governor Whitman had replaced a retiring state supreme court justice with the court's first African American, James Coleman Jr., who had attended segregated public schools as a child in Virginia. Then, the spring after Sciarra joined ELC, Chief Justice Robert Wilentz was hospitalized with mysterious leg pains that doctors soon traced to a lethal melanoma. A month later, Wilentz resigned from the court, and a month after that, he was dead. Whitman replaced him with her attorney general, Deborah Poritz, the first woman to hold the chief justice's job. Sciarra had taken over the *Abbott* case at the very moment the architect of the eloquent *Abbott II* ruling had left the stage.

The court had given the state until September 1996 to replace the despised QEA with a new funding formula, but ELC was not optimistic about the Whitman administration's response. Like former Governor Kean, Whitman had grown up in a wealthy family with long-standing Republican ties: her father, a contractor who had helped build Rockefeller Center, was a state Republican chairman and an advisor to President Eisenhower. Whitman had spent five years as a county official in affluent, pastoral central New Jersey and two years heading the state's public utilities board before her near-upset of U.S. Senator Bill Bradley had made her a statewide star. Her friendly, down-to-earth style had neutralized the political dangers of her privileged background, but during the 1993 gubernatorial campaign, Whitman had explained her failure to vote in school board elections by noting that her own children attended private schools. ''I didn't have children in those schools and I didn't think I ought to be telling them how to run those schools,'' she had said. Her most strident critics saw the remark as evidence of a rich woman's deep indifference to the communal responsibility for public schooling.

Whatever the significance of Whitman's campaign gaffe, it was clear that her political base lay in the wealthy suburbs with the least to gain from *Abbott*, and she bore little allegiance to the public education establishment that, thanks to Morheuser's rapprochement with the teachers' union, now firmly supported the rulings. For education commissioner, Whitman had chosen Leo Klagholz, a respected state bureaucrat whose signature initiative—the Kean-era opening up of teacher certification— had faced stiff union opposition. A key plank in Whitman's education platform was a pilot program to give Jersey City parents publicly funded vouchers for private school tuition, a pet project of the city's maverick Republican mayor but anathema to the teachers' union. Although Whitman had quickly backed off the voucher proposal—legislators were unenthusiastic about incurring union wrath over a program benefiting only one city—Klagholz was forging ahead with a broader reform effort with potentially greater impact on New Jersey's school-funding dilemma.

The 1990s had seen the birth of a national education reform movement that advocated a new basis for schooling—academic standards spelling out what skills and knowledge students were expected to acquire by the time they finished high school. Academic standards were the cornerstone of many other countries' education systems, but in the United States, where schooling was traditionally a local matter, the call for across-the-board curriculum standards was controversial. Who would decide what those standards should include—how the biology curriculum should treat evolution, or how the history syllabus should handle the most controversial episodes of the American past? How should states assess whether students had achieved the standards? What sanctions should students face if they could not measure up? Despite these knotty issues, by decade's end, virtually every state was involved in standards-based reform, and New Jersey had taken its first steps in that direction more than a year before Whitman's election. Nevertheless, ELC and its allies suspected that Klagholz and Whitman had ulterior motives for pursuing standards-based reform. In its *Robinson* and *Abbott* rulings, the state supreme court had repeatedly explained that it used school spending as a proxy for educational quality because the state had supplied no alternative measure. Perhaps, advocates on the left thought, the new Republican administration hoped to use academic standards as an alternative measure of quality, a measure the court could substitute for the expensive requirement of spending parity between rich and poor school districts. After all, Whitman had a costly campaign promise to pay for: she was forging ahead with plans to cut the state income tax by 30 percent.

Years later, an important Whitman adviser would insist that Klagholz had been given no marching orders to cut school spending. But the new commissioner made little secret of his belief that New Jersey's schools, urban and suburban alike, spent profligately, largely because each district was free to set its own budget, subject to voter approval, with no independent gauge of what programs were educationally necessary. The *Abbott* decision, Klagholz argued, had codified that irrationality by forcing the state to match every dollar of suburban spending with a dollar of urban spending, regardless of whether that suburban dollar had any educational justification. "Livingston has Astroturf on its football field. Is that guaranteed by the Constitution?" Klagholz liked to ask.

As long as urban-suburban parity remained the law, however, simple arithmetic showed that there were only two ways to achieve it: spend more in urban districts, or spend less in suburban ones. The administration set out to rein in the suburbs. A year into Whitman's administration, her budget proposed levying financial penalties on school districts with administrative costs 30 percent or more above the state average. Among the seventy districts in danger of losing a collective $11 million in state aid were some wealthy and academically successful suburbs, and, despite their reputation for waste and bloat, only one of the QEA's thirty urban special needs districts. The administrative penalties made some sense: New Jersey spent more than the national average on educational administration, and most policy wonks assumed its profusion of small school districts was one reason why. If a town wanted to keep its boutique school district with one building and no high school, well—fine, the Whitman administration was saying, but the state would no longer help pay for that particular luxury.

The neatly plausible theory looked messier in practice, however. The state, it turned out, was including nurses, librarians, and guidance counselors in its definition of school administrators, and suburban parents rebelled against the implication that such services were a waste of money. The Garden State Coalition of Schools, the suburban alliance born out of opposition to QEA, held a meeting in affluent Livingston, and an impressive five hundred people showed up, galvanized by a direct threat to their spending prerogatives. The newly vocal suburbs were filled with voters who had elected the Republican-dominated legislature, and their representatives were listening. That year, the legislature watered down the penalty program, and within two years, it was gone.

The battle over administrative penalties was just a warm-up for the far more important battle over the new school-funding formula. The 1994 *Abbott III* ruling had given the Whitman administration two years to develop a new funding law, and the legally easiest approach was obvious: spend whatever was required for parity, find a few extra millions to placate the neglected middle class, and leave the broader contours of the system untouched. Klagholz had greater ambitions, however. He was determined to change the terms of the debate: to stop using money as a proxy for educational quality and to brake the eternal school-spending increases. In February 1995, a year after the bruising battle over administrative penalties, the Department of Education released an interim report on what it called a "comprehensive plan for educational improvement and financing." The report struck some familiar notes in its critique of QEA and its distaste for New Jersey's profusion of tiny school districts, but it also took some surprising new tacks. Throughout the QEA debate, legislators and advocates alike had praised the state's high-spending, high-achieving suburban districts as "lighthouses," beacons of academic excellence showing their lesser peers the way. The new report adopted an entirely different tone. These districts, Klagholz dared to argue, flourished not because they spent lavishly on excellent programs but because their students came from privileged backgrounds. Furthermore, not all high-spending suburbs achieved at high levels, and some successful districts spent far less. "New Jersey's current system is based on, and it leaves entirely unchallenged, the established practices of the public education system, particularly as those practices are embodied in districts in wealthier communities," the report said. "It sets as its standard the existing spending levels of those districts without scrutinizing the educational and fiscal practices that produce those spending levels."

The administration envisioned a new system that for the first time would give substantive meaning to the constitutional guarantee of a thorough and efficient education. First would come curriculum standards, defining the "thorough" in T&E. Next would come a costing-out of the programs required to educate students up to those standards, defining the "efficient" half of the equation. At one end of the spectrum, poor districts would get extra financial help, but only to meet poor children's academic needs, not to alleviate their myriad other disadvantages: schools could not be expected to solve every social problem. At the other end of the spectrum, wealthy districts would be permitted to spend above the state-determined T&E funding level, even though such excess spending would by definition be unnecessary: efforts to block such spending were doomed to failure anyway, since the rich would inevitably find a way around strict limits. Like the architects of every school-funding formula since Bateman's time, the Whitman administration would not force the rich to make do with less. "The purpose of this plan is to define and equitably fund a statewide system of education that is thorough and efficient," Klagholz's report said. "It is not to achieve absolute social uniformity through a broad redistribution of wealth and draconian governmental controls."

Years later, even David Sciarra would acknowledge that the comprehensive plan was a conceptual advance in the school-funding debate. At last, the state would decide what students were supposed to learn in thirteen years of public education; at last, the state would determine how much it cost to deliver that instruction. The February 1995 interim plan omitted one key piece of information, however: the spending level at which the state believed school districts could deliver a standards-based T&E education. In further refinements issued over the next fifteen months of public hearings and political jockeying, the administration filled this hole, adding spending numbers derived from a hypothetical model school district designed to deliver the curriculum standards in accord not with New Jersey's bloated status quo but with ideally efficient practices. The new foundation formula would assure every district, no matter its wealth, the state aid it needed to spend as much as the model, and although suburbs could choose to spend more, they would get no state aid to cover the excess. Most significant, they would have to label the extra spending "not constitutionally required," right there on the ballot presented to voters during school budget elections. That, thought the Garden State Coalition's lobbyist, was like hanging up a brightly colored piñata and inviting tax-weary voters to take a whack.

Those piñatas would be everywhere, she thought: the model district was about as realistic as Brigadoon. Pinning down the details was as complicated as ever—the model district spent either $7,194 per student, if you listened to ELC, or $8,285, if you listened to the state—but by some measures, Whitman's plan called for lower spending than QEA did, even though the state expected students to meet newly rigorous curriculum standards. One Rutgers study estimated that three-quarters of the state's school districts had spent more in 1993–94 than one version of Klagholz's model would have allowed, a total of $869 million in spending now branded "not constitutionally required." In some districts, excess spending amounted to 10, 20, even 40 percent of the budget. Since few New Jersey school systems resembled the model in size or grade configuration, districts faced two choices: conform to the model by changing rapidly and radically, or continue supposedly inefficient spending and pay for it out of local property taxes. And choosing the second option required districts to hang up that tempting piñata, labeling as "not constitutionally required" spending needed just to maintain existing programs.

What were all these supposedly excessive dollars buying? Klagholz's reports were notably short of examples. Although the reports asserted that school salaries and benefits were too generous and that districts were too small and too numerous, the reports did not specify what salaries would be appropriate or which districts should consolidate their operations. The reports offered only one specific example of nonessential spending— night-game lighting on athletic fields. Looking back, combatants on both

sides of the Whitman-era school-funding wars offered an array of explanations for this curious omission. Perhaps the department, racing a court-
ordered deadline, had no time to mine colorful nuggets from hundreds of
local school budgets; perhaps naming names seemed unproductively divisive; perhaps little truly excessive spending was there to be found. Or
perhaps the problem lay in the inevitably subjective nature of the judgment about what adequate schooling entailed, about what was essential
and what expendable. At one hearing, a suburban principal testified
that living within the T&E numbers would force his district to cut back
football, Italian, and instrumental music—core school services to some,
unnecessary frills to others. The administration's proposal demanded
substantive sacrifices—not only darkened sports fields, but also stingier
teacher contracts, bigger classes, and fewer course offerings—but the administration's rhetoric hid that unpleasant reality behind talk of waste
and excess.

The truth was more complicated, the department's top finance offi-
Everyone hated the administration proposal—school boards, administrators, teachers, parents. "It would put the light out in our lighthouse
districts," the teachers' union testified at the first legislative hearing, during which only Klagholz spoke in favor of the plan. Opponents suspected
that the model-district budget was a bureaucratic fiction, that rather than
building the number from a ground-up study of schools' needs, as the Department of Education claimed to have done, the administration had decided what it wanted to spend and had worked backward to arrive at a
per-pupil amount.

The truth was more complicated, the department's top finance official said years later. The department had derived its spending figures
honestly, he said, but it had begun with assumptions that ensured a conservative result. The administration plugged average teacher salaries into
its model, even though wealthy suburbs often paid more. It gave most
teachers only one class period for preparation, even though New Jersey
districts commonly allowed two. It assumed the burgeoning core curriculum would leave no time for Advanced Placement courses or vocational
training, and so the model district budgeted nothing for teachers of AP biology or home economics. Support for the state's funding model was not
universal, even within the Education Department: as late as April 1996,
colleagues warned Klagholz that delivering the new curriculum standards

might require extra spending. Still, plenty of education officials believed sincerely in the model's validity. "If the numbers were cooked, they weren't heated in an oven," a Republican legislative leader said years later. "It was just a little across the flame."

In May 1996, the state Board of Education formally adopted the long-debated core curriculum standards in seven subjects: English, math, science, social studies, foreign languages, health/physical education, and the arts. Soon after, the Education Department released the final draft of its funding plan, quickly introduced in legislation as the Comprehensive Educational Improvement and Financing Act, or CEIFA. On top of its much-disputed T&E funding level, the package included a school-aid increase of $235 million to cover rising enrollments, subsidize property tax relief for high-taxing districts, and pay for preschool in poor districts. For much of the recession-plagued early 1990s, most districts had seen little or no increase in school aid, despite growing enrollments, but under the new plan, most districts would initially get more money, and only a handful would lose more than 1 percent of their budgets.

The administration had hoped the new money would blunt criticism, but the bill was soon under attack from all sides. ELC had one set of objections. Although the bill gave poor districts extra money to educate disadvantaged students, the amounts involved were apparently arbitrary: the Education Department had never studied what programs poor children needed and how much those programs would cost, even though the court had twice ordered such a study. Furthermore, although CEIFA forced rich districts to tell voters when planned spending would exceed the T&E level, the bill neither required the rich to spend down to that level nor enabled the poor to spend above it. CEIFA would never close the spending gaps outlawed in *Abbott*. Adding insult to injury, CEIFA limited its extra help to the twenty-eight urban districts on the supreme court's original *Abbott II* list, removing the two that QEA had added.

If ELC was angry, the suburbs were enraged. Before CEIFA was even introduced, the Garden State Coalition of Schools began mobilizing its articulate, determined parents. One wintry February night in 1996, an astonishing one thousand people streamed into a coalition-organized forum on the issues. These people had moved to the suburbs because of suburban schools' reputation for excellence, and, rightly or wrongly, they believed such excellence required high spending. Most of that high spending was paid for with local property taxes, and although the state supreme court and the Education Law Center called that public money, suburbanites called it something else: their own money. They might not expect the state to give them much help, but they certainly would not let the state make it hard for them to help themselves. Through the spring and summer of 1996, suburban opposition to CEIFA gathered strength. Thousands of angry letters arrived at Whitman's office. Behind the scenes, the Garden State Coalition's chief lobbyist encouraged Democratic legislative staff to request a study of CEIFA's likely impact on school districts. When the legislature's nonpartisan research arm found that 309 of the state's districts—more than half the total—spent more than CEIFA recommended, the lobbyist orchestrated a complicated handoff ensuring the information would leak to the newspapers.

Administration officials labored in vain to win legislators' support. CEIFA had a plausible logic: decide what students should learn, figure out what it costs to teach them, enable every district to spend that much, and discourage districts from spending more. If that final provision were eliminated and the suburbs were allowed to spend whatever they wanted, undiscouraged, CEIFA's logic would be fatally undermined, the administration argued. "For the foundation amount to make sense, we can't allow districts to be spending far above it," one official said years later. "Clearly, there should be local prerogatives, but once you get above 15 percent or 10 percent, you're really leaving local prerogative and you're getting into a territory of suburban districts know something we don't." Whitman's Republican Party controlled both houses of the legislature, but nevertheless, solutions were elusive. Assembly Speaker Jack Collins, a South Jersey Republican whose folksy manner masked political steel, refused to consider setting a special, higher foundation amount for the expensive districts of North Jersey; other legislators wanted protection for the biggest towns they represented. Few had the stomach to demand that their constituents renegotiate teacher contracts and cut back football to live within CEIFA's T&E amounts. Republicans saw CEIFA as a fancy variant of the hated QEA, Robin Hood plundering the rich. They remembered the fate of Democrats who had backed Governor Jim Florio when the Republicans refused to lend him even a single vote. Now the Democrats were returning the favor, refusing to help pass CEIFA, and the Republicans feared they might be walking into their own version of the Democrats' 1991 electoral disaster.

By July 1996, the administration had lost its battle to preserve CEIFA's logic. That month, Republican legislators introduced an amended bill giving in to the suburbs' chief demands. Although the new bill required suburban districts to limit their annual budget increases, it calculated those annual increases from the suburbs' existing spending levels, rather than forcing spending down to the T&E amount. Furthermore, districts that wanted to exceed even those budget caps could seek voter approval to do so, and they would no longer have to describe any spending above T&E as "not constitutionally required." The grandfathering provision, as the CEIFA amendment was called, openly flouted the *Abbott* parity requirement. The state would fund the urban special needs districts up to the T&E level; the suburbs would be free to spend far more. The provision enshrined the very spending disparities that *Abbott* had outlawed.

Plenty of legislators and lobbyists knew the court was likely to find CEIFA unconstitutional if it included the grandfathering provision. Sciarra predicted that his toddler could win the case, and even the governor reportedly had her doubts. Still, not everyone thought CEIFA's potential unconstitutionality was a drawback. Assembly Speaker Collins, for one, had no objection to provoking a constitutional crisis; the *Abbott* rulings, he thought, were a liberal court's power grab. "There are *three* branches of government," Collins was fond of intoning to reporters—his way of reminding them that the legislature, not the courts or the governor, decided what the state should spend on schooling.

The maneuvering over CEIFA stretched into the fall as the court extended its September 1996 deadline to December 31, but the basic contours of the bill had been established in the summer. All that remained were the tortuous details—a few million dollars more for middle-class districts, a sop or two to towns with powerful legislative patrons. Decades earlier, school-funding bills had filled a few pages of relatively plain English, but CEIFA was such a morass of figures, algorithms, and convoluted prose that few legislators understood it well enough to cast their votes, pro or con, on principle: instead, they checked the computer runs showing how much state money was coming to their constituents and voted accordingly. In the end, the bill increased school aid by $286 million, with half the increase going to poor urban districts. Although the administration could have saved money by spending just the $270 million required to bring those districts to parity, "that wouldn't have solved the education problem," Whitman said. "That's what this whole thing is about, from my perspective. This isn't an argument about money. It's an issue of what happens in the classroom." Six days before Christmas, the legislature passed CEIFA largely along party lines, with the usual partisan posturing: as assembly Democratic leader Joe Doria Jr., a veteran of the QEA battle, declaimed, "The light of learning will be extinguished by the passage of this bill," Democrats en masse switched off their desk lamps. Out of the gloom rolled the voice of Republican Speaker Collins: "How dare you! What pomposity and demagoguery!" The next day, a beaming Whitman signed the bill in front of a statehouse Christmas tree.

Everyone knew the *Abbott* case was headed back to court. Whitman Chief of Staff Peter Verniero had shaken his head over the complex school-funding bill, thinking, "Someone's going to have to argue this someday and really put this statute in plain language." By the time CEIFA passed, Verniero had been appointed attorney general, and although he had never before argued a case in the state supreme court, he decided to argue *Abbott*, to underline the administration's commitment to the issues. Suddenly, the unenviable task of putting CEIFA into plain language belonged to him. ELC staff worked through the holidays preparing their supreme court brief. Sciarra was so busy that his wife barely saw him for a month and so preoccupied that, dressing their son one morning, he put the toddler's shoes on the wrong feet.

The new litigation would focus squarely on the Whitman administration's efforts to reframe the school-funding debate. Since the 1990 *Abbott II* decision, the court's pressure had brought progress toward spending parity between rich and poor districts. ELC's own figures showed the gap shrinking from $1,700 per student in 1989–90 to $1,000 per student in 1996–97—from 25 or 30 percent to as little as 10 or 11 percent—and using different assumptions, the state calculated the remaining parity gap at just 4 percent. CEIFA, however, rejected *Abbott II*'s use of spending parity as a proxy for T&E in favor of defining T&E directly: thoroughness would mean compliance with curriculum standards, and efficiency would mean spending like that in the hypothetical model district.

ELC's case rejected this reframing, questioning the state's new definitions of both thoroughness and efficiency. The new curriculum standards might be worthwhile, ELC argued, but they were aspirations rather than guarantees of a high-quality educational program, and the state had done no study of the extra programs that poor children would need to help them achieve the standards. Even worse, the funding level derived from the hypothetical model district was hopelessly inadequate, a poor substitute for parity with wealthy suburbs. Parity was still the law, ELC argued, and CEIFA, like QEA, did nothing to guarantee it. In the two and a half years since *Abbott III* had rejected as unacceptable a 16 percent spending gap between rich and poor districts, the disparity had shrunk only slightly, ELC asserted, and the grandfathering of suburban spending levels ensured it would never narrow further. CEIFA's T&E spending level would be a ceiling for the poor and a floor for the rich. The legislative history of CEIFA itself proved that the rich would spend more: that very imperative had dictated the grandfathering compromise.

The state argued vigorously for its new approach. For years, Verniero noted, the court had lamented the lack of a substantive, nonfiscal gauge of T&E; now, for the first time, the state had devised one. At last, desired educational outcomes lay at the heart of the state's funding plan; at last, the cost of delivering those outcomes dictated spending. Suburban districts' spending levels, the standard under the old parity measure, were now irrelevant: whatever extras those districts provided were unnecessary to achieving the constitutional level of education. The court should let CEIFA take effect, deferring to the good-faith efforts of the other two branches of government to solve the decades-old school-funding problem.

Few expected the state to win its case. The grandfathering amendment, the legislature's capitulation to suburban pressure, had knocked a huge hole in the logic of the state's position. Although Wilentz was gone, five of the seven justices who had concurred with the *Abbott II* parity mandate remained on the court, and one of the newcomers, Chief Justice Deborah Poritz, was sitting out the new litigation, since she had been Whitman's attorney general during much of the legislative maneuvering over CEIFA.

Sciarra was confident his case was strong; Verniero knew he faced an up-hill battle.

The *Abbott IV* decision came swiftly, just five months after Whitman had signed CEIFA. Inside the court, the most liberal justices had quickly decided that CEIFA was hopelessly inadequate. With Wilentz gone, Justice Gary Stein, Governor Kean's former policy advisor, led the charge. The grandfathering of suburban spending levels made CEIFA "almost a para-digm of a statute that violated the intent and spirit of *Abbott II*," Stein said years later. "I mean, it didn't come close." The unrealistically hypotheti-cal school district, the legislature's political maneuvering over suburban spending, the Department of Education's failure to study the program-matic needs of the poor: to Stein, they all suggested deliberate evasion of the *Abbott* decree.

Stein's colleagues, even the most liberal among them, did not share his jaundiced view of the state's motives. Where he saw stonewalling, they saw bureaucratic apathy and political compromise. Nevertheless, *Abbott IV* gave the state little to celebrate. Writing for the court's five-person ma-jority, Justice Alan Handler praised the new core curriculum standards but agreed with ELC that CEIFA's financial structure provided no guaran-tee that poor districts would be able to meet them. The hypothetical school district whose spending was supposedly a model of efficiency bore little resemblance to poor urban districts in, for example, the number of security guards it employed. And while the state had argued that extra spending was unnecessary and wasteful, the court majority was uncon-vinced: the very suburban anger that had forced the legislature to grand-father in higher spending levels suggested otherwise. Voters, educators, and interest groups "were seeking something more than the right to waste money," Handler wrote; they were expressing the "common understand-ing that those expenditures secure genuine educational benefits." The legislative capitulation to those demands meant that "CEIFA will perpetu-ate a two-tiered school system in which the students in the wealthier dis-tricts will have the resources necessary either to meet or to exceed the standards, and in which the poorer urban districts will be asked to do the same or more with less." Although CEIFA remained law for most New Jersey districts, it was unconstitutional for the poorest urban schools, the court ruled.

The court's remedy was the same as it had been seven years earlier, in
Abbott II: parity in spending between rich and poor school districts. But
the spending gap remained at 11 percent, or something over $200 million,
and CEIFA promised to halt further progress. After seven years, the court
was no longer willing to wait. The gap had to be closed—by September
1997, four months away. Still, Handler took pains to answer critics who
accused the court of merely throwing money at urban schools. Parity, he
wrote, was an interim remedy that would probably become "obsolete"
once the state made a careful study of what it cost to deliver the curriculum standards. Then that number, whatever it turned out to be, could
serve as the benchmark for T&E.

If Stein shared Wilentz's passion, however, he lacked the old chief's
persuasiveness, and for the first time in the *Abbott* litigation, the court
could not muster a unanimous front. Justice Marie Garibaldi, who had
suppressed her qualms about the role of money in school improvement to
join the majority in *Abbott II*, dissented in *Abbott IV*. The parity remedy
had been tried, Garibaldi argued, and it had failed: in the years since
Abbott II, millions more had flowed into the special needs districts, with
little result. Although the richest suburbs spent far more than the CEIFA
T&E level, most middle-class districts spent roughly that much. Why
shouldn't the special needs districts be able to do the job for similar
sums? Garibaldi asked. The majority saw parity as an interim remedy
headed for eventual obsolescence, but Garibaldi was skeptical: inevitably,
she argued, the interim remedy would harden into permanence, and each
year state aid to the urban districts would fluctuate with suburban spending, turning budgeting into guesswork. The parity mandate forced the
state to sign a blank check whose amount suburban voters would fill in
every year.

Parity had always constituted only half the *Abbott* mandate, however.
The court had also ordered the state to study what special programs poor
children needed to overcome their disadvantages, and just as the *Abbott IV*
majority was no longer willing to wait for parity, so too it would no longer
wait for the programmatic study. Again, the court ordered the commissioner of education to study the needs of the poor, but this time it put
teeth in that order: by year's end, a lower court was to examine the commissioner's report and make recommendations that the supreme court

would review. *Abbott IV* contained a last surprise: the court also ordered the commissioner to devise a plan for solving the glaring facilities problems of poor districts. ELC had always assumed it would take another lawsuit to establish that crumbling buildings violated the T&E clause, but the court majority had just decided that such a requirement was already implicit in *Abbott*.

For ELC and its allies, *Abbott IV* merited all the hackneyed adjectives— landmark, watershed, bombshell. Twenty-seven years after the filing of *Robinson v. Cahill*, the New Jersey Supreme Court had, in a manner that brooked no further delay, ordered spending parity for urban districts and a detailed study of their programmatic needs. Riding back to his office in the passenger seat of a venerable Honda, David Sciarra read aloud excerpts from the decision while his driver, a longtime League of Women Voters activist, pumped her fist out the window and punctuated his recital with cries of "Right on!" and "Way to go, supreme court!" At his press conference, exultant and angry, Sciarra called for Klagholz to resign in response to the court's criticism. Sciarra hadn't planned the incendiary demand, and he quickly regretted it; inevitably, such a personal attack would color his relationship with the man who would now be overseeing a complicated reform effort. But it was too late to take back the words.

Predictably, the governor and legislative leaders hated the decision, although privately many were not surprised. Echoing Garibaldi's dissent, Assembly Speaker Collins predicted the parity requirement would forever raise the bar on state spending. "It is unending," Collins said. "We could literally be spending billions and billions and billions." Discontented legislators suggested resurrecting the effort to amend T&E out of the constitution, but the administration tamped down such talk. New Jersey, like the country as a whole, was enjoying an economic boom, and legislators had just heard that tax receipts would come in hundreds of millions above budget. Absorbing the new parity requirement might not be that hard after all.

As the legislature prepared to comply grudgingly with the court's parity order, the lawyers turned their attention to the second part of the court's ruling, the required hearing on the programs poor children needed—the "remand hearing," as everyone soon called it. The justices had quickly accepted Stein's suggestion that the case go to a well-regarded appeals court judge, Michael Patrick King. Pat King had been born in Camden during the Depression; his mother taught public school in the city, but King went to private elementary school and later graduated from high school in the wealthy suburb of Haddonfield. King's father, who had died when King was eleven, was a lawyer, and King followed in his footsteps, becoming a judge in 1972. He was a history buff—he gave every new law clerk a map of New Jersey and took detours to visit state landmarks—and he was a stickler for good writing, handing out copies of Strunk and White's famous style manual and delivering forty-five-minute lectures on the merits of the dash or the semi-colon. He was also a kind and compassionate man. In the 1970s, he presided temporarily in family court, where judges wrestled with the system's saddest cases—family breakdown, child neglect, domestic violence. Sometimes, when he learned of children facing a weekend with no foster-family placement, King took them home to his own wife and four children. By the time the state supreme court chose him to preside over the remand hearing, King was the state's third most senior appellate judge, a twenty-five-year veteran with a reputation for intelligence, thoroughness, and independence. In legal circles, he was mentioned as a potential future state supreme court justice himself.

King was no education expert, however, and Stein was determined to enlist such an expert—in legal parlance, a "special master"—to help King evaluate the state's proposals. Stein worked the phones, talking to university professors and authors of significant education finance articles, asking everyone for names. Over and over, he heard about Allan Odden, a professor at the University of Wisconsin in Madison, who was both a respected researcher and an experienced policy analyst. Odden had taught high school math in East Harlem in the 1960s before earning a Ph.D. in education administration. For nine years, he had run the school finance center at the Denver-based Education Commission of the States, a policy clearinghouse for governors and state legislatures. When King called to discuss the job, Odden was intrigued. No other state had appointed a special master in a school-finance case, and Odden, who strongly supported standards-based reform, admired CEIFA's effort to tie funding to academic standards. Plus, as a rich state, New Jersey had the resources to carry out whatever reforms it chose. For a fee of fifty thousand dollars, Odden agreed to work as King's special master. ELC was wary. In his published work, Odden wrote more about how schools spent their money than about how much they spent, and he had worked closely with policymakers. Would that make him inherently sympathetic to the state's concerns?

Preparations for the November remand hearings consumed the summer and fall of 1997. The judge devoured books and articles on school funding and education reform and made ten visits to Camden's public schools, to see firsthand the kinds of programs the hearings would dissect. At ELC, Sciarra lined up expert witnesses, but mostly he waited to see what the state would propose: its court-ordered reform plan would necessarily take center stage at the hearing. Twice before, in *Abbott II* and *Abbott III*, the court had ordered such a plan, and in 1991 the legislature had made a similar demand, but governors, education commissioners, and legislators of both parties had come and gone, and no study had ever been done. Years later, no one was quite sure why. Perhaps, as Justice Stein believed, the state had been stonewalling, deliberately ignoring the court order to avoid discovering which expensive programs it had to launch. Perhaps, as more charitable observers suggested, the bureaucracy had been otherwise engaged, or perhaps no one had been quite sure how to undertake the work. Whatever the reason, procrastination had now run its course. Governor Whitman told the Education Department to develop a program the court would accept, Klagholz assigned staff to the project, and lawyers on both sides sparred over the details.

Odden's presence was already shaking up the debate. *Abbott II* had called for parity in spending for what might be called general education— schooling offered to children with no need for such services as special education, bilingual education, or remedial tutoring. Atop this general education base, the court had said, the state should layer the extra programs that poor children needed to wipe out their disadvantages. King's remand hearing was supposed to hash out exactly which supplemental programs this extra layer should include. In meetings with the judge and the lawyers, however, Odden questioned the validity of the court's bright line between base and supplemental. He drew an analogy with shopping for a new car. In some models, little more than brakes, engine, and vinyl seats come standard, and customers pay extra for moonroofs and leather seats; in some luxury sedans, the standard package already includes moonroofs and leather. Similarly, Odden thought, until you knew what programs the suburbs bought with their base funding, you could not know what supplemental services urban districts needed, or how much it would cost to provide them. ELC was appalled. Blur the line between the parity-funded base and the extra-cost supplemental programs, they feared, and the state would cut corners by using parity funds to pay for supplemental programs. Fifteen years of legal trench warfare had established that the cities were entitled to both parity funding and supplemental programs. That was what *Abbott* required.

Odden's view was a natural corollary of his interest in a then-popular education reform approach known as whole-school reform. Traditionally, reformers had tried to fix schools by adding new programs—a reading curriculum here, an anti-truancy effort there—to whatever a school was already doing, funding the new programs with their own separate grants. That approach had failed, whole-school reformers argued. Instead, schools needed unified, top-to-bottom reform efforts that pulled together all available funding streams and focused every person and every program on the same ends. The best-known of these whole-school reform models was Success for All (SFA), a program developed by Johns Hopkins academics that had raised test scores in inner-city schools. SFA featured tightly scripted, ninety-minute-long reading lessons, specially developed curricular materials, frequent tests to gauge progress, and intensive tutoring for struggling students; among whole-school reform models, it was one of the most expensive and prescriptive. The twenty-eight poor, urban districts—CEIFA called them "*Abbott* districts," dispensing with QEA's "special needs" terminology—needed such radical change, Odden thought: he had seen the plans they had submitted for spending their *Abbott IV* parity windfall, and he was deeply unimpressed. Although poor by New Jersey standards, the *Abbott* districts spent more than almost any other American city, and yet many had no idea how to spend effectively, he thought. In their parity plans, districts without effective reading programs proposed devoting their new money to useless initiatives, like hiring extra teachers' aides. Odden admired SFA, and when state officials conferred with him six or seven weeks before the start of the remand hearing, he made no secret of his view that whole-school reform was a promising strategy.

Years later, Odden could not remember exactly what he had said, but one state official recalled him examining a department-commissioned study of existing *Abbott* programs and saying, "You're never going to win with this—this is a hodgepodge."

Whatever Odden's words, the state soon made Success for All the centerpiece of its reform effort. Just weeks before the remand hearing opened, the department's finance officials began plugging SFA's staffing requirements into the same computer model that had churned out the controversial CEIFA efficiency standards. This time, however, to placate the court that had recently rejected those standards, the state used assumptions guaranteed to produce higher spending levels: suburban teacher salaries, rather than the lower state averages, for example, and security costs based on the needs of the edgy inner city rather than the placid suburbs. The illustrative budget the department produced showed that New Jersey could install SFA in urban elementary schools without spending a dime more than those schools already got. Indeed, within the existing budget, the state proposed supplementing SFA with a half day of preschool for four-year-olds, reduced class sizes, and such extras as computers.

The state's sudden embrace of SFA startled ELC, and at first blush the proposal seemed problematic. The state hoped to put SFA into every *Abbott* district elementary school, but SFA had been designed as a voluntary program available only to schools where at least 80 percent of the teachers had voted to adopt it. SFA also applied only to elementary schools: the state's report frankly acknowledged that research on whole-school reform programs for middle and high schools was spotty. For older children, the state reverted to a more conventional supplemental approach, recommending such add-ons as dropout prevention programs, alternative schools for disruptive students, and college counseling or workplace transition programs for graduates.

Still, ELC could hardly argue strenuously against Success for All: a year earlier, seeking to influence the CEIFA debate, ELC had issued its own report on supplemental programs for *Abbott* children, and that report had praised Success for All as the type of research-based instructional program the state needed. ELC found itself in the uncomfortable position of nitpicking a reform effort that, under different circumstances, it might well have embraced. Similarly, the state's proposed half day of preschool for four-year-olds was unexceptionable—decades of research showed that good preschool programs improved poor children's chances of school success. The most ELC could argue was that the state's proposal was too timid: instead of a half day, ELC advocated a full day, for both three- and four-year-olds.

In one area, however, the two sides clashed over principles, not just details. ELC wanted to give inner-city schools an expansive role in meeting students' health and social-services needs: *Abbott* district schools would become "community schools," providing one-stop shopping for everything from vaccinations to pregnancy tests to counseling. New Jersey's Department of Human Services already ran a well-regarded school clinic program in a handful of urban schools, and ELC wanted a clinic in every *Abbott* school. Children facing hunger, violence, illness, or family turmoil risked school failure, Sciarra argued; the question was not whether schools would deal with those problems, but how. Would troubled children disrupt classes, or would schools find ways to address nonacademic needs and free teachers to teach? Inner-city schools already employed armies of nurses, guidance counselors, and truant officers: why not accept that reality and find a way to make it work? The Education Department saw nothing but danger in such a broadened mission. Schools' primary job was academic preparation, state officials thought, and that task was hard enough. If schools tried to become all things to all people, they risked doing nothing well. The state did not plan to ignore students' health and social service needs, but Klagholz proposed hiring staff to refer students to community programs, rather than bringing such programs into the schools. ELC's experts believed such an approach would never work; students with disorganized lives would never make it to outside appointments.

The remand hearing opened the week before Thanksgiving 1997. King had divided the proceedings into two parts: first, both sides would present testimony on the supplemental programs *Abbott* children needed, and then the hearing would move on to urban districts' facilities needs. Like the administrative law court hearing a decade earlier, the remand hearing was short on dramatics: day after day, state education officials, academic researchers, and local school administrators took the stand to explain the latest thinking on, say, preschool education, class size, or school-based clinics.

To ELC, the weaknesses in the state's case were obvious. Although the supreme court had ordered the state to study what *Abbott* children needed and which programs would meet those needs, state officials conceded under cross-examination that they had done no detailed needs assessment before recommending programs; they had not even examined whether test scores had risen at the handful of New Jersey schools already using Success for All. Instead, the officials said, they had relied on national research and their own professional expertise in deciding which programs would help. To ELC, it was clear that the state was once again trying to sidestep the court order in an effort to fit programs into a predetermined fiscal box. The state's illustrative school budgets, with their acknowledged link to the disputed CEIFA model, made Sciarra especially suspicious. Did the state plan to impose these budgets on *Abbott* schools, even though the court had invalidated the CEIFA model for those very schools? Klagholz denied it. The illustrative budgets were just that— illustrations of how the state could pay for whole-school reform, he testified. If schools turned out to need more money, he would ask the legislature to supply it.

ELC's witnesses had problematic moments, too. A Columbia University sociologist described the virtues of an array of supplemental programs— preschool, summer school, reduced class size, school-based clinics—but refused to say which would most improve the achievement of low-income kids. "I cannot choose one over the other, because my reading of the research suggests that you need to do each of those things if you want to achieve success," he insisted under cross-examination. The state's litigator, thirty-eight-year-old Assistant Attorney General Jeffrey Miller, thought his side had scored a point. Liberal idealism was all very well, but the state had to make hard choices about how best to deploy limited resources, and one of the plaintiffs' chief witnesses had just refused to choose. That all-or-nothing stubbornness encapsulated the differences between the two sides, Miller thought.

Inevitably, the cost of the reforms loomed large. Miller sought to show that the price of ELC's proposals could soar as high as $811 million; ELC's longtime ally, Margaret Goertz, insisted the true cost was at least $150 million less. No one disagreed, however, that ELC's expansive vision would cost far more than the state's plan. By Goertz's estimate, the administration's proposals for kindergarten through high school would require only $17.6 million more than the state was already spending, and the administration's preschool proposal would actually cost $131 million less. The cost estimates for supplemental programs were dwarfed, however, by assessments of the building program. Even the relatively superficial survey the state had found time to do before the remand hearing suggested that repairing or replacing hundreds of dilapidated inner-city schools would cost $1.8 billion, and on the stand the state's own witness said that number was certainly too low.

Special master Allan Odden inadvertently provided the hearing's most dramatic sideshow. Sciarra had spent the third day of testimony hammering Klagholz over the missing needs assessment, but chatting with reporters in the hallway during a break, Odden suggested that omission was insignificant. "We don't need to catalog the needs of these kids," Odden said. "It has been done a zillion times." The reporters seemed to know little about Success for All's research base, so Odden described the "spectacular" track record of the state's preferred reform. For good measure, he praised New Jersey's efforts to link curriculum standards to school funding—efforts embodied in the very law the supreme court had partially invalidated. Odden had said all these things before, in published articles and conference presentations, but when Sciarra saw the next day's newspapers, he demanded that the judge fire his consultant. "The very integrity of this process has now been tainted by Dr. Odden," Sciarra said. "He is, in effect, an advocate for the state now." Judge King was unsympathetic. "Shall we muzzle him, is that your proposal?" he asked sarcastically. Odden stayed on the case, and the issue faded. Behind the scenes, however, Odden apologized to the judge. In retrospect, he realized, he should have kept his mouth shut.

Three days before Christmas 1997, the eighteen-day hearing ended, after testimony by twenty-four witnesses that filled nearly 3,500 transcript pages. In his closing argument, state lawyer Miller called ELC's community-school vision "pie in the sky," an overblown liberal solution to problems schools were never meant to address. Sciarra "believes more is better—more programs, more money, more everything," Miller said. "The department believes the school's mission is to educate." In his turn, Sciarra accused the state of offering a bare-bones program to children who brought huge problems to school. By contrast, he said, ELC envisioned schools that would "place these children at an equal starting line and prepare them to assume their rightful place in our economy and in our democracy."

Judge King retired to spend the holidays hashing out alternatives. Soon, he had the help of Odden's report, which, despite ELC's fears, steered a middle course between the two proposals. Like the state, Odden recommended that schools adopt a whole-school reform model, preferably Success for All; like ELC, Odden called for two years of full-day preschool, rather than just half a day for four-year-olds. ELC wanted smaller classes, but Odden doubted they were worth the cost; the state wanted schools out of the health and social services business, but Odden recommended school-based clinics in middle and high schools. The state's proposal preserved the traditional structure of the school year; Odden, like ELC, recommended summer school. Three weeks into the new year, Judge King issued his report, which largely adopted Odden's programmatic recommendations and put their cost at $312 million. The state would have to spend another $2.8 billion on facilities, King estimated.

King's recommendations carried no legal weight until the state supreme court ratified them, but Republican legislators nonetheless protested loudly at the price tag. Around Trenton, talk turned to legislative defiance and Byrne-era constitutional crisis; a bill was introduced calling for a constitutional convention to water down the T&E clause. The legislature's top Republicans wrote directly to the supreme court, arguing that King's expensive recommendations lay beyond the scope of the T&E clause. Preschool, health clinics, and all the rest might be good policy, but the courts could not turn policy choices into constitutional mandates. Spending so much on urban districts would inevitably mean shortchanging middle-class ones, the legislators warned, not to mention a host of other state priorities, from mass transit to prescription drugs for the elderly.

Once again, Verniero pored over boxes of documents, mastering the record of the remand hearing. This time, though, he felt more confident about the strength of his case. A nationally known education expert and a respected state appellate judge had accepted the central elements of the state's proposal: preschool, Success for All, and a construction program.

Now the state would urge the supreme court to respect the power of the executive branch by deferring to the commissioner of education's proposals. The justices should steer clear of specific mandates, Verniero would argue, to avoid setting in court-ordered concrete programs that might later need to be scrapped. And, certainly, the court should not mandate the extras King had called for—summer school, school-based clinics, and full-day preschool—since it was unclear whether those programs improved student achievement.

ELC attacked each element of the state's case, offering its now-familiar arguments for an expansive vision of community schools and against deference to an executive branch with a long history of noncompliance with *Abbott*. Most crucially, ELC rejected the state's insistence that only supplemental programs that improved students' academic achievement were required for T&E. In *Abbott II*, describing the deprivation poor children faced, Wilentz had written, "The goal is . . . to wipe out their disadvantages as much as a school district can, and to give them an educational opportunity that will enable them to use their innate ability." The court's marching orders were clear, ELC insisted: schools could not limit their mission to instruction alone. They had to do what they could to improve students' lives.

Now the justices retired to deliberate, and contentious negotiations over the *Abbott V* ruling began. As usual, Justice Gary Stein pressed for a more ambitious and prescriptive decision; after decades of state neglect and judicial patience, now was no time for timidity, he thought. Other justices were more cautious. They were not sure the remand hearing record showed that every urban school needed such programs as school-based clinics, and they did not want to put New Jersey's supreme court in the business of running schools. Justice Alan Handler was again writing the opinion, and Stein peppered him with suggestions. The two men spent hours in telephone conferences, as Stein pressed his case for a more comprehensive reform package. His colleagues teased Stein about his passion, suggesting that after he retired from the court, he should become education commissioner.

The unanimous *Abbott V* decision, released on May 21, 1998, did not go as far as Stein had hoped, but it still issued an extraordinarily detailed and prescriptive set of mandates. The court ordered New Jersey to put full-day kindergarten and half-day preschool for three- and four-year-olds in place in the twenty-eight *Abbott* districts by the fall of 1999. It endorsed the state's plan to institute whole school reform models, presumptively Success for All, in three hundred elementary schools within three years. It ordered the state to pay the full cost of repairing or replacing aging inner-city school buildings, with construction to begin by the spring of 2000. The court did not endorse Judge King's call to mandate summer school and school-based clinics; instead, it ordered the state to fund those programs and an array of others—everything from security guards to extra computers—if districts could show they needed them.

The recommendations were sweeping—the preschool mandate alone was the nation's first—but the press was most intrigued by two sentences in the opinion. "We anticipate that these reforms will be undertaken and pursued vigorously and in good faith," Handler had written. "Given those commitments, this decision should be the last major judicial involvement in the long and tortuous history of the State's extraordinary effort to bring a thorough and efficient education to the children in its poorest school districts." The New Jersey Supreme Court was surrendering its jurisdiction over the *Abbott* case, relinquishing to the administrative law courts the job of adjudicating the state's compliance with the *Abbott V* orders. The justices wanted, some of them said years later, to make clear that they did not run the schools, that the commissioner of education was responsible for implementing the programs they had called for. But the press heard a rather different message: the *Abbott* case was over.

Stein was dismayed. Inside the court, he had argued against surrendering jurisdiction, fearing the move would be interpreted in just this way, as an end to court involvement. Still, he thought such an interpretation misread *Abbott V*: nothing in the decision precluded the Supreme Court from returning to the *Abbott* fray if it chose. On his way to Martha's Vineyard the morning after the decision's release, Stein dialed the *New York Times* reporter who had authored that day's piece—"The court said it was giving up its oversight," she had written—and asked her, off the record, where she got that from. "That's not what we meant," he told her. A few days later, Handler sounded a similar note: during a panel at his forty-fifth Princeton reunion, the author of *Abbott V* pointed out that the court's ruling made the commissioner's proposals into court-ordered remedies, not just executive-branch policy choices. "The courts will always be available if there is an impasse," Handler added.

Whatever the liberal justices' gloss, however, *Abbott V* was widely viewed as a Whitman victory. The administration had proposed half-day preschool, whole-school reform, and a facilities program, and the court had essentially endorsed that proposal. The administration had urged restraint in expanding the schools' mission to include health and social services, and the court had left decisions about funding those services up to the commissioner. The administration had asked the court to let the executive branch implement the new reforms, and the court had announced it was giving up its jurisdiction. By making most supplemental programs optional, the ruling had taken the pressure off the current budget. The preschool program would be a huge challenge, but it did not have to be in place for a year. School construction would be tremendously expensive, but the legislature had two years to craft a bill. "By not putting a dollar value on it, it gives the Whitman administration tremendous ability to deal with these issues," a former Republican Senate staffer told reporters. "The heat's off."

David Sciarra held his own press conference with his own victory declaration, but the brash anger that had tripped him up the year before had dissipated. He felt humbled by the work that lay ahead. The state had just a few years to enroll thousands of children in preschool, to start hundreds of troubled schools on the road to comprehensive reform, to launch a multi-billion-dollar school construction program. How could ELC influence events when it had no working relationship with the Whitman administration? All Sciarra could think was how hard everything was going to be.

PART THREE

The Never-Ending Story

Implementing *Abbott*, 1998–2006

10

"We Do Not Run School Systems"

For seventeen years, the *Abbott* case had turned on large questions: the role of money in schooling, the power of education to overcome poverty, the fairest way to apportion billions in taxpayer dollars. The 1998 *Abbott V* ruling changed the terms of the debate, opening a new chapter in New Jersey's long struggle over equal educational opportunity. The state supreme court had ordered a comprehensive reform package only reluctantly, after a succession of legislatures and executives had failed to act. By surrendering their jurisdiction over the case, the justices had hoped to signal that they did not run the schools, that the hard work of implementing programs was up to the other branches of government. Instead, the ruling's detailed reform prescriptions inaugurated an era of hand-to-hand combat over inches of territory—fierce, technical battles that, in the eight years after *Abbott V*, would spawn ten more Roman-numeraled court rulings.

The first battleground was the preschool mandate. Nothing in *Abbott V* had thrilled the Education Law Center more, but even ELC founder Paul Tractenberg thought the court had a tenuous legal basis for ordering half-day classes for poor three- and four-year olds: the New Jersey Constitution's T&E guarantee explicitly applied only to "all the children in the State between the ages of five and eighteen years." To extend the entitlement backward, the court had cobbled together an argument based on the CEIFA law's provision of preschool funding, sidestepping the question of whether preschool were *constitutionally* required. Then the court had doubled back to add that, since poor children struggled academically

281

without it, preschool had "strong constitutional underpinning." It wasn't pretty, but from ELC's point of view, it did the job.

ELC had good reasons, both substantive and political, for making the preschool mandate its top priority. Preschool, with its adorable little pupils and its support from both left and right, was as close as education reform came to a motherhood-and-apple-pie issue. More important, in the fad-driven world of school reform, it was that rarest of creatures, a program with long-term research vouching for its effectiveness. Two respected studies had shown that early education significantly reduced the likelihood that poor children would drop out of school, get arrested, have babies out of wedlock, or fail to find work as adults; every dollar spent on a good preschool program saved society nine dollars in future spending on special education, welfare, and delinquency. Even though research showed poor children typically made a year's worth of progress for every year they spent in school, they began so far behind—*Abbott* kindergartners' communication skills lagged by eighteen months, one study found—that they could never catch up. Preschool could help put poor and middle-class children at the same starting line.

The preschool portion of the remand hearing had done nothing to erase ELC's congenital suspicions of the state. Education officials had tied themselves in knots testifying that a full-day preschool program was no better than a cheaper half-day program, despite research suggesting the contrary, and now ELC doubted it could trust Governor Christie Whitman's administration to implement even the half day the court had ordered. Soon after *Abbott V*, ELC head David Sciarra and Education Commissioner Leo Klagholz had tried to mend fences, meeting semisecretly at a diner a safe distance from Trenton. Before one meeting, Klagholz had glanced up at Whitman's photo on the diner wall and remarked that he would have to watch what he said, since his boss would be listening. Sciarra found the joke revealing: Klagholz, he speculated, was on a short leash.

Still, no one could accuse the Whitman administration of giving preschool planning low priority: the governor's leading policy advisor, Eileen McGinnis, headed an implementation group that was meeting weekly, visiting schools, and investigating other states' preschool initiatives. McGinnis wanted the program to succeed, since she believed broken governmental promises fed public cynicism, but she thought the supreme court's time line extraordinarily unrealistic. The court had ordered preschool to be in place by September1999, less than sixteen months after its ruling, and dozens of major decisions had to be made before then. Where would all the new preschool classes be housed? Who would ensure those new classrooms were clean and safe? Where would the teachers come from? What credentials would they have? How many children would each class hold? How long would the school day and year last?

ELC believed many of these questions had been answered months before. At remand, ELC's expert, Rutgers economist W. Steven Barnett, a coauthor of one of the seminal preschool studies, had argued for an intensive program, with classes of fifteen children taught by two adults, one of them a certified teacher. He had recommended a comprehensive curriculum, social services for families, generous supplies of everything from finger paints to jungle gyms, and a full six-hour school day, plus before- and after-school child care. Such a program would not come cheaply— Barnett estimated the costs at $9,000 to $14,000 per child, considerably more than the average $8,194 the state was already spending for public schooling—but nothing less would produce the big gains, the $9-for-$1 payoffs, that research showed were possible, he argued. The state's preschool proposal had been far more modest—$3,000 per child for a half day of schooling, minus the extra child care. But even Klagholz's cost estimates had assumed classes of fifteen children taught by two adults, one a teacher earning a public-school salary of $51,000. At remand, the two sides had certainly had their differences, but on preschool class size and teacher credentials, they had apparently agreed, and as far as ELC was concerned, *Abbott V* had put the court's imprimatur on that agreement.

McGinnis, however, saw the state's remand proposal not as an iron-clad commitment but as a planning document that her team was free to remodel. And remodel they did, in a surprising direction. In January 1999, Whitman announced that, far from cutting corners, the state would do *more* than the court had ordered, phasing in a full-day preschool program rather than the half day *Abbott V* required. Coming a year after top education officials had testified against full-day preschool, the about-face was dizzying. The state had changed course, McGinnis told reporters, after learning that half the *Abbott* preschoolers already got some kind of early child care; now, the state hoped to build on that foundation by improving those services. Years later, other officials suggested alternative explanations. Perhaps those who disagreed with Klagholz's position were gaining influence, while his power was waning—weeks later, he would announce his resignation. Or perhaps officials had testified against full-day preschool as a *constitutional* mandate but had decided the program made good policy sense anyway. ELC suspected Whitman knew litigation was looming and hoped to convince the justices of her commitment to their pet program.

Regardless, the policy reversal was shrewd PR: ELC had wanted full-day preschool for three- and four-year-olds, and now the state was planning full-day preschool for three- and four-year-olds. In a replay of its remand-hearing dilemma over whole-school reform, ELC found itself in the uncomfortable position of refusing to take yes for an answer. Still, ELC's experts were unconvinced by the state's plans. Whitman proposed spending $8,000 per child—a princely sum by the standards of most public preschools, but well below Barnett's minimum estimate. Her program would permit larger classes—twenty children with three adults, rather than fifteen children with two adults—and would not require preschool teachers to hold college degrees. "Three- and four-year-olds should be doing what they do best: playing, not cramming for kindergarten," the governor said. But Barnett insisted that Whitman's program would never produce the big gains preschool could bring. "Rather than one-on-one with mom, now you're in a group of twenty kids with three adults, none of whom is better educated than your mom," Barnett said. "What's the point?"

By then, the debate over preschool quality had simmered for months, and the crux of the argument was fast becoming a little-noticed sentence in *Abbott V* permitting the state to provide preschool in collaboration with community day care centers. McGinnis' team had seized on collaboration as the obvious way to find classroom space for thousands of new pupils, and indeed, such partnerships made sense: local child-care centers were woven into the fabric of inner-city life, freeing some single mothers to work and giving others teaching jobs. Since the launch of federal welfare-reform efforts, public money had poured into the centers, and that investment would be wasted if public schools took over the care of three- and four-year-olds.

But standards for class size and teacher credentials in state-licensed day care centers were far lower than the standards ELC believed the court had adopted for the new *Abbott* preschool program; as it stood, child care was babysitting, not education, and licensed child-care centers ran the gamut from cheerful, nurturing places run by well-trained teachers to sparsely furnished church basements staffed by high school graduates. ELC's remand proposal—drafted by economist Barnett and developmental psychologist Ellen Frede, his wife and research partner—had also promoted collaboration with existing day care centers, but only if the state paid to improve those centers' facilities, reduce their class size, and upgrade their teachers' credentials. Soon, however, it became clear that the state would not fund such improvements, at least initially. The state's strategy, it seemed, was to serve as many children as possible as quickly as possible, with quality upgrades coming later, when there had been time to recruit new staff, develop preschool teacher certification programs, and find classroom space. Barnett and Frede thought the state had it backward: better, they argued, to start with a small, high-quality program and then expand to serve more children. The state's approach would accustom some child-care centers to getting state funding for lower-quality care, and those centers would likely resist efforts to make them change their ways. A two-tiered preschool system would emerge, with well-paid, certified teachers heading classes in the public schools and low-paid, undereducated child-care workers providing glorified babysitting in community day care centers.

Years later, Whitman advisor McGinnis would insist that cost cutting had played no role in the state's preschool planning: her team had sought only to design a feasible, efficient program, she said. But ELC was sure the state's sudden interest in collaborating with child-care centers was a cynical cover for just such cost cutting. State officials were equally skeptical of ELC's criticism. They suspected that the teachers' union, a major ELC financial backer for more than five years, was eager to ensure that new preschool classes would be located in unionized public schools. As the contentious planning process unfolded, mutual acquaintances arranged for McGinnis, Barnett, and Frede to meet over dinner, but the effort to clear the air was not a success: the two sides argued all night long. McGinnis was already furious about a preschool survey Barnett had sent school districts, with a cover page explaining that any data collected might prove useful in future litigation. ELC's insistent litigiousness was making a hard job even harder, she thought.

By midsummer 1999, ELC was indeed back in court, accusing the state of "a classic 'bait-and-switch'"—winning supreme court approval for a high-quality educational program and replacing it with state-sanctioned babysitting the moment the court's back was turned. The state insisted ELC's demands were unreasonable; inevitably, it would take time to phase in a huge, complex program. Procedural rules allowed ELC to make its new case directly to the supreme court, and barely a year after optimistically surrendering jurisdiction, the justices were back in the thick of *Abbott*. On a Martha's Vineyard beach that summer, Justice Gary Stein ran into his fellow liberal, Justice Daniel O'Hern, and alerted him to the pending case. Stein was already upset. "The court believed the preschool program would be the foundation for reform of the entire school system for these districts. The result has been chaotic," Stein told the lawyers during oral arguments that fall. "My question is, how did this happen?"

As the justices deliberated, Stein fought hard to shape the new opinion, *Abbott VI*, into a ringing denunciation of the state's approach to preschool, which he believed irresponsibly ignored the court's crystal-clear directives. Stein struggled to win over his colleagues, however. The strong liberal majority that had decided earlier cases was depleted. Wilentz was dead, Handler had retired, and O'Hern, Stein's closest remaining ally, believed that state officials, struggling with an enormously complex job, had simply misconstrued the court's expectations. Stein was a perfectionist who expected little less than perfection from others, O'Hern thought. "Delivering programs is extremely difficult stuff," O'Hern said years later. "I have a more tolerant view of human capacity. People try; they don't always make it." Chief Justice Deborah Poritz, Whitman's former attorney general, was writing the decision, and she too did not share Stein's anger. Poritz drafted the opinion; Stein annotated her drafts. "I was not the soul of tact," he admitted years later.

The final version, issued in March 2000, found middle ground. The court refrained from questioning the administration's good faith, attributing "discrepancies" in the implementation of preschool to "misunderstandings"—though, in a separate concurrence, Stein called himself "somewhat less sanguine" about the state's motivations. But the court largely accepted ELC's argument that the administration's plans to deliver preschool via licensed child-care centers staffed with uncertified teachers fell unacceptably short of the program proposed at remand and endorsed in *Abbott V*. Collaborating with day care centers was appropriate, but those centers had to go beyond minimum licensing rules to meet the higher standards of *Abbott* preschool—fifteen children and two adults per class, certified teachers, and high-quality curricula. The state had promised some of these improvements, but the court ordered a faster timetable and once again left it to the administrative law courts to iron out disputes along the way. Wearily, the court urged the parties to find a way to get along. "For too long, there has been suspicion and distrust. . . . It is our hope that the adversarial relationship between the parties will give way to a cooperative effort," Poritz wrote. "The children deserve no less."

As the 2000–01 school year progressed, the wrangles over preschool implementation continued. A state-commissioned study of the program gave it decent marks overall but found that in nearly one in five classrooms, the teaching was of such poor quality that the students would have been better off staying home. In their own report, ELC allies Barnett and Frede found a comparable number of poor classrooms and far fewer good ones, and their evaluators returned from screening visits horrified at what they had seen. Poorly educated teachers were passing their limited skills onto their students—one had told her class that diamond shapes were triangles—or were maintaining discipline through yelling. In administrative proceedings, ELC complained about low enrollments, inadequate budgets, and snail's-pace dispute resolution. Once more, *Abbott* worked its way through the system, and in February 2002, a splintered supreme court ruled again, praising the state's progress but ordering it to ensure adequate funding and resolve disputes more efficiently. "We do not run school systems," the majority pointed out, not for the first time.

Abbott V was full of expensive mandates, but none were as astronomically expensive as the school-construction program. In its ruling, the supreme court had ordered the state to pay the full cost of repairing or replacing deteriorating inner-city schools, with work to begin within two years, by the spring of 2000. No one really knew how much that work would cost: the remand court's estimate, $2.8 billion, had been derived from a year-old study that did not even pretend to be exhaustive. In any case, every practical politician in the state knew the legislature could not pass a school construction bill that paid only for schools in the *Abbott* districts. The suburbs might lack crumbling, century-old buildings, but their schools were overflowing with children who lived in the new houses springing up on acres of former farmland. The state's coffers were full, and a school-construction bill was the perfect way to distribute largesse to communities that seldom qualified for much state aid. The court had taken care of the *Abbott* districts by ordering the state to pay 100 percent of their construction costs. The only remaining question was how the legislature would take care of the suburbs, and how well the bill would serve every interest group from architects to construction unions.

By the fall of 1998, five months after *Abbott V*, the outlines of a bill were starting to emerge. The administration was floating plans to split $5.3 billion in school-construction money between *Abbott* and non-*Abbott* districts, with the wealthiest districts getting no state aid. To cut costs, districts would select their schools from a limited number of prototype designs. Months passed; interest groups lobbied. The affluent suburban districts in the Garden State Coalition of Schools worried that the prototype schools were too small and lacked such now-standard amenities as art rooms, music rooms, and middle-school science labs. The prototypes were redesigned; the program's cost rose to $6 billion. The prototypes were caricatured as "cookie-cutter schools"; then they were abandoned. Each district would now be free to design its own schools. The wealthiest districts found their way into the program; the state would cover 10 percent of their construction bonds. Still, no bill had been formally introduced in the legislature. As the fall of 1999 arrived, the education commissioner began clearing the way for the most urgent *Abbott* district projects to start by spring. With just months to the court-ordered deadline, legislative wheels began to turn at last. The state senate introduced a bill paying the full cost of *Abbott* district construction and offering non-*Abbott* districts $1 billion in low-interest loans.

Three weeks before Christmas 1999, the wheels screeched to a stop. Republican Assembly Speaker Jack Collins, rumored to be considering a gubernatorial run, announced his own school-construction bill. It was more generous to the Republican-leaning suburbs—his loans were no-interest—and less generous to the heavily Democratic *Abbott* districts: the state would pay 90 percent, not 100 percent, of their costs. The supreme court had not really ordered full payment, Collins declared, even though virtually everyone else who had read *Abbott V* believed it had. For three months, as Collins persisted in his eccentric interpretation of *Abbott V*, the legislation stalled while the spring 2000 construction deadline drew ever closer. Finally, a month after the start of spring, Collins asked the supreme court to clarify its ruling, and the court obliged: its call for full state funding of *Abbott* district construction had meant, the court explained, full state funding of *Abbott* district construction.

The logjam was broken, but during the months of delay, anxieties had festered. Suburban districts had begun carefully examining their building needs, and their neighbors' building needs, and suddenly even $1 billion in loans was looking skimpy. Districts wanted protection in case the money ran out, and Ocean County legislators introduced a set of amendments, carefully written to steer aid to seven Ocean County school districts. To short-circuit such special pleading, the whole bill was recast: instead of loans, the state would offer grants, paying at least 40 percent of the construction costs for every district, no matter how wealthy. Now districts that had recently completed construction projects complained. They had undertaken necessary work without delay, and districts that had irresponsibly procrastinated were about to be rewarded with state aid. Legislators began considering making school construction aid retroactive.

Even before this late-spring feeding frenzy, costs had begun to balloon. The *Abbott* districts' detailed facilities plans had yielded a bottom line of $7.3 billion, more than two and a half times higher than the remand court's estimate. No one knew how much the suburbs planned to spend, and the bill's estimate of construction costs per square foot seemed unrealistically low, especially for expensive North Jersey. Legislators wanted to appear fiscally responsible, even as they authorized billions in new state debt; centralizing oversight of the costliest building projects seemed a logical way to ensure efficiencies. But no agency had ever managed such a vast program. Drafts of the bill passed the job around from one state authority to another. Meanwhile, urban advocates worried

that centralization would yield bureaucratic gridlock. Would it take another century to replace those century-old schools?

The jerry-built juggernaut creaked on toward its destination. It was
mid-July 2000, more than two years after *Abbott V*, when the legislature finally finished its work. The school construction program had become the
most expensive public works project in New Jersey history; the court's
open-ended guarantee to the cities, coupled with the legislature's extraordinary generosity to the suburbs, had produced a program with a
truly staggering price tag. In its final form, the bill provided $6 billion in
state money to the *Abbott* districts and $2.6 billion to everyone else—
when combined with local contributions, enough to fund $12 billion in
school construction, most of it paid for with borrowed money. The state
would cover 100 percent of the construction costs for the *Abbott* districts
and at least 40 percent for everyone else, with limited retroactive funding.
The small, well-regarded Economic Development Authority would manage
construction in poor districts getting high levels of state aid, including the
Abbott districts. As Whitman signed the bill into law and legislators con-
gratulated themselves on their achievement, everyone agreed that the really hard work—building schools—was about to begin.

The Education Law Center had played a relatively small role in the endless
legislative wrangling over school construction. Except for Speaker Collins's
quixotic crusade against the plain language of *Abbott V*, most of the controversy concerned funding for the suburbs, not for ELC's urban clients.
With its energies consumed by litigation over the shape of the preschool
program, ELC also watched from the sidelines as the state worked on the
third major element of the *Abbott V* package, whole-school reform. Even
from the sidelines, however, serious problems were obvious.

Whole-school reform models promised total school restructuring
in one convenient package: teacher training, classroom materials, and
sometimes curriculum would be supplied, for a price, by a whole-school
reform developer. Often, the developer was a university-based researcher
with a big idea about how to reorganize schools to produce better results—
say, by giving all students the enriched program typically available only to
the gifted, or by integrating technology into instruction, or by orienting
the curriculum around themes instead of traditional academic subjects.

At the *Abbott* remand hearing, the state's witnesses had described just one whole-school reform model, the well-known, solidly researched Success for All. The *Abbott V* court, impressed by evidence of SFA's success at raising inner-city test scores, had endorsed it as the "presumptive" reform model for the three hundred *Abbott* elementary schools.

The court's formulation had always carried the seeds of contradiction, however, since SFA's developers would work only with schools where 80 percent of the faculty had voted to adopt the program. In essence, the state was trying to impose a bottom-up reform from the top down. Four months after *Abbott V*, when the state announced which elementary schools would participate in the first year of whole-school reform's three-year phase-in, that fundamental contradiction became impossible to ignore. Only twenty-seven of the first seventy-two schools had chosen to implement the "presumptive" SFA model, and fourteen of those twenty-seven had been using SFA since well before *Abbott V*. A year later, eighty-three more schools launched whole-school reform, but only twenty-two chose SFA. The trend troubled one key observer, Supreme Court Justice Gary Stein; in his separate concurrence to the March 2000 *Abbott VI* pre-school opinion, Stein called it "disconcerting and inauspicious" that so few schools were choosing SFA. A month later, citing Stein's concerns, the state Department of Education told schools that had not yet chosen a whole-school reform model that picking SFA would mean tens of thousands of dollars in extra start-up grants. Even that plea failed, however: by fall, all but a handful of the 314 *Abbott* elementary schools had chosen a whole-school reform model, but only sixty-six, just over one in five, had chosen SFA.

The other schools picked their reform models from a menu of alternatives supplied by the state; in some districts, two, three, even five different whole-school reform models were in use. The proliferation of models posed clear problems. In New Jersey's urban schools, as in poor districts everywhere, students changed schools often, as families moved across town when their precarious living arrangements fell apart. The proliferation of reform models ensured that students changing schools would face especially difficult transitions. And, in marked contrast to SFA, many of the alternative models suggested by the state had little research supporting their effectiveness. Perhaps they would work better than what the struggling *Abbott* schools were already doing; perhaps not. No one knew for sure. No one even knew how well the models meshed with New Jersey's core curriculum standards, the foundation for reform in all the state's schools.

How had whole-school reform veered so far from the court's expectations, and so quickly? Academic research conducted in the first years of implementation suggested some reasons why.

In theory, each school should have chosen its reform model after careful deliberation; principal and teachers alike should have accepted the need for change, assessed their school's weaknesses, and looked for models designed to address those weaknesses. Everyone should have understood the research base for each model under consideration. But in many *Abbott* elementary schools, the academic studies found, the reform process bore little resemblance to this ideal. Especially in the first year of implementation, schools rushed to choose models; teachers barely understood what they were picking or why. After years of half-baked reforms that had come and gone, teachers and principals assumed this effort would be no different, and they feared committing themselves to an expensive and complicated program, like SFA, lest state money should dry up and leave them stranded. "Many felt that this was simply one more edict from either the district or the state department that would pass in a few short years," one Rutgers study concluded. (As if to confirm that cynicism, the $50,000 start-up grants the state had promised failed to materialize in the first year of implementation, forcing some schools to delay crucial training.) Perhaps most fundamentally, despite the desperately low test scores that plagued many of the *Abbott* elementary schools, their staffs felt little urgency for change. They looked for whole-school reform models that required less of it, and less than the relatively rigorous and scripted SFA. "It seemed to me to be the least intrusive of the models," one principal said about the program his school eventually chose. "You could continue to do what you were pretty much doing."

If the flawed model-selection process had confused some schools, the flawed budgeting process completely befuddled them. Site-based management—educational jargon for putting a team of teachers, parents, and administrators in charge of decisions affecting their own school— was a centerpiece of whole-school reform; in theory, a local team would understand local needs better than a far-off central office bureaucrat would. The state had taken this theory to an extreme, however. Eager to cut district central offices, reputed headquarters of wasteful spending, out of the budget process, the state required individual schools to write their own budgets, based on the staffing, training, and materials required by their whole-school reform models. Not only would the school management teams set budgeting priorities—say, deciding that their school needed another librarian; they would also build detailed schoolwide budgets—say, figuring out how to tap federal grants and state funding sources for the new librarian's salary. Then these schoolwide budgets would be submitted directly to the state Education Department for approval. The laypeople on the school management teams found the work complicated, technical, and time consuming. Teachers spent hours sitting in budget workshops instead of teaching classes; even the advisors sent from Trenton to provide technical help did not always understand the new procedures. At remand, state officials had promised not to impose their "illustrative" budget on individual schools, but in practice the illustrative budget guided the school management teams as they felt their way through the process. Funding levels varied from school to school, but that variation had little to do with which whole-school reform model was in place. Often, funding was decided the traditional New Jersey way: savvy administrators found helpful state bureaucrats and cut good deals for their schools. Schools with less-effective leadership ended up with less.

As the 2001 gubernatorial elections approached, the Education Law Center was eager for change. The *Abbott V* reforms were struggling: the preschool program was mired in litigation, urban districts had seen more red tape than school construction, and whole-school reform remained problematic. Christie Whitman had left the governorship early in 2001 to take a job in the new presidential administration, and with the Republicans' conservative gubernatorial candidate given little chance of winning in moderate New Jersey, all eyes were on the Democrat, James McGreevey, the mayor of the sprawling central New Jersey township of Woodbridge. McGreevey had grown up blue-collar, Irish Catholic, and ambitious, with a ferocious work ethic, an obsessive attention to detail, and a budding politician's gift for telling people what they wanted to hear. Single-mindedly, he had worked his way up through the Democratic machine, winning the favor of party bosses, serving two terms in the state legislature, and nearly beating Whitman in her 1997 reelection bid. He could be a wooden public speaker, and sometimes, with his closely cropped hair and play-it-safe blue suit, he cut an awkward figure, like the nerdy dad chaperoning the middle-school dance. But, at forty-four, he still worked harder than anyone else—reading more briefing books, marching in more small-town parades, and staying later at every chicken dinner to shake just one more hand. Politically, he was a classic left-of-center urban Democrat, dutifully stamping his ticket with endorsements from labor unions, environmentalists, and abortion-rights groups. ELC and its supporters had high hopes for a McGreevey administration. The constant battles with the Whitman administration over every inch of territory had worn Paul Tractenberg down, but the McGreevey campaign was reaching out to ELC. McGreevey's education advisor, a lawyer and one-time math teacher named Lucille Davy, who was married to one of McGreevey's closest aides, was calling often, thirsty for information about the *Abbott* reforms.

McGreevey won as handily as expected and chose as his education commissioner a little-known fifty-five-year-old school superintendent, William Librera, who had grown up working class in North Jersey. For ELC, Librera's best quality was his open enthusiasm for the *Abbott* decisions; the day McGreevey announced his appointment, Librera called *Abbott* a decision to "celebrate." Like ELC, Librera believed *Abbott* implementation had gone off course. To beef up the preschool program, fix the unwieldy school budget process, evaluate the effectiveness of the whole-school reform models, and streamline the construction program, he thought, the Education Department needed to consolidate the work in a single division headed by an assistant education commissioner—an *Abbott* czar. Librera wanted the famous urban educator Anthony Alvarado for the job, but when that possibility fizzled, he looked closer to home. Steve Block, ELC's longtime researcher, recommended Gordon MacInnes.

Tall and craggy, MacInnes was something of a jack-of-all-trades in New Jersey policy and politics. In the 1960s, after graduate school at Princeton, he had helped shape Governor Richard Hughes's urban policy in the wake of the Newark riots. Later, he ran a major state charity, headed New Jersey's public broadcasting network, chaired his father-in-law's $300 million manufacturing company, wrote a book on race in American politics, and founded a nonprofit school reform group. He worked on the presidential campaigns of Robert Kennedy and Walter Mondale and twice served in the New Jersey legislature, though, as a Democrat in staunchly Republican Morris County, he never managed to win back-to-back terms. He was smart, savvy, and almost unstoppably articulate. Block had known MacInnes for years, and throughout the Whitman-era preschool litigation, MacInnes had been a firm ELC ally. When Librera gave MacInnes the job, Block was sure he would make a fine *Abbott* czar.

Within a month of McGreevey's January 2002 inauguration, the administration put its new attitude toward the *Abbott* decisions on very public display. In a Trenton elementary school's gym, the governor and ELC's David Sciarra held a joint press conference to announce a collaboration between the former adversaries. ELC would join key state officials on a new Abbott Implementation and Compliance Coordinating Council, which would meet monthly to hash out the details of the *Abbott* reforms. "It's time for the state to stop being an obstacle to change," McGreevey said. "We've got to commit ourselves toward improving education in our urban school districts. This is not a partisan issue. It's not a regional issue. It's a moral imperative." Behind the scenes, not everyone shared the enthusiasm. Sciarra and Block, thrilled at the state's new embrace of *Abbott*, had consulted only minimally with most of ELC's board, and lawyers in the attorney general's office, which had fought ELC in court for years, warned Librera that the advocates would never be capable of real compromise. The doubters were silent that day, however. The official position was optimism.

Two months later, the new relationship bore its first fruit. Although New Jersey was facing a huge budget deficit—Whitman had increased state debt and cut the income tax, and now those choices, combined with a national recession, were yielding rivers of red ink—McGreevey promised to invest $140 million more in the *Abbott* preschool program, now run by preschool researcher Ellen Frede. In return, ELC had agreed to a one-year freeze on spending for all other *Abbott* programs—in effect, a small budget cut, since districts would have to pay next year's cost-of-living-increases out of last year's budget. Both the state and ELC characterized the freeze as a one-year time-out on implementing the *Abbott* reforms, a pause to allow the new partners to figure out what programs the state's money was paying for and whether those programs were working. The *Abbott* districts were certainly not suffering alone: virtually every school district in the state was facing a similar aid freeze, and most already spent far less than the *Abbott* districts, with their court-ordered parity with wealthy suburbs. Still, for the advocacy community, the time-out came as a shock. For the first time in *Abbott*'s twenty-one-year history, ELC was supporting a state effort to curb urban school spending.

Years later, Sciarra acknowledged mishandling the time-out. In retrospect, he believed, he had not given either his board or the larger school community a full enough explanation of ELC's decision. Furthermore, he had come to realize, he should never have appropriated to ELC the power to agree to school districts' funding levels. ELC had always insisted it represented children, not school systems; in agreeing to the spending time-out, it had behaved as if it spoke for the districts. Whatever the technicalities, the rage that ELC's decision unleashed bespoke a primal sense of betrayal. "This is the rape of the *Abbott* districts," announced Patricia Bombelyn, a New Brunswick lawyer who had once studied under Tractenberg. Soon, Bombelyn founded an online forum, AbbottWatch, where ELC's critics vented their frustration. At an information meeting in New Brunswick, angry parents berated Sciarra for selling out. ELC had its doubts about AbbottWatch's motives—the group's founders were strong supporters of tuition vouchers—but behind the scenes, others in the liberal advocacy community voiced quieter concerns about whether Sciarra had too quickly thrown in his lot with an untested administration. With the state's fiscal problems stretching to the horizon, how could Sciarra be sure the one-year time-out would not last indefinitely?

Block had taken the initial criticism in stride, certain the anger would subside as the collaboration yielded real improvements in *Abbott* implementation. At first, the monthly meetings of the high-level *Abbott* council and its subcommittees went well, but quickly the mood began to sour. The room was filled with healthy egos—Block, the impassioned reformer; Sciarra, the tenacious advocate; MacInnes, the opinionated administrator—and participants grew to dread the inevitable shouting matches. Soon, education commissioner Librera decided these "root-canal meetings," as he called them years later, were an unproductive use of his time. If his staff chose not to prepare for the next meeting, so that it had to be postponed, he had no objections. By fall 2002, the council had stopped meeting.

At the heart of the disagreement between ELC and the state lay perhaps the most contentious part of the *Abbott* reform package: supplemental programs, the extra services that urban schools would layer atop their regular educational program in order to wipe out the special disadvantages of children growing up in poverty. Although the 1990 *Abbott II* opinion had ordered such programs, that mandate had been eclipsed by the court's dramatic call for spending parity between rich and poor school districts; the parity question had been settled once and for all only in the 1997 *Abbott IV* opinion, when the court had ordered equal spending almost immediately. Controversial as the parity mandate was, fulfilling it was merely a matter of arithmetic: after *Abbott IV*, the legislature allocated enough money each year to ensure that every *Abbott* district could spend as much as the wealthy suburbs. By contrast, the question of supplemental programs was far more complicated, a matter not just of arithmetic but of judgments about what tasks schools could or should take on and how best to carry them out. The remand hearing had hashed out these very questions, with the state arguing that schools should focus on their educational mission and ELC countering that inner-city schools could not educate unless they also helped students who came to class hungry, sick, or traumatized.

In its 1998 *Abbott V* decision, the supreme court had largely stayed out of this debate, noting only that students' health and social service needs had to be met one way or another. Although the court had mandated a few supplemental offerings—not only preschool and whole-school reform, but also computer specialists, dropout-prevention coordinators, and the like—it had consigned most others to the discretionary category, required only if districts could demonstrate their necessity. Since the state Education Department had still never determined what supplemental programs New Jersey's urban schools needed, the court had little basis for mandating any particular program.

Without such a study to provide a rigorous reality check for school district requests, however, the supplemental-programs funding process soon degenerated into Trenton's customary fiscal improvisation. *Abbott V* had given the Education Department new responsibilities without corresponding increases in staff or funding, and as overburdened bureaucrats struggled to cope, the definition of a supplemental program deserving extra funding developed "an understandable looseness," Librera said years later. *Abbott* districts devised their budgets, explaining what parity funding would cover and what more they needed. Then they cut deals for the excess, the education commissioner got what he could out of the legislature, and everyone lived to fight another day. Was the extra money paying for the supplemental supports the supreme court had envisioned, or was it covering the usual costs of doing school business? No one really knew.

Under the Whitman administration, the supplemental funding process was fraught with conflict. The first year after *Abbott V*, districts initially asked for $294.5 million, later cut their requests to $152.5 million, and were eventually awarded $37 million. Klagholz's successor as education commissioner, David Hespe, had trouble extracting even that much from a reluctant legislature: after *Abbott V*, most state officials had assumed urban districts could manage just fine with parity funding—which, after all, was far more than most middle-class districts spent. The next year, the districts requested $478 million and Hespe approved $156.6 million; the following year, the districts asked for $1.2 billion and got $315 million. Disagreements wound up in administrative law court, where hearings dragged on for months. By the time ELC and the new McGreevey administration agreed to the one-year time-out, the supplemental funding process had become "almost like a blank check," the state's lawyer argued in court. In the time-out year, the state was supposed to get its house in order.

Soon, however, it became clear that the remand-hearing dispute over the mission of the schools had survived the change of administration. While ELC saw supplemental programs, with their promise of wiping out the disadvantages of poverty, as an integral part of *Abbott*, *Abbott* czar Gordon MacInnes had been suspicious of such grandiose liberal idealism for three decades, ever since working in a Trenton antipoverty program after graduate school. As MacInnes saw it, the real goal of *Abbott* was not some woolly antipoverty agenda but the elimination of the academic achievement gap between rich and poor, minority and white. Research showed that children who could not read well by third grade fell further and further behind in every subject as they got older; therefore, MacInnes decided, he must focus on early literacy in the *Abbott* districts. Schools needed to concentrate on the difficult but doable job of educating, not on the monumental job of wiping out disadvantage. Preschool was crucial, yes, but for MacInnes, the other *Abbott V* mandates—the computer specialists, the dropout-prevention coordinators—were distractions from the real work of teaching young children to read. ELC believed MacInnes had drawn a false dichotomy between instructional programs, the proper work of schools, and supplemental ones, an unnecessary distraction. Summer school, after-school tutoring, hot breakfasts—all of them helped city kids keep up in class. Even extra security guards and school health services, ostensibly noninstructional supplemental programs, helped clear a space in which teachers could teach. Those services might not translate into extra points on a test, but the court had never made test-score gains the sole gauge of *Abbott*'s success.

To MacInnes, no *Abbott V* mandate seemed more distracting than whole-school reform, the centerpiece of the Whitman administration's remand proposal. Since 1996, most New Jersey school districts had spent their time aligning their curricula with the state's new academic standards and tests—ensuring that students studied algebra, grammar, and the Civil War at the grade level and in the detail the state required. But most *Abbott* districts had spent those same years picking whole-school reform models, training their teachers in this or that new approach, hiring the facilitators and tutors their models required. No wonder, MacInnes thought, that *Abbott* students performed miserably on state tests: in many districts, the curriculum they were following had never been properly aligned with the standards on which the tests were based. In October 2002, MacInnes told the *Abbott* districts that their elementary schools were no longer required to adopt whole-school reform models, as long as they found another way to help all students read by third grade and master the core curriculum standards. A few *Abbott* districts consistently earned relatively high elementary school test scores, MacInnes had learned, and they were districts that had deliberately chosen unobtrusive whole-school reform models. In districts that had embraced *Abbott V*'s prescriptions wholeheartedly, scores were stagnating. Perhaps the key to closing the achievement gap lay in replicating the high-achieving districts' approaches elsewhere, MacInnes thought. It certainly didn't lie in a blind commitment to the programs enshrined in *Abbott V.*

MacInnes's decision should have been a victory for ELC—after all, at the remand hearing five years earlier, ELC had argued against making whole-school reform mandatory. Sciarra and Block had spent many hours successfully convincing Lucille Davy, now McGreevey's education advisor, that whole-school reform was a failure. To Davy's astonishment and frustration, however, ELC's views had apparently changed; now it opposed MacInnes's efforts to scrap whole-school reform. Years later, Sciarra would explain the reversal as a simple evolution in ELC's views: despite well-documented growing pains, whole-school reform was beginning to take root, ELC had come to believe, and scrapping the models would only bring further chaos. Test scores at *Abbott* elementary schools finally seemed to be moving upward; surely the state should evaluate what was working before abandoning everything. But Sciarra's account, however sincere, ignores the psychological context of the confrontation. By the fall of 2002, the rocky months of collaboration had eroded ELC's trust in the good intentions of the McGreevey administration, and so ELC reverted to the default position it had maintained ever since Morheuser's day: suspicion of state motives. With trust gone, Sciarra no longer felt safe abandoning the bird-in-the-hand certainties of the *Abbott V* reform prescriptions. Those prescriptions might not be ideal, but they were better than a future in which urban students were left to the tender mercies of an administration that Sciarra no longer believed had children's best interests at heart.

Why had trust vanished so quickly? MacInnes's vision of *Abbott* had not really changed in the years since he had fought side by side with ELC against the Whitman administration's implementation of preschool, but agreement on that issue had masked the deeper divergence between the two sides. Now, as those differences became unmistakable, ELC's Block felt blindsided: the man he had recommended for the czar job because of his deep commitment to *Abbott* was not committed to *Abbott* after all, at least not to ELC's vision of *Abbott*. Frustration blossomed on both sides. MacInnes wanted to follow his promising research into high-scoring urban districts wherever it led, even if that meant jettisoning parts of *Abbott V*. Blocking his way he found ELC, with—as he and Education Commissioner Librera saw it—a lawyerly attachment to every comma in the prescriptive opinion. ELC wanted the state to do what it had promised under the time-out agreement: figure out what supplemental programs were in place, evaluate how well they were working, and straighten out the flawed funding process. Blocking its way it found MacInnes, with—as ELC saw it—an ideological antipathy to crucial parts of its hard-won court victories.

Years after the collaboration had unraveled, each side would accuse the other of one final betrayal—making the divorce public without advance notice. The writing had been on the wall for weeks, however. By the fall of 2002, as state officials spoke publicly of a return to court to ask permission to relax some of *Abbott V*'s requirements, especially the whole-school reform mandate and the directives to hire particular staff, Sciarra was insisting ELC had not yet agreed to any such court filing. Finally, in January 2003, less than a year after the hopeful Trenton press conference, Sciarra made public a stinging letter to Education Commissioner Librera. The state's proposals were "clearly designed to eliminate, undermine and weaken the *Abbott* programs and reforms," Sciarra wrote. "As a result, ELC cannot and will not support this plan." The collaboration was officially over. Sciarra felt used: ELC had given the state a year of budgetary grace, but now, he thought, it was clear the administration had never really intended to implement *Abbott*. McGreevey advisor Davy wondered if anything would ever satisfy ELC.

In March, the state returned to court, asking permission to make whole-school reform optional and to ignore the *Abbott V* mandates to staff particular supplemental positions. Like the Republican Whitman administration before it, the Democratic McGreevey administration insisted that cost cutting was not its goal, but deep in the state's court filing was a piece of fiscal news that infuriated ELC. In 2002 Sciarra had agreed to the fiscal time-out because he believed the spending freeze would last only one year. That belief had been staggeringly naïve: the state's budget problems were monumental, and *Abbott* spending was a tempting multibillion-dollar target for cost cutters. The March filing made clear that state officials were seeking a second year's budgetary grace—"a maintenance year," they called it. Although the state planned to spend an extra $209 million to ensure parity and expand preschool, that money was to be deducted from the $380 million the state was already spending on *Abbott* supplemental programs—a budgetary shell game, in ELC's view. The state was also demanding that eleven of the *Abbott* districts raise their school taxes, frozen at 1997 levels since the *Abbott IV* parity order, but that incendiary proposal quickly evaporated in the heat of legislative opposition.

The supreme court tried once more to stay out of the detailed, technical disagreements that the *Abbott* case had become, assigning the latest dispute to mediation. Over the spring of 2003, with a judge's help, the two sides hashed out their differences over whole-school reform and supplemental programs. The state won the right to try new reform approaches in low-performing schools and to give high-performing ones extra flexibility; ELC won agreement that *Abbott* schools would continue to implement a list of agreed supplemental programs; and both sides promised to work together to design a formal evaluation of the *Abbott* reforms. Still, the court could not stay entirely above the fray: that July, it ruled on the one issue the mediation had left unresolved, the state's request for a second year's funding time-out. The eventual ruling—a partial victory for the state, allowing it to delay new programs but requiring it to keep funding existing ones—would cost the McGreevey administration $200 million more.

For the next three years, *Abbott* never left the courts for long, as the state, the *Abbott* districts, and sometimes the Education Law Center jousted over fiscal technicalities—the precise definition of a "maintenance budget," for example, or the mechanics of preschool funding. The issues had become so baroque, the amounts of money so relatively small, that it was no longer easy to declare winners and losers. The McGreevey administration ended in scandal, and a billionaire Democrat, Jon Corzine, succeeded to the governorship, vowing to put New Jersey on the road to fiscal responsibility. In April 2006, Corzine made his own application to the court for a freeze in *Abbott* supplemental funding; to longtime *Abbott* watchers, the state's plea for a year's grace to determine what programs it was paying for and how well they were working had a curiously familiar ring. A month later, the court gave the new administration the breathing room it sought, as well as the right to demand school tax increases in eight *Abbott* districts with especially low rates. By then, New Jersey's ten-year-old CEIFA school funding formula, which the *Abbott IV* court had invalidated only for poor urban districts, had become irrelevant to the rest of the state's schools as well. Over the previous four years, with budget crisis succeeding budget crisis, the legislature had abandoned all pretense of adhering to a formula and had begun divvying up education dollars according to ad hoc rules based on political clout rather than policy principles. In the thirty-six years since the filing of *Robinson v. Cahill*, the state supreme court had invalidated four school-funding laws, and less than a year after his election, Corzine was already promising to propose a school-funding formula of his own.

11

The Children Grow Up

By the early twenty-first century, New Jersey had spent two generations wrestling with the question of equal educational opportunity, but that titanic legal and political struggle had barely touched the lives of the twenty children who were named plaintiffs in *Abbott v. Burke*. By the time the state supreme court invalidated Governor Jim Florio's QEA in the 1994 *Abbott III* decision, all the plaintiff children had left New Jersey's public schools. Until a newspaper sought them out soon after the 1997 *Abbott IV* decision, none but Ray Abbott had ever been the subject of a press account; some had never even known they were involved in the case, however peripherally. Growing up is hard work under the best of circumstances, and few of the *Abbott* children had enjoyed that ideal. Some had suffered early deprivation, at home and in school; some had gotten little adult guidance as they looked ahead to life after graduation. And as they would readily admit years later, some had compounded the damage with shortsighted, self-destructive choices. Nevertheless, their stories bore witness to the indomitable spirit of their parents, to the extraordinary resilience of children, and to the human capacity for growth.

Ray Abbott

Ray Abbott was paroled at the end of 1997, halfway through his eight-year sentence. Jean had stuck by him, bringing their baby daughter on prison visits, and the summer before his release, they were married. In prison, Ray had finally discovered the motivation he had lacked before: eager to fill his empty days and impress the parole board, he had enrolled in anger management classes, begun attending Narcotics Anonymous meetings, and started studying for a GED. The day he learned he had passed the test on his second attempt, he was "so proud of me," he remembered years later. Reading still challenged him, but in prison, with time to spare, he had discovered a passion for Sidney Sheldon novels and taught himself to pore over a dictionary to decode unfamiliar words. Sometime during his prison stay, he would say years later, he had also stopped using drugs.

Out of prison and living with Jean on Long Island, Ray at first found work at McDonald's, but soon a far better opportunity presented itself. Anthony, a friend from long-ago summer basketball games, offered him a job in a sheet-metal shop, and by watching the experienced workers, Ray picked up the trade. Book learning had always come hard to him, but he loved reading blueprints. He could grasp the information encoded visually in shapes and spaces. Eventually, he found work for an air-conditioning company, making ductwork in its shop and installing central air in homes and businesses. Watching units he had installed hum into life, with air flowing through the ductwork he had made, Ray felt a sense of accomplishment for the first time.

In May 1999, Ray and Jean had a second child, a son. Jean wanted to raise her children away from the fraying, blue-collar towns of Long Island, and at her insistence the family moved to upstate New York and bought a house. An out-of-county move was a violation of Ray's parole, which still had more than a year to run, and as he remembered it years later, the parole department refused to do the paperwork to transfer such a short-term case to another county. Ray and Jean moved anyway, but the violation was quickly detected; rather than send Ray back to New York's overcrowded prisons, the authorities placed him in a twenty-eight-day drug rehabilitation program, even though, Ray insisted years later, he had been sober for years. With the parole violation resolved, he spent his weekdays working on Long Island and his weekends sneaking upstate to see his wife and children. The strain of the long, expensive trips began to tell, however. Gradually, his visits decreased to every other week. When Ray's parole ended in 2001, he moved back upstate, but he could not get a job in his newfound trade, and eventually he returned to work on Long

Island and sent money to his family. After a while, Jean told him she had found another man, and the divorce became final in 2003.

Still, Ray Abbott soldiered on. Although he had heard nothing from his grandparents, stepfather, or siblings since the disastrous fight at his mother's funeral and had not seen his oldest daughter since her babyhood, he stayed in touch with his two younger children, even when the transmission on his car failed and he had to travel six and a half hours by bus to see them. He sent Jean money when he had it, and at Christmas 2004 he showered the kids with toys, clothes, and jewelry. A serious on-the-job knee injury, to the same knee he'd hurt playing football as a teenager, lost him his best job, an on-the-books position with real benefits, but he found off-the-books work for a subcontractor.

Was his sobriety secure? Ray insisted it was, even though he was too tired after a long day at work to attend twelve-step meetings, even though he had a beer now and then during a Friday night poker game or a Sunday football broadcast. His friends were few, but he shared a close bond with Anthony, who had given him his start in sheet metal. Uncle Ray was the only friend Anthony and his wife trusted to babysit for their three young children. Twenty years earlier, Ray Abbott marveled, no one would have trusted him with anything. He knew he was responsible for many of the wrong turns his life had taken, that his addiction, his lies, and his thieving had driven away his family. He wondered if better schools could have reached him—perhaps if the classes had been smaller, someone could have kept him from falling so far behind, from giving up. In the end, however, he blamed only himself. "It just took me thirty-three years to grow up," he said.

Two days after Christmas 2004, thirty-six-year-old Ray Abbott, a slightly built man with close-cropped dark hair, high cheekbones, and gold-rimmed glasses, sat in a bleak Wendy's restaurant on Long Island and, as "Silent Night" played over the sound system, told his story to the writer of this book. Nowhere seems lonelier than a fast-food joint at holiday time. But searching for Ray had reawakened dormant family connections. Soon after the interview, for the first time since his mother's funeral twelve years earlier, Ray heard from his younger half-brother, and some time later, Ray moved back to New Jersey to be closer to family.

He found work as a truck driver and began dating someone new, a school-teacher in an *Abbott* district.

Henry Stevens Jr.

Henry Stevens Sr. spent seventeen years working for the Ohio teachers' union before health problems forced him into early retirement. In his desk drawer, he always kept a copy of the original complaint in *Abbott v. Burke*. Somewhere along the line, his oldest son, Henry Jr.—by 2006, a corporate manager married to his high school sweetheart, and the father of three—heard something about his own connection with the case.

Back in South Jersey in 2000 for his best friend's wedding, Henry Stevens Jr. decided to show his girlfriend the Camden neighborhood he had last seen fourteen years earlier. On Saturday afternoon, they drove into town, parked the car, and strolled over to the green house on Berkley Street where Henry had grown up, played backyard basketball, and turned the family garage into a neighborhood hangout. But the scruffy block he remembered fondly had deteriorated in the years since he had left. In the neighborhood park, the same park where the big kid had stolen his bike all those years earlier, money and drugs were changing hands openly, in broad daylight. Henry's old house hadn't had a paint job since his father's day, the old basketball hoop had been replaced by an orange crate with its bottom knocked out, and dog feces littered the pavement in front of the garage he had loved. Henry had hoped to knock on the door and take a look around, but the neighbors who remembered him advised him not to risk that knock—better still, not even to stand around in front. His childhood home had become a drug house. Henry stayed for less than an hour, and as he drove out of town, he felt grateful, not for the first time, that his parents had left Camden when they did.

Michael Hadley

Lola Moore retired from the Camden schools in 2005. She had held two jobs till the end, running the youth services center at Woodrow Wilson High School every day and spending three evenings a week and part of her

Saturdays teaching a computer class for local families. Her years of work inside the high school had given her a new appreciation for the challenges inner-city teachers faced—the babies having babies, the students calling their teachers "bitch," the racial and economic isolation that affluent New Jersey tolerated in its cities. "They couldn't pay me enough money to be a teacher," Moore said now. Still, she had never given up on her community. Years earlier, Lynnette, by then a well-paid manager in the federal housing department, had offered to buy her mother a house in any suburb she liked, but Moore had never wanted to leave the neat brick rowhouse in east Camden where she had raised her children. She still gave school board members an earful at every meeting, as furious as ever about exorbitant administrative salaries and textbook shortages, and now that those meetings were a staple of local public-access TV, her fans recognized her in the grocery store.

For several years after his pro football dreams ended, Lola Moore's son, Michael Hadley, worked as a substitute teacher and teacher's aide in Camden, filling in wherever the school system sent him. His favorite job was a long-term assignment as an elementary school gym teacher. Eventually, he found work as a laborer with the city housing authority. Laid off perhaps five years later, he spent time in another position or two before settling into a job as a laborer for a home builder. In 1998, a girlfriend gave birth to his son, and Michael began planning for the baby's future, determined that his little boy would grow up to earn a college degree, or at least to hold a better job than his father's. By the time his son was an honor-roll first grader at the same Camden elementary school Michael himself had attended, Michael had already saved enough, he said, to ensure that by third grade, the little boy could attend private school, or perhaps move to the suburbs. Two years later, though, his son was still in public school, and Michael had extended his deadline to fourth or fifth grade.

When he spoke about his own school days, Michael sounded ambivalent. His teachers had been caring and committed, he insisted; only he was to blame for the opportunities that had slipped through his fingers. Still, he concluded, "I'm not going to sit here and let my son get cheated like I got cheated." He honored Lola Moore's struggles, but he knew he had missed something in not having a father. If he'd had a dad to throw a football with him, to teach him the positions and hone his natural talent, he would have ended up in the pros.

Dorian and Khudayja Waiters

One day in the mid-1990s, Dorian Waiters called his sister Khudayja at work. By then, she had left Bloomingdale's, taken a computer job at a clothing company, and begun classes at a technical school. Dorian said he needed to see her—immediately—and right there on the phone, Khudayja burst into tears. She knew that his AIDS test must have been positive.

For perhaps three years, Dorian's illness took its course. He shuttled in and out of hospitals, but when he was well enough, he still went clubbing, and once he insisted that a friend bring a fashionable outfit to the hospital so he could be well dressed for a pending doctor visit. On Memorial Day 1996, Khudayja and some friends took him to a club in Washington, D.C. By then, AIDS had left Dorian nearly blind, but Khudayja sat next to him, holding his hand, just to let him know she was there. He was ashamed of his physical decline: he had shrunk to a gaunt ninety pounds, his ribs and facial bones stood out, and sometimes he walked with a cane. Most painful for Khudayja, dementia had invaded his mind: he had become spacey and forgetful and would lose his train of thought in midsentence. His hospital stays grew longer, and in between he lived in a New York hospice and spent most of his time sleeping, frightened and deeply depressed. In the spring of 1997, Khudayja visited him in the hospital one day after work. As he held her hand, he urged her to earn her college degree and keep her faith in God. That fall, three weeks before his twenty-seventh birthday, Dorian Waiters slipped into a coma and died.

Even as she struggled with grief and loss, Khudayja soared professionally. She finished her two-year associate's degree and held a succession of technical jobs with investment firms. When Merrill Lynch offered to promote her to assistant vice president, give her a big raise, and relocate her to California, she negotiated an even bigger raise and took the job. In Los Angeles, she juggled long work hours with college classes, but the grind made her unhappy. At last, she quit, moved to North Carolina, earned a bachelor's degree in psychology, and went on to a master's. She planned to look for a job in organizational development, to mesh her corporate experience with her psychology training. In 2005, she married an engineer; a year later, they had a baby girl. Although Khudayja still wept, even years later, as she described her brother's slow, agonizing death, she had come to terms with her loss. She missed Dorian, but she knew he was with her.

Caroline and Jermaine James

One day in 1993, Caroline James and her toddler son were sitting in their car at a stop sign on Eighteenth Avenue in Newark when a boy put a gun to the window and ordered them out. Her car turned up later in Queens; the thief, Caroline eventually learned, was all of ten years old. The trauma of the carjacking, coupled with her grief at her big brother Bunny's death, soured Caroline on New Jersey. She decided to move back to North Carolina, to the same town her mother had been so happy to leave decades earlier. Visiting her paternal grandmother in Wilmington one day, Caroline glimpsed a familiar face. "Daddy?" she asked, shocked. But her father retreated upstairs, unable to face the daughter he had abandoned sixteen years earlier. Caroline didn't go after him.

In Wilmington, she found work as a medical assistant; in 1998, she married a truck driver, and they had a daughter. But the marriage went bad, and in 2001, Caroline decided she had had enough of the supposed peace and quiet of college town North Carolina. She returned to the New York area in June and took her children to the observation deck of the World Trade Center a few months before the buildings fell to terrorists. By now, her mother, Mattie James, had left East Orange, and when she returned to her hometown for a visit, Caroline understood why. The city seemed sadder and dingier than she remembered. At a park a few blocks from her childhood home, she ran into the man who had coached her on the city track team when she was a kid. Caroline was just arranging a spot on the team for her own son when a gunshot echoed through the park. She never went back.

Caroline had promised herself that she would return to North Carolina if she could not get a job by the beginning of the school year, but she met her self-imposed deadline, finding work with her mother's latest employer, a firm that managed mostly low-income housing. Caroline moved into one of the firm's properties in Jersey City and looked into Catholic school for her son, but the tuition was more than she could afford. Nervously, she enrolled him in the Jersey City public schools. A few years later, she pronounced herself satisfied. Like her mother before her, Caroline James rode herd on her kids, and on their teachers. Maybe once her kids were older, she thought, she would finally go to college.

Her younger brother, Jermaine, had kept his graveside pledge to Bunny, finishing his political science degree at Hampton University in 1997. He planned on law school, although his enthusiasm for that career path dimmed when he worked as a law firm temp after graduation and noticed that some workaholic attorneys kept cots in their offices. In January 1998, however, Jermaine's plans changed. A mutual friend introduced him to a Newark City Council candidate named Cory Booker. Although Booker was just six years older than Jermaine and had never been elected to anything, his nascent political career was generating disproportionate excitement, for his résumé read like a Democratic campaign manager's dream: he was an African American from a North Jersey suburb, a graduate of Stanford University and Yale Law, and a Rhodes Scholar. More important, Booker spoke with articulate passion about the imperative need for new approaches to urban reform. Already, people were whispering those magic words: first black president. Jermaine James heard Booker speak and decided to defer his law school plans. In the five months before the May 1998 council election, he volunteered on Booker's campaign; when Booker won, Jermaine went to work for him in city hall, serving as his chief of staff for the last half of his four-year council term.

In 2002, Councilman Booker made an audacious run at the mayoralty, campaigning in the nonpartisan election as a reformer attacking the sclerotic incumbency of Sharpe James, Newark's second black mayor and an old lion of Jersey Democratic politics. The national press cast the bitter 2002 campaign in resonant terms: a new generation of African American leaders was challenging the civil rights movement's old guard. Inadvertently, Jermaine James—no relation to the mayor—gave Booker a political headache when, seven weeks before the election, he was briefly detained during a police raid on a strip club said to be promoting prostitution. He was never charged with any wrongdoing, but the mayor survived Booker's challenge.

To prepare for the 2006 rematch, Booker's administration-in-waiting set up shop on the twenty-first floor of an office building in downtown Newark. Truth sometimes is stranger than fiction: Jermaine James, *Abbott v. Burke* plaintiff and senior Booker advisor, was working just eighteen floors above the offices of the Education Law Center. As the years passed, Jermaine pursued a master's degree in public administration, and he and his fiancée had a baby boy. When election season arrived, Mayor Sharpe James kept everyone guessing about his intentions until the eleventh hour, but finally he bowed out, and Booker coasted to a coronation. By the fall, Jermaine James was the deputy chief of staff for the mayor of New Jersey's largest city.

The Knowles Children

Dan Knowles joined the marines in 1994, the same year he finished high school. His twenty-one-year-old brother, Guy Knowles Jr., had been drifting aimlessly since dropping out four years earlier, but Dan's new direction shook Guy Jr. out of his long sleep, and he quickly earned his GED and followed Dan into the marines. Both brothers thrived instantly. In boot camp on Parris Island, Dan found the discipline he had missed all his life; finally, he glimpsed the possibility of another life. Guy Jr. discovered that the tough years after his parents' split, the many times he'd been the new kid in school, had left him with a flexibility that served him well. Perhaps the marines didn't make a man of him—he liked to think he was a man before he joined—but they taught him how to set goals more ambitious than earning one more paycheck.

Their sister Cristina had dropped out of college after a year: the financial pressure of full-time studies supported with part-time work had finally become too much. For the next few years, she worked in social service jobs—as a group-home counselor, at a training center for the mentally disabled—and returned to college briefly to study social work. She had left school again by twenty-two, when she married a computer programmer; at twenty-three, she gave birth to a son. She had always liked children—even as a teenager, she had dreamed of becoming a foster parent or adopting—and over the next eight years, as she juggled jobs, family, and schooling, children became the center of her life. She found work as a teacher's assistant for disabled children and returned to college a third time, to study for a special education degree. When she and her husband found a house in rural Pennsylvania, they opened their home to a succession of foster children, had three more babies of their own, and invited Cristina's mother to live with them. By 2006, Cristina had earned more than half the college credits she needed. She still hoped to finish one day.

The Knowles brothers spent four years in the marines. Guy Jr. worked presidential guard duty in Washington, D.C., and then spent two years at Camp Pendleton in California before leaving the service when his next assignment seemed unpalatable. Dan was an administrative assistant at Camp Lejeune in North Carolina, where he met the daughter of a fellow marine. He left the service in 1998, because his girlfriend, soon to be his wife, was pregnant and the marines were planning to deploy him overseas.

Back in civilian life, Guy Knowles Jr. felt his new sense of direction desert him; though he stayed in California and found work as a security guard, he felt stuck. Within a year, however, he had met the woman he would marry, and through that new relationship, he rediscovered his ambition. He earned a truck driver's license and drove for a recycling company; he moved up to dispatcher, then to operations manager, then to plant manager, and he and his wife bought a house. Dan was living in a nearby town, with his wife and two children. After leaving the marines, he had worked in a series of clerical jobs before moving to California and finding a job driving a garbage truck. He dreamed of going back to school, perhaps to become a counselor for children as troubled as the boy he had once been.

Guy Knowles Sr. had left his post office job in 1999 and become a case manager for a Newark social service program, but in 2004, his oldest son invited him to California. There, Guy Sr. connected with the Veterans Administration's health care network and learned for the first time that his frequent job changes, his troubled relationships, and his Vietnam-inflected dreams were legacies of combat trauma. Though he liked the weather in southern California, by 2006, already restless, he was planning to send his résumé to Newark's new mayor, Cory Booker. His children knew little about *Abbott v. Burke*. Once, Dan wondered aloud how much money they were in line for. "Oh, no, it's not about money," his father told him. "It's about empowerment."

Leslie and LaMar Stephens

LaMar Stephens was working the St. Peter's College grill one day when a familiar face came through the cafeteria line—Gerard, his former colleague from the local cable TV franchise, who now worked for the Fox TV network and taught at St. Peter's. "LaMar, what are you doing?" Gerard asked. "You want to work for Fox?" "Hell, yes," LaMar replied. "What am I, stupid?" LaMar lacked only one prerequisite for an editing job, familiarity with a particular editing machine, so he borrowed the manual from Gerard, devoured it in a night, bluffed his way through the interview, and got the job. He was still there more than ten years later; on the side, he produced rap DVDs. By then, his son was a teenager attending public high school in middle-class Woodbridge, the sprawling township where Governor McGreevey had once been mayor. Although LaMar was not convinced that suburban schools offered a better education than urban ones, he had never wanted his son to attend public school in Jersey City. The violence had intensified since his own day, he felt. Proving yourself now might entail not a fistfight, but a homicide.

By the time Leslie Stephens moved to the suburbs in the late 1990s, she and her husband had four daughters, and the two oldest had spent years in the Jersey City schools. Leslie had never been much impressed with the district: "They don't care about their children," she told a newspaper in 1997. But eight years later, her oldest daughters were college graduates, and her mother, Tommi, had never given up hope that Leslie herself, still working in medical billing, would go back to school too, one of these days.

By then, Eddie Stephens had remarried and moved to Newark with his wife and two younger children; he was still teaching in the public schools. Tommi Stephens, too, remained a teacher. Once, she had considered becoming a principal and had earned her master's degree in preparation, but eventually she realized that principals spent more time completing paperwork and coordinating bus schedules than shaping how children were taught. Instead, Tommi trained in Reading Recovery, a tutoring program for struggling first-graders, spending eight years teaching children before becoming a mentor to other teachers learning the program's techniques. By 2004, she could see the *Abbott* preschool program bearing fruit in the classrooms she supervised. Years earlier, the children in the bottom fifth of first grade knew almost none of their letters and could barely write their first names. A decade later, she still saw the children in the bottom fifth of first grade, but now they knew most of their letters and could write a few simple words. All those years earlier, she had wondered whether to let her children join their names to *Abbott v. Burke*, but now she felt proud they had been a part of the case.

Liana Diaz

Liana Diaz kept her job at the Jersey City job training program for eight years. By then, her younger siblings had finished high school in Jersey City and gone on to work and family lives, and her mother, Lucila, was remarried, to a Jersey City firefighter. Lucila and her new husband decided to live frugally, saving for the day when they could take their generous public-sector pensions to retirement in a place with lower taxes and more sunshine. Lucila kept her job at the Jersey City school district's central office until the end, retiring in 2005 after twenty-six increasingly embittered years. By then, she knew, she was difficult to work with, even nasty. Her self-esteem was battered; she felt she had never done anything with her education, never been more than a secretary. A year into her Arizona retirement, however, she felt her spirits reviving. Eventually, she thought, she might return to school.

Liana had made her own break with the past years before. By 1998, at twenty-eight, she was tired of the snowy mid-Atlantic winters and, still single and childless, she had few strings tying her to Jersey City. Before another winter came, she left for Los Angeles. Eventually, she settled into a job at a mortgage company, where she worked her way up from bookkeeper to account manager. Her mother had nagged her for years to finish her college degree, and at last Liana realized it was time. She knew she could not move up without that piece of paper, and she wanted the closure. "I needed to be finished," she said years later. She sat down at her computer, created a spreadsheet of the courses she needed to take at the local Cal State campus, and made her way systematically through the program. For the first time, she realized how good it felt to earn the best grades she could. In December 2004, she finished her bachelor's degree in accounting, and fifteen months later, she left California's superheated real estate market and bought a house near her mother. Soon, she found work with a tax-advising firm; she hoped to become a certified public accountant, earn a master's degree in finance, and perhaps start her own business one day. At thirty-six, she looked forward to a bright future, but she couldn't help wondering how far she might already have come if only she had finished college at twenty-two.

Zakia and Aisha Hargrove

Years later, Zakia Hargrove would say that her stay in the psych ward after her suicide attempt had scared her straight. Although she still struggled with eating problems, she took medication, got therapy, and began working on a psychology degree at Jersey City State College. She would go on for a master's, she had decided, and become a psychologist specializing in the treatment of abused children. In her sophomore year, however, she became pregnant, and although she was determined to finish her bachelor's degree—and did, graduating in 1997, only one semester late—she shelved her plans for further education. She stayed on at the private preschool where she had been working, eventually becoming the kindergarten teacher. She had been living with her baby's father, a fellow college student, but when he began hitting her, she took their son and moved into a shelter in central New Jersey.

At a church Bible study one night, she got to talking with a factory worker named John. As their friendship grew, he started leaving dinner in a bag on her doorstep, where she would find it when she came home from work each night. On Valentine's Day 1998, he left flowers and balloons, and the next year they married and had a baby. Within four years, they had three children of their own. Zakia had enrolled her oldest son in private school, but after the third baby, the tuition became unaffordable. She switched her oldest to public school and began homeschooling her second, who had learned to read as a toddler. Zakia still fought her demons; a relapse into bulimia sent her to the hospital in 2004, and eating normally remained a struggle. But she tried to feel proud of how far she'd come.

Aisha Hargrove attended special education classes until age twenty-one, the legal limit, but she never learned to do much more than write her name. She lived with her grandmother in Jersey City until Alzheimer's disease began to cloud the older woman's mind. Then, the family found Aisha a placement nearby, and she moved into her own room in a residential group home with five other disabled adults and round-the-clock staff. There, Aisha learned to bathe and dress herself and to speak in full sentences, not baby talk. She fixed her own lunch the night before the workshops she attended. She made the Kool-Aid for the group home's nightly dinners and chatted to her aunts on the telephone. In 2004, her grandmother died, and as the family sat talking one night before the funeral, Aisha surprised them all with her simple, eloquent statement of grief. "I have a pain in my heart," she said. She had, her aunts thought, become her own person.

The Figueroas

Eighteen months after the birth of her son, Vivian Figueroa went back to school, and in December 1999 she graduated from a New Jersey state college with a teaching degree. Originally, she had planned to teach in Camden, to help students like her younger self struggle against poverty and despair, so she had done her student teaching in the city. The work was extraordinarily draining. Her first week on the job, a student called her "bitch." She met third graders who couldn't read, elementary school pupils with no respect for authority, and children whose mothers were dying of AIDS. An older colleague urged her not to read her students' cumulative files, lest the record of suffering prove too devastating to bear. Vivian's own personal life was in turmoil: her marriage had begun failing after the baby's birth, and by the time she finished college, she and her husband had separated. Finally, Vivian decided she did not have the emotional strength to support both her own son and the schoolchildren of Camden. She got a job teaching elementary school Spanish in affluent, suburban Haddonfield.

Vivian had been living in Pennsauken, Camden's blue-collar neighbor, but she was eager to leave. During substitute-teaching stints in the

Pennsauken schools, she had come to dislike the mouthy attitude of some of her students, and she wanted better for her own son. After two years of separation, she reconciled with her husband, and with the new beginning came a move to an affluent suburb with reputedly better schools. But the reconciliation proved short-lived. Vivian took her son and moved out, found a teaching job on the Jersey Shore, and started over.

Her siblings made their own way into adulthood. Orlando Figueroa rose through the ranks of the Camden police, becoming one of the first Hispanics to make lieutenant. He began work on a community college degree and moved to the suburbs with his family. Guarded and private, he preferred not to show his wife and children the devastated city where he had grown up.

Frances Figueroa had been raising her children alone in suburban Cherry Hill for about a year when one of her sisters introduced her to a man named Angel. Like her, he was a high school dropout with a hankering for a better life, and soon they became a team. Angel spent his days doing auto-body work while Frances cleaned the house and watched the kids, who eventually included a daughter of their own. When Angel got home, Frances left for her waitressing job while he made dinner, supervised homework, and put the children to bed. In 1997, they married. One of Frances's brothers helped Angel find a better-paying job with a chemical-cleanup company, and the family bought a four-bedroom colonial in Pennsauken, down the street from a day care center where Frances worked.

Like Vivian, however, Frances soon grew dissatisfied with the town. In the morning, she found empty drug bags on her front lawn; her son's preteen friends were already smoking, and the scent of marijuana wafted from the groups of kids who hung out at the local park. Frances thought she could see Pennsauken turning into Camden before her very eyes, and that she could not tolerate. Even though it meant settling for a smaller house, Frances insisted on moving her family to the suburbs. She found work doing billing for an optical lab. Although she had tried five or six times to earn a GED, she had never gotten very far. In her thirties, Frances was a bright, articulate woman who still found schoolbooks hopelessly intimidating. Her children, she hoped, would go to college one day. Meanwhile, she poured her energy into her house—she loved vacuuming—intent on making it the kind of place her kids would be happy to come home to. She had always wanted that as a child.

The Camden Police Department finally called Hector Figueroa in August 1999, after years of frustrating bureaucratic and political shenanigans had repeatedly blocked his hiring. At the police academy, he studied with far-better-educated recruits and still passed every test and earned dean's list grades. "When that happened, I felt my attitude change toward college," he said years later. "I said, I could have done it. I could have done something." He found he loved his job, and he stuck with it through a painful divorce from the woman he had loved since his teenage years. In mid-2006, he won promotion to detective. Hector still suffered from his lost years of schooling—he had never mastered cursive writing, for instance, and he wrote his reports in capital letters, since he wasn't sure about all the lower-case ones. He mourned the prom he had never attended, the reunions he would never go to. His teachers had failed him, he thought: despite the chaos of his family life, he had had it in him to learn. "If there's one thing I think all kids, even problem kids, should have, they should have at least their school," he said years later. "You're not guaranteed a home life, but you should be guaranteed a school life."

When Arlayne Figueroa left her violent boyfriend, she decided to study cosmetology: despite her training, she had never managed to convince anyone to hire a young, Hispanic woman for an accounting job. The state's welfare-reform program would pay for child care but not for cosmetology training—apparently, the state had decided cosmetology was oversubscribed—so Arlayne took out loans, got a contraceptive implant, and plunged into her studies. A week into her first cosmetology job, she found out she was pregnant again. The Norplant had failed her. The pregnancy left her too sick to work, so she moved in with her new boyfriend and went back on welfare. After their daughter arrived, Arlayne pieced together a living, driving school buses so she could be home with her children. She never found steady work in cosmetology. Apparently, those welfare reform bureaucrats had been onto something.

By the time her daughter was school age, Arlayne and her boyfriend had split up. She and the kids ended up in subsidized housing in Pennsauken; she drove buses during the day and used her accounting background working for a tax service at night. She was frustrated, barely getting by, close to an emotional breakdown. "I can't do this," she told a niece one day. "You have to go back to school," her niece said. "That's the only way you're going to make it. You can struggle for the rest of your life, or you can struggle for the next three years and just do it." Arlayne knew her niece was right. On the Internet, she searched for careers she could pursue close to home, careers combining good money with minimal extra training, and finally she decided to become an optician. For the next three years, she juggled full-time schooling and part-time work. She drove buses, worked twenty or twenty-five hours a week in an optical lab and a lens store, and accepted help from her mother.

Two years along, the whole precarious structure almost collapsed. Arlayne's oldest son was struggling emotionally, final exams were approaching, and she had just ended another relationship. As she lay in bed one morning, she felt strange, disembodied; she felt like giving up. None of her children got to school that day, and Arlayne missed crucial exams. But before day's end, she had stepped back from the brink. "You know what? I can't give up," she told herself. "If I don't get up and go to work, I'm going to lose my job, and things are going to be worse." She couldn't afford to have a nervous breakdown, she realized. Over the next year and a half, she made up the school work she had missed, and by 2006, she had finished her training, found work as an optician on a South Jersey military base, and moved her family to a middle-class suburb.

By rights, Blanca Figueroa's children should have had no chance. They began the game with far more than three strikes against them. Their mother was alone, uneducated, emotionally fragile, ethnically marginalized; her limited resources were divided among far too many offspring; she made her home in a city whose desperate circumstances mirrored her own. As they grew to adulthood, her children coped with sexual abuse, family chaos, school failure, and domestic violence; some of them flirted perilously with drugs and street gangs. But against the odds, Blanca Figueroa's children made it out of poverty: by the first decade of the twenty-first century, they were all alive and drug-free, working, paying mortgages, and raising kids. They knew theirs was an extraordinary story. Sometimes, they wondered how they had done it. Blanca still melted easily into anguished, guilty tears when she recalled the early troubles she had failed to protect them from. But her children paid tribute to the gifts she had given them: unshakable love, a nonnegotiable insistence on respectful good manners, and a fierce dedication to their survival. The state had defended *Abbott v. Burke*, in part, by arguing that some children can't be saved, but Blanca's kids were living proof that no child is beyond saving.

CONCLUSION

Other People's Children

Did it work?

Sooner or later, every conversation about New Jersey's school-funding battle arrives at that perfectly reasonable, deceptively simple question. Were they worth it, all those years of litigation and legislation and angry argument? Did *Abbott v. Burke* succeed?

Given *Abbott*'s tortuous journey, it is no surprise that answering that question remains far more difficult than asking it, for reasons both practical and philosophical. Although the state supreme court has called more than once for an independent evaluation of the *Abbott* remedies, to date the state has never commissioned one. Lawyers, bureaucrats, and scholars have failed to reach consensus on the goals and methods of such a study, and even if such a consensus does eventually emerge, any research project launched years into the reform effort will have to proceed without benefit of baseline data. Red tape also repeatedly delayed the creation of a statewide database capable of tracking individual students over time, information increasingly seen as crucial to education research. The database was expected to be ready only in 2007.

Perhaps more important than these practical roadblocks, however, is a philosophical problem: the criteria for judging *Abbott*'s effectiveness—what it would mean to say that *Abbott* "worked"—remain as contested as anything in the long history of New Jersey's school-funding fight.

The supreme court's 1990 *Abbott II* ruling implicitly proposed one standard for evaluating the success of the reform effort the court was about to set in motion. Poor urban districts, Chief Justice Robert Wilentz wrote, "are entitled to pass or fail with at least the same amount of money as their competitors." By that standard—funding equity for poor urban districts—New Jersey's school-finance struggle has been astonishingly successful. When Wilentz wrote those words, the thirty school systems that would soon be labeled "special needs districts" spent about 26 percent less per pupil than the wealthiest suburban districts, a difference of $1,700 per student, or $42,500 for every classroom of twenty-five children. By 2006, as the legislature prepared to resume the search for a politically palatable school funding formula, *Abbott*'s "parity plus" mandate had pushed average spending in the poor urban districts to 20 percent *above* suburban spending—nearly $3,000 per pupil, or $74,000 for a class of twenty-five. Nor had the state achieved funding equity by depressing overall spending levels: New Jersey consistently ranked among the highest-spending states in the nation, and some of the *Abbott* districts were among the highest-spending school systems in New Jersey. If justice demands that a roughly equal share of society's wealth be expended on the schooling of rich and poor, New Jersey has achieved some measure of justice.

But funding equity is not what most citizens have in mind when they ask whether *Abbott* worked. What they expect, they would probably say, are results. Of course, even this demand is not as straightforward as it sounds. The results we expect from schooling are many, some measurable, some not. We expect students to attend school regularly, take rigorous academic courses, finish high school, get into college, find good jobs. We also expect them to reap less tangible benefits: to develop an appreciation for music, art, and literature; to gain the scientific literacy necessary for informed citizenship; to acquire a work ethic and the habits of respect and common courtesy; to learn how to be good friends and good parents. Still, when citizens ask whether *Abbott* worked, most of them probably have in mind a single, specific criterion: standardized testing. Tell me, they ask: did all the money New Jersey pumped into inner-city schools raise those perennially low test scores?

Even this simple question has a complicated answer, however, for New Jersey's protean testing program supplies no uniform yardstick against which to measure both the schools of twenty-five years ago and the schools of today. In some states, scores on the National Assessment of Educational Progress (NAEP), the respected test known as the "Nation's

Report Card," might constitute such a standard, but until 2003, when the federal No Child Left Behind law first required every state to participate in NAEP, New Jersey seldom did. Furthermore, frequent revisions to the state's own testing program make assessing progress over time a treacherous business. At various periods since the early 1980s, New Jersey has mandated two different fourth-grade tests, two different eighth-grade tests, and three different high school tests, with experts often cautioning that scores on the new tests should not be compared with scores on the old ones. Sometimes reading and writing have been tested separately, sometimes combined as "language arts." Sometimes science has been tested, sometimes not. The state has increased testing time, to ensure coverage of more material, and decreased it, to placate parents worried about overstressed children. Controversies over the validity of test questions and the accuracy of scoring protocols have erupted with the regularity of sunspots.

Still, despite the twists and turns in the state's testing program, test scores provide some real information. No matter how many different tests the state has required over the years, in any given year every student took the same test; therefore, while it is difficult to draw conclusions about the absolute performance of the *Abbott* districts, it remains feasible to examine their relative performance—the size of the gap between the test scores of *Abbott* students and those of their non-*Abbott* peers. The analysis of relative performance also speaks to something fundamental. The American Dream depends upon public schools that level the playing field for the impoverished children of the inner city and their better-off peers, and the size of the *Abbott* test-score gap graphically illustrates how closely New Jersey's reality approximates to this ideal.

The picture is mixed. Look at elementary school scores, and it is difficult not to feel optimistic; look at middle and high school scores, and it is difficult not to feel discouraged. The good news: in the six years beginning in 1998–99, when the state first began measuring how well younger students were meeting the new core curriculum standards, the gap between the scores of *Abbott* fourth graders and those of their non-*Abbott* peers decreased by half, shrinking steadily each year in both language arts and math. The bad news: in that same period, the eighth-grade score gap shrank by far less. For high school students, the picture is cloudier, because the state introduced a new eleventh-grade test in 2001–02. The gap between *Abbott* and non-*Abbott* scores is significantly smaller on the new test than on the old, but only in math has the gap on the new test narrowed over the succeeding years. At all grade levels, too, the variation in performance among *Abbott* districts is striking. A handful of districts have virtually closed the gap between their scores and those of non-*Abbott* districts; a few are even nearing the proficiency rates of the wealthiest suburbs, which perennially outperform even the middle class. Other *Abbott* districts, however, remain mired in failure, with proficiency rates that are 30, 40, even 50 percentage points below those in better-off communities. Only the most determined critic of standardized testing could dismiss such dismal numbers outright, for while it is likely that a passing mark on a standardized test does not guarantee academic achievement, a failing mark probably does guarantee the reverse. It is hard to imagine that *Abbott* district teenagers who cannot pass these tests are well equipped for adulthood.

Hungry for evidence that *Abbott* has indeed worked, advocates offer plausible explanations for the discrepancy between test-score gains at the elementary level and test-score stagnation at the secondary level. Preschool and whole-school reform, the *Abbott* remedies that have claimed the lion's share of attention, targeted younger children, advocates note; by contrast, until the launch of a secondary-school reform initiative in 2005, middle- and high school programs were barely an afterthought. *Abbott* is working where *Abbott* has been tried, the advocates argue. Try it with older children, and it will work for them, as well. Perhaps the advocates are right to see elementary school progress as an unambiguous harbinger of hope, but the history of New Jersey's testing program suggests that caution should temper optimism. Over the six-year lifespan of New Jersey's ninth-grade test, urban districts came close to closing the once-yawning gap between their test scores and those of their wealthier peers. But when a new eleventh-grade test replaced the old ninth-grade one, those gaps reappeared, as large as ever and far more stubborn. Only time will tell if recent improvements in elementary school performance will persist or evaporate.

Certainly, New Jersey is not alone in struggling with secondary education: a raft of national reports have criticized the nation's middle schools and high schools as impersonal, unfocused, and insufficiently rigorous. It is not only in New Jersey that elementary schools, with their malleable children and involved parents, seem more amenable to change. If this context makes the struggles of New Jersey's older students easier to understand, however, it does not necessarily offer grounds for optimism: why should New Jersey succeed where other states are failing? Today's fourth-graders will be tomorrow's middle school and high school students, and it remains to be seen whether they will consolidate their gains or instead lose their way amid all the distractions that make growing up in the inner city so much harder than growing up in the suburbs. In 2004–05, *Abbott* eighth graders' math proficiency was 34.8 percentage points below that of their non-*Abbott* peers. That same year, the math proficiency gap for *Abbott* fourth-graders was 18.7 percentage points. Those fourth-graders will take the eighth-grade math test in 2008–9, and then we will learn something important about how *Abbott* is working.

Abbott's critics sometimes blame disappointing test scores on inner-city corruption and incompetence; decades after the state's lawyers first used the mismanagement argument, periodic scandals ensure that it never loses its relevance. In 2006 alone, Camden's superintendent resigned amid reports that she had collected improper salary bonuses, the Asbury Park school board offered its superintendent a $600,000 contract buyout, the state investigated allegations that Camden school officials had countenanced cheating on standardized tests, and Jersey City's state-appointed superintendent—seventeen years after takeover, the district was still state-run—was criticized for spending taxpayers' money lavishly while attending an overseas conference. Non-*Abbott* districts have seen scandals of their own—a 2000 state investigation found rampant waste and fraud in school roofing projects, for example—but the *Abbott* districts' high state-aid levels ensure that their failings will always be big news. It is difficult to know whether the officials of urban school districts are uniquely susceptible to the temptations of power. Perhaps they simply have more opportunities to abuse their prerogatives: in New Jersey's big urban school systems, political considerations often trump accountability, and citizens lack the time and expertise to keep close watch. Certainly, nothing is more contemptible than stealing from impoverished children, but it is no clearer than it ever was that these abuses are responsible for educational failure. Three *Abbott* districts with especially impressive records of test-score improvement are located in Hudson County, historically New Jersey's epicenter of big-city political corruption.

Whatever the explanation for disappointing school performance, New Jersey has no shortage of voices arguing that the lack of across-the-board test-score gains is proof positive that *Abbott* has failed. But Marilyn Morheuser's case was about opportunity—giving inner-city children access to the public services enjoyed by their more affluent fellow citizens, whether or not that access translated directly into test-score gains. Suburban parents seldom require proof that every school program—every music class, every field trip, every hour of counseling—helps maintain the high test scores their communities take for granted. Suburban parents want art classes, foreign language programs, even football teams and chess clubs, not only because they believe these offerings give their children an edge in college admissions, but also because they want their children to sample the full richness of human experience. Surely, *Abbott* children are also entitled to opportunity for its own sake.

The preschool program is the most promising of the new opportunities *Abbott* has spawned. Between 2002 and 2005, with researcher Ellen Frede in charge and stepped-up funding in place, the program's enrollment grew rapidly; by 2006, the state was projecting that 80 percent of eligible *Abbott* preschoolers would soon be enrolled. The program's quality was also rising, research commissioned by Frede suggested. By 2005, virtually every *Abbott* preschool teacher, whether employed by a public school or a community child-care center, held a bachelor's degree; six years earlier, only 38 percent of preschool teachers had finished college. Improved teacher training was showing up in classroom practice: in 2004–05, researchers rated only 2.5 percent of state-funded preschool classrooms in the lowest quality category, down from 21 percent four years earlier. Anecdotally, Frede had heard that some *Abbott* districts were revising their curricula to keep up with the improved skills of entering kindergartners. Decades of national research suggest that a good preschool education will improve *Abbott* students' odds of finishing school—and, perhaps, of passing state tests. Still, only a strong elementary and secondary education can maximize the preschool advantage. "It's not fair to expect preschool to be a magic bullet," Frede said, months after leaving state government to return to academia, "although it's pretty phenomenal what preschool can do."

If preschool is widely viewed as a success, other *Abbott* remedies remain more problematic. The whole-school reform models the Whitman administration once championed are embraced in some districts and ignored in others; under *Abbott* czar Gordon MacInnes, who left his job in early 2007, the Education Department preferred to promote a state-developed early literacy initiative drawing on the work of Union City, a North Jersey *Abbott* district with especially high test scores. The Corzine administration is reexamining supplemental programs; the new secondary school reforms are ambitious but still embryonic.

No *Abbott* remedy has generated more controversy than the school construction program, however. In the program's first two years, its centralized management process—which the legislature had established to ensure that the best-funded districts, including the *Abbotts*, did not squander the lavish state funding to which the school construction law entitled them—slowed the repair and replacement of urban schools to a crawl. Meanwhile, affluent suburbs and poor rural districts alike collected their smaller state funding allocations and moved ahead with their projects. In mid-2002, Governor Jim McGreevey reorganized the program to speed construction in the cities that were the law's original inspiration—not to mention his political base—and the pace of work accelerated. Less than three years later, however, a newspaper investigation found that the speed-up had spawned huge cost overruns. A subsequent state investigation uncovered rampant waste and mismanagement, and the school construction agency announced it would soon run out of money. By mid-2006, six years into the program, the *Abbott* districts had seen forty new schools and thirty-seven additions or major renovations completed; a few dozen more were in the pipeline. Hundreds of other projects remained in limbo, however, while legislators debated whether to commit billions more to an agency still in the midst of reforming itself. A process designed to keep local officials from wasting public money had degenerated into a textbook case of government waste. None of it had much to do with *Abbott*, but children were still attending school in aging, dilapidated buildings.

Did it work? Ten years after CEIFA, the question of *Abbott*'s efficacy had become increasingly urgent to supporters of the rulings, for political pressure was mounting to modify the spending regime those rulings had ushered in. By 2006, just as New Jersey Supreme Court Justice Marie Garibaldi had predicted nine years earlier, the parity remedy that her colleagues had called an interim measure had become entrenched in the state's school-funding system. Each year, the wealthiest suburban districts struck the school budgets their citizens were willing to pay for, subject only to state-dictated limits on spending increases; then the state calculated the suburbs' average per-pupil spending and gave the *Abbott* districts the aid they needed to match that spending. By 2006, the *Abbott* districts, which enrolled 23 percent of New Jersey's public school students, were getting 57.6 percent of the state's school aid. Exacerbating the political problem that imbalance created were the successive state budget crises that, since 2002–03, had convinced the legislature to abandon the CEIFA funding formula. The formula would have entitled many districts to extra money to cover growing enrollments, new special-education costs, and the like, but instead, for five successive fiscal years, most of the state's school districts had gotten little or no extra state aid, and they had made up the difference in the usual ways, with service cuts and property tax increases.

The supreme court had limited its remedy to a small group of poor districts, and a succession of governors and legislators had failed to integrate the court's mandates for those districts into a unified statewide funding formula. As a result, school spending in New Jersey had come to resemble an upside-down bell curve, with rich and poor districts spending at the highest levels while districts in the broad middle range made do with less. A spending-adequacy study commissioned by the McGreevey administration but made public only in 2006, after a court fight, concluded that, as a group, the *Abbott* districts were spending about what they needed, and the wealthy suburbs were spending 5 percent more than they needed. But in the socioeconomic groups between those extremes, spending was falling as much as 17 percent below the levels required for adequacy, the study found.

Abbott-district status had become an all-important designation, entitling the lucky winner to such valuable benefits as universal preschool and full state funding for school construction, and yet only the most improvisational of processes determined which districts were entitled to that status. The court's original grouping of twenty-eight districts had been assembled from lists that were themselves based on U.S. Census figures that were almost out of date. The Democratic Florio administration had increased the number of districts to thirty, and the Republican Whitman administration had cut that number back to twenty-eight, in equally ad hoc decisions. Three years after CEIFA, political and legal pressure convinced the legislature to restore the two rejected districts to the list. Four years later, after a group of poor, rural districts brought a legal case arguing that their plight was no less pressing than that of their urban cousins, the legislature voted to make one small, rural South Jersey school system the thirty-first *Abbott* district. Meanwhile, gentrification had improved the economic circumstances of several of the original *Abbott* districts, but the legislature lacked the stomach for the fight it would undoubtedly take to remove their coveted *Abbott* status.

With property taxes rising in middle-class towns and wealthy suburbs, more and more legislators were finding it politically untenable to continue funding the *Abbott* districts at levels far above those of most other districts. Even *Abbott* advocates were uncomfortably aware that plenty of poor children lived in working-class towns whose non-*Abbott* status deprived their students of guaranteed access to full-day preschool, intensive literacy instruction, and the other *Abbott* programs. By the fall of 2006, the legislature was promising to design a new funding formula that would eliminate *Abbott*-district designation in favor of delivering services to disadvantaged children no matter where they lived, and the Education Law Center was promising a court battle if the new formula threatened to undo years of hard-won gains.

Another administration, another funding formula: New Jersey's struggle over the *Abbott* rulings remains, it seems, eternally unresolved. Could it all have turned out differently? From the start, New Jersey's school-funding battle has seemed in some ways exceptional. The state's tradition of extreme localism sharpened the contrasts between rich and poor; the liberal, activist state supreme court stepped into a fight that more cautious courts might have avoided; New Jersey's great wealth permitted unusually sweeping remedies. And, of course, the *Abbott* battle was waged by an unusually committed advocate, Marilyn Morheuser. Certainly, Morheuser did not work alone: many others helped organize the case in her lifetime and picked up the torch after her death. But her passionate tenacity sustained *Abbott* through years of delay and uncertainty. No matter the setback, she never gave up. Morheuser's near-fanatical intensity sometimes made her difficult, but without it, her case might not have survived.

Nevertheless, despite all that makes New Jersey's story unique, the contingent confluence of particular individuals cannot fully explain this long struggle. Over two generations, from *Robinson* through *Abbott*, the same themes of urban decline, suburban resistance, and political accommodation resurface again and again. The motives of individuals—however admirable, however suspect—matter less than the broader social forces that have influenced the state's battle over equal education.

The never-ending turmoil points up both the limitations and the necessity of litigation that shapes public policy while circumventing democratic decision making. Because the *Abbott* plaintiffs won their case in court, not through democratic give-and-take, their gains seem fragile, forever up for grabs. A legislative fight over school funding for the poor might have forged enduring coalitions between idealistic liberals committed to social equality and pragmatic conservatives convinced that economic competitiveness requires an educated workforce. With the court making funding decisions for them, legislators never had to find that common ground.

Ultimately, though, it is hard to believe that without the pressure of litigation, New Jersey's legislators would ever have granted poor schools the abundant resources and expansive programs the *Abbott* plaintiffs won in court. It is especially hard to believe in such an outcome given that, even *with* the pressure of litigation, legislators resisted equalization efforts so fiercely. The income tax passed only after the court closed the schools; the modestly redistributive QEA I quickly evolved into the far less powerful QEA II; CEIFA grandfathered in high suburban spending levels. Suburbanites believe their privileges are earned, not conferred, and with a vigor born of that conviction, they defend those privileges and push their legislators to do the same. In a majority-rule democracy, in a state dominated by suburbanites, their claims will inevitably prevail. Only the courts can speak for the voiceless.

As a tool of policy development, however, litigation is a blunt instrument with which to perform delicate social surgery. Ideally, policy develops through a predictable process that preserves flexibility and moderates extremism, and litigation seldom promotes any of these ends. Court rulings are unpredictable, as the Florio administration discovered to its cost, when it banked on a pension-aid ban that never materialized. Court orders are inflexible, as New Jersey's battles over preschool and whole-school reform suggest; judges cannot easily strike a balance between a prescriptiveness that handcuffs policy makers and a vagueness that makes noncompliance tempting. Perhaps most important, the imperatives of litigation encourage an absolutism that precludes sensible compromise. For years, ELC argued that money would cure urban districts' ills; for years, the state argued that money would make no difference at all. The state spotlighted mismanagement in urban districts, and therefore Marilyn Morheuser refused to discuss it. Common sense suggested that the truth lay somewhere between these exaggerated extremes—that money mattered, but that spending it on the right programs mattered just as much, that mismanagement was important, but not all-important. As the two sides argued their corners in court, however, that common-sense middle ground lay empty. It took seventeen years—from the filing of the *Abbott* case in 1981 until the issuing of the *Abbott V* opinion in 1998—for the two sides to turn their attention to implementing programs. Seventeen years: a child grows up in seventeen years.

Lawyers, legislators, and bureaucrats always have another chance to get school funding right—another case, another session, another law—but children only go through school once. Liberals often dismiss the conservative call for greater school choice, whether in the form of charter schools or tuition vouchers, as a diversion from the real work of improving traditional public schools, but the stories of the *Abbott* families challenge this tenet of the liberal faith. The *Abbott* parents, watching their children's precious years of education slip away, had no time to wait for the public schools to improve, and over and over, they found ways to choose something better—by moving to a wealthier town, by scraping together private school tuition, by fudging the residency laws. In the face of their desperate determination to secure the best possible opportunities for real-life children with only so much time, liberal denunciations of privatized schooling ring hollow indeed.

If the stories of the *Abbott* families challenge the antiprivatization pieties of the left, however, those stories also challenge the right's readiness to blame inner-city parents for the failures of inner-city education, and thus to elide the communal responsibility for schooling. Education begins at home, the argument goes; if inner-city schools are failing, it must be because inner-city parents are lazy and disengaged, their children too damaged to learn. Yet the *Abbott* families do not fit this convenient stereotype. In the stories of Mattie James and Lola Moore, who worked extra jobs to pay tuition, or of Lucila Diaz, who rejected the stigma of welfare for the dignity of work, or of Frances Figueroa, who walked three miles in the cold to get her children a ticket out of Camden, the suburban middle class can see, if they choose to look, a reflection of their own commitment to work and family, education and self-improvement. Each day, urban parents, like suburban ones, trust their children to the competence of professional educators. It is unjust to demand that these brave and hardworking parents do what no suburban parents are expected to do—ensure the quality of their children's schools. Schooling is a public responsibility, not the private burden of parents whose lives are already far harder than those of most of their critics.

Not all the *Abbott* parents were equally competent, of course, but even the most troubled cared deeply about their children: fragile Blanca Figueroa did her best to nurture her brood, and mentally ill Patricia Watson advocated tirelessly for her disabled daughter. Certainly, their children carried scars from their difficult upbringing, but in the end almost all the *Abbott* children fought their way to a decent adulthood, whatever the mistakes of their parents, whatever the failings of their schools.

How much did school matter to the *Abbott* children, in the end? The real lives of real people are more complicated than the stereotypes of right or left, and the *Abbott* children's lives were shaped not only by schooling but by divorce and remarriage, love and abuse, illness and addiction, poverty and luck. No one person, no one institution, deserves all the credit or all the blame.

Still, as they looked back, many of the *Abbott* children—even those with the hardest family lives and the unhappiest school experiences—remembered teachers who illuminated their darkness with moments of faith and kindness. The persistence of these memories suggests the power that school does have—the power to give children strength and hope and a vision of the future. "You're not guaranteed a home life, but you should be guaranteed a school life," Hector Figueroa said, and his words express something profound. Public institutions matter, even if they are not the only things that do. We cannot fix everything that is wrong in the lives of other people's children, but we can fix some things. Surely we should try.

NOTES

These notes are intended to supplement, not duplicate, the attribution provided in the text. Therefore, when the text identifies a legal brief, a judicial opinion, or an interview subject as the source of a quotation, I do not give a more precise reference here. Chapter notes identify the interviews, archives, and published sources on which the text is based; supply references for anecdotes or direct quotations from published or archival sources; and identify the speaker when the text quotes directly from an unnamed interview subject. The "Works Cited" section supplies full publication information for printed sources. Because the archives of the Education Law Center ("ELC archives") and the Morheuser papers held by Thomas Cioppettini ("Cioppettini papers") are uncataloged, it is impossible to indicate with precision where documents from those collections can be found.

I use the following abbreviations:

Asbury Park Press: APP
Bergen Record: Record
Jersey Journal: JJ
Milwaukee Sentinel: MS
New Jersey Law Journal: NJLJ
New York Times: NYT
Philadelphia Inquirer: PI
Star-Ledger: S-L
Times of Trenton: TT

INTRODUCTION. THE INHERITANCE

The suburban dentist is quoted in Iver Peterson, "Jersey Education: $ + $ = Quality," *NYT*, February 5, 1975. In our interview, Thomas Corcoran called education the middle-class property right. For the distinction between equity and adequacy suits, see, e.g., Rebell, "Educational Adequacy, Democracy and the Courts"; Reed, *On Equal Terms*; and Thro, "Judicial Analysis During the Third Wave of School Finance Litigation." The "Litigation" page of the National Access Network's Web site discusses the proportion of plaintiff victories in the two types of cases. The Peter Schrag statement comes from *Final Test*, 85.

CHAPTER 1. JERSEY CITY'S TAX WAR

In this and the next chapter, my account of the lives of Betty and Kenneth Robinson is based on the following sources: birth certificates, yearbooks, and obituaries; Patrick Ford, "A Mother's Legacy: Her Lawsuit Led to State T. and E. Law," *JJ*, August 8, 1979; Kelman, "Time Erodes Family's Hope"; Mary Jo Patterson, "T&E Plaintiff Looks Back on Landmark Case," *S-L*, August 14, 1979; and interviews with Frances Charles, Saundra Green, Cheryl Howard, Wilbur Robinson Jr., Annie Ruth Rock, and Thomasena Simmons.

The history of the Booker T. Washington Apartments is drawn from accounts in the *JJ*, which described the project as "exclusively for colored people" in "Low-Rent Housing Bids Ready Soon," June 18, 1941. In a September 22, 2004, letter to me, Sandra Robertson described Booker T's apartments. New Jersey's 1960s welfare stipends are listed in New Jersey Legislature, Welfare Investigating Committee, *Report*, 26.

I base my account of conditions at School 22 on interviews with Philip Feintuch and Terence Matthews. The experiences of the young art teacher, Anthony Guadadiello, are described in his November 6, 1986, testimony at the *Abbott v. Burke* administrative hearing. Jersey City school enrollment numbers come from an enrollment analysis provided to me by the school district on January 5, 2004. Thomas, *Education in Jersey City*, 3, describes the demographics of the city and its schools. Jersey City students' performance on national tests and the district's attitude toward science instruction are discussed in Aaron Schulman's testimony at the *Robinson v. Cahill* superior court trial, November 9, 1971.

For the history of politics, public education, and school finance in New Jersey, see Anyon, *Ghetto Schooling*; Bole and Johnson, *The New Jersey High School*; Parciak, "Equality of Educational Opportunity in New Jersey"; the *Robinson v. Cahill* superior court ruling; *Robinson I*; Salmore and Salmore, *New Jersey Politics and Government*; State Aid to School Districts Study Commission, "A Commitment to New Jersey"; and West, *Elementary Education in New Jersey*. West, *Elementary Education*, 102, gives the state share of school spending in 1963. Spending and taxation in Newark and Millburn are detailed in New Jersey Department of Education, *Sixteenth Annual Report*, 229, 231. The description of Newark's disaffected youth comes from Governor's Select Commission, *Report for Action*, 78.

The mechanics of school aid formulas are discussed in, e.g., Coons, Clune, and Sugarman, *Private Wealth and Public Education*.

My account of the *Robinson* litigation is based on press reports; Lehne, *The Quest for Justice*; Lehne and Rottenberg, "The Real Story of the Income Tax"; the transcript of the superior court trial; legal briefs and opinions; and interviews with Theodore Botter, Harold Ruvoldt Jr., William Shine, Paul Tractenberg, and Stephen Weiss. The Jersey City mayor's speech is reprinted in *JJ*, "Mayor Whelan's Seventh Annual State of the City Message," January 15, 1970. Harold Ruvoldt Sr. is described as the "boy orator of the Democratic Party" in *JJ*, April 4, 1950. The "right to learn" quotation comes from Ruvoldt, "The Right to Learn," 19. Ruvoldt's exchange with a former education official comes from Joseph E. Clayton's testimony at the *Robinson v. Cahill* superior court trial, November 3, 1971. Ronald Sullivan, "Most Communities in Jersey Facing School-Aid

Loss," *NYT*, January 24, 1972, characterizes the significance of the *Robinson* ruling. Kenneth Robinson's reaction is reported in Robert J. Braun, "Property Tax Quashed for School Financing," *S-L*, January 20, 1972.

CHAPTER 2. CELEBRATING THE BICENTENNIAL

My account of conditions at Ferris High School is based on interviews with Thomas Favia, Joanne Kenny, Anthony Nicodemo, and Gabriel Taverney. Ferris's "modern design" is described in *JJ*, "Highlights of Ferris High School Dedication," May 8, 1969. Kenneth Robinson's academic struggles are mentioned in Kelman, "Time Erodes Family's Hope."

For Brendan Byrne's background, I rely on press accounts. The wiretapped mobsters are quoted in Fecht, "Brendan T. Byrne."

In our interview, Herbert Green told me the anecdote about the lunchtime encounter between two school board members.

I base my account of the T&E law and the income tax battle on press reports; Lehne, *The Quest for Justice*; Lehne and Rottenberg, "The Real Story of the Income Tax"; and interviews with Raymond Bateman, Fred Burke, Albert Burstein, Brendan Byrne, Thomas Cochran, Frank J. Dodd, James Dugan, Jerry Fitzgerald English, Clifford Goldman, Herbert Green, Lewis Kaden, Jeffrey Laurenti, Richard Leone, Paul Muller, Marvin Reed, Ernest Reock Jr., Richard Roper, William Shine, S. Herbert Starkey Jr., John White, and Stephen Wiley. For the *Robinson* litigation, I use press reports; legal briefs; *Robinson III–VII*; and interviews with Mary Cheh, John Finnerty, Charles Friedrich, Dominick Mazzagetti, Kenneth Meskin, Marianne Espinosa Murphy, Harold Ruvoldt Jr., Sidney Schreiber, and Paul Tractenberg.

The quotation from Byrne's address to the supreme court comes from an audiotape of the March 18, 1975, oral argument. Byrne's prediction of "fiscal chaos" is quoted in Bob Cunningham, "Byrne: Income Tax or Fiscal Chaos," *Record*, June 27, 1975. Jan Schaffer, "Tax Pressure Fizzles in Steaming Senate," *PI*, June 28, 1975, describes the telegrams on legislators' desks and the circulation of Byrne's horoscope. In our interview, Tractenberg told me the "tedious and exasperating" anecdote. The 150 telephone calls and the amended lyrics to the "Battle Hymn of the Republic" are described in Bob Cunningham and Allan F. Yoder, "A Tax Bill Nobody Liked," *Record*, June 18, 1976. The cries of "tax strike!" are reported in James McQueeny, "A Scenario Finally Played to Conclusion," *S-L*, June 18, 1976. The voices calling "Nine to two!" are described in Dan Weissman, "2 % Tax Plan Rejected; Assembly Still at Work," *S-L*, July 1, 1976. The arm-twisting of Democratic legislators is detailed in Alfonso A. Narvaez, "Jersey Assembly Defers Tax Issue," *NYT*, July 3, 1976, and Vincent "Ozzie" Pellecchia's report of the reaction to his resistance comes from Ronald Sullivan, "What School Crisis?" *NYT*, July 7, 1976. Byrne's statement at the bill signing is quoted in Alfonso A. Narvaez, "New Jersey Votes State Income Tax; Byrne Signs Bill," *NYT*, July 9, 1976. The racing fans' reaction to Byrne is recounted in Herb Jaffe, "Meadows Track Filled for Post Time," *S-L*, September 2, 1976. Byrne's memorable response to the Bateman-Simon plan is quoted in Philip Lentz, "Governor Criticizes Bateman Tax Plan," *S-L*, September 27, 1977.

CHAPTER 3. THE TRUE BELIEVER

For general background on Marilyn Morheuser's life, I use résumés, college transcripts, letters, newspaper articles, and personal documents from the Cioppettini papers; Kathy Barrett Carter, "A Labor of Love," *S-L*, May 1, 1994; Anthony DePalma,"About New Jersey," *NYT*, June 24, 1990; Jo Astrid Glading, "Ex-Nun, Baseball Fan Goes to Bat for Poorly Funded School Districts," *Press of Atlantic City*, August 27, 1989; Christopher Kilbourne, "Former Nun Fighting for N.J. Schools and Her Life," *Record*, May 2, 1994; Ladd, "She Gave Up the Church to Challenge the State"; Marian McBride, " 'Rights' Action Difficult in Cloister," *MS*, January 26, 1966; Craig R. McCoy, "The Holy Crusade of Marilyn Morheuser," *PI*, December 10, 1989; and Kimberly J. McLarin, "A 1960's Throwback Leads the Challenge to the Financing of Public Schools in New Jersey," *NYT*, July 22, 1994.

For Morheuser's family and childhood, I rely on interviews with Margaret Benben, Mary Brinovec, Marie Casey, Marilyn Casey, and Margaret Gaskill. I am especially grateful to Marie Casey for generously sharing her research into her family's history. Morheuser's description of her family's "typical Mason-Dixon Line blindness" is quoted in McBride, " 'Rights' Action."

My account of Morheuser's college and convent years is based on the Cioppettini papers and on interviews with Magdalen Seaman, Jacqueline Grennan Wexler, and Sisters Mary Rhodes Buckler, Theresa Coyle, Pat Kenoyer, and Patricia Jean Manion, S.L. For the history of the Sisters of Loretto, see H. Sanders, *More Than a Renewal*; I also rely on my interview with Sister Katherine Misbauer, S.L. Morheuser described her desire to be "one with the world" in McCoy, "The Holy Crusade." She described the Las Vegas, New Mexico, school as "an oasis" in Morheuser, "Saturday Afternoon on Doorbell Duty," 56, and said her students' lives contained "nothing colorful" in McBride, " 'Rights' Action." The racist remark overheard by her former student is described in Glading, "Ex-Nun." Morheuser's description of her dissatisfaction with the "box" of convent life is quoted in McBride, " 'Rights' Action." The James Baldwin quotation is from "Letter from a Region in My Mind," 144. The account of Morheuser's conversation with the head of her order comes from McCoy, "The Holy Crusade."

For Morheuser's Milwaukee years, I rely on interviews with Jay Anderson, Daphne Barbee-Wooten, Lee Berthel, Richard G. Carter, Rev. Bertraim S. Gregg, Reuben Harpole, Joan Franklin Mosley, George Sanders, Richard Slippen, Robert Stuckert, Barbara Symmes, Ann Tevik, Leon Todd, Rev. Lucius Walker Jr., and Martin Wheelwright. Morheuser explained the Freedom School's curriculum in Marian McBride, "Former Nun Directs Freedom School," *MS*, May 18, 1961. She discussed her attitude toward "Negro revolution" in *Jet* 29, no. 12 (December 30, 1965), 8. The witness account of Morheuser as "a glorious gazelle" comes from McCoy, "The Holy Crusade." Morheuser's protest against "Mississippi justice" is quoted in Bernice Buresh, "Jail for Miss Morheuser," *MS*, February 8, 1966. Morheuser discussed her jail stay in Carter, "A Labor of Love." The gift of daffodils is mentioned in *MS*, "Miss Morheuser Ends Jail Term," March 3, 1966, and Morheuser's immediate return to protesting is noted in *MS*, "Labor Council Won't Meet at Eagles Club," March 3, 1966.

For Lloyd Barbee's background and the history of Milwaukee's civil rights move-ment, I use press reports; Aukofer, *City with a Chance*; and Dougherty, *More Than One Struggle*. I am grateful to Jack Dougherty for permitting me to read portions of his book before its publication. Barbee described his relationship with Morheuser as near mind reading in McCoy, "The Holy Crusade."

For the *Amos* lawsuit, I use computer printouts and research reports from the Wheelwright papers. My account of the Benton Harbor episode is based on interviews with Stuart Dunnings Jr., Louis Lucas, Mosley, and Wheelwright.

For Morheuser's law school experiences, I use interviews with James Louis, An-namay Sheppard, Paul Tractenberg, and Wheelwright.

CHAPTER 4. SON OF *ROBINSON*

Letters, memos, witness reports, and ELC annual reports referenced in this chapter come from the ELC archives.

My account of the Education Law Center's early days is based on the ELC archives and on interviews with James Kelly, Michael Lottman, and Paul Tractenberg. The num-ber of applicants for the executive director job is mentioned in ELC's FY 1979 Annual Report, 27. The quotation about school district mismanagement comes from ELC's FY 1978 Annual Report, 13.

For ELC's *Abbott* case preparation and the *Abbott* court proceedings, I use the ELC archives and interviews with Steven Block, Kathryn Brock, Stephen Eisdorfer, Bertram P. Goltz Jr., Peter Herzberg, Fredrica Hochman, Helen Lindsay, David Long, Lawrence Lustberg, Debra Matrick, Joyce Miller, Tractenberg, and Steven Wallach. The reports detailing failures of the T&E law include, for example, Goertz, *Where Did the 400 Mil-lion Dollars Go?*; the seven reports prepared for the New Jersey legislature or its Joint Committee on the Public Schools, 1978–1990; and the two Rubin reports for the New Jersey Education Reform Project. The analysis of how much money reached poor dis-tricts is in Goertz, *Where Did the 400 Million Dollars Go?* 2; the description of "the broad outcome" of the new law is in Goertz, *Where Did the 400 Million Dollars Go?* 4. The teacher-salary comparison is based on "New Jersey Teachers' Salary Survey," *NJEA Re-view* 52, no. 4 (December 1978), 36.

The quotation about "the cost-quality issue" comes from an Eisdorfer memo, March 16, 1978. The description of the "fine educator" is in a 1983 witness-interview report. The conversation with Jersey City administrators is described in a Kathleen Mor-risett memo, April 5, 1983. Morheuser's account of the end of the *Sharif* case is in a March 12, 1983, memo. Her account of the meeting with the NJEA is in a May 7, 1982, memo. ELC's suspicions about the state's exhaustion motion are detailed in ELC's *Abbott* brief, October 26, 1983, 70–71. Morheuser described her fear that ELC would run out of money in a March 16, 1984, letter to Susan Wilson. She discussed "the Abbott plaintiffs' 'motion to survive' " in an October 27, 1983, letter to Tractenberg and Annamay Shep-pard. She discussed the wait for the appellate ruling in a January 13, 1984, letter to Long.

For Marilyn Morheuser's personal life, I rely on the Cioppettini papers and on interviews with Block, Marie Casey, Thomas Cioppettini, James Louis, Sheppard,

Janet Stotland, Tractenberg, and Martin Wheelwright. Kathy Barrett Carter, "A Labor of Love," *S-L*. May 1, 1994, describes Morheuser's temporary estrangement from her sister.

Thomas Kean's background is detailed in Kean, *The Politics of Inclusion*. For Kean administration policies, I use press accounts and interviews with Saul Cooperman and Thomas Kean. Kean's description of the funding formula as "outdated and unjust" comes from Dan Weissman, "Kean Warns on School Aid in His Final State of State," *S-L*, January 10, 1990.

CHAPTER 5. THE FAMILIES

In this and later chapters, my account of the *Abbott* plaintiffs' lives is based on birth certificates, obituaries, yearbooks, and property records, but primarily on the following interviews: *Abbott*—Raymond Abbott, Samuel Appel, Frances Bell; *Diaz*—Liana Diaz, Lucila Rivera Mangels; *Figueroa*—Joy Appel Brown, Arlayne Figueroa, Blanca Figueroa, Frances Figueroa, Hector Figueroa, Orlando Figueroa, Vivian Figueroa; *Hadley*—Michael Hadley, Lola Moore; *Hargrove*—Evanett Fields, Zakia Hargrove, Deborah Jackson, Cora Watson; *James*—Caroline James, Mattie James, Jermaine James; *Knowles*—Cristina Knowles, Daniel Knowles, Guy Knowles Jr., Guy Knowles Sr.; *Stephens*—Eddie Stephens, LaMar Stephens, Tommi Stephens; *Stevens*—Henry Stevens Jr., Henry Stevens Sr.; *Waiters*—Khudayja Waiters, Lynn Waiters.

Mary Jo Patterson and Ted Sherman, "20 Pupils from 1981: Where Are They Now?" *S-L*, June 8, 1997, gives general background on the *Abbott* plaintiffs.

Details about Raymond Abbott's life can also be found in Associated Press, "For Him, a Lawsuit Far Too Late," *PI*, March 24, 1990, and "Inmate Abbott Hopes Ruling Helps Others," *Record*, June 6, 1990; Steve Chambers, "Case's Namesakes Are Far Removed: Abbott, Now 21, in Prison," *APP*, March 23, 1990; Sherry Conohan, "For This Mother, a Simple Matter of Fairness," *APP*, September 24, 1989; Robert Hanley, "Plaintiff Regards Schools Ruling from a New Jersey Jail," *NYT*, June 12, 1990; Rudy Larini, "Abbott Faults Choices More Than School," *S-L*, May 18, 1997; Thomas Moran, "Decision Is Too Late to Help Abbott: Lead Plaintiff Landed in Jail," *Record*, June 6, 1990; Nancy Phillips,"For Plaintiff in N.J. School Funding Suit, a Troubled Life," *PI*, May 17, 1990; and Joseph A. Slobodzian, "School Funding Formula Being Challenged," *PI*, September 4, 1984. Frances (Luci) Abbott's anger at the deficiencies in Camden's music program is described in Jane M. Von Bergen, "Seeking Equal Schools for Kids 'We Dare Not Scar,'" *PI*, March 13, 1989. Luci's concern over Raymond's camouflaged potential is noted on her intake form in the ELC archives.

The description of the *Abbott* children as "phantom clients" comes from Paris, "Legal Mobilization and Social Reform," 448.

I base my account of the history, demographics, and schools of Camden, East Orange, Irvington, and Jersey City on press accounts; U.S. Census records; relevant articles in the *Encyclopedia of New Jersey*; *Abbott v. Burke*, Initial Decision; Appel, "Finding the Point Again!"; Kirp et al., *Our Town*; Kozol, *Savage Inequalities*; New Jersey Department of Education, *A Survey of the Camden City Public Schools*; Siegel, *An Outline History of Irvington*; and Vespucci and Goldberg, *A History of East Orange*. The comparison between the value of a single casino and the sum total of Camden's property wealth comes from *Abbott v. Burke*, Initial Decision, 17. The description of Camden's school district as "a system in trouble" is in New Jersey Department of Education, *Survey of the Camden City Public Schools*, III-1. The description of an East Orange street as "the Fifth Avenue of the suburbs" is quoted in Vespucci and Goldberg, *History*, "Business and Industry"; praise for East Orange High School is quoted in Vespucci and Goldberg, *History*, "Not So Long Ago." In our interview, Saul Cooperman described the dust-covered desk in the Jersey City central office.

CHAPTER 6. "THE SYSTEM IS BROKEN"

Letters and memos referenced in this chapter come from the ELC archives, unless otherwise indicated.

For the *Abbott* legal proceedings, I rely on press accounts; the transcript of the administrative hearing; legal briefs and rulings, especially *Abbott v. Burke*, Initial Decision; the ELC archives; the Cioppettini papers; and interviews with Shirley Brandman, Ida Castro, Sheila Dow-Ford, Margaret Goertz, Bertram P. Goltz Jr., E. Philip Isaac, Lillian Kaminer, David Long, Joyce Miller, Sandrya L. Porter, Florence Schreiber Powers, Michael Rubin, Annamay Sheppard, and Paul Tractenberg.

For Steven Lefelt's background, see FindLaw, "Hon. Steven L. Lefelt." The story of Castro's childhood encounter with a racist teacher is told in Fletcher, "Childhood Lessons Still Inspire." Since Alfred Ramey Jr. declined to be interviewed for this book, my discussion of his views is based on accounts he gave during a March 12, 1986, preliminary hearing and in a motion and affidavit filed on March 19, 1986. Marilyn Morheuser's account of her conversation with Ramey about the case's political context is contained in a November 13, 1985, memo.

The courtroom where the first half of the administrative hearing was conducted is described in David Corcoran, "City Schools Fight On for Their Fair Share," *Record*, December 18, 1986. Associated Press, "Wider Gap Cited Between Poor, Rich School Districts," *Record*, October 16, 1986, describes the case as "half-forgotten."

Eric Hanushek explained his skepticism about the relationship between school spending and educational quality in May 4, 1987, testimony in the *Abbott v. Burke* administrative hearing. The danger of wearing good sneakers and the importance of field trips are mentioned in Robert Giordano's testimony, November 19, 1986. Aletha Wright described the kindergartner's rape in October 14, 1986, testimony. Michael Ross discussed the Jersey City schools' unpopularity in October 28, 1986, testimony. Riletta Cream called the schools "the hub" of Camden children's lives in October 15, 1986, testimony. James Kimple described the impact funding cuts would have on South Brunswick in October 22, 1986, testimony. Harry Galinsky described political corruption in Hoboken in March 18, 1987, testimony. Charles Williams described Jersey City's atmosphere in November 20, 1986, testimony. The ticketing of Williams's car is described in Charles Weening's testimony, February 11, 1987. Walter McCarroll called urban districts "among the most inefficient" in February 2, 1987, testimony. Donald Beineman called Camden's principals "incompetent" in February 3, 1987, testimony.

Lefelt's suggestion that the state might be deliberately delaying the proceedings came during an *Abbott v. Burke* preliminary hearing, March 12, 1986. Lefelt questioned the length of the state's cross-examination on October 8, 1986, and raised concerns about the size of the record on February 11, 1987 ("bordering on being unmanageable"), April 28, 1987 ("mountain of documents"), and July 13, 1987 ("the only case"). He counted 745 exhibits in *Abbott v. Burke*, Initial Decision, 7. He described the filings as "'briefs'" and declined to accept any more of them in an April 14, 1988, ruling.

ELC's spending on the *Abbott* case is mentioned in the Morheuser affidavit filed with ELC's *Abbott v. Burke* brief, December 13, 1983. ELC's 1988 funding crisis is described in Joan Verdon, "Finances Imperil School Aid Suit: Non-Profit Law Group Going Broke," *Record*, February 2, 1988. Morheuser's inability to fund-raise in 1987 and the "LUCK" of the Clark grant are detailed in undated, but post-1990, notes in the Cioppettini papers.

Morheuser's "ecstatic" reaction to the appellate ruling is noted in Priscilla Van Tassel, "Poor Districts Gain in Battle on School Funds," *NYT*, May 27, 1984. ELC's proof plan is called the "trial preparation 'Bible' " in a Long memo, March 24, 1982. Priscilla Van Tassel, "School Financing Challenged at Trial," *NYT*, October 5, 1986, quotes Morheuser saying that the state "can't guarantee results," and Craig R. McCoy, "Opening Round Nearly Over in N.J. School-Aid Case," *PI*, October 4, 1987, quotes her discussion of the importance of money. The Irvington superintendent's view of Lefelt's ruling is quoted in Jo Astrid Glading, "Former Nun Wins Legal Battle Against New Jersey Law on Funding for Education," Associated Press, August 29, 1988. Morheuser's preference for spending limits on the rich is summarized in Joan Verdon, "School Ruling May Mean New Tax," *Record*, August 28, 1988; a Republican assemblyman's objections to such limits are described in Joan Verdon, "Judge: Revamp School Funding," *Record*, August 26, 1988.

Rubin's interview with the Princeton guidance counselor is reported in a January 12, 1986, memo. Morheuser discussed the need for "true believers" in a January 12, 1986, memo. Morheuser referred to the "war on poor children" in a September 4, 1986, letter to Anthony Scardaville and to the danger of delay in a November 28, 1984, letter to Gustavo Mellander.

For the Kean administration's reaction to the case, I rely on interviews with Saul Cooperman and Thomas Kean.

I base my account of the state supreme court's view of the case on interviews with Marie Garibaldi, Alan Handler, Daniel O'Hern, and Gary Stein.

For Morheuser's personal life, I rely on the ELC archives and the Cioppettini papers and on interviews with Margaret Benben, Steven Block, Thomas Cioppettini, James Louis, Lawrence Lustberg, Tractenberg, and Martin Wheelwright. The description of Morheuser's self-medication with megavitamins comes from Morheuser's letter to Flora Kimmich, February 15, 1984. Morheuser's poem "Found Again" is in the Cioppettini papers.

CHAPTER 7. THE TWENTY-ONE/FORTY-ONE RULE

Letters, memos, and reports referenced in this chapter come from the ELC archives, unless otherwise indicated.

For Jim Florio's background, see Kerr, "Read His Lips" and Turcol, "The Return of Jim Florio."

For the backgrounds of David Wilentz and Robert Wilentz, I rely on press reports, the *Encyclopedia of New Jersey*, and "Chief Justice Robert N. Wilentz: A Tribute," *Rutgers Law Review* 49, no. 3 (Spring 1997). The lobbyist's description of Wilentz's influence comes from Robert Cohen, "Wilentz Choice May Usher in New Court Era," *S-L*, March 18, 1979. Richard Hughes's tribute to Wilentz's "moral leadership" is quoted in Charles Q. Finley, "Wilentz Greets Challenge: New Chief Justice Adjusts to 'Changed Life,'" *S-L*, April 29, 1979. Wilentz's reserve is described by Daniel O'Hern in his interview with McGovern and Honecker.

For *Abbott II*, I rely on legal briefs; *Abbott II*; and interviews with Marie Garibaldi, Alan Handler, O'Hern, and Gary Stein. Marilyn Morheuser called the wait for the ruling "nail-biting" in ELC's FY 1990 Annual Report, 5. Her dramatic announcement about the ruling's release is reported in Rich Heidorn Jr., "Ruling Due Today in N.J. Schools Suit," *PI*, June 5, 1990. In our interview, O'Hern compared a unanimous ruling to a "thunderclap." Christopher Kilbourne, "Still Miles to Go Till Equality," *Record*, June 7, 1990, describes ELC's ringing telephones; the pink message slips, letter from the incoming education commissioner, and note addressed to "Madam Freedom Fighter" are in the ELC archives. Morheuser reports her three-day smile in ELC's quarterly report to donors, July 19, 1990, 7. The Ford/Mercedes analogy is quoted in Tom Hester, "Decision Draws Mixed Reaction from Leaders," *S-L*, June 6, 1990. The ruling's propensity for fostering resentment is described in Corcoran and Scovronick, "More Than Equal," 66.

For the Florio administration, the legislature, and QEA, I rely on press accounts and on interviews with Douglas Berman, Thomas Corcoran, Dolores Corona, Joseph Doria Jr., John Ellis, John H. Ewing, Jim Florio, Betty Kraemer, John Lynch, James Reilly, Nathan Scovronick, Jon Shure, and Melvin Wyns.

The administration's initial desire to avoid developing a new formula in secret is discussed in the executive summary of the Department of Education transition report, 7, located in the New Jersey State Archives, Governor James Joseph Florio record group, Office of Management and Planning subgroup, records of Brenda J. Bacon, G-035 (Box 2: Departmental Information 1990),"Education Initiatives" folder. The executive summary is undated and unsigned, but a cover letter identifies it as Corcoran's work. The Republican assemblyman's prediction that funding caps would inspire a "revolution" is quoted in the online version of Kathy Barrett Carter, "State's Top Court Ready To Take Up School Funding Case," *S-L*, September 24, 1989. The suburban superintendent's prediction that QEA will spawn mediocrity is quoted in Robert Hanley, "New Jersey Suburbs Attack Florio's Plan to Shift Their School Aid," *NYT*, May 26, 1990. In our interview, Harry Galinsky described the danger that suburban protests might look like "crying into our beer." The "gold Assemblyman badges" and "lavish lunches" are described in Sandy McClure, " 'Arrogant' Assembly Ups Its Budget $5.6M," *Trentonian*, June 21, 1990. John Budzash is quoted in Hoyt and Schoonmaker, "Robin Hood's Merry Plan," 630. The Republicans' red bandanas are mentioned in Wayne King, "The 2d Man at the Helm of New Jersey's Taut Ship of State," *NYT*, June 18, 1990, and the toilet-paper-stuffed envelopes in Wayne King, "New Jersey Democrats Wary of Tax Issue," *NYT*, July 29, 1990. Joseph Doria Jr.'s description of the Democratic caucus is quoted in Tom Johnson and Donna Leusner, "Long Night of Arm-Twisting Brings Florio Victory . . . and New Enemies," *S-L*, June 22, 1990. Morheuser's angry description of QEA II is in a fund-raising proposal, June 1991, 4.

For QEA's fiscal mechanics, see Goertz, *The Development and Implementation of the Quality Education Act of 1990* and *A Quest for Equal Educational Opportunity in New Jersey*. For an analysis of how school districts used QEA money, see Firestone et al., *From Cashbox to Classroom*, "The QEA: Myth and Reality," and *Where Did the $800 Million Go?*

My account of Morheuser's dispute with the Association for Children of New Jersey is based on interviews with Herbert Green and Cecilia Zalkind. Morheuser's denunciation of the report is in a September 4, 1992, letter to urban superintendents. The report's conclusion is quoted from Zalkind, *Keeping the Focus on Children*, 13.

My account of the pension-aid issue and ELC's changing stance relies on Block, "Comparing the Adequacy of New Jersey and Kentucky Court Mandates, Statutes and Regulations to Remedy Unconstitutional Public Education"; Paris, "Legal Mobilization and Social Reform"; and interviews with Steven Block, Robert Bonazzi, Corona, Galinsky, Reilly, Mark Smith, Paul Tractenberg, and James Zazzali. Morheuser calls pension aid "high-class welfare" in an August 2, 1990, analysis of QEA sent to state and local officials, 17. Corcoran's prediction that "NJEA will be divided" is made on the first page of an April 10, 1990, memo in the New Jersey State Archives, Governor James Joseph Florio record group, Office of Management and Planning subgroup, records of Brenda J. Bacon, G-035 (Box 2: Departmental Information 1990), "Education Initiatives" folder. In our interview, Reilly said that NJEA "dodged a bullet." Morheuser's astonishment at NJEA's lukewarm response to the proposed T&E amendment is described in Paris, "Legal Mobilization and Social Reform," 375. Her explanation of ELC's changed stance is included in ELC's report to the Norman Foundation, August 1992, 4. In our interview, Reilly described Morheuser asking herself what she should do. ELC's political "maturing" is asserted in Block, "Comparing the Adequacy," 78.

My account of the QEA litigation relies on the ELC archives; legal briefs; the *Abbott v. Burke* Superior Court ruling; *Abbott III*; the superior court trial transcript; and interviews with William Brown, Benjamin Clarke, Jonathan Feldman, Margaret Goertz, Paul Levy, and Lawrence Lustberg. The need to update statistics is discussed in the quarterly report of ELC's Equal Educational Opportunity Project, February 10, 1992. The pros and cons of readjusting the special needs weight are discussed in a memo from Robert DeCotiis, William Harla, and Nancy Kaplen Miller, March 31, 1992, 2, in the New Jersey State Archives, Governor James Joseph Florio record group, records of Diane Quinton, G-425 (Box 26: Subject Files–QEA Property Tax; Department Files–Agric. to OLS), "QEA—Property Tax Rates" folder.

Testimony at the QEA trial is described as "dense" and "tedious" in Kathleen Bird, "Adversary's Expert Boosts School Funding Plaintiffs," *NJLJ*, July 13, 1992. Elena Scambio described the costs of educational failure in August 5, 1992, testimony. Levy questioned statistics' validity on July 8, 1992, and expressed frustration at "buzz words" on July 9, 1992. Morheuser described Levy's decision to delay the trial in a report to the Norman Foundation, August 1992. Garibaldi's assertion of state stonewalling is quoted in Kathy Barrett Carter, "School Aid Debate Heard by Court," *S-L*, May 25, 1994. Morheuser boasted of her influence over the state's funding allocation in a February 11, 1993, letter to the Fund for New Jersey.

ELC's continuing financial woes are detailed in ELC's archives. Morheuser requested money for copying costs in a May 24, 1991, letter to Mutual Benefit Life and for deposition transcripts in a May 12, 1992, letter to law firm Crummy Del Deo. She detailed one foundation's decision to cut off funding in an October 13, 1992, memo. She estimated that *Abbott* accounted for 69 percent of ELC's work in a June 27, 1991, letter to a donor. Her empathetic reaction to Newark's treatment of homeless children is contained in a June 25, 1992, letter to Eugene Campbell.

For Morheuser's last years, I rely on the Cioppettini papers and on interviews with Block, Paula Bryant, Thomas Cioppettini, H. Kit Ellenbogen, Helen Lindsay, James Louis, Judy Miller, Annamay Sheppard, and Tractenberg. Morheuser described her unspecified "health problem" in a June 1, 1993, memo and her "more invasive" treatment in a March 1, 1994, memo. Morheuser's decision to "formalize" her relationship with the Sisters of Loretto is explained in the co-membership contract, dated July 20, 1994, in the Cioppettini papers. Supreme Court Justice Robert Clifford's tribute to her is reported in Michael Booth, "An Academic Freedom," *NJLJ*, June 13, 1994.

CHAPTER 8. THE CHILDREN OF *ABBOTT*

My account of Project U.S.E. is based on interviews with Michael Bagley and Andy Hensch. The description of the case that sent Raymond Abbott to state prison comes from defense and prosecution appeal briefs. Abbott's conversation with the police arresting him is in the defense brief, 4, and the juror's impressions of Abbott are in the same brief, 46.

Camden dropout statistics are in Burch, *The Dropout Problem in New Jersey's Big Urban Schools*, 9.

Leslie Stephens did not respond to requests for an interview for this book. My account of her perceptions comes from Mary Jo Patterson and Ted Sherman, "20 Pupils from 1981: Where Are They Now?" *S-L*, June 8, 1997.

CHAPTER 9. A CONSTITUTIONAL RIGHT TO ASTROTURF

For David Sciarra's background, I rely on Lisa Brennan, "New School-Funding Advocate Gears Up for Next Battle," *NJLJ*, December 4, 1995; Mancino, "The Advocate"; James M. O'Neill, "A Voice for N.J.'s Education Underdogs," *PI*, January 6, 1997; and interviews with David Sciarra and Ellie Sciarra.

For Christie Whitman's background, see Jerry Gray, "Whitman Pursues 'Family Business,'" *NYT*, June 9, 1993; and David Wald, "Low-Key Style Traced to Whitman's Traditions," *S-L*, October 10, 1993. Whitman's explanation of her failure to vote in a local school election is quoted in *S-L*, "Whitman Revises Voting Story Again," May 3, 1993.

For standards-based reform in New Jersey, see Doolan, "Systemic Change and Standards-Based Reform."

For the legislative battle over CEIFA, I rely on press reports; the ELC archives; the three drafts of the New Jersey Department of Education's *Comprehensive Plan for Educational Improvement and Financing*; and interviews with Michael Azzara, Jack Collins, Dolores Corona, Donald DiFrancesco, David Hespe, Robert Martin, Eileen McGinnis, James Reilly, David Sciarra, and Lynne Strickland.

Leo Klagholz's Astroturf remark is quoted in O'Dea, "The Price of Parity," 10. The critique of New Jersey's school-funding system is in New Jersey Department of Education, *Comprehensive Plan for Educational Improvement and Financing: An Interim Report*, 2, and the rejection of "draconian" controls is in the same report, 27. The Rutgers study estimating that three-quarters of the state's school districts spent more than one version of CEIFA allowed is mentioned in O'Dea, "The Price of Parity," 13. The suburban principal discussed cutting football and Italian during testimony delivered to the Senate Education Committee, July 17, 1996; the testimony is included in ELC's archives. The teachers' union's testimony is quoted in Donna Leusner, "Some Fear State Plan Would Pit Property Taxes Against School Funding," *S-L*, December 6, 1995. Colleagues' warnings to Klagholz are described in Doolan, "Systemic Change," 212. In our interview, Collins discussed the possibility of "cooked" numbers. The thousands of angry letters from the suburbs are mentioned in Jennifer Preston, "3 More Months to Answer a 20-Year-Old Riddle," *NYT*, September 15, 1996. In our interview, Hespe discussed the importance of maintaining the foundation amount. David Sciarra's prediction that his toddler could win the case is quoted in John McLaughlin, "Court Will Have Final Say on School Plan," *S-L*, November 17, 1996; the governor's doubts are reported in Preston, "3 More Months." I frequently heard Collins enumerate the branches of government during my years as a statehouse reporter. Whitman's explanation for her approach to CEIFA is quoted in Nick Chiles, "26 School Districts Perplexed by Plan," *S-L*, December 19, 1996. The legislative histrionics during the CEIFA debate are described in Cynthia Burton and Ron Marsico, "Legislature Adopts Overhaul of School Aid Standards," *S-L*, December 20, 1996.

For Michael Patrick King's background, see Carla Anderson, "Future of Poor, Urban Schools in Judge's Hands," *TT*, December 14, 1997; Abby Goodnough, "Judge Weighing New Jersey's Spending On Urban Schools Offers Few Clues on Ruling," *NYT*, January 4, 1998; Robbins, "The Mentoring King"; Sanders, "On School Funding, Remands, and Chosen Wise Men"; and Robert Schwaneberg, "Tough Jurist Tapped to Oversee Urban Schools," *S-L*, June 1, 1997. King's love of history is described in Robbins, "The Mentoring King," xiii–xv; his lectures on punctuation in Schwaneberg, "Tough Jurist Tapped"; his kindness to foster children in Sanders, "On School Funding," xlvii; and his possible future on the state supreme court in Anderson, "Future of Poor, Urban Schools."

For the legal proceedings, I use press accounts; legal briefs; the *Abbott v. Burke* remand hearing transcript and ruling; *Abbott IV* and *V*; and interviews with Steven Block, James Coleman Jr., Marie Garibaldi, Alan Handler, Jeffrey Miller, Allan Odden, Daniel O'Hern, David Sciarra, Gary Stein, and Peter Verniero. Sciarra's mistake with his son's shoes is described in O'Neill, "A Voice." ELC's funding numbers are noted in Goertz and Edwards, "In Search of Excellence for All," 20; the state's numbers are in its

Abbott v. Burke brief of January 31, 1997. The jubilant ride back to ELC's offices after the *Abbott IV* ruling is described in Robert J. Braun, "With Their Vigor and Pride Renewed, Critics Bash Whitman and Klagholz," *S-L*, May 15, 1997. Collins's condemnation of the ruling is quoted in Dunstan McNichol, "School Aid Decision Outrages Lawmakers," *Record*, May 16, 1997.

In our interview, Azzara remembered Odden describing the *Abbott* programs as "a hodgepodge"; Hespe also remembered Odden advocating whole-school reform at this meeting. The state's whole-school reform proposal is detailed in New Jersey Department of Education, *A Study of Supplemental Programs and Recommendations for the Abbott Districts*; ELC's earlier report is Education Law Center, *Wiping Out Disadvantages*.

Klagholz testified about illustrative budgets during the *Abbott v. Burke* remand hearing, November 19, 1997. Gary Natriello refused to choose the most important supplemental program in December 8, 1997, testimony. Margaret Goertz offered cost estimates during December 9, 1997, testimony. Odden's controversial remarks to reporters are quoted in Kathy Barrett Carter, "Expert Favors Reform Plan for Schools," *S-L*, November 20, 1997. (Abby Goodnough, "Schools Chief in New Jersey Is Pressed on Education Plan," *NYT*, November 20, 1997, renders the quotes somewhat differently.) The argument between Sciarra and King over Odden's comments is contained in the remand hearing transcript for November 20, 1997. No transcript was made of the closing arguments, but Sciarra and Miller's remarks are quoted in Kathy Barrett Carter, "School Funding Hearings Conclude," *S-L*, December 23, 1997. The analysis of *Abbott V* that irritated Stein is in Jennifer Preston, "Plan by Whitman on Urban Schools Backed by Court," *NYT*, May 22, 1998. Handler's gloss on the ruling is quoted in Peter Aseltine, "Justice: Court Hasn't Closed Door on Schools," *TT*, May 30, 1998. The former Republican staffer's view is quoted in Dunstan McNichol, "Court Clears Plan for Poor Schools," *S-L*, May 22, 1998.

CHAPTER 10. "WE DO NOT RUN SCHOOL SYSTEMS"

I base my account of the disputes over *Abbott* preschool on press reports; legal briefs; *Abbott VI*; *Abbott VIII*; *In re: Abbott Global Issues*, Initial Decision; studies by Barnett et al. and Lamy et al.; and interviews with Steven Block, James Coleman Jr., Lucille Davy, Ellen Frede, William Librera, Eileen McGinnis, Gordon MacInnes, Daniel O'Hern, David Sciarra, Gary Stein, and Paul Tractenberg. The "two respected studies" of preschool's efficacy are the High/Scope Perry Preschool study and the Abecedarian study. W. Steven Barnett described the Perry study's $9-for-$1 finding in testimony at the *Abbott v. Burke* remand hearing, December 1, 1997. (In a more recent follow-up study of the Perry program, researchers have adjusted that ratio upward, to $17-for-$1.) Abbott kindergartners' communication skills are assessed in Barnett et al., *Early Childhood Education in the Abbott Districts*, 2. New Jersey's per-pupil K–12 spending is listed as $8,194 in the actual costs section of the New Jersey Department of Education, *Comparative Spending Guide*. Governor Christie Whitman's caution against kindergarten cramming is quoted in Maria Newman, "New Jersey to Provide Full-Day Preschool in Its 28 Poorest Districts," *NYT*, January 7, 1999; Barnett's critique of the state's preschool

proposal in quoted in Dunstan McNichol and Donna Leusner, "Whitman Details Plans
for Full-Day Preschool," *S-L*, January 7, 1999. Stein's assessment of the preschool program as "chaotic" is quoted in Maria Newman, "Justices Fault Pace of Preschool Program," *NYT*, October 13, 1999. The state-commissioned study that gave the preschool
program decent marks is Resnick, *The Evaluation of Early Childhood Education Programming in the 30 Abbott School Districts*. The competing report from ELC allies is Barnett
et al., *Fragile Lives, Shattered Dreams*.

My account of the disputes over whole-school reform is based on press reports;
legal briefs; *Abbott VI* and *Abbott IX–XI*; studies by Erlichson et al., Erlichson and Goertz, Muirhead et al., and Walker et al.; and interviews with Block, Librera, MacInnes,
Sciarra, Stein, and Tractenberg. The schools' suspicion of state edicts is described in
Erlichson et al., *Implementing Whole School Reform in New Jersey*, 22. The principal who
sought a relatively nonintrusive reform model is quoted in Erlichson and Goertz, *Implementing Whole School Reform in New Jersey*, 20.

My account of legislative wrangling over school construction is based on press reports, especially Dunstan McNichol, "How School Repair Plan Ballooned," *S-L*, May 14,
2000; *Abbott VII*; and my own observations as a statehouse reporter in 1999–2000.

For Jim McGreevey's background, see McGreevey, *The Confession*. For Gordon
MacInnes's background, see MacInnes, *Wrong for All the Right Reasons*.

Librera's desire to "celebrate" *Abbott* is quoted in John Mooney, "McGreevey
Chooses Leader for Education," *S-L*, January 8, 2002. McGreevey's explanation of his
decision to collaborate with ELC is quoted in David Kocieniewski, "Panel Created in
New Jersey to Aid Poor School Districts," *NYT*, February 20, 2002. Patricia Bombelyn's
view of that collaboration as a "rape" is quoted in Mary P. Gallagher, "Collaboration
with Regulators Causes Rift among Traditional Abbott Allies," *NJLJ*, May 24, 2002.

The state's description of the supplemental funding process as "almost like a
blank check" is quoted in Brian Kladko, "$500M in School Aid Lost in Shuffle," *Record*,
June 5, 2002. Sciarra's repudiation of the state's return to court is in a January 28,
2003, letter to Librera.

CHAPTER 11. THE CHILDREN GROW UP

The anecdote about Lola Moore's grocery-store encounters with her admirers comes
from Kristen A. Graham, "Retiring Won't Stop This School Activist," *PI*, June 20, 2005.
Leslie Stephens is quoted in Mary Jo Patterson and Ted Sherman, "20 Pupils from 1981:
Where Are They Now?" *S-L*, June 8, 1997.

CONCLUSION. OTHER PEOPLE'S CHILDREN

Reock, *State Aid for Schools in New Jersey*, table 39, puts the pre-*Abbott* spending disparity at 26 percent. The post-*Abbott* disparity is put at 20 percent (in the other direction) in the state brief in *Abbott v. Burke*, April 7, 2006, 12.

The state's preschool enrollment projections are contained in New Jersey Department of the Treasury, *Fiscal 2007 Budget in Brief*, 24. The proportion of preschool teachers with bachelor's degrees in 2005 is reported in Lamy et al., *Giant Steps for the Littlest
Children*, 14; the proportion six years earlier is reported in Lamy et al., *Inch by Inch*,

Row by Row, 7. The 2004–05 quality ratings are discussed in Lamy et al., *Giant Steps*, 5; the quality ratings from four years earlier are detailed in Barnett et al., *Fragile Lives, Shattered Dreams*, 9.

The number of projects spawned by the *Abbott* school construction program is reported in Dunstan McNichol, "SCC Makes Its Case for More Funding," *S-L*, May 26, 2006.

Abbott enrollment and aid numbers are reported in Settle, testimony, 42.

Details of the spending adequacy study are in Education Law Center, summary of state spending adequacy study, 1.

WORKS CITED

ARCHIVAL SOURCES

Cioppettini, Thomas. Uncataloged papers. Ocean Grove, New Jersey.

Education Law Center. Uncataloged archives. Newark, New Jersey.

New Jersey State Archives. Governor James Joseph Florio record group. Trenton, New Jersey.

——. Office of Management and Planning. Records of Brenda J. Bacon, chief, 1990–94.

——. Records of Diane Quinton, legislative liaison, 1989–93.

Wheelwright, Martin. Uncataloged papers. Lambertville, New Jersey.

INTERVIEWS

Abbott, Raymond: December 27, 2004.

Anderson, Jay: May 14, 2004.

Appel, Reverend Samuel: June 4, 2004.

Azzara, Michael: April 3, 2006.

Bagley, Michael: February 14, 2006.

Barbee-Wooten, Daphne: August 14, 2004.

Bateman, Raymond: May 1, 2003.

Bell, Frances: September 15, 2004.

Benben, Margaret: April 14, 2004.

Berman, Douglas: September 15, 2005.

Berthel, Lee: January 7, 2004.

Block, Steven: June 12, 2003; April 11, September 16, and October 7, 2005; May 3, 2006.

Bonazzi, Robert: May 25, 2005.

Botter, Theodore: March 13 and March 17, 2003.

Brandman, Shirley: April 26, 2005.

Brinovec, Mary: December 9, 2003.

Brock, Kathryn: December 16, 2003.

Brown, Joy Appel: February 19, 2005.

Brown, William: July 6, 2005.

Bryant, Paula: September 15, 2003.

Buckler, Sister Mary Rhodes: August 27, 2003.

Burke, Fred: April 24, 2003.

Burstein, Albert: April 2, 2003.

Byrne, Brendan: March 24, 2003.

Carter, Richard G.: April 7, 2004.

Casey, Marie: January 26, 2004.

Casey, Marilyn: March 18, 2004.

Castro, Ida: January 14, 2004.

Charles, Frances: July 17, 2003.

Cheh, Mary: July 9, 2003.

Cioppettini, Thomas: August 5, 2003.

Clarke, Benjamin: June 3, 2005.

Cochran, Thomas: April 13, 2003.

Coleman, James Jr.: May 25, 2006.

Collins, Jack: October 20, 2005.

Cooperman, Saul: September 23, 2004.

Corcoran, Thomas: April 22, 2005.

Corona, Dolores: November 3, 2005.

Coyle, Sister Theresa: September 8, 2003.

Davy, Lucille: August 17, 2006.

Diaz, Liana: June 21, 2006.

DiFrancesco, Donald: October 11, 2005.

Dodd, Frank J.: May 2, 2003.

Doria, Joseph Jr.: June 15, 2005.

Dow-Ford, Sheila: January 20, 2004.

Dugan, James: June 26, 2003.

Dunnings, Stuart Jr.: September 15, 2004.

Eisdorfer, Stephen: August 15 and August 21, 2003.

Ellenbogen, H. Kit.: December 17, 2003.

Ellis, John: May 26, 2005.

English, Jerry Fitzgerald: May 19, 2003.

Ewing, John H.: June 10, 2005.

Favia, Thomas: December 8, 2003.

Feintuch, Philip: December 10, 2003.

Feldman, Jonathan: December 18, 2003.

Fields, Evanett: August 16, 2005.

Figueroa, Arlayne: May 26, 2005.

Figueroa, Blanca: June 9, 2004.

Figueroa, Frances: June 18, 2004.

Figueroa, Hector: May 13, 2004.

Figueroa, Orlando: June 7, 2004.

Figueroa, Vivian: July 14, 2004.

Finnerty, John: July 18, 2003.

Florio, Jim: June 30, 2005.

Frede, Ellen: May 23, 2006.

Friedrich, Charles: June 9, 2003.

Galinsky, Harry: May 14, 2005.

Garibaldi, Marie: June 23, 2005.

Gaskill, Margaret: January 2, 2004.

Goertz, Margaret: June 22, 2005.

Goldman, Clifford: April 30, 2003.

Goltz, Bertram P. Jr.: July 6, 2004.

Green, Herbert: March 26, 2003; April 20, 2005.

Green, Saundra: June 16 and July 14, 2003.

Gregg, Reverend Bertraim S.: May 14, 2004.

Hadley, Michael: July 13, 2004.

Handler, Alan: June 8, 2005; March 30, 2006.

Hargrove, Zakia: August 16, 2005.

Harpole, Reuben: March 23, 2004.

Hensch, Andy: April 27, 2006.

Herzberg, Peter: April 7, 2005.

Hespe, David: March 30, 2006.

Hochman, Fredrica: January 7, 2004.

Howard, Cheryl: June 25 and July 9, 2003.

Isaac, E. Philip: April 13 and April 26, 2004.

Jackson, Bobby. October 3, 2006.

Jackson, Deborah. May 2, 2006.

James, Caroline: July 22, 2004.

James, Jermaine: July 8, 2004.

James, Mattie: October 2, 2004.

Kaden, Lewis: April 1, 2003.

Kaminer, Lillian: September 9, 2004.

Kean, Thomas: June 6, 2005.

Kelly, James: April 8, 2003.

Kenny, Joanne: December 8, 2003.

Kenoyer, Sister Pat: December 8, 2003.

Knowles, Cristina: December 19 and December 20, 2006.

Knowles, Daniel: June 22, 2006.

Knowles, Guy Jr.: May 11, 2006.

Knowles, Guy Sr.: May 18, 2006.

Kraemer, Betty: May 19, 2005.

Laurenti, Jeffrey: April 19, 2003.

Leone, Richard: April 7, April 28, and May 22, 2003; November 3, 2005.

Levy, Paul: September 9, 2005.

Librera, William: May 5, 2006.

Lindsay, Helen: August 4, 2003.

Long, David; September 9, 2003.

Lottman, Michael: August 27 and August 28, 2003.

Louis, James: August 12, 2003.

Lucas, Louis: September 9, 2004.

Lustberg, Lawrence: September 22, 2003.

Lynch, John: June 21, 2005.

MacInnes, Gordon: May 11, 2006.

Mangels, Lucila Rivera: March 31, 2006.

Manion, Sister Patricia Jean: September 3, 2003.

Martin, Robert: February 17, 2006.

Matrick, Debra: January 19, 2004.

Matthews, Terence: December 10, 2003.

Mazzagetti, Dominick: June 9, 2003.

McGinnis, Eileen: April 21, 2006.

Meskin, Kenneth: June 24, 2003.

Miller, Jeffrey: February 10, 2006.

Miller, Joyce: December 23, 2003.

Miller, Judy: August 1, 2003.

Misbauer, Sister Katherine: August 18, 2003.

Moore, Lola: May 26, 2004.

Mosley, Joan Franklin: January 13, 2005.

Muller, Paul: May 21, 2003.

Murphy, Marianne Espinosa: June 24, 2003.

Nicodemo, Anthony: December 8, 2003.

Odden, Allan: April 27, 2006.

O'Hern, Daniel: June 2, 2005; March 9, 2006.

Porter, Sandrya L.: August 11, 2004.

Powers, Florence Schreiber: April 13, 2005.

Reed, Marvin: April 29, 2003.

Reilly, James: November 3, 2005.

Reock, Ernest Jr.: May 7, 2003.

Robinson, Wilbur Jr.: July 13, 2003.

Rock, Annie Ruth: June 16, 2003.

Roper, Richard: June 12, 2003.

Rubin, Michael: January 10, 2004.

Ruvoldt, Harold Jr.: May 2 and May 6, 2003.

Sanders, George: January 6, 2004.

Schreiber, Sidney: May 20, 2003.

Sciarra, David: October 14 and October 28, 2005; May 16, 2006.

Sciarra, Ellie: February 8, 2006.

Scovronick, Nathan: May 26, 2005.

Seaman, Magdalen: December 8, 2003.

Sheppard, Annamay: August 11, 2003.

Shine, William: June 4, 2003.

Shure, Jon: April 25, 2005.

Slippen, Richard: December 18, 2003.

Smith, Mark: April 20, 2005.

Starkey, S. Herbert Jr.: May 16, 2003.

Stein, Gary: June 13, 2005; March 6, 2006.

Stephens, Eddie: July 21, 2004.

Stephens, LaMar: July 30, 2004.

Stephens, Tommi: November 2, 2004.

Stevens, Henry Jr.: May 6, 2004.

Stevens, Henry Sr.: May 6, 2004.

Stotland, Janet: December 16, 2003.

Strickland, Lynne: May 3 and September 28, 2005.

Stuckert, Robert: March 15, 2004.

Symmes, Barbara: January 11, 2004.

Taverney, Gabriel: December 8, 2003.

Tevik, Ann: May 11, 2004.

Todd, Leon: April 15, 2004.

Tractenberg, Paul: March 14 and August 20, 2003; October 21, 2005; May 17, 2006.

Verniero, Peter: February 15, 2006.

Waiters, Khudayja: June 15, 2004.

Waiters, Lynn: May 12, 2004.

Walker, Reverend Lucius Jr.: September 22, 2004.

Wallach, Steven: June 2, 2005.

Watson, Cora: November 5, 2005.

Weiss, Stephen: April 3, 2003.

Wexler, Jacqueline Grennan: October 2, 2003.

Wheelwright, Martin: August 28, 2003; September 15, 2004.

White, John: April 25, 2003.

Wiley, Stephen: April 24, 2003.

Wyns, Melvin: June 7, 2005.

Zalkind, Cecilia: April 22, 2005.

Zazzali, James: April 21, 2006.

LEGAL RULINGS

Abbott v. Burke, 195 N.J. Super. 59 (1984).

Abbott v. Burke I, 100 N.J. 269 (1985).

Abbott v. Burke. Initial Decision, Office of Administrative Law. OAL Docket No. EDU 5581–85, August 24, 1988.

Abbott v. Burke. Commissioner of Education decision. OAL Docket No. EDU 5581–85, February 22, 1989.

Abbott v. Burke II, 119 N.J. 287 (1990).

Abbott v. Burke. Unpublished decision of Superior Court of New Jersey, Docket No. 91-C-00150, August 31, 1993.

Abbott v. Burke III, 136 N.J. 444 (1994).

Abbott v. Burke IV, 149 N.J. 145 (1997).

Abbott v. Burke, 1998 N.J. Super. Lexis 25.

Abbott v. Burke V, 153 N.J. 480 (1998).

Abbott v. Burke VI, 163 N.J. 95 (2000).

Abbott v. Burke VII, 164 N.J. 84 (2000).

Abbott v. Burke VIII, 170 N.J. 537 (2002).

Abbott v. Burke IX, 172 N.J. 294 (2002).

Abbott v. Burke X, 177 N.J. 578 (2003).

Abbott v. Burke XI, 177 N.J. 596 (2003).

Abbott v. Burke XIV, 185 N.J. 612 (2005).

Abbott v. Burke XV, 2006 N.J. Lexis 655.

Asbury Park Board of Education et al. v. New Jersey Department of Education ("Abbott XII"), 180 N.J. 109 (2004).

In re: Abbott Global Issues. Initial Decision, Office of Administrative Law. OAL Docket No. EDU 3246–01, April 20, 2001.

Millville Board of Education et al. v. New Jersey Department of Education and *Neptune Township Board of Education v. New Jersey Department of Education ("Abbott XIII")*, 183 N.J. 264 (2005).

Robinson v. Cahill, 118 N.J. Super. 223 (1972) and 119 N.J. Super. 40 (1972).

Robinson v. Cahill I, 62 N.J. 473 (1973).

Robinson v. Cahill II, 63 N.J. 196 (1973).

Robinson v. Cahill III, 67 N.J. 35 (1975).

Robinson v. Cahill IV, 69 N.J. 133 (1975).

Robinson v. Cahill V, 69 N.J. 449 (1976).

Robinson v. Cahill VI, 70 N.J. 155 (1976).

Robinson v. Cahill VII, 70 N.J. 464 (1976).

San Antonio Independent School District v. Rodriguez, 411 U.S. 1 (1973).

Serrano v. Priest, 5 Cal. 3d 584 (1971).

NEWSPAPERS

Asbury Park Press, 1976–1998.

Bergen Record, 1970–2003.

Camden Courier-Post, 1968–1989.

Jersey Journal, 1941–1989.

Milwaukee Journal, 1963–1965.

Milwaukee Sentinel, 1963–1966.

Newark Star-Ledger, 1970–2006.

New Jersey Law Journal, 1973–2002.

New York Times, 1972–2006.

North Jersey Herald and News, 1990.

Philadelphia Inquirer, 1975–1990.

Press of Atlantic City, 1989–1990.

Times of Trenton (formerly *Evening Times*), 1972–1998.

Trentonian, 1975–1990.

PRINTED SOURCES, PUBLISHED AND UNPUBLISHED

Anyon, Jean. *Ghetto Schooling: A Political Economy of Urban Educational Reform*. New York: Teachers College Press, 1997.

Appel, Sam. "Finding the Point Again! A Report and Reflections on 25 Years of Urban Ministry in Camden, New Jersey." Typescript, November 1988.

Aukofer, Frank A. *City With a Chance*. Milwaukee: Bruce Publishing, 1968.

Baldwin, James. "Letter from a Region in My Mind." *The New Yorker*, November 17, 1962.

Barnett, W. Steven, Julie Tarr, and Ellen Frede. *Early Childhood Education in the Abbott Districts: Children's Needs and the Need for High Quality Programs*. Rutgers University Center for Early Education Research, New Brunswick, NJ, January 5, 1999.

Barnett, W. Steven, Julie Tarr, Cindy Esposito Lamy, and Ellen Frede. *Fragile Lives, Shattered Dreams: A Report on Implementation of Preschool Education in New Jersey's Abbott Districts*. Rutgers University Center for Early Education Research, New Brunswick, NJ, May 31, 2001.

Block, Steven G. "Comparing the Adequacy of New Jersey and Kentucky Court Mandates, Statutes and Regulations to Remedy Unconstitutional Public Education." Ph.D. diss., Seton Hall University, October 2002.

Bole, Robert D., and Laurence B. Johnson. *The New Jersey High School: A History*. Princeton, NJ: D. Van Nostrand, 1964.

Burch, Philip. *The Dropout Problem in New Jersey's Big Urban Schools: Educational Inequality and Governmental Inaction*. Rutgers University Bureau of Government Research, Department of Government Services, New Brunswick, NJ, May 1992.

"Chief Justice Robert N. Wilentz: A Tribute." *Rutgers Law Review* 49, no. 3 (Spring 1997).

Coons, John E., William H. Clune III, and Stephen D. Sugarman. *Private Wealth and Public Education*. Cambridge, MA: Harvard University Press, 1970.

Corcoran, Thomas and Nathan Scovronick. "More Than Equal: New Jersey's Quality Education Act." In *Strategies for School Equity: Creating Productive Schools in a Just Society*, ed. Marilyn J. Gittell, 53–69. New Haven, CT: Yale University Press, 1998.

Doolan, Edward J. "Systemic Change and Standards-Based Reform: An Historical Analysis of Educational Policy Formation in New Jersey." Ph.D. diss., Rutgers University, May 2004.

Dougherty, Jack. *More Than One Struggle: The Evolution of Black School Reform in Milwaukee*. Chapel Hill: University of North Carolina Press, 2004.

Education Law Center. Summary of state spending adequacy study. http://www.edlawcenter.org/ELCPublic/elcnews_061020_DOE_EducationCostFigures.pdf

———. *Wiping Out Disadvantages: The Programs and Services Needed to Supplement Regular Education for Poor School Children*. October 1996.

Erlichson, Bari Anhalt, and Margaret Goertz. *Implementing Whole School Reform in New Jersey: Year Two*. Rutgers University Center for Government Services, New Brunswick, NJ, January 2001.

Erlichson, Bari Anhalt, Margaret Goertz, and Barbara J. Turnbull. *Implementing Whole School Reform in New Jersey: Year One in the First Cohort Schools*. Rutgers University Center for Government Services, New Brunswick, NJ, October 1999.

Fecht, Audrey. "Brendan T. Byrne: Name in the News." *Newark News*, January 11, 1970.

FindLaw. "Hon. Steven L. Lefelt." http://pview.findlaw.com/cmd/profileview?wld_id = 2333468_1&channel = &print = 1.

Firestone, William A., Margaret E. Goertz, Brianna Nagle, and Marcy F. Smelkinson. *Where Did the $800 Million Go? The First Year of New Jersey's Quality Education Act*.

Center for Educational Policy Analysis, Rutgers University, New Brunswick, NJ, March 1993.

Firestone, William A., Gary J. Natriello, and Margaret E. Goertz. *From Cashbox to Classroom: The Struggle for Fiscal Reform and Educational Change in New Jersey*. New York: Teachers College Press, 1997.

———. "The QEA: Myth and Reality." *New Jersey Reporter*, September/October 1994.

Fletcher, Michael A. "Childhood Lessons Still Inspire New Leader of EEOC." *Washington Post*, November 30, 1998.

Goertz, Margaret E. *The Development and Implementation of the Quality Education Act of 1990*. Consortium for Policy Research in Education, Eagleton Institute of Politics, Rutgers University, New Brunswick, NJ, November 1992.

———. *A Quest for Equal Educational Opportunity in New Jersey: Abbott v. Burke and the Quality Education Act of 1990*. Program for New Jersey Affairs, Woodrow Wilson School of Public and International Affairs, Princeton University, Princeton, NJ, January 1991.

———. *Where Did the 400 Million Dollars Go? The Impact of the New Jersey Public School Education Act of 1975*. Education Policy Research Institute, Educational Testing Service, Princeton, NJ, March 1978.

Goertz, Margaret E., and Malik Edwards. "In Search of Excellence for All: The Courts and New Jersey School Finance Reform." *Journal of Education Finance* 25, no. 1 (Summer 1999): 5–31.

Governor's Select Commission on Civil Disorder, State of New Jersey. *Report for Action*. February 1968.

Hoyt, Michael, and Mary Ellen Schoonmaker. "Robin Hood's Merry Plan: Educating the Garden State." *Commonweal*, November 9, 1990.

Kean, Thomas H. *The Politics of Inclusion*. New York: Free Press, 1988.

Kelman, Susan. "Time Erodes Family's Hope of School Reform." *Hudson Dispatch*, August 9, 1979.

Kerr, Peter. "Read His Lips: More Taxes." *New York Times Magazine*, May 20, 1990.

Kirp, David L., John P. Dwyer, and Larry A. Rosenthal. *Our Town: Race, Housing, and the Soul of Suburbia*. New Brunswick, NJ: Rutgers University Press, 1995.

Kozol, Jonathan. *Savage Inequalities: Children in America's Schools*. New York: Crown, 1991.

Ladd, Scott. "She Gave Up The Church to Challenge the State." *National Law Journal*, January 30, 1995.

Lamy, Cynthia Esposito, Ellen Frede, Holly Seplocha, Janis Strasser, Saigeetha Jambunathan, Jo Anne Juncker, and Ellen Wolock. *Giant Steps for the Littlest Children: Progress in the Sixth Year of the Abbott Preschool Program*. Early Learning Improvement Coalition, May 18, 2005.

Lamy, Cynthia Esposito, Ellen Frede, Holly Seplocha, Janis Strasser, Saigeetha Jambunathan, Jo Anne Juncker, Heidi Ferrar, Lorraine Wiley, and Ellen Wolock. *Inch by Inch, Row by Row Gonna Make This Garden Grow: Classroom Quality and Language Skills in the Abbott Preschool Program*. Early Learning Improvement Coalition, March 26, 2004.

Lehne, Richard. *The Quest for Justice: The Politics of School Finance Reform*. New York: Longman, 1978.

Lehne, Richard, and Dan Rottenberg. "The Real Story of the Income Tax." *New Jersey Monthly*, November 1976.

Lurie, Maxine, and Marc Mappen. *Encyclopedia of New Jersey*. New Brunswick, NJ: Rutgers University Press, 2004.

MacInnes, Gordon. *Wrong for All the Right Reasons: How White Liberals Have Been Undone by Race*. New York: New York University Press, 1996.

Mancino, Colleen. "The Advocate." *New Jersey Monthly*, October 1998.

McGreevey, James E. *The Confession*. New York: Regan, 2006.

Morheuser, Marilyn. "Saturday Afternoon on Doorbell Duty." *Lorettine Quarterly* 47, no. 4 (May 1953).

Muirhead, Marilyn Savarese, Ryan L. Tyler, and Madlene P. Hamilton. *Study of Whole School Reform Implementation in New Jersey Abbott Districts: Perceptions of Key Stakeholders*. George Washington University, Washington, DC, April 2001.

National Access Network. "Litigation." http://www.schoolfunding.info/litigation/litigation.php3.

New Jersey Department of Education. *Comparative Spending Guide*. March 2000. http://www.state.nj.us/njded/guide/2000/.

———. *Comprehensive Plan for Educational Improvement and Financing: An Interim Report*. February 1995.

———. *Comprehensive Plan for Educational Improvement and Financing*. November 1995.

———. *Comprehensive Plan for Educational Improvement and Financing*. May 1996.

———. Division of Business and Finance. *Sixteenth Annual Report of the Commissioner of Education: Financial Statistics of School Districts, School Year 1966–67*.

———. *A Study of Supplemental Programs and Recommendations for the Abbott Districts*. November 1997.

———. *A Survey of the Camden City Public Schools*. November 1969.

New Jersey Department of the Treasury. *Fiscal 2007 Budget in Brief*. http://www.state.nj.us/treasury/omb/publications/07bib/pdf/bib.pdf

New Jersey Education Association. "New Jersey Teachers' 1978–79 Salary Survey." *NJEA Review* 52, no. 4 (December 1978).

New Jersey Legislature. *New Jersey School Budgets and Property Taxes, 1980 to 1982. Part I—Statewide Data* and *Part II—Equalization and Equity Among Taxing Districts*. Prepared by Rutgers University, Bureau of Government Research, January 1983 (Part I), October 1983 (Part II).

———. *State Aid for Schools in New Jersey, 1976–1989*. Prepared by Rutgers University, Bureau of Government Research and Department of Government Services, January 1990.

New Jersey Legislature. Joint Committee on the Public Schools. *The Impact of State School Aid on Property Taxes in 1977*. Report prepared by Rutgers University, Bureau of Government Research, August 15, 1978.

———. *Maintenance of Local Effort Under the Public School Education Act of 1975*. Report prepared by Rutgers University, Bureau of Government Research, January 1981.

———. *New Jersey School Budgets and Property Taxes in 1979*. Report prepared by Rutgers University, Bureau of Government Research, September 1980.

——. *School Budget Caps in New Jersey 1976–1980: Four Years of Experience with Expenditure Limitations.* Report prepared by Rutgers University, Bureau of Government Research, May 1980.

——. *School Budgets and Property Taxes in 1978.* Report prepared by Rutgers University, Bureau of Government Research, April 2, 1979.

New Jersey Legislature. Welfare Investigating Committee. *Report on the Aid to Dependent Children Program in New Jersey.* January 1963.

O'Dea, Colleen. "The Price of Parity: Once More Into the School Aid Breach." *New Jersey Reporter*, May/June 1996.

O'Hern, Daniel. Interview by James M. McGovern Jr. and Robert Honecker, for "Remembering the 20th Century: An Oral History of Monmouth County." August 4, 2000. http://www.visitmonmouth.com/oralhistory/bios/OHernDaniel.htm.

Parciak, Thomas C. "Equality of Educational Opportunity in New Jersey: A Case Study of the Public School Education Act of 1975." Ph.D. diss., Teachers College, Columbia University, 1979.

Paris, Michael. "Legal Mobilization and Social Reform: A Comparative Study of School Finance Litigation in New Jersey and Kentucky." Ph.D. diss., Brandeis University, February 1998.

Rebell, Michael. "Educational Adequacy, Democracy and the Courts." In *Achieving High Educational Standards for All: Conference Summary*, ed. Timothy Ready, Christopher Edley Jr., and Catherine E. Snow, 218–267. Washington, DC: National Academies Press, 2002.

Reed, Douglas S. *On Equal Terms: The Constitutional Politics of Educational Opportunity.* Princeton, NJ: Princeton University Press, 2001.

Reock, Ernest C., Jr. *State Aid for Schools in New Jersey, 1976–1996.* Rutgers University Center for Government Services, New Brunswick, NJ, June 1996.

Resnick, Gary, with Ruth Hubbell McKey and Douglas Klayman. *The Evaluation of Early Childhood Education Programming in the 30 Abbott School Districts: First-Year Report on Program Implementation and Descriptions of Children and Families.* Prepared for the New Jersey Department of Human Services and the New Jersey Department of Education, June 25, 2001.

Robbins, Ruth Anne. "The Mentoring King." *Rutgers Law Journal* 35, no. 4 (Summer 2004): xii–xxiii.

Rubin, Larry. *A Discussion of the Expenditure Cap Provision of the New Jersey Public School Education Act of 1975.* New Jersey Education Reform Project, Newark, NJ, May 1978.

——. *An Evaluation of the Fiscal Impact of New Jersey's Public School Education Act of 1975 on the State's Low Wealth and Urban School Districts.* New Jersey Education Reform Project, Newark, NJ, June 1978.

Ruvoldt, Harold J., Jr., "The Right to Learn." *New Jersey State Bar Journal* 14, no. 51 (May 1970): 16–20.

Salmore, Barbara G., and Stephen A. Salmore. *New Jersey Politics and Government: Suburban Politics Comes of Age.* Lincoln: University of Nebraska Press, 1993.

Sanders, Deborah L. "On School Funding, Remands, and Chosen Wise Men: Judge King and the Remand Opinion Aimed at Fulfilling the Constitutional Mandate for a

Thorough and Efficient Education." *Rutgers Law Journal* 35, no. 4 (Summer 2004): xxxix–1.

Sanders, Helen. *More Than a Renewal: Loretto Before and After Vatican II: 1952–1977.* Nerinx, KY: Sisters of Loretto, 1982.

Schrag, Peter. *Final Test: The Battle for Adequacy in America's Schools.* New York: New Press, 2003.

Settle, Theodore. Testimony before Joint Legislative Committee on Public School Funding Reform, August 10, 2006. http://www.njleg.state.nj.us/PropertyTaxSession/OPI/jcsf081006.pdf

Siegel, Alan A. *An Outline History of Irvington, New Jersey.* Irvington Historical Society, 1998.

State Aid to School Districts Study Commission. *A Commitment to New Jersey's Children: A State School Support Program for New Jersey.* Final report to the governor and the legislature, December 19, 1968.

Thomas, Earl Preston. *Education in Jersey City: An Assessment of the Impact of Robinson v. Cahill.* New Jersey Education Reform Project, Newark, NJ, July 1979.

Thro, William E. "Judicial Analysis During the Third Wave of School Finance Litigation: The Massachusetts Decision as a Model." *Boston College Law Review* 35, no. 3 (May 1994): 597–617.

Turcol, Tom. "The Return of Jim Florio." *New Jersey Reporter*, April 2000.

Vespucci, Richard, and Donna Lee Goldberg. *A History of East Orange.* Worrall Publications, 1976.

Walker, Elaine, and Dan Gutmore, with Mary Kildow. *The Quest for Equity and Excellence in Education: A Study on Whole School Reform in New Jersey Special Needs Districts.* Seton Hall University, South Orange, NJ, March 2000.

West, Roscoe L. *Elementary Education in New Jersey: A History.* Princeton, NJ: D. Van Nostrand, 1964.

Zalkind, Cecilia. *Keeping the Focus on Children: Accountability for Educational Improvement in the Special Needs Districts.* Association for Children of New Jersey, October 1992.

INDEX

All places named are in New Jersey.

Abbott, Frances (Luci), 113–115, 116, 118, 214–216, 218
Abbott, Howard, 113–115
Abbott, Raymond, 99, 113–115, 162, 214–219, 226, 304–307
Abbott districts: corruption in, 326–327; designation of, 270, 330; funding of, 295–296, 301–303, 322–323, 329–330; school construction in, 288–290, 328–329; test scores of, 4, 299–300, 322–327. See also Asbury Park; Camden public schools; East Orange public schools; Irvington; Jersey City public schools; special needs districts; Union City; urban school districts
Abbott Implementation and Compliance Coordinating Council, 295–297
Abbott v. Burke, New Jersey Supreme Court rulings in: Abbott I, 147–149, 154, 160, 164, 174, 175; Abbott II, 176, 187, 189–193, 199, 201–203, 206, 260, 263–266, 269, 297, 322–323; Abbott III, 209–211, 256, 264, 269, 304; Abbott IV, 263–267, 270, 273–274, 297, 302–303; Abbott V, 276–278, 281–283, 287–291, 293, 297–301; Abbott VI, 286–287, 291. See also minimum aid; parity; preschool; school construction; supplemental programs; teacher pensions; whole school reform
Abbott v. Burke litigation: administrative hearing of, 160–167; administrative ruling in, 168–171, 174–175; choice of plaintiffs for, 110–111, 115, 117, 120, 126, 129, 132, 134–135, 139, 140–141, 144; complaint and response in, 98–101, 157; dismissal of, 107–109, 145–147; evaluation of results of, 302, 322; filing of, 99; implementation proceedings in, 281, 286–287, 295–298, 301–303; plaintiffs' case in, 93–94, 149–151; political context of, 104, 158, 177; remand hearing in, 266–275, 297; state's case in, 107, 155–159, 321; Superior Court trial of, 199–200, 204–206; trial preparations for, 95–96, 102, 104, 147–148, 152–154. See also Abbott v. Burke, New Jersey Supreme Court rulings in; Block, Steven; Education Law Center; Long, David; Morheuser, Marilyn; Sciarra, David; Tractenberg, Paul
AbbottWatch, 296
ACLU. See American Civil Liberties Union
ACNJ. See Association for Children of New Jersey
Administrative Law, New Jersey Office of, 101, 107, 145–147
Advocates for Education, 113, 118
American Civil Liberties Union (ACLU), 24, 46, 86, 148, 160
Amos v. Board of School Directors of Milwaukee. See Morheuser, Marilyn
Anderson, Jay, 73
Appel, Joy, 125–126
Appel, Samuel, 112–113, 117, 125–126
Archway School, 229
Asbury Park, 326
Assembly, New Jersey. See legislature, New Jersey
Association for Children of New Jersey (ACNJ), 199
Atlantic City, 106, 112, 192, 251–252
Attorney General, New Jersey Office of, 22, 26, 107, 154–155, 200, 204, 295

Barbee, Lloyd, 67–68, 70–71, 74, 76, 78, 80–85, 97
Barnett, W. Steven, 283–287. See also Frede, Ellen; preschool
Bateman, Raymond, 15–16, 17–18, 29, 42, 51–52

Bateman Commission, 15–17
Bergen County, 41, 51
Berman, Douglas, 180–181, 194, 195. *See also* Corcoran, Thomas; Florio, Jim
Black People's Unity Movement, 113
Block, Steven, 106; background of, 95–96; involvement in McGreevey collaboration of, 294–296, 300; relationship with Marilyn Morheuser of, 176–177, 209–210; role in finding *Abbott* plaintiffs of, 111, 129–130, 140; views on corruption of, 103–104, 164, 198; views on teacher pensions of, 203–204. *See also* Education Law Center
Bombelyn, Patricia, 296
Booker, Cory, 311–312, 313
Botter, Theodore, 22–23, 24, 25, 27–30, 33, 35, 45, 171
Bradley, Bill, 195, 196, 207, 254
Brown, William, 200
Brown v. Board of Education, 19, 34, 70, 72, 76, 101, 130, 200
Bryant, Paula, 208–209, 213
Budzash, John, 185, 186
Burke, Fred, 99, 157
Byrne, Brendan: background of, 36–37; and income tax, 37–39, 41–42, 44–45, 47–48, 50–51, 89, 92, 177–178; and legislature, 38, 39; reelection of, 47, 51–52, 195; and *Robinson* case, 40, 46–47, 104; and school funding formula, 44–45, 92. *See also* Goldman, Clifford; Kaden, Lewis; Leone, Richard

Cahill, William, 20, 24, 29, 33–34, 36, 37, 104, 188
Camden, 99, 100, 177, 217, 268, 318, 333; in *Abbott* plaintiffs' lives, 113–126; decline of, 105, 111–113, 126, 132, 134, 220, 307
Camden Metropolitan Ministry, 113
Camden public schools, 27, 43, 93–94, 102, 151, 163, 165, 169, 269, 326; in *Abbott* plaintiffs' lives, 113–126, 214, 219–221, 222–225, 308, 317; Camden High School, 112, 119, 163; East Camden Middle School, 220–221, 222; Forest Hill Elementary School, 117; Veterans Memorial Middle School, 115, 229–230; Woodrow Wilson High School, 112, 118, 119, 123, 221, 222–225, 307
Cape May, 179
Castro, Ida, 149, 152, 162
CEIFA. *See* Comprehensive Educational Improvement and Financing Act
Cherry, George, 114, 214–216

Cherry Hill, 43, 93, 112, 120, 151, 229, 318
Cioppettini, Thomas, 97–98, 175, 212–213
Clarke, Benjamin, 200, 202, 205, 206, 211
Clark Foundation. *See* Edna McConnell Clark Foundation
Coleman, James, Jr. (New Jersey Supreme Court justice), 253
Coleman, James (sociologist), 26
Collins, Jack, 261, 262, 263, 267, 288–289, 290
Comprehensive Educational Improvement and Financing Act (CEIFA), 256–266, 268, 271, 281, 303, 329–330, 331
construction, school. *See* school construction
Cooperman, Saul, 105, 146, 157, 160, 172–175. *See also* Kean, Thomas
Corcoran, Thomas, 177, 179–182, 184–185, 186–187, 194, 195. *See also* Berman, Douglas; Florio, Jim
core curriculum standards, New Jersey, 254–255, 257–260, 263–264, 265, 299
Corzine, Jon, 302–303, 328
Coulter, Kenneth, 71, 73
Coyle, Theresa, 64–65

Davy, Lucille, 294, 300. *See also* Frede, Ellen; Librera, William; MacInnes, Gordon; McGreevey, James
Diaz, Justo, 140, 244
Diaz, Liana, 140–141, 244–245, 315–316
Diaz, Lucila Rivera, 139–141, 244–245, 315, 333
Dodd, Frank (Pat), 39
Doria, Joseph Jr., 178, 195, 263
Dow-Ford, Sheila, 148, 153, 160–161, 166
Dreier, William, 102, 104

East Orange, 23, 99, 126–132, 231, 234–236, 310, 326
East Orange Housing Authority, 131, 234
East Orange public schools, 102, 126–132, 146, 159, 169, 173, 232–237; Clifford J. Scott High School, 127; East Orange High School, 126, 127, 131–132, 159, 234, 235; Nassau School, 130
East Orange Tenants Association, 129, 231, 232
Economic Development Authority, New Jersey, 290
Edna McConnell Clark Foundation, 167
Education, New Jersey Department of, 27, 36, 98, 112, 172–173, 176, 189, 294; and *Abbott* case, 101, 107, 152, 156, 157, 165, 192, 269, 272; and CEIFA, 256,

259–260, 265; and QEA, 179, 198, 199, 200, 201; and *Robinson* case, 25; and supplemental programs, 297–298; and T&E law, 42–44, 89; and whole school reform, 291, 293, 328
Education Commission of the States, 268
Education Law Center, 302, 312, 330, 332; and *Abbott* administrative hearing, 162–166; and *Abbott* filing, 99–104; and *Abbott* Superior Court trial, 204–206; and *Abbott II*, 193; and *Abbott IV*, 267; and *Abbott V*, 278; board of, 108, 113, 204, 211–212, 295, 296; and CEIFA, 260, 262; finances of, 90, 108, 146, 167–168, 171, 207–208, 253; founding of, 87–89; leadership of, 86, 89–90, 208–213, 249–50; litigation preparation of, 107–109, 146–149, 152–153, 159–161, 200–202, 263–265; partnership with McGreevey administration of, 293–301; preparing *Abbott* complaint, 93–99; and preschool, 271–272, 281–287, 295; and *Robinson* case, 45, 89, 93; relationship with NJEA of, 106, 202–204; and remand hearing, 272–276; staff of, 88, 146, 148–149, 160, 162, 176, 200; and supplemental programs, 272, 297–299; and whole school reform, 271, 290, 299–301. See also *Abbott v. Burke* litigation; Block, Steven; Lottman, Michael; Morheuser, Marilyn; Sciarra, David; *Sharif v. Byrne*; Tractenberg, Paul
Educational Testing Service (ETS), 23, 26, 27
ELC. *See* Education Law Center
Elizabeth, 87, 179
Essex County, 36, 134, 238
Essex County Community College, 96, 243
ETS. *See* Educational Testing Service

Feldman, Jonathan, 200
Figueroa, Arlayne, 125, 227, 230–231, 319–320
Figueroa, Blanca, 120–126, 225–228, 229–231, 320–321, 333
Figueroa, Frances, 124, 126, 226–227, 228–229, 231, 318–319, 333
Figueroa, Hector, 124–125, 126, 227, 229–230, 319, 334
Figueroa, Orlando, 123–124, 125, 126, 226, 230, 318
Figueroa, Vivian, 123–124, 126, 225–226, 228, 317–318
Flaherty, Thomas, 20
Florio, Jim, 253; background of, 177; and *Abbott II*, 194, 332; electoral defeats of,

177, 207; electoral victory of, 177; and QEA, 182–184, 187, 194, 195–196, 202, 207, 261, 304, 330; and tax increases, 177–179, 182, 186, 194–197. *See also* Berman, Douglas; Corcoran, Thomas
Ford Foundation, 86–87, 88, 108
Fowler, William, Jr., 156, 158, 162
Franklin, Joan, 80–82, 84–85
Frede, Ellen, 285–286, 287, 295, 327–328. *See also* Barnett, W. Steven; Davy, Lucille; MacInnes, Gordon; McGreevey, James; preschool

Garden State Coalition of Schools, 183–184, 203, 256, 258, 260–261, 288
Garibaldi, Marie, 190, 211, 266, 329
Glassboro State College, 224
Goertz, Margaret, 152, 162, 181, 198, 201, 273–274
Goertz, Robert, 181
Goldman, Clifford, 42–43, 92. *See also* Byrne, Brendan; Kaden, Lewis; Leone, Richard
Goltz, Bertram, Jr. (Skip), 154–155, 159
Groppi, James, 72

Haddonfield, 220–221, 268, 317
Hadley, Lynnette, 118–119, 222, 308
Hadley, Michael, 119, 222–225, 308–309
Hague, Frank, 19, 135
Hamilton, 39
Handler, Alan, 265–266, 276–278, 286
Hands Across New Jersey, 185–186
Hanushek, Eric, 157
Hargrove, Aisha, 142–144, 246–247, 317
Hargrove, James, 141–142
Hargrove, Zakia, 142–144, 245–248, 316–317
Hauptmann, Bruno, 187
Head Start, 73, 137
Hespe, David, 298. *See also* Klagholz, Leo; McGinnis, Eileen; Verniero, Peter; Whitman, Christie
Hoboken, 103–104, 164, 176
home rule, 13, 30, 42, 45, 91, 157–158, 179
Hudson County, 19, 22, 99, 103, 327
Hughes, Richard, 15, 24, 37, 39–40, 46, 51, 188, 294
Human Services, New Jersey Department of, 138, 272

income tax: in Byrne era, 1, 37–42, 44–45, 47–52, 89, 92, 93, 106, 177, 331; in Cahill era, 24, 33–34, 104; in Florio era, 178–183, 185–187, 194–195, 197; in Hughes era, 14, 15, 188; in Kean era, 177; in Whitman era, 207, 255, 295

Irvington: city, 99, 132–134, 163, 235; Grove Street School, 134; public schools, 132–134, 146, 159, 163, 169, 172, 238
Isaac, Eldad Philip, 155, 159, 164, 165, 166

Jackson, Bobby, 136
James, Caroline, 130–132, 234–237, 310–311
James, Jermaine, 130–132, 234–237, 311–312
James, Julian (Bunny), 130–132, 234–235, 237, 310, 311
James, Mattie, 130–132, 234–237, 310, 333
James, Sharpe, 311–312
Jersey City, 19–20, 134–136, 164; and *Abbott* case, 99, 100; in *Abbott* plaintiffs' lives, 136–144, 241–248, 311, 314–317; and *Robinson* case, 18–20, 23, 25, 28, 30, 40, 93; in Robinson family's life, 9–12, 31, 54–55
Jersey City public schools, 12; Academic High School, 244–245; in *Abbott* plaintiffs' lives, 135, 137–144, 241, 244–245, 247, 314; conditions in, 22, 26–27, 31, 159, 163; corruption in, 103, 134–135, 164–165, 169, 173, 326; Ferris High School, 32; Lincoln High School, 32, 139, 141, 241–243; in Robinson family's life, 12, 21–22, 55; School 3, 140, 244; School 14, 138, 241; School 16, 140, 244; School 22, 21–22; School 29, 241; and school vouchers, 254; state takeover of, 173, 205, 326
Jersey City State College, 142, 316

Kaden, Lewis, 38. *See also* Byrne, Brendan; Goldman, Clifford; Leone, Richard
Kean, Thomas, 252, 265; background of, 104–105, 177, 253; and education issues, 105, 158, 196, 254; and electoral victories, 105, 238; and New Jersey Supreme Court, 188–189; and school funding, 105–106; and school takeover, 105–106, 205. *See also* Cooperman, Saul
Kelly, James, 87–90
King, Michael Patrick, 268–269, 272–275, 276, 277
Klagholz, Leo, 254–259, 267, 272–274, 282–284, 298. *See also* Hespe, David; McGinnis, Eileen; Verniero, Peter; Whitman, Christie
Knowles, Cristina, 133–134, 238–240, 312–313
Knowles, Daniel, 133–134, 237–240, 312, 313

Knowles, Gladys, 133–134, 237–239, 313
Knowles, Guy, Jr., 133–134, 237–240, 312, 313
Knowles, Guy, Sr., 133–134, 237, 313–314
Krieger, Harold, 20

Lawyers' Committee for Civil Rights Under Law, 93, 147, 148
League of Women Voters, 148, 267
Lefelt, Steven, 175, 176, 199, 202, 204; and *Abbott* hearing delays, 161, 205; and *Abbott* hearing record, 164, 166–167; and *Abbott* ruling, 168–174, 189, 190, 192; background of, 160
Legal Services of New Jersey, 24, 250, 251, 253
legislature, New Jersey, 5, 14, 157, 294, 295, 303, 323, 330, 331–332; in Byrne era, 36–52, 89, 91–92, 191; in Cahill/Hughes era, 17–18, 27, 28, 29, 36, 188; in Florio era, 172, 178–179, 181, 185, 187, 191–98, 200, 201, 203, 269; in Kean era, 105–106, 158, 188–89, 252; in Whitman era, 254, 256–265, 267, 273, 278, 287–290, 297, 298; reaction to *Abbott* rulings of, 171–172, 193–194, 267, 275; representativeness of, 13, 36
Leone, Richard, 37–38, 41, 42, 47–48, 51–52. *See also* Byrne, Brendan; Goldman, Clifford; Kaden, Lewis
Levy, Paul, 204–206
Librera, William, 294, 295, 297, 298, 301. *See also* Davy, Lucille; Frede, Ellen; MacInnes, Gordon; McGreevey, James
local control. *See* home rule
Long, David, 93, 109, 147–148, 151, 153, 162, 166, 202
Long, Virginia, 104, 107, 109, 145, 146, 147
Lottman, Michael, 89–90, 100
Lucas, Louis, 81
Lynch, John, 196, 198

MacInnes, Gordon, 294–295, 296, 298–301, 328. *See also* Davy, Lucille; Frede, Ellen; McGreevey, James; Librera, William
Maple Shade, 229
Maplewood, 232
Martin, Fred, 21
Matrick, Debra, 102, 109
MBST. *See* Minimum Basic Skills Test
McGinnis, Eileen, 282–286. *See also* Hespe, David; Klagholz, Leo; Verniero, Peter; Whitman, Christie
McGreevey, James, 293–295, 314, 328. *See also* Davy, Lucille; Frede, Ellen; MacInnes, Gordon; Librera, William

Millburn, 15, 43, 88, 193
Miller, Jeffrey, 273–274
Miller, Joyce, 102, 109, 148
Milwaukee United School Integration
     Committee (MUSIC). *See* Morheuser,
     Marilyn
minimum aid, 18, 29, 33, 40, 42, 92, 182,
     192
Minimum Basic Skills Test (MBST), 93,
     105
monitoring of school districts, 92, 157,
     170, 173, 174, 182
Montclair, 115
Montclair State College, 137, 233
Moore, Lola, 117–120, 136, 222–225,
     307–308, 333
Morgan, Ivy, 75
Morheuser, Celeste, 60, 61, 62
Morheuser, Joseph (grandfather), 61
Morheuser, Joseph (uncle), 60
Morheuser, Marie Werthe (mother),
     59–60
Morheuser, Marie (sister), 60, 61, 62, 66,
     69, 97, 212–213
Morheuser, Marilyn: arrests and jailing
     of, 74, 75–76; attitude toward
     adversaries of, 80, 107, 153–154, 160,
     165–167, 196, 198–199, 206; attitude
     toward school corruption of, 103–104,
     120, 198–199, 332; childhood of,
     59–61; civil rights movement
     interest of, 66–69, 71–74, 85, 101;
     college years of, 61–62; continuing
     relationship with Sisters of Loretto of,
     175, 211, 213; convent years of, 62–69;
     death of, 213; departure from Sisters
     of Loretto of, 69; friendships of,
     83–84, 97–98, 208–209, 331; hiring by
     Education Law Center of, 86, 90;
     illnesses of, 78–79, 108, 145, 208–213;
     journalism of, 67, 71, 73; law school
     years of, 82–84; and legislators, 187,
     194, 196, 207; personality of, 59,
     96–97, 110, 154, 159, 209, 249–250;
     post-law school employment of, 84,
     86; preparation for *Abbott* case of, 96,
     98–99, 106–107, 110–111, 147–152,
     199–200; reaction to *Abbott* rulings of,
     109, 146, 147, 193; relationships with
     colleagues of, 79, 96–97, 103–104, 148,
     153, 160, 176–177, 200, 209–210;
     relationship with Lloyd Barbee of,
     67–68, 70–72, 81–83; role in
     Milwaukee United School Integration
     Committee (MUSIC) of, 71–77; work
     habits of, 78–79, 96–97, 200; work on
     *Amos v. Board of School Directors of
     Milwaukee* of, 76–82, 84–85; work on
     Benton Harbor, Michigan, case of,

80–81. See also *Abbott v. Burke*
     litigation; Education Law Center
Morheuser, Martin (brother), 60, 61, 62
Morheuser, Martin (father), 59–60, 66,
     97, 213
Morheuser, Pauline, 60
Morheuser, Rose, 60, 62
Morris County, 295
Mount Laurel (affordable housing cases),
     86, 188
municipal overburden, 18, 26–27, 46,
     169, 190

NAACP. *See* National Association for the
     Advancement of Colored People
NAEP. *See* National Assessment of
     Educational Progress
National Assessment of Educational
     Progress (NAEP), 323–324
National Association for the Advancement
     of Colored People (NAACP), 46, 67,
     68, 70, 71, 77, 78, 80–81
National Commission on Excellence in
     Education, 105
National Rifle Association (NRA), 197
Newark, 24, 44, 84, 95, 149, 161, 213; in
     Abbott plaintiffs' lives, 133, 139,
     232–240, 310–314; as largest city in
     N.J., 12, 134; as location of ELC offices,
     86, 88, 148, 312; as Marilyn
     Morheuser's home, 96, 145; riots in,
     15, 82–83, 96, 126, 132, 295
Newark Boys Chorus School, 235, 236
Newark public schools, 15, 43, 95,
     137–138, 151, 180, 184, 193, 208; Arts
     High School, 234; corruption in, 89,
     98–99, 106, 173; Science High School,
     236–237; Weequahic High School, 87.
     See also *Sharif v. Byrne*
New Brunswick, 296
New Jersey Board of Education, 146, 158,
     169, 172, 174, 260
New Jersey Education Association
     (NJEA), 105, 254, 259, 285; attitude
     toward *Abbott* case of, 106, 185; and
     pension shift, 182, 184–185, 195–196,
     202–204, 257; relationship with ELC
     of, 106, 203–204, 209, 285; in
     Robinson era, 43, 46, 106
New Jersey 101.5 (radio station), 185, 195
New Jersey School Boards Association
     (NJSBA), 25, 46
New Jersey Supreme Court. *See* Supreme
     Court, New Jersey
New York Times, 127, 277
NJEA. *See* New Jersey Education
     Association
NJSBA. *See* New Jersey School Boards
     Association

No Child Left Behind Act, 3, 324
NRA. *See* National Rifle Association

Ocean City, 100
Ocean County, 289
Odden, Allan, 268–271, 274, 275
O'Hern, Daniel, 286
Orange, 242

Paramus, 100
parity, 296, 298, 302, 323, 329; in
    Abbott II, 192, 203, 297; in *Abbott IV*,
    266–267, 297, 302; in CEIFA, 255,
    256, 262, 263–264; in QEA, 193–194,
    201–202, 205–206, 210–211; at
    remand hearing, 269–270. See also
    Abbott v. Burke, New Jersey Supreme
    Court rulings in; *Abbott v. Burke*
    litigation
Pashman, Morris, 46
Passaic County, 49
Paterson, 23, 33
Pellecchia, Vincent (Ozzie), 49, 50
Pennsauken, 121, 215, 216, 226, 228, 229,
    230–231, 317–318, 319
pensions. *See* teacher pensions
Perth Amboy, 187
Plainfield, 23, 208
Poritz, Deborah, 253, 264, 286–287
Powers, David, 155, 166
pre-kindergarten. *See* preschool
preschool, 205, 260, 290, 293–295, 330;
    in *Abbott* rulings, 276–278, 281–82,
    286–287, 291, 297, 299, 332; at
    remand hearing, 271–276, 282–283;
    research supporting effectiveness of,
    282; results of, 315, 325, 327–328;
    state efforts to implement,
    282–287, 295, 300, 302. *See also*
    Barnett, W. Steven; Frede, Ellen;
    McGinnis, Eileen
Princeton, 44, 151, 152, 193
Princeton University, 36, 38, 141, 277,
    294
Project U.S.E. (Urban Suburban
    Environments), 216
property tax, 13, 16, 192, 329; efforts to
    reduce, 33, 37–39, 150, 183, 186,
    195–196, 260; to fund schools, 19, 24,
    30, 46, 99, 181, 195, 258, 261, 330;
    statewide, 14, 33, 46, 171–172; in
    urban and suburban school districts,
    15, 30, 35, 44–46, 91, 179, 183, 261
Public Advocate, New Jersey Department
    of, 38, 86, 148–149, 252–253
Public Defender, New Jersey, 84, 86
Public School Education Act of 1975
    ("T&E Law"), 42–46, 48, 89–96,
    99–100, 107, 150, 152, 157, 170

Puerto Rican Congress of New Jersey,
    134
Puerto Rican Socialist Party, 133

Quality Education Act (QEA), drafting of,
    178–182; impact of, 197–199;
    introduced, 182; litigation over,
    199–202, 204–207, 209–211, 304;
    opposition to, 183–187, 195–196, 256;
    phasing out of, 207, 253; provisions
    of, 182–183, 200–202, 256, 258, 261,
    264, 331; QEA I passed, 194–195; QEA
    II passed, 196–197, 203; special needs
    districts under, 194, 260. See also
    Abbott v. Burke, New Jersey Supreme
    Court rulings in; *Abbott v. Burke*
    litigation; Berman, Douglas; Corcoran,
    Thomas; Florio, Jim; minimum aid;
    New Jersey Education Association;
    parity; special needs districts; teacher
    pensions
QEA. *See* Quality Education Act

Ramey, Alfred, Jr., 154, 155, 158, 159, 161,
    164, 166
Reock, Ernest, Jr., 152
Ridgewood, 179
Robinson, Ernestine Betty, 9–12, 15, 21,
    25, 28–29, 32, 52–53, 110
Robinson, Gwen, 53, 55
Robinson, Joan, 11, 52, 53, 55
Robinson, Kenneth (Babe), 9, 12, 21, 25,
    30, 31–33, 52–55, 110, 162
Robinson, Larry (Tank), 9, 32–33, 52, 53,
    54, 55
Robinson, Lydia, 9, 11, 53, 55
Robinson, Patricia, 9, 11, 55
Robinson, Saundra, 11, 53–55
Robinson, Tony, 32–33, 53, 55
Robinson, Wilbur, 11, 15
Robinson v. Cahill, New Jersey Supreme
    Court rulings in, 42, 51, 94, 100, 101,
    157–158, 172, 174, 178, 190, 191, 193,
    255; *Robinson I*, 34–37, 39–40, 42;
    Robinson II, 40; *Robinson III*, 40;
    Robinson IV, 40; *Robinson V*, 45–46,
    94; *Robinson VI*, 46–47, 49
Robinson v. Cahill litigation, 4–5, 21, 43,
    45, 88–89, 96, 110–111, 147; filing of,
    22–23, 267, 303; New Jersey Superior
    Court ruling in, 28–30, 34; political
    context of, 18–20, 23, 24–27, 104; trial
    of, 25–27, 94, 147, 161; trial
    preparations for, 23–25. See also
    Robinson v. Cahill, New Jersey
    Supreme Court rulings in
Rock, Annie Ruth, 10, 12
Rock, Thomasena, 10, 11
Rubin, Michael, 146, 147, 148, 152

Rutgers Law School, 24, 25, 45, 82–84, 87, 88, 149, 154, 159, 160, 210
Rutgers University, 152, 258, 283, 292
Ruvoldt, Harold, Jr., 19–21, 22–29, 30, 40, 93, 110
Ruvoldt, Harold, Sr., 19, 20
Ryan, Jimmy, 20

Saint Peter's College, 140, 243–244, 314
sales tax, 13–15, 24, 177–182, 185–186, 194–195, 197
San Antonio v. Rodriguez, 19, 34–35
school construction, 182, 267, 274–275, 277–278, 287–290, 293–294, 328–329
school funding, New Jersey, 13–14, 15, 17–18, 25, 28, 29, 35, 42, 45, 46, 90. See also *Abbott v. Burke*, New Jersey Supreme Court rulings in; *Abbott v. Burke* litigation; *Robinson v. Cahill*, New Jersey Supreme Court rulings in; *Robinson v. Cahill* litigation
school funding formulas, types of, 4, 12–13, 16–17, 91, 150, 168–169, 171, 179
school funding litigation, New Jersey, 3–4, 176, 330–332. See also *Abbott v. Burke*, New Jersey Supreme Court rulings in; *Abbott v. Burke* litigation; *Robinson v. Cahill*, New Jersey Supreme Court rulings in; *Robinson v. Cahill* litigation
school funding litigation, U.S., 2–4, 176
school spending, New Jersey, 14–15, 256–259, 270, 275, 323; discrepancies between rich and poor, 29–30, 35–36, 45, 90–92, 99–100, 150, 155, 168–169, 171–172, 192–193, 198, 200–202, 265, 322–323; and educational quality, 25–26, 29, 94, 146, 156–157, 173, 190, 332; and suburban districts, 253–258, 260–265, 329. See also *Abbott v. Burke*, New Jersey Supreme Court rulings in; *Robinson v. Cahill*, New Jersey Supreme Court rulings in
school takeover, 173–174, 205, 326
school vouchers, 254, 296, 332
Schoolwatch, 96
Schrag, Peter, 3
Sciarra, David: background of, 249–253; and CEIFA, 257, 262, 265; hiring by ELC of, 249, 253; and Leo Klagholz, 267, 282; and McGreevey partnership, 295–296, 300–301; preparations for *Abbott* litigation of, 253, 263; reactions to *Abbott* rulings of, 267, 278; and remand hearing, 269, 272–274. *See also* Education Law Center
Sciarra, David (father), 250
Sciarra, Ellie, 250, 251
Sciarra, Fay, 252, 263

Sciarra, Helen, 250–251
Senate, New Jersey. *See* legislature, New Jersey
Serrano v. Priest, 19, 24–25, 27
Seton Hall University, 19, 128
SFA. *See* whole school reform
Shapiro, Peter, 134, 238
Sharif v. Byrne, 98–99, 104, 110
Sheppard, Annamay, 84, 90, 108, 209–210
Shine, William, 43, 92
Simon, William, 51–52
Sisters of Loretto at the Foot of the Cross. *See* Morheuser, Marilyn
Smith, Mark, 184
Somerset County, 16
South Brunswick, 163
South Orange-Maplewood public schools, 232–233
special needs districts, 208, 255; designation of, 191–192, 194, 270, 330; funding of, 194, 197–198, 201–202, 205, 262, 266, 323; test scores of, 197–198; use of QEA funds by, 198–199. See also *Abbott* districts; Asbury Park; Camden public schools; East Orange public schools; Irvington; Jersey City public schools; Union City; urban school districts
standardized tests, 3, 77, 105, 173, 180; in urban schools, 4, 22, 126, 133, 135, 169, 174, 197–198, 227, 244, 292, 323–328; use of in litigation, 25, 100, 111, 150–152, 156–157; use of in monitoring, 28, 43–44, 89, 93, 151; and whole school reform, 270, 273, 291, 299–300. See also *Abbott* districts; Minimum Basic Skills Test; special needs districts
Stein, Gary, 189, 265, 266, 268, 269, 276–277, 286–287, 291
Stephens, Eddie, 136–139, 242, 314
Stephens, LaMar, 137–139, 241–244, 314
Stephens, Leslie, 137–139, 241, 314
Stephens, Tommi, 136–139, 241–242, 314–315
Stevens, Henry, Jr., 116–117, 219–221, 307
Stevens, Henry, Sr., 112, 116–117, 118, 220–221, 307
Stevens, Nezettia, 116
Stewart, Clifford Gregory, 149
Story, Harold, 70, 72
Success For All (SFA). *See* whole school reform
supplemental programs, 192, 211, 264, 266–278, 297–299, 301–303, 328
Supreme Court, California, 24–25, 34
Supreme Court, Kentucky, 176
Supreme Court, Montana, 176

Supreme Court, New Jersey, 36, 86, 107, 172, 189, 252, 253, 268; in *Abbott* case, 180, 182, 255, 261, 275, 329, 331; in *Robinson* case, 89, 94, 255, 261, 331. See also *Abbott v. Burke*, New Jersey Supreme Court rulings in; *Robinson v. Cahill*, New Jersey Supreme Court rulings in

Supreme Court, U.S., 19, 34–35, 72, 76, 83

T&E clause of New Jersey Constitution: adopted, 14; meaning of, 28, 35, 88, 100, 158, 275; and preschool, 281; proposed repeal of, 158, 203, 275; and school construction, 267; use in school funding litigation of, 19–20, 26, 101

"T&E law." *See* Public School Education Act of 1975

takeover. *See* school takeover

taxes. *See* income tax; property tax; sales tax

teacher pensions, 181–185, 192–194, 196, 198, 201–204, 207, 332. *See also* New Jersey Education Association

testing. *See* standardized tests

Tobin, Mary Luke, 68–69

Tractenberg, Paul, 249, 281, 294–296; background of, 87–88; and finances of Education Law Center, 108; and founding of Education Law Center, 45, 87–89; illness of, 210, 212; and Marilyn Morheuser's illness, 209–210, 212; work on *Abbott* case of, 108, 209–210; work on *Robinson* case of, 24, 25, 28, 45, 88–89. *See also* Education Law Center; Morheuser, Marilyn

Trenton, 29, 106, 160, 204, 252, 275, 282, 293, 298; as site of courts, 162, 166, 210; as site for lobbying, 187, 194, 212; as site for protests, 47–48, 185; public schools, 152, 163, 193, 295, 301

Trentonian, 185

Union City, 328

Urban League, 148

urban school districts: conditions in, 95–96, 99, 150, 157, 159, 162–164, 189, 193; corruption in, 89–90, 100, 103–106, 155–156, 164–165, 168–170, 173, 174, 198, 332; funding of, 17, 19, 105, 151, 155–156, 168–171, 180, 189–93. See also *Abbott* districts;

Abbott v. Burke, New Jersey Supreme Court rulings in; Asbury Park; Atlantic City; Camden public schools; East Orange public schools; Irvington; Jersey City public schools; Newark public schools; *Robinson v. Cahill*, New Jersey Supreme Court rulings in; special needs districts; Union City

Verniero, Peter, 263–265, 275–276. *See also* Hespe, David; Klagholz, Leo; McGinnis, Eileen; Whitman, Christie

vouchers. *See* school vouchers

Waiters, Dorian, 127–129, 231–234, 309–310

Waiters, Khudayja, 127–129, 231–234, 309–310

Waiters, Lynn, 127–129, 130, 231–234

Watson, Clementine, 141, 246–248, 317

Watson, Cora, 141

Watson, John, 141, 142

Watson, Patricia, 141–144, 245–246, 333

Weintraub, Joseph, 23, 35, 36, 39

Weiss, Stephen, 24, 25, 26–27

West Orange, 238–240

Westfield, 33, 184

Wheelwright, Martin, 79, 83, 84

Whelan, Thomas, 18–19, 20, 25

Whitman, Christie, 253, 293; and *Abbott* rulings, 211, 278; background of, 253–254; and Bill Bradley race, 195, 207; and CEIFA, 253, 261–263, 265; and curriculum standards, 254–255; electoral victories of, 207, 294; and income tax cut, 207, 255, 295; and preschool, 282–284, 295; and remand hearing, 269; and school construction, 290; and school vouchers, 254. *See also* Comprehensive Educational Improvement and Financing Act; Hespe, David; Klagholz, Leo; McGinnis, Eileen; Poritz, Deborah; Verniero, Peter

whole school reform, 270–271, 273–275, 277–278, 284, 290–294, 297, 299–302, 325, 328

Wildwood, 250–251

Wilentz, David, 187

Wilentz, Robert, 5, 187–193, 210–211, 253, 264, 265, 266, 276, 286, 322–323

Williams, Charles, 165

Woodbridge, 293, 314

Zazzali, James, 204

ABOUT THE AUTHOR

DEBORAH YAFFE has worked as a newspaper reporter for the *Jersey Journal*, the *Recorder* of San Francisco, the *Asbury Park Press*, and the Trenton bureau of the Gannett chain. She holds a bachelor's degree from Yale University and a master's degree from Oxford University. She lives in West Windsor, New Jersey, with her husband and two children.